Communications in Computer and Information Science 2609

Rationale
The CCIS series is devoted to the publication of proceedings of computer science conferences. Its aim is to efficiently disseminate original research results in informatics in printed and electronic form. While the focus is on publication of peer-reviewed full papers presenting mature work, inclusion of reviewed short papers reporting on work in progress is welcome, too. Besides globally relevant meetings with internationally representative program committees guaranteeing a strict peer-reviewing and paper selection process, conferences run by societies or of high regional or national relevance are also considered for publication.

Topics
The topical scope of CCIS spans the entire spectrum of informatics ranging from foundational topics in the theory of computing to information and communications science and technology and a broad variety of interdisciplinary application fields.

Information for Volume Editors and Authors
Publication in CCIS is free of charge. No royalties are paid, however, we offer registered conference participants temporary free access to the online version of the conference proceedings on SpringerLink (http://link.springer.com) by means of an http referrer from the conference website and/or a number of complimentary printed copies, as specified in the official acceptance email of the event.

CCIS proceedings can be published in time for distribution at conferences or as post-proceedings, and delivered in the form of printed books and/or electronically as USBs and/or e-content licenses for accessing proceedings at SpringerLink. Furthermore, CCIS proceedings are included in the CCIS electronic book series hosted in the SpringerLink digital library at http://link.springer.com/bookseries/7899. Conferences publishing in CCIS are allowed to use our online conference service (Meteor) for managing the whole proceedings lifecycle (from submission and reviewing to preparing for publication) free of charge.

Publication process
The language of publication is exclusively English. Authors publishing in CCIS have to sign the Springer CCIS copyright transfer form, however, they are free to use their material published in CCIS for substantially changed, more elaborate subsequent publications elsewhere. For the preparation of the camera-ready papers/files, authors have to strictly adhere to the Springer CCIS Authors' Instructions and are strongly encouraged to use the CCIS LaTeX style files or templates.

Abstracting/Indexing
CCIS is abstracted/indexed in DBLP, Google Scholar, EI-Compendex, Mathematical Reviews, SCImago, Scopus. CCIS volumes are also submitted for the inclusion in ISI Proceedings.

How to start
To start the evaluation of your proposal for inclusion in the CCIS series, please send an e-mail to ccis@springer.com

Daniel Vasić · Emil Brajković
Editors

Digital Transformation in Education and Artificial Intelligence Application

Third International Conference, MoStart 2025
Mostar, Bosnia and Herzegovina, April 23–25, 2025
Proceedings

Springer

Editors
Daniel Vasić
University of Mostar
Mostar, Bosnia and Herzegovina

Emil Brajković
University of Mostar
Mostar, Bosnia and Herzegovina

ISSN 1865-0929 ISSN 1865-0937 (electronic)
Communications in Computer and Information Science
ISBN 978-3-032-02800-6 ISBN 978-3-032-02801-3 (eBook)
https://doi.org/10.1007/978-3-032-02801-3

This Springer imprint is published by the registered company Springer Nature Switzerland AG
The registered company address is: Gewerbestrasse 11, 6330 Cham, Switzerland

Preface

The 3rd International Conference on Digital Transformation in Education and Artificial Intelligence Applications (MoStart 2025) marked an important milestone in promoting research and innovation at the intersection of education, artificial intelligence, and digital technologies. This year's conference was held in Mostar, Bosnia and Herzegovina, at the newly inaugurated University Center for IT (SUMIT), a modern facility that reflects the University of Mostar's commitment to advancing scientific and academic infrastructure. Thanks to the dedicated efforts of the University's academic and technical teams, MoStart 2025 was for the first time hosted entirely within its own institutional premises, showcasing both organizational maturity and infrastructural advancement.

The conference offered a dynamic and interdisciplinary platform for exchanging knowledge across a wide spectrum of domains, including computer science, educational technologies, AI, data science, cybersecurity, and robotics. The program featured keynote speeches from internationally recognized experts, focused thematic sessions, and the unique "Scientific Coffee Break" – an informal mentoring and discussion format especially designed to support doctoral students in refining their research and connecting with experienced scholars.

Key topics addressed during the conference included advanced educational technology, intelligent systems, robotics in education, security within Industry 4.0 frameworks, the implementation of large language models in personalized learning environments, and broader cross-disciplinary applications of AI. Among the program highlights were keynote lectures on extracting concept maps from semantic hypergraphs and recent developments in medical image analysis using machine learning techniques.

MoStart 2025 attracted a vibrant and diverse community of participants, including researchers, educators, practitioners, and students from around the world. The conference received 39 full paper submissions, all of which underwent a rigorous double-blind peer review process, with papers receiving 2.77 reviews each, on average. Following a careful and selective evaluation, only the 19 most impactful and methodologically sound contributions were accepted for presentation, ensuring that the final program met the highest academic standards and reflected the core themes of the event.

The scientific program was structured into two principal tracks: Advanced Technologies in Education and Artificial Intelligence Applications. Both tracks featured high-quality research addressing critical challenges and emerging trends in their respective domains. Contributions came from a range of countries, with particularly strong representation from Bosnia and Herzegovina, Croatia, India, Belgium, and Bulgaria. Notably, the conference saw substantial participation from regional researchers, underscoring the growing academic engagement and international collaboration potential within Southeast Europe.

We extend our deepest appreciation to all authors, reviewers, session chairs, and attendees whose enthusiasm and scholarly contributions made MoStart 2025 a success. Special recognition goes to the Organizing Committee and the University of Mostar's support teams, whose tireless work enabled the successful realization of this year's event within our own facilities—marking not only a major step for the conference itself, but also a significant advancement in the University's ongoing commitment to excellence in research, innovation, and international collaboration.

June 2025

Daniel Vasić
Emil Brajković

Organization

General Chair

Daniel Vasić	University of Mostar, Bosnia and Herzegovina
Emil Brajković	University of Mostar, Bosnia and Herzegovina

Program Committee Chair

Daniel Vasić	University of Mostar, Bosnia and Herzegovina

Steering Committee

Boris Crnokić	University of Mostar, Bosnia and Herzegovina
Tomislav Volarić	University of Mostar, Bosnia and Herzegovina
Emil Brajković	University of Mostar, Bosnia and Herzegovina
Mirela Kundid Vasić	University of Mostar, Bosnia and Herzegovina
Krešimir Rakić	University of Mostar, Bosnia and Herzegovina
Davorka Topić Stipić	University of Mostar, Bosnia and Herzegovina
Daniel Vasić	University of Mostar, Bosnia and Herzegovina
Damir Vasilj	University of Mostar, Bosnia and Herzegovina
Ivan Šabić	Croatian Academic and Research Network, Croatia
Marin Bošnjak	University of Mostar, Bosnia and Herzegovina
Hrvoje Ljubić	University of Mostar, Bosnia and Herzegovina
Maja Marić	University of Mostar, Bosnia and Herzegovina
Vedran Mihalj	University of Mostar, Bosnia and Herzegovina
Manlio Napoli	University of Mostar, Bosnia and Herzegovina
Hrvoje Puljiz	Croatian Academic and Research Network, Croatia
Robert Rozić	University of Mostar, Bosnia and Herzegovina
Franjo Vučić	University of Mostar, Bosnia and Herzegovina

Program Committee

Sanja Bijakšić	University of Mostar, Bosnia and Herzegovina
Mirjana Bonković	University of Split, Croatia
Geoffrey Dick	St John's University, USA
Ivo Čolak	University of Mostar, Bosnia and Herzegovina
Juan Manuel Fernández Luna	University of Granada, Spain
Irena Galić	University of Osijek, Croatia
Puya Ghazizadeh	St John's University, USA
Suzanna Schmeelk	St John's University, USA
Sven Gotovac	University of Split, Croatia
Tamara Grujić	University of Split, Croatia
Rainer Herpers	Bonn-Rhein-Sieg University of Applied Sciences, Germany
Branko Katalinić	Vienna University of Technology, Austria
Zdenko Klepić	University of Mostar, Bosnia and Herzegovina
Goran Martinović	University of Osijek, Croatia
Pedro Miguel Moreira	Polytechnic Institute of Viana do Castelo, Portugal
Vladan Papić	University of Split, Croatia
Marko Rosić	University of Split, Croatia
Slavomir Stankov	University of Split, Croatia
Zoran Tomić	University of Mostar, Bosnia and Herzegovina
Drago Žagar	University of Osijek, Croatia
Boris Crnokić	University of Mostar, Bosnia and Herzegovina
Ani Grubišić	University of Split, Croatia
Tonćo Marušić	University of Mostar, Bosnia and Herzegovina
Jonathan Schler	Holon Institute of Technology, Israel
Jan Šnajder	University of Zagreb, Croatia
Danijel Topić	University of Osijek, Croatia
Tomislav Volarić	University of Mostar, Bosnia and Herzegovina
Branko Žitko	University of Split, Croatia
Krunoslav Žubrinić	University of Dubrovnik, Croatia
Elisabete Cunha	Polytechnic Institute of Viana do Castelo, Portugal
Bárbara Cristina Dos Santos Gaspar Cleto	Polytechnic Institute of Porto, Portugal
Angelina Gašpar	University of Split, Croatia
Janez Gotlih	University of Maribor, Slovenia
Miroslav Grubišić	University of Mostar, Bosnia and Herzegovina
Lada Maleš	University of Split, Croatia
Benny Johnson	Vitalsource, USA

Timi Karner	University of Maribor, Slovenia
Mirela Kundid Vasić	University of Mostar, Bosnia and Herzegovina
Nikola Ljubešić	University of Ljubljana, Slovenia
Željko Marušić	University of Mostar, Bosnia and Herzegovina
Ivan Peko	University of Split, Croatia
Krešimir Rakić	University of Mostar, Bosnia and Herzegovina
Višnja Simić	University of Kragujevac, Serbia
Suzana Tomaš	University of Split, Croatia
Daniel Vasić	University of Mostar, Bosnia and Herzegovina
Josip Vasilj	University of Split, Croatia
Željko Šeremet	University of Mostar, Bosnia and Herzegovina
Goran Zaharija	University of Split, Croatia

Additional Reviewers

Benčević, Marin
Bročić, Lucija

Contents

Brain in a Jar: Demystifying AI for Elementary Schoolers

Dino Nejašmić(✉), Monika Mladenović, Saša Mladenović, and Andrina Granić

Faculty of Science, University of Split, Rudera Boskovica 33, Split, Croatia
{dino.nejasmic,monika.mladenovic,sasa.mladenovic, andrina.granic}@pmfst.hr

Abstract. This article describes a workshop designed to introduce artificial intelligence (AI) concepts to elementary school students using interactive tools and discussions. The workshop, attended by over 50 fifth and sixth-grade students in several sessions, aimed to demystify AI principles by incorporating the "Brain in a Jar" concept and exploring the "Chinese Room Argument". The workshop's centerpiece was a "smart box", made especially for the workshop, symbolizing AI, which engaged students in understanding how machines learn and make decisions. Through hands-on activities, such as interaction with NAO robots and the "smart box", students learned about AI's basic concepts like object recognition and decision-making processes. The "Brain in a Jar" concept was used to provoke discussions on the nature of intelligence and the potential for machines to replicate human-like cognitive functions. Meanwhile, the "Chinese Room Argument" raised ethical and philosophical questions about AI's understanding versus true comprehension. Pre-workshop and post-workshop surveys were conducted to gauge participants' understanding and perceptions of AI. Initial findings indicate increased awareness and curiosity about AI technology among students, highlighting the effectiveness of interactive learning experiences in fostering technological literacy and critical thinking. This article provides insights into effective pedagogical approaches for integrating AI concepts into elementary school curricula, highlighting interactive tools and philosophical discussions. The presented model offers teachers innovative ways to introduce complex technological concepts, improve digital literacy, and incorporate new technologies into education.

Keywords: Artificial Intelligence · Education · AI literacy · NAO Robot · Interaction · Hands-on · Critical Thinking · Survey · Teaching First

1 Introduction

Given that artificial intelligence (AI) has been rapidly transforming our world for the past few years, it is crucial to introduce the younger generation to this groundbreaking technology [1]. Children frequently interact with AI, but still their understanding of it is often limited. To increase awareness and knowledge about AI among K-12 students, it is crucial to introduce AI learning activities to young learners consistently and from

D. Vasić and E. Brajković (Eds.): MoStart 2025, CCIS 2609, pp. 1–11, 2026.
https://doi.org/10.1007/978-3-032-02801-3_1

an early age [2]. Computational thinking [3] is now recognized as a key component of digital literacy, alongside reading, writing, and arithmetic. AI literacy further extends the concept of literacy by encompassing the skills needed to understand, use, and critically evaluate AI technologies and their societal impact [4–6]. AI literacy involves understanding AI concepts and technologies, which is foundational for students' learning intentions. AI literacy predicts students' confidence and perceived relevance of learning AI, influencing their readiness to engage with AI. Furthermore, AI literacy also includes primary constructs: awareness, use, evaluation, and ethics [7]. Even if AI literacy is crucial, it alone may not be enough to motivate continuous learning intention among students. While children's perceptions of AI can be improved, their attitudes towards engineering and science can remain unchanged [8]. In order to effectively develop AI curricula, it is crucial to understand what children already know and how they feel about AI. Some curricula employ play-based, story-based, and project-based learning methods to facilitate understanding of AI concepts and use interactive tools like Teachable Machine, AI for Oceans, and Quick, Draw! to engage children in learning about AI and machine learning through play and games [9]. Some other examples offer interactive and engaging learning experiences that blend STEM with the arts, making complex concepts more tangible and relatable. They aim to enhance understanding of AI concepts among K-12 students, such as perception, representation, reasoning, and generation [10].

Although incorporating basic AI concepts early in learning brings many of the aforementioned benefits, there are still some topics that need to be addressed. Effective teaching strategies are needed, that can leverage children's pre-existing knowledge and experiences with technology. The challenges are rooted in the abstract nature of AI, making it difficult for students to grasp its relevance and purpose. Finally, understanding students' preconceptions is crucial for creating meaningful education that connects with their daily interactions involving technology and AI [11].

1.1 The Brain in a Jar

The "Brain in a Jar" workshop serves as an educational initiative aimed at demystifying AI for elementary school students. Through interactive tools and engaging activities, the workshop strives to stimulate curiosity and foster a fundamental understanding of artificial intelligence among fifth and sixth graders.

The workshop's innovative approach utilizes the "Brain in a Jar" metaphor and the "Chinese Room Argument" to provoke thought and discussion on the nature of intelligence. By interacting with NAO robots and a specially designed "smart box," students explore AI's basic concepts, such as object recognition. These hands-on experiences are instrumental in challenging defined notions of machine intelligence and encouraging critical thinking.

The "Brain in a jar" or "Brain in a vat" theory is a philosophical thought experiment that questions the nature of reality. It explores the idea that our senses might not be reliable, and we could be brains in a vat, experiencing a simulated reality. The theory is rooted in Rene Descartes' skepticism, famously encapsulated in "Cogito, ergo sum" – "I think, therefore I am." While the theory is hypothetical, it encourages us to critically examine our perceptions and the world around us. It's a modern take on Cartesian skepticism, questioning the certainty of our existence. The concept of "Brain in a jar" was used to stimulate students to think about how AI system could perceive and interpret its environment, and develop a form of consciousness or understanding of reality [12]. The "Brain in a Jar" experiment serves as a metaphor to illustrate the distinction between simulated understanding and genuine comprehension, which lies at the heart of AI systems that mimic intelligent behavior without possessing consciousness or awareness.

"Chinese Room Argument", a thought experiment by John Searle argues that instructing the person or implementing a program for translation of Chinese symbols does not equate to actual understanding of language, as the person (or computer) would only manipulate symbols without comprehending their meaning.

The argument was used to help students to distinguish between strong AI, which posits that a correctly programmed computer has cognition like a human, and weak AI, which views computers as tools to study cognition. It emphasizes that syntactical manipulation of symbols (syntax) is not the same as understanding the meaning (semantics) associated with them. Furthermore, it asserts that simulating cognitive processes is not the same as duplicating them [13].

This article outlines a workshop aimed at introducing elementary school students to artificial intelligence (AI) concepts through interactive tools and discussions, with the goal of demystifying how AI operates. Furthermore, the article describes the conducted workshop's methodology, its impact on students' AI literacy and the significance of integrating AI education into early curricula. With analysis of pre- and post-workshop surveys, it gives insights into the effectiveness of such interactive learning experiences and the importance of fostering technological literacy from a young age.

The rest of the paper is organized as follows. The Methodology chapter provides a detailed description of the research design, including the context, participants, instruments, and procedures used in the study. The Results chapter presents the findings from both the quantitative and qualitative analyses, addressing the research questions posed. Finally, the Conclusion chapter discusses the implications of the findings, highlights the limitations of the study, and suggests directions for future research.

2 Methodology

The research was conducted from April to May 2024 during workshops for fifth and sixth-grade elementary school students (ages 10–11). Three workshops were held at the Department of Computer Science, Faculty of Science, University of Split. Students attended the workshops with their informatics teachers as part of extracurricular activities. Participation was voluntary, and the collected data was anonymized. Parents provided informal consent for their children's participation and the collection of data during the workshops.

The focus of the study is to investigate AI literacy among elementary school students and awareness of AI. Since girls are still an underrepresented group in the Computer science field, we also wanted to explore whether there are differences in attitudes toward AI. Therefore, we posed two research questions:

RQ1: Are there differences in motivation for learning about AI between genders?

RQ2: Are there differences in students' recognition of AI-driven devices and systems after the workshop?

2.1 Research Context

In Croatia, the informatics course is mandatory for fifth and sixth-graders, though it does not yet explicitly cover AI topics. Given the rapid growth of AI, there is a pressing need to develop AI literacy from an early age. To address this need, the first and third authors designed a workshop titled "Brain in a Jar" to introduce AI concepts to K-12 students using a NAO robot and interactive activities.

a) Box from the outside *b) Box from the inside*

Fig. 1. "Brain in a jar" box.

Before the workshop students took a pre-survey about AI awareness. The workshop featured a "smart box," or "brain in a jar" metaphor, a physical box with input and output mechanisms. Figure 1 shows the box. Students were asked if they could, for example, find which two 4-digit numbers multiplied give certain large number. To demonstrate the "Brain in a Jar" concept, many papers with large numbers, such as 23002644 or 76263082, were prepared. Inside the box, a table with instructions, such as 23002644 = 7637 * 3012, was prepared to help the person behind the box to map certain tasks to their solution. Similarly, for the Chinese language task, several Chinese symbols for different colors and objects were prepared. Students placed papers with tasks containing one color and one object into the input slot. Another student behind the box would find the correct answer on the table and place the corresponding paper through the output slot. This activity aimed to show that the "intelligence" behind the box's responses was merely a mapping process, not genuine understanding.

Subsequently, the same tasks were demonstrated using a NAO robot programmed by the first author to provide correct answers. Nao is programmed using predefined markers, that can easily be recognized by NAO. Each marker is associated with a certain object displayed in the picture, demonstrating similar functionality as "Brain in a jar". Figure 2 shows the NAO robot and markers used for the mentioned task.

This highlighted the distinction between AI and human intelligence, emphasizing that AI's ability to quickly map many operations is not equivalent to human cognitive functions. After the workshop, students took a post-survey containing the same questions as the pre-survey, along with six additional Likert-style questions about attitudes toward AI. We aimed to determine if the workshop changed students' awareness of AI and whether they would like to learn more about AI in the future.

Fig. 2. NAO and markers.

2.2 Participants

The workshops were attended by a total of 59 students, with 44 of them completing both the pre- and post-surveys. Therefore, we analyzed data from these 44 students. Among them, there were 23 boys and 21 girls. Most students were fifth-graders (n = 37), while the others were sixth-graders (n = 7). Of all the students, 14 reported that they had used ChatGPT, mostly for homework, while 30 stated that they had not used ChatGPT yet.

2.3 Instruments

Pre-workshop and post-workshop surveys were conducted to determine any changes in students' awareness and understanding of AI. The first part of the post-test was identical whereas the second part contained an additional six Likert-style questions to determine attitudes towards AI and AI education.

The pre-survey contained 16 items. The first question with three items collected socio-demographic data (gender, school, grade). The second question was related to the usage of ChatGPT. The third question contained six images, and students were asked to mark the ones they believed were AI-driven. Figure 3 shows these pictures.

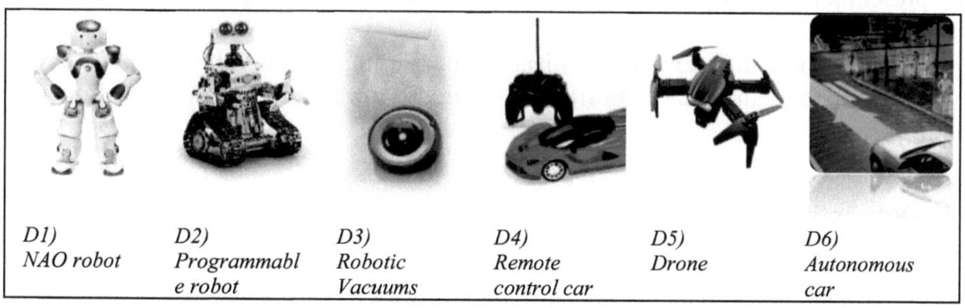

Fig. 3. Listed devices (third survey question).

In the following, fourth question, students could mark one or more systems from five systems that they thought were AI-driven. The offered systems were:

S1 – Autonomous car.

S2 – Music or movie recommendation (like on Spotify or Netflix).

S3 – Remote control boat.

S4 – ChatGPT.

S5 – Photo editing.

Post-survey contained a total of 22 questions. The first 16 items were the same as the pre-test, with an additional six Likert-style questions (options 1–5) related to attitudes towards AI and AI education. These Likert-style questions demonstrated good reliability, determined by a Cronbach alpha coefficient of 0.731. Table 1 shows Likert-style questions.

Table 1. Post-survey Likert-style questions.

Question	Statement	Question type
Q1	Artificial intelligence is interesting	Likert style (1–5)
Q2	I want to learn more about Artificial intelligence	Likert style (1–5)
Q3	I want to learn more about Artificial intelligence in the future	Likert style (1–5)
Q4	I like lectures with a robot	Likert style (1–5)
Q5	I would like to learn more about robots	Likert style (1–5)
Q6	Using Artificial intelligence in communication with the robot is fun	Likert style (1–5)

Questions Q1, Q4, and Q6 were related to the attitudes toward AI presented during the workshop (the "fun" part of AI), while Q2, Q3, and Q5 were related to attitudes toward AI education.

3 Results

We present our findings in the following sections, addressing the posed research questions:

RQ1: Are there differences in motivation for learning about AI between genders?

RQ2: Are there differences in students' attitudes towards AI and AI education after the workshop?

3.1 Descriptive Statistics

Table 1 shows Likert-style questions in the post-survey. As mentioned earlier, questions Q1, Q4, and Q6 were related to the attitudes toward AI presented during the workshop (the "fun" part of AI), while Q2, Q3, and Q5 were related to attitudes toward AI education. The descriptive statistics related to those questions are presented in Table 2.

Table 2. Descriptive statistics for Likert-style questions.

	Q1	Q2	Q3	Q4	Q5	Q6
n	44	44	44	44	44	44
Mean	4.86	4.45	3.14	4.91	4.48	4.84
Median	5.00	5.00	3.00	5.00	5.00	5.00
Mod	5	5	3	5	5	5
Range	3–5	1–5	1–5	4–5	2–5	3–5

When analyzing the questions related to attitudes towards AI and robots (Q1, Q4, and Q6), a higher level of satisfaction is evident based on the descriptive statistics (median, mode, and range). On the other hand, when it comes to attitudes toward learning AI (Q2, Q3, and Q5), it is clear that students are not as enthusiastic about learning AI, with Q3 showing the lowest indicators among the questions.

3.2 Differences in Motivation for Learning About AI Between Genders

The Mann-Whitney U test was used to determine the differences in motivation for learning about AI between genders. The questions were Likert-style (Table 1) with options from 1 (I completely disagree) to 5 (I completely agree). Table 3 shows descriptive statistics for these questions.

Table 3. The Mann-Whitney U test results.

Question	Q1	Q2	Q3	Q4	Q5	Q6
Mann-Whitney U	227.000	206.500	145.000	239.500	211.500	240.000
p	0.536	0.317	**0.020**	0.925	0.368	0.953

As Table 3 shows, the only statistically significant difference between gender attitudes was found for Q3 (I want to learn more about Artificial intelligence in the future). To determine where these differences lie, we additionally analyzed frequencies by gender, which is shown in Table 4.

Table 4. Frequencies based on the gender for Q3.

	1	2	3	4	5	Total
Boys	1	3	7	6	6	23
Girls	4	7	5	2	3	21
Total	**5**	**10**	**12**	**8**	**9**	**44**

Based on the results, it is evident that girls are less prone to learn about AI in the future compared to boys.

Interestingly, these results are not in line with the outcomes of a workshop with the NAO robot conducted a year ago [14]. The previous workshop focused on programming, and all workshop teachers were women. In that workshop, girls were more inclined to learn about programming and robots compared to boys. This current workshop focused on AI, with the main teacher being a man (the first author), who might have influenced the boys through his role as a role model, similar to how women teachers could affect girls as role models.

The lower enthusiasm among girls could also be attributed to several factors, such as a lack of role models in the AI field, societal stereotypes, or differing levels of prior exposure to technology. These findings highlight the need for targeted interventions to encourage girls to engage with AI and computer science more broadly, ensuring balanced representation and opportunities for all students.

3.3 Comparison of Students' Recognition of AI-Driven Devices and Systems After the Workshop

As mentioned, both surveys (pre- and post-) contained several identical questions. We aimed to determine whether there would be differences in recognizing AI-driven devices (third survey question with the prefix D) or systems (fourth survey question with the prefix S). The details are presented in the Instruments section.

To determine whether there are differences between the options in pre- and post-tests, we used McNemar's test because all items were dichotomous. Table 5 shows McNemar's test results.

Table 5. McNemar's test results.

	D1 pre-post	D2 pre-post	D3 pre-post	D4 pre-post	D5 pre-post	D6 pre-post	S1 pre-post	S2 pre-post	S3 pre-post	S4 pre-post	S5 pre-post
N	44	44	44	44	44	44	44	44	44	44	44
p	0.500	0.625	1.000	0.065	0.227	0.344	0.063	1.000	0.227	0.727	0.375

According to the results presented in Table 5, there were no statistically significant differences in recognizing AI-driven devices and systems. This suggests that the workshop may not have influenced students' ability to recognize AI-driven systems.

3.4 Qualitative Analysis

In all workshops, besides the teacher, at least three additional people were present as observers: two students' schoolteachers and the second author. Teachers and authors discussed their observations during the workshop, and there was no doubt that students enjoyed it. This observation is supported by survey data, as the last survey question was an open-ended question inviting comments on the workshop. Among the 44 participants, only one did not leave a comment. In all 43 comments, students used keywords like "*fun*," "*I liked it very much*," "*super*," "*I liked everything*," or similar expressions. Figure 4 shows the students in one of the workshops.

Fig. 4. Students during the workshop.

However, while there is no doubt about the motivational factor of robots, there is an impression that the focus was on the robot as a device for fun, while the educational factor remained neglected. The robot as a device took all the focus, so the students were more interested in what the robot could do, asking questions like "*Can it sing?*", "*Can it dance?*", "*Can it speak Croatian?*" and so on. This observation is also supported by the survey results, particularly the Likert-style questions related to attitudes towards AI education (Q2, Q3, and Q5), which received lower ratings compared to the questions related to "fun". This is especially evident in Q3, which is related to learning about AI in the future, as shown in Tables 2 and 3.

4 Conclusion

The findings indicated that while students found the activities fun and educational, their awareness of AI did not significantly change. The robot was perceived more as a novelty or distraction rather than an educational tool. This suggests a need for further research, focusing on educational content with the robot serving as a demonstrative aid.

Our study aimed to investigate AI literacy among elementary school students and their attitudes toward AI education. The pre- and post-workshop surveys revealed that students enjoyed the workshop, as evidenced by the high ratings for the "fun" aspects of AI (Q1, Q4, and Q6) and the overwhelmingly positive comments. However, the enthusiasm for learning more about AI (Q2, Q3, and Q5) was notably lower, indicating that while the workshop was engaging, it did not significantly enhance students' motivation to learn about AI in the future.

Additionally, our analysis of gender differences highlighted that boys showed more interest in learning about AI compared to girls, as reflected in Q3's statistically significant results. This discrepancy suggests that boys might have been more influenced by the male instructor, whereas previous workshops with female instructors showed higher engagement from girls. These findings emphasize the importance of role models in STEM education and suggest that diverse teaching staff could help balance gender interests.

The qualitative analysis supported these findings, showing that students were fascinated by the robot's capabilities, asking questions about its functions rather than its educational content. This aligns with the lower ratings for AI education-related questions, suggesting that while robots can captivate students, they need to be integrated into the curriculum in a way that emphasizes their educational value.

Seymour Papert's critique in "Does Easy Do It?" [15] warns against the potential pitfalls of "edutainment"—the blend of education and entertainment. While the premise is to get the best of both worlds, there is a concern that we might end up with the worst of both. In our workshop, while the robot successfully engaged students, it may have overshadowed the educational content, making the experience feel more like entertainment rather than a meaningful learning opportunity. This could lead to students enjoying the experience without gaining a deeper understanding of the subject matter.

To address this, the "hard fun" [16] approach should be considered in designing such activities. As Papert suggests, if the activity is just "fun," the learning outcomes may be missed, and if it is just "hard," the motivational factor may be lost. The key is to find a balance between hard and fun.

In conclusion, while interactive tools like robots can make AI workshops enjoyable, they must be carefully integrated to ensure educational objectives are met. Future workshops should focus on creating a balanced approach where robots are used to demonstrate AI concepts clearly and engagingly without overshadowing the educational content. Additionally, targeted interventions to encourage girls to engage with AI and computer science are necessary to ensure balanced representation and opportunities for all students. Further research is required to explore how best to achieve these goals and enhance AI literacy among elementary school students.

References

1. Goralski, M.A., Tan, T.K.: Artificial intelligence and sustainable development. Int. J. Manage. Educ. **18**(1), 100330 (2020). https://doi.org/10.1016/j.ijme.2019.100330
2. Vandenberg, J., Mott, B.: 'AI teaches itself: exploring young learners' perspectives on artificial intelligence for instrument development'. In: Proceedings of the 2023 Conference on Innovation and Technology in Computer Science Education V. 1, pp. 485–490. ACM, Turku Finland (2023). https://doi.org/10.1145/3587102.3588778
3. Wing, J.M.: Computational thinking. Commun. ACM **49**(3), 33–35 (2006). https://doi.org/10.1145/1118178.1118215
4. Kong, S.-C., Man-Yin Cheung, W., Zhang, G.: Evaluation of an artificial intelligence literacy course for university students with diverse study backgrounds. Comput. Educ. Artific. Intell. **2**, 100026 (2021). https://doi.org/10.1016/j.caeai.2021.100026

5. Ng, D.T.K., Leung, J.K.L., Chu, S.K.W., Qiao, M.S.: Conceptualizing AI literacy: an exploratory review. Comput. Educ.: Artific. Intell. **2**, 100041 (2021). https://doi.org/10.1016/j.caeai.2021.100041
6. Lišnić, B., Zaharija, G., Mladenović, S.: Integration of artificial intelligence in K-12: analysis of a three-year pilot study. AI **6**(3), 49 (2025). https://doi.org/10.3390/ai6030049
7. Wang, B., Rau, P.-L.P., Yuan, T.: Measuring user competence in using artificial intelligence: validity and reliability of artificial intelligence literacy scale. Behav. Inform. Technol. **42**(9), 1324–1337 (2023). https://doi.org/10.1080/0144929X.2022.2072768
8. Chai, C.S., Wang, X., Xu, C.: An extended theory of planned behavior for the modelling of chinese secondary school students' intention to learn artificial intelligence. Mathematics **8**(11), 2089 (2020). https://doi.org/10.3390/math8112089
9. Su, J., Yang, W.: AI literacy curriculum and its relation to children's perceptions of robots and attitudes towards engineering and science: an intervention study in early childhood education. Comput. Assist. Learn. **40**(1), 241–253 (2024). https://doi.org/10.1111/jcal.12867
10. Mitchell, J.J., et al., 'Bridging the gap: early education on robot and AI ethics through the robot theater platform in an informal learning environment. In: Companion of the 2024 ACM/IEEE International Conference on Human-Robot Interaction, pp. 760–764. ACM, Boulder CO USA (2024). https://doi.org/10.1145/3610978.3640581
11. Axell, C., Berg, A.: "You give a little bit more love to animals than to robots": primary pupils' conceptions of "programming" and programmable artefacts. Int. J. Technol. Des. Educ. **34**(2), 505–530 (2024). https://doi.org/10.1007/s10798-023-09838-6
12. Putnam, H.: Reason, truth and history, 1st edn. Cambridge University Press (1981). https://doi.org/10.1017/CBO9780511625398
13. Moural, J.: The chinese room argument. In: Smith , B. (ed.) John Searle, 1st edn, pp. 214–260. Cambridge University Press (2003). https://doi.org/10.1017/CBO9780511613999.010
14. Prnjak, A., Mladenović, M., Prnić, M., Mladenović, S.: Community-engaged Informatics education: a robot-assisted approach to STEM learning. In: Higher Education in the Service of Society, Cadiz (2024)
15. Papert, S.: Does easy do it? Children, games, and learning (2010)
16. Papert, S.: Hard fun. Bangor Daily News, vol. 2 (2002)

Humanoid Robots in Education: A Systematic Review of Pedagogical Approaches and Impact

Gordana Jugo[1](✉), Boris Crnokić[2], and Vlado Grubišić[3]

[1] CARNET, 10000 Zagreb, Croatia
gordana.jugo@carnet.hr

[2] Faculty of Mechanical Engineering, Computing and Electrical Engineering, University of Mostar, Mostar 88000, Bosnia and Herzegovina
boris.crnokic@fsre.sum.ba

[3] University of Mostar, Mostar 88000, Bosnia and Herzegovina
vlado.grubisic@fsre.sum.ba

Abstract. Humanoid robots in education present both promising opportunities and considerable risks. This review explores the use of humanoid robots in formal education, focusing on pedagogical approaches, their impact, challenges and ethical considerations. Most studies employed constructivist and socio-cultural approaches, like problem-based and game-based learning. The results revealed that humanoid robots enhance learning effectiveness, student engagement, motivation, enjoyment, confidence, and 21st-century skills, including digital competence. However, ethical concerns persist, including privacy, data security, and reduced social engagement due to over-reliance on robots. Implementation challenges include technical issues, high costs and a lack of trained personnel. The review provides recommendations for implementation, future research and development to ensure the responsible and effective integration of robots into formal education.

Keywords: Educational Robotics · Robotics in Education · Humanoid Robots · Pedagogical Approaches

1 Introduction

Rapid technological and societal transformations have created considerable challenges for educational systems, such as addressing diverse student needs, coping with teacher shortages, and managing inadequate funding. Consequently, education systems must evolve to embrace these changes and equip students with the skills necessary to thrive in a dynamic future. One promising way to tackle these challenges is by integrating educational technologies, including robots, into classrooms.

Humanoid robots, resembling humans in shape, sensing, communication, and movement, offer unique educational opportunities. According to [1], implementing humanoid robots in education integrates the advantages of technology with the human component. As this study will demonstrate, incorporating humanoid robots into education

D. Vasić and E. Brajković (Eds.): MoStart 2025, CCIS 2609, pp. 12–26, 2026.
https://doi.org/10.1007/978-3-032-02801-3_2

can enhance effectiveness, foster 21st-century skills, and boost student engagement, including students with special needs. When used properly, humanoid robots can boost educational efficiency and inclusivity. Poor management, however, may lead to wrong pedagogical choices, reinforce negative social values, and deepen the digital divide. Therefore, the application of robots in education must be grounded in robust pedagogical approaches. Teachers, policymakers, and other stakeholders should fully grasp the potential and implications of humanoid robots in education to ensure their responsible, effective and sustainable integration.

The research questions addressed are as follows:

- What pedagogical approaches do teachers adopt when using humanoid robots in formal education?
- What are the benefits and challenges of using humanoid robots in education?
- What implementation challenges and ethical considerations arise when employing humanoid robots in education?

The paper is structured as follows: the research problem, background, significance, and objectives are provided in the Introduction, followed by existing research and theoretical frameworks related to the topic in the Literature review section. The Methodology section describes the research design, data collection methods, analysis procedures and limitations. Results and Discussions sections provide and interpret the results, comparing them with existing research, and explaining their implications. The Conclusion section summarises the key insights and recommendations for future research.

2 Review of Literature

This section outlines the characteristics of humanoid robots used in education, the pedagogical approaches implemented, and the positive, negative, and inconsistent impacts of robots in educational settings. It also addresses ethical issues and explores the potential for collaboration between human teachers and robots.

The most frequently used robot was NAO, appearing in nine studies [2–10], followed by Pepper in three studies [1, 2, 11]. Other robots include Darwin [12], JACO2 [2], and Robonova-1 [13]. However, this research adopts a generic approach, disregarding specific robot models due to the substantial similarities among the robots in these studies. This approach ensures broader applicability and aligns with the paper's objective to provide comprehensive insights into using humanoid robots in education.

Humanoid robots feature speech recognition, tactile sensors, computer vision, and mobility, and some can speak over 20 languages (SoftBank Robotics, 2020, in [7]). However, they struggle with object recognition and face major design challenges, including the complexity of realistic movement and the need for independent power sources [14]. Despite advances in learning algorithms, their cognitive abilities are still far from human intelligence.

The reviewed literature describes pedagogical approaches from traditional direct instruction to novel approaches, such as robot-assisted language learning (RALL). However, most approaches are based on constructivist and socio-cultural learning theories, such as problem-based or situated learning. The roles of humanoid robots include teaching assistants, learning assistants for students, tutees, teachers, peers, assistive technology, learning tools, and learning materials.

Robots' positive impact on learning performance is demonstrated by [6]. Other reported benefits include high learner engagement [3, 10, 15–17], increased enjoyment of learning [6, 10, 12], high enthusiasm and improved confidence. Robots support the development of various skills, such as creativity, critical thinking, collaboration, computational thinking, problem-solving, resilience, and decoding skills [3]. According to [18], humanoid robots can address the specific learning needs of each student. However, [19] argues it is difficult, if not impossible, to reprogram the robot quickly enough to adapt to students' ever-changing intellectual, mental, physical, and emotional states.

A comparative study of robots' impact on academic performance reports inconsistent results [15]. Students' excitement about interacting with robots may decline over time [7]. Moreover, specific gestures, such as thumbs-up or applauding, can increase confidence in some students but may decrease the performance of others [21].

Several studies reported technical challenges in the classroom [2, 3, 5, 7], including speech and face recognition, connectivity, malfunctions, and repairs. Technical issues may result in distractions among students waiting for the robot to reset [10].

Despite significant technological advancements, robots' communication skills remain inferior to human teachers due to their lack of emotional intelligence [18].

Compared to the selected studies, this review emphasises pedagogical approaches underpinning the use of humanoid robots in education and relates them to an analysis of benefits, challenges, and ethical considerations.

3 Methodology

A systematic literature review was chosen to address the research questions as it provides comprehensive and objective insights into the subject. A broad and relevant search was conducted using the following academic databases: ACM Digital Library, ERIC, IEEE Xplore, Scopus, and Web of Science.

Keywords related to pedagogical approaches for using humanoid robots in formal education were identified and combined into an effective search string: humanoid AND robot* AND education* AND (pedagog* OR didactics OR teaching).

The initial search across these five databases yielded 752 articles. After applying inclusion and exclusion criteria, the pool was reduced to 65 papers. Following abstract reviews, 33 articles were selected: ACM Digital Library: 0, ERIC: 7, IEEE Xplore: 4, Scopus: 12, and Web of Science: 10.

The selection process employed the following inclusion criteria for studies:

- Focus on pedagogical approaches to using humanoid robots in formal education.
- They are research or review articles published in academic journals, or
- They are conference papers published in conference proceedings.
- The full text is available in the selected databases.

The exclusion criteria were as follows:

- The source is a book, dissertation, thesis, or other non-peer-reviewed publication.
- The content is unrelated to the topic, such as a focus on technical aspects.

- The educational level falls outside the range of pre-school to higher education.

Due to the novelty of humanoid robots in education, no specific year range was defined. However, all selected papers were published in the last 15 years, starting from 2010.

The first phase of data extraction was conducted through a systematic analysis, during which relevant data were categorised as follows:

- Study Details: Title, authors, publication year and type.
- Methodology: Research design, sample, and data collection methods.
- Limitations and Future Research
- Intervention: Pedagogical approach, type of robot, and roles of the teacher and robot.
- Findings: Quantitative and qualitative results related to pedagogical approaches for using humanoid robots in formal education settings.
- Technical and Other Challenges: Challenges faced, including ethical considerations.

Analysing the full texts, 3 papers were excluded for not meeting the inclusion criteria. The final selection of 30 studies includes 22 research articles and 8 review articles.

In the second phase, a qualitative synthesis approach was used for an in-depth data review, leading to a comprehensive synthesis of findings.

A limitation of this review is that the selection process was confined to specific databases and English-language publications, which may have led to the exclusion of relevant studies. Additionally, the selected keywords may have overlooked alternative formulations of key concepts.

4 Results

4.1 Pedagogical Approaches and Impact of Humanoid Robots in Education

RALL is the most common learning method in the reviewed articles [6, 7, 11, 15, 18, 21, 22]. Other methods include problem-based learning [3, 13, 23, 24], game-based learning [17, 22, 23, 25], learning by teaching [4, 17, 25], inquiry-based learning [3, 13, 23], project-based learning [13, 23], situated learning [10], and culturally responsive pedagogy [26]. Some pedagogical approaches focused on assessment [7, 12, 20]. In some cases, two or multiple methods were applied, with the results reported jointly rather than separately for each method [8, 11, 15, 20, 23, 24].

Robot-Assisted Language Learning. RALL is not a single method but a collection of different approaches to using robots to enhance language skills [21]. The reviewed papers introduce methods such as storytelling [22], total physical response [11, 21], game-based learning [6], and robotic progressive assessment [7].

Alemi et al. [4] compared three groups of English as a Foreign Language (EFL) learners: RALL, GBLL (Game-Based Learning), and a control group using traditional methods. The RALL group outperformed others in immediate and delayed post-tests in acquisition and retention of grammar. Additionally, the RALL group enjoyed learning, participated actively, and showed a positive attitude toward robots in the classroom.

Alemi and Khatoony [22] studied a humanoid robot facilitating a Virtual Reality game for EFL learners. Students engaged in scenario-based conversations, followed by the robot asking related questions. Pre and post-tests indicate significant improvements in young EFL learners' pronunciation accuracy.

Ao and Yu [14] studied factors affecting learning performance in RALL. Verbal interactions like pre-recorded voices, quizzes, and feedback enhance learning, while synthesised voices, small talk and bilingual robots hinder it. Nonverbal cues, such as moderate gaze, adequate positioning, and iconic gestures, enhance performance. However, gestures like thumbs up, applause, and dancing boosted confidence for some but distracted others, reducing performance.

Ouafa et al. [15] note RALL benefits such as increased engagement, personalised support, and tailored interactions. However, they argue that the impact of RALL on academic performance is inconsistent.

Problem-Based Learning. In problem-based learning (PBL), students collaborate in groups, gain knowledge by facilitated problem-solving, with teachers guiding the process [27]. Most studies combined PBL with other methods, so its impact is unclear. Nasir et al. [24] conducted a PBL study to improve computational thinking. A humanoid robot, acting as a CEO, asked students to solve a problem while providing guidance, feedback, and support. Participants perceived the robot as competent, friendly, and likeable, with performance showing no significant impact on their perception.

Learning by Teaching. In learning by teaching, tutors engage in reflective knowledge-building by explaining concepts to tutees, benefiting both sides [28]. Reviewed articles [4, 17, 25] describe students tutoring humanoid robots, where the robots take on the role of tutees.

Ekström and Pareto [17, 25] combined learning by teaching with game-based learning, where a robot and a child played a digital math game. The robot acting as a tutee asked the child to explain math concepts. Children readily accepted the role, and teachers valued the robot's diverse questions but found the activity slower and less effective than traditional methods, with verbal communication limitations.

Tanaka et al. [11] examined human-robot interaction in children's learning activities at home. Lessons were delivered through pre-recorded videos displayed on the robot's chest, while the robot interacted with the children. Key findings included children's preference for brief instructions, boredom caused by monotone speech, the importance of eye contact, and the value of physical contact in interactions.

Jamet et al. [4] found that learning by teaching improves children's skills in reading, writing, language, reasoning, and focus, benefiting all ages and children with special needs. Clear communication of the tutor's role is essential for its effectiveness.

Situated Learning. Situated learning defines learning as a social process where learners move from peripheral to central roles as they gain expertise [29]. So and Lee [10] designed a learning approach using a humanoid robot to teach young children measurement. Children were asking questions and touching the robot, feeling comfortable and enthusiastic. Despite technical issues that sometimes led to distractions, children enjoyed learning with the robot, even preferring it over human teachers for being friendlier and more entertaining. The study showed the robot's ability to foster engagement and create a positive learning environment while achieving learning outcomes.

Pedagogical Approaches Focused on Assessment. Chew and Chua [7] employed a humanoid robot to assess students' Chinese pronunciation and provide personalised feedback. The method enhanced engagement, enthusiasm, and motivation. Students found the robot easy to interact with and useful, enjoyed learning and appreciated the personalised feedback. While initial excitement waned slightly, the robot sustained positive emotional and cognitive engagement.

Khairy et al. [20] developed an algorithm for humanoid robots to assist higher education students during oral assessments, addressing challenges like shyness, dissatisfaction, hesitation, and a lack of confidence. Results showed that robots boosted students' self-confidence and promoted active learning.

Brown and Howard [12] tested the hypothesis that a robotic educational agent could improve test performance by adaptively engaging with students. Analysis of test completion times, survey responses, and comments showed the robot reduced idle time, maintained attention, and enhanced participants' enjoyment of the exam.

Culturally Responsive Pedagogy. Williams et al. [26] developed a program to increase middle school girls' participation in social robotics through a culturally responsive curriculum. It integrates robot programming and ethics with asset building, reflection, and community connections. This approach promotes engagement and improves learning outcomes, focusing on students' strengths. The program enhances students' understanding of technology's role in social justice and their self-concept and self-efficacy in computer science and technology.

Mixed Pedagogical Approaches. Morita et al. [2] combined direct instruction with experiential learning. Teachers developed a learning scenario with a tool based on knowledge chunk reuse. Two robots assisted in engaging students and demonstrating the concept of pendulum movement. Teachers found the tool useful but were concerned it could inhibit creativity and result in an inflexible teaching approach. Students enjoyed the robots' speech and humour.

Riojas et al. [13] examined various educational technologies, including humanoid robots, in pre-college engineering education. They proposed criteria for selecting appropriate technologies, including cost, learning activities, and required expertise. They suggest some technologies suit deductive methods like direct instruction, while others support inductive approaches like problem, inquiry, and project-based methods. Problem-Based Learning (PBL) and Inquiry-Based Learning (IBL) focus on knowledge construction by solving problems or answering questions through self-directed learning. Project-Based Learning promotes practical application of knowledge by creating a final product. According to Riojas et al. [13], humanoid robots are particularly effective in problem-based learning due to their programmability. They recommend balancing deductive and inductive teaching methods to support diverse learning objectives, using humanoid robots to complement, not replace, instructor guidance.

In a three-year study by Chalmers et al. [3], 29 teachers in 10 schools used two humanoid robots in subjects like programming, mathematics, and languages, employing social constructivist methods such as collaborative, inquiry-based, and problem-based learning. Each school had a robot for 8 weeks to 9 months. Teachers attended a professional development session beforehand and were encouraged to design challenging, open-ended learning activities. They valued the robots' ability to boost student engagement, provide immediate feedback, and foster problem-solving and persistence. Students showed enthusiasm, motivation, and confidence in computer science, developing 21st-century skills like creativity, critical thinking, collaboration, and computational thinking, with no gender differences in engagement. Teachers were surprised by the feelings students developed toward the robots, often treating them as companions. Overall, the robots enhanced understanding, deep learning, and sustained interest.

Students with Special Educational Needs (SEN). Studies on humanoid robots involving students with SEN [8, 9, 16, 19, 30, 31] employed various pedagogical approaches and found high engagement, interest, and enthusiasm [9, 16]. Aziz et al. [8] noted that autistic children enjoyed interacting with robots and showed emotional responses.

Gouraguine et al. [9] developed a methodology to improve visual learning for children with specific needs, focusing on understanding mathematical concepts through human-robot interactions. Three strategies were tested: robot (TAT), traditional aids (TT), and both combined (BT). The robot proved more effective than traditional methods. Additionally, TAT was the most popular approach. Children formed strong bonds with the robot while appreciating its ability to recognise handwritten digits.

Sigacheva et al. [19] proposed RALL to teach autistic children EFL, with robots acting as teachers in individual communication sessions. Robots excelled in encouraging communication and tactile interaction, creating a safe and supportive learning environment. However, human teachers were superior in problem-solving, individualised education plans, and flexibly addressing children's changing emotional and intellectual needs, particularly in homeschooling contexts.

Tuna [16] conducted a pilot study to assess whether humanoid robots could help children with autism spectrum disorder (ASD) improve symbolic play. Using targeted scenarios and a least-to-most prompting (LMP) procedure, robots encouraged high engagement in children and improved their symbolic play skills.

Alcorn et al. [30] explored educators' views on using humanoid robots with pupils with ASD. While most were open to their use, they raised concerns about over-reliance on robots limiting engagement with people and other activities. Educators emphasised the need for personalisation, with robots supporting learning rather than replacing teachers, and highlighted the importance of human interaction.

4.2 Implementation Challenges

Several studies highlight technical challenges in using robots in education, including speech recognition issues in noisy environments, limited face recognition, and connectivity problems causing slow responses or disrupted robot operation [2, 3, 7, 10, 17]. Malfunctions requiring resets or repairs lead to idle time, distracting students [8]. Integration also requires additional time for programming and setup [2].

Psychological and classroom management challenges also arise. Students, especially first-time users, might struggle interacting with humanoid robots [7]. Robots could increase classroom disorder [18], while limited robot availability may cause boredom and distraction among students waiting for their turn [10].

Cost is another limiting factor, with expenses ranging from tens to thousands of dollars [12, 13, 19]. However, some researchers argue that robots can be more cost-effective than hiring and training human instructors [15].

4.3 Ethical Considerations

Integrating humanoid robots in education raises significant ethical challenges, including privacy, data security, and transparency. Robots' ability to assess responses, store personal profiles, and provide feedback can enhance teaching but poses risks if data is stored and accessed without proper consent, particularly for minors [32].

Robots' decisions about educational appropriateness may differ from those made by human teachers, who consider students' goals, emotions, and values [32]. Over-reliance on robots could also limit creativity and lead to inflexible teaching methods [2].

Potential societal disruptions, such as labour market displacement and underestimating AI's long-term impacts, could prevent economic and social opportunities [7].

Anthropomorphism is another challenge since attributing human-like characteristics to robots could influence children's developmental processes [12]. Emotional attachment to robots may harm children's social skills and interactions with peers and adults [30]. Additionally, robots may be perceived as friendlier and favoured over human teachers [10].

To ensure children's safety during interactions, various precautions were reported, such as testing scenarios with simulated robots before introducing real ones [16] and establishing specific rules, including the mandatory teacher presence, maintaining a safe distance between children and the robot, and promptly terminating sessions if children showed discomfort [8].

The high cost of robots limits their accessibility, potentially widening educational gaps [13]. Additionally, robots may reflect social and cultural biases, reinforcing inequities [15, 32].

Newton and Newton [32] propose a code of practice for the ethical integration of robots in education. It emphasises the importance of assessing values in robot-assisted teaching while preserving key roles for human educators, such as classroom management and ensuring teaching quality. Special attention is given to limiting young children's interactions with robots to foster interpersonal skills and higher-order thinking, promoting robots as complements to teachers rather than replacements.

Additionally, Newton and Newton [32] highlight the emotional aspect of teaching, questioning whether robots can develop a genuine passion for the subject or inspire a love of learning in students.

4.4 Limitations and Potential Gaps in the Selected Studies

A key limitation in the reviewed studies is small sample sizes, with some involving as few as two students and only a few exceeding 40 participants. Teacher samples were generally larger, but some studies had limited teacher participation. Additionally, most studies were brief, with some including only one session.

Research design limitations have also been noted. For example, social robotics research for autism often involves single interactions in controlled, laboratory-based settings rather than real-world environments, raising validity concerns [30]. Similarly, findings based on a single Australian school sector using only one type of robot, the NAO robot, cannot be generalised [3].

Gaps also exist in exploring pedagogical approaches. While RALL and learning by teaching are well-studied, other methods are rarely addressed, and some studies lack a defined approach or use mixed strategies without separate results.

In addition, Morita et al. [2] emphasise the need for tailored learning theories to support the effective use of robots in education.

5 Discussion

5.1 Pedagogical Approaches and Robotic Impact

The reviewed literature explores various pedagogical approaches to using robots in education, spanning traditional direct instruction to innovative methods like RALL. These approaches are often student-centred, rooted in constructivist and socio-cultural learning theories, such as problem-based learning, game-based learning, and learning by teaching. Some studies effectively combine multiple strategies. In addition, incorporating robots encouraged some teachers to rethink their pedagogy, emphasising the need to adapt teaching methods to leverage emerging technologies [3].

The impact of using robots in education is presented through various pedagogical approaches. However, it is difficult to determine the impact of specific pedagogical approaches, as they are often combined, with results not reported separately [2, 3, 11, 13, 17, 23, 25]. Additionally, certain approaches, such as situated learning [10] and culturally responsive pedagogy [26], are underrepresented and insufficiently elaborated. For these reasons, the impact of robots will be examined from the common perspective of approaches rooted in constructivist and socio-cultural learning theories.

Although the integration of humanoid robots in education presents benefits and challenges, positive outcomes dominate the findings. Robots are frequently reported to enhance student engagement, interest, motivation, enjoyment, enthusiasm, self-confidence, and social interaction. Robots also elicited emotional responses in autistic children, but occasionally distracted some students. Concerns include a potential decline in excitement as the novelty wears off.

Robots positively impact cognitive outcomes by enhancing understanding and promoting deep learning. They foster skill development, such as reading, writing, and language. While some studies question robots' ability to foster critical and creative thinking [32], others report positive impacts on critical thinking and problem-solving skills [3]. Students learning grammar through RALL outperformed students using traditional or game-based methods [6]. However, some studies report ambiguous or negative results, such as robots reducing academic performance or causing distractions [21].

Students view robots positively, appreciating their competence, intelligence, and personalised feedback [6, 7]. Interactions with robots create safe and friendly environments, with some students forming emotional attachments. This might benefit special educational needs (SEN) students, who prefer assistive technologies over traditional tools.

However, concerns have been expressed regarding the potential over-reliance on robots and their impact on students' social and emotional development.

A study by Chalmers et al. [3], conducted with a robust sample over an extended period and demonstrating promising results, presents an example of good practice. Robots enhanced student engagement, deep learning, and skill development, including critical and creative thinking, while maintaining high interest and enthusiasm. In addition to a robust sample and an extended period, key factors for success included professional development sessions for teachers and the opportunity for educators to select their preferred pedagogical approach, which, in this case, was a social constructivist method.

Considering teachers' perspectives is essential as they are crucial for the implementation of robots into education. Teachers welcome robots but emphasise the need to balance technology with human interaction, while over-reliance on robots may prevent flexibility and limit peer engagement.

Overall, robots show promise in fostering interactive, motivating learning environments and inspiring pedagogical innovation. However, their integration must be carefully managed to address potential drawbacks. While robots may surpass humans in some respects, no evidence suggests they are more effective than human teachers [18], who remain essential in orchestrating all aspects of the learning process, including defining learning objectives, choosing methods and tools, designing learning activities, and fostering meaningful connections in education.

5.2 Ethical Considerations

Several studies acknowledge significant ethical challenges, including privacy, data protection, societal disruptions, anthropomorphism, and equity of access.

Collaboration among robot engineers, programmers, teachers, sociologists, and ethicists is essential to ensure that human rights and ethical considerations are respected and protected [32]. Global and national policies must be established to guide the responsible use of humanoid robots in education. These policies should be supported by organisational guidelines and codes of practice that align with broader policies while being tailored to specific contexts and needs.

The possibility that robots could replace human teachers and diminish social engagement raises a pressing ethical concern. As robots become increasingly autonomous and capable, teachers should adapt their practices and rethink their roles, ensuring that learning experiences continue to prioritise human values. Importantly, the presence of robots should not overshadow the fundamental purpose of education: teaching students what it means to be human (Macmurray, 2012 in [32]).

Another concern is the potential over-reliance on robots. In the digital age, teachers are not merely expected to be managers of teaching and learning but also creative and imaginative designers of meaningful learning experiences, effectively using available resources [32]. Robots should be regarded as one of these resources. Ideally, teachers and robots may work together to enhance learning, with human teachers maintaining oversight and guiding the educational process.

In summary, while humanoid robots have the potential to transform education, their integration must be guided by a robust ethical framework. This approach will address pressing concerns and ensure that robots are deployed responsibly and inclusively, complementing the indispensable role of human educators.

5.3 Recommendations for Implementation

When designing educational activities with robots, teachers must align robot selection and teaching methods with learning goals, clearly defining the roles of teachers, students, and robots for effective integration. Robots' lack of advanced cognitive abilities, emotional intelligence, and intuition limits their role, making them suitable for repetitive tasks [18].

The integration of humanoid robots in education faces challenges such as technical difficulties, safety concerns, and high costs. Technical issues, including unreliable speech and face recognition, connectivity problems, and robot malfunctions, have proven distracting and remain significant barriers. Further, programming, setting up, and maintaining robots require extra time and expertise. The novelty and complexity of robots exceed current teacher competencies.

To enable effective use and avoid challenges at the organisational level, factors such as classroom management, technical support, teacher training, financial resources, and a stable internet connection are essential [13]. Policies should be established and regularly updated to reflect advancements in robotics and evolving user needs. Teachers and students may also require guidance and training to interact with robots effectively [32].

Since humanoid robots have the potential to improve teaching effectiveness and enrich learning experiences, developing appropriate standards and procedures is crucial to improving the overall quality of education. Given the lack of a well-defined curriculum and learning materials for teachers working with humanoid robots, creating these resources is essential for effective implementation [14]. Furthermore, addressing public concerns and establishing legal frameworks are critical steps in integrating robots into educational settings [14].

5.4 Future Directions and Research

Despite advances in humanoid robot functionalities, including face and speech recognition and multilingual abilities, significant progress is still required in sensing, cognition, manipulation and power systems [14]. Therefore, their abilities in emotion recognition, expression, and adaptability to human feelings should be improved [18].

Continued research in experimental settings, baseline studies and multi-dimensional evaluation metrics is needed to assess robotic impact [24], and empirical evaluations of robots' effectiveness in education [13]. Collaboration between researchers and educational organisations is crucial for developing specific applications, implementing interventions, and conducting contextual studies in formal education environments [11].

Since most studies involve limited sample sizes, future research with a larger and more diverse group of participants is necessary [8, 16]. Research methods, sampling, and implementation should be carefully planned to ensure robust research results while facilitating meaningful learning. Ethical considerations and the safety of both students and educators must remain a priority. Robots should be used under teacher supervision, as fully autonomous behaviour still requires further research and development [14].

To conclude, designing human-robot interaction that positively impacts participants' learning and accurately measuring such impact remains an ongoing challenge [24].

6 Conclusion

Research findings reveal several advantages of using humanoid robots in formal education, combined with pedagogical approaches rooted in constructivist and socio-cultural learning theories, including increased student engagement, motivation, and enjoyment of learning. Students demonstrated high levels of enthusiasm, confidence and improved 21st century skills. Some studies indicate that robots can foster critical thinking and problem-solving skills and outperform traditional teaching methods. However, a smaller number of studies report ambiguous or negative results. To maximise the benefits of humanoid robots, it is essential to carefully define their role in the classroom and ground their implementation in solid pedagogical frameworks.

Despite the benefits, challenges remain. The design of humanoid robots encounters issues with movements, sensing, and cognitive abilities. Their implementation in education faces practical barriers like technical challenges, high costs and lack of trained personnel, which must be addressed for widespread adoption.

Many students positively perceive robots, valuing their competence, intelligence, and ability to provide personalised feedback. While generally positive about robots, teachers express valid concerns about over-reliance on technology, which could reduce social interaction between students and teachers.

Although humanoid robots may offer advantages over human teachers, such as tirelessness, multilingual abilities, and real-time feedback, they still lack emotional intelligence and spontaneity, which limits their ability to respond to students' needs. Robots are not intended to replace human teachers, but to serve as supportive tools, handling routine tasks so teachers can focus on orchestrating the teaching and learning process to enhance the educational experience, fostering deeper understanding.

The design and development of educational robots should be a collaborative effort involving a multidisciplinary team, including programmers, educators, psychologists, and ethicists, alongside key stakeholders such as students, teachers and policymakers.

Additionally, children and adults alike must be educated on the responsible use of robotic technologies. The increasing sophistication of AI raises significant ethical concerns, including those related to privacy, data security, surveillance, and anthropomorphism. Addressing these issues requires comprehensive national and global policies, institutional guidelines, and collaborative engagement among educators, technologists, and ethicists. Ensuring the safety, privacy, and well-being of both students and teachers.

To conclude, humanoid robots in education offer promising opportunities and significant challenges. They have the potential to create motivating learning environments, enable innovative teaching methodologies, and prepare students for an AI-driven future in which interactions with such technologies will become increasingly common. However, further research is necessary to assess their impact and identify optimal ways to use robots to enhance educational outcomes, while minimising potential drawbacks.

Acknowledgments. This paper is part of the Postgraduate doctoral programme "Information management and application of information and Communication technologies" offered by the University of Mostar.

References

1. Pande, A., Mishra, D.: Humanoid robot as an educational assistant–insights of speech recognition for online and offline mode of teaching. Behav. Inform. Technol. **44**, 975–992 (2024). https://doi.org/10.1080/0144929X.2024.2344726
2. Morita, T., Takahashi, N., Kosuda, M., Yamaguchi, T.: A teaching assistant robot design tool based on knowledge chunks reuse. In: Proceedings - International Computer Software and Applications Conference, pp. 68–73. IEEE Computer Society (2019). https://doi.org/10.1109/COMPSAC.2019.10185
3. Chalmers, C., Keane, T., Boden, M., Williams, M.: Humanoid robots go to school. Educ Inf Technol (Dordr). **27**, 7563–7581 (2022). https://doi.org/10.1007/s10639-022-10913-z
4. Jamet, F., Masson, O., Jacquet, B., Stilgenbauer, J.L., Baratgin, J.: Learning by teaching with humanoid robot: a new powerful experimental tool to improve children's learning ability. J. Robot. **2018** (2018). https://doi.org/10.1155/2018/4578762
5. Budiharto, W., Cahyani, A.D., Rumondor, P.C.B., Suhartono, D.: EduRobot: intelligent humanoid robot with natural interaction for education and entertainment. In: Procedia Computer Science, pp. 564–570. Elsevier B.V. (2017). https://doi.org/10.1016/j.procs.2017.10.064
6. Alemi, M., Bakhtiari Fard, N., Rezanejad, A.: The triumph of human-robot interaction: employing humanoid robot to boost grammar acquisition and retention among iranian young EFL learners 1. MEXTESOL J. **47**, 1 (2023). https://doi.org/10.61871/mj.v47n3-5
7. Chew, E., Chua, X.N.: Robotic Chinese language tutor: personalising progress assessment and feedback or taking over your job? Horizon. **28**, 113–124 (2020). https://doi.org/10.1108/OTH-04-2020-0015
8. Aziz, A.A., Moganan, F.F.M., Ismail, A., Lokman, A.M.: Autistic children's kansei responses towards humanoid-robot as teaching mediator. In: Procedia Computer Science, pp. 488–493. Elsevier B.V. (2015). https://doi.org/10.1016/j.procs.2015.12.322
9. Gouraguine, S., Qbadou, M., Rafik, M., Riad, M., Mansouri, K.: A new knowledge primitive of digits recognition for NAO robot using MNIST dataset and CNN algorithm for children's visual learning enhancement. J. Inform. Technol. Educ.: Res. **22**, 389–408 (2023). https://doi.org/10.28945/5194
10. So, S., Lee, N.: Pedagogical exploration and technological development of a humanoid robotic system for teaching to and learning in young children. Cogent Educ. **10** (2023). https://doi.org/10.1080/2331186X.2023.2179181
11. Tanaka, F., Isshiki, K., Takahashi, F., Uekusa, M., Sei, R., Hayashi, K.: Pepper learns together with children: development of an educational application. In: 2015 IEEE-RAS 15th International Conference on Humanoid Robots (Humanoids), pp. 270–275. IEEE (2015). https://doi.org/10.1109/HUMANOIDS.2015.7363546
12. Brown, L., Howard, A.M.: Engaging children in math education using a socially interactive humanoid robot. In: 2013 13th IEEE-RAS International Conference on Humanoid Robots (Humanoids), pp. 183–188. IEEE (2015). https://doi.org/10.1109/HUMANOIDS.2013.7029974
13. Riojas, M., Lysecky, S., Rozenblit, J.: Educational technologies for precollege engineering education. IEEE Trans. Learn. Technol. **5**, 20–37 (2012). https://doi.org/10.1109/TLT.2011.16

14. Tuna, G., Tuna, A., Ahmetoglu, E., Kuscu, H.: A survey on the use of humanoid robots in primary education: Prospects, research challenges and future research directions. Cypriot J. Educ. Sci. **14**, 361–373 (2019). https://doi.org/10.18844/cjes.v14i3.3291
15. Ouafa, S., Nadir, Y., Qbadou, M., Mansouri, K.: Comparative study of the impact of robot-human integration in the context of learning scenarios: literature review. In: 2024 4th International Conference on Innovative Research in Applied Science, Engineering and Technology, IRASET 2024, pp. 1–7. Institute of Electrical and Electronics Engineers Inc. (2024). https://doi.org/10.1109/IRASET60544.2024.10548633
16. Tuna, A.: Inclusive education for young children with autism spectrum disorder: use of humanoid robots and virtual agents to alleviate symptoms and improve skills, and a pilot study. J. Learn. Teach. Digital Age **7**, 274–282 (2022). https://doi.org/10.53850/joltida.1071876
17. Ekström, S., Pareto, L.: The dual role of humanoid robots in education: as didactic tools and social actors. Educ. Inf. Technol. (Dordr) **27**, 12609–12644 (2022). https://doi.org/10.1007/s10639-022-11132-2
18. Tuna, A., Tuna, G.: The use of humanoid robots with multilingual interaction skills in teaching a foreign language: opportunities, research challenges and future research directions. CEPS J. **9**, 95–115 (2019). https://doi.org/10.25656/01:18142
19. Sigacheva, N., Baranova, A.R., Makaev, K.F.: Communication problems: advantages and disadvantages of teaching autistic children with humanoid robots. In: VI International Forum on Teacher Education, pp. 2387–2396. Pensoft Publishers (2020). https://doi.org/10.3897/ap.2.e2387
20. Khairy, D., Alkhalaf, S., Areed, M.F., Amasha, M.A., Abougalala, R.A.: An algorithm for providing adaptive behavior to humanoid robot in oral assessment. IJACSA Int. J. Adv. Comput. Sci. Appl. **13**, 2022 (2019). https://doi.org/10.14569/IJACSA.2022.01309119
21. Ao, Y., Yu, Z.: Exploring the relationship between interactions and learning performance in robot-assisted language learning. Educ. Res. Int. **2022** (2022). https://doi.org/10.1155/2022/1958317
22. Alemi, M., Khatoony, S.: Virtual reality assisted pronunciation training (VRAPT) for young EFL learners. Teach. English Technol. **20**, 59–81 (2020)
23. Sannicandro, K., De Santis, A., Bellini, C., Minerva, T.: A scoping review on the relationship between robotics in educational contexts and e-health. Front. Educ. (Lausanne) **7**, (2022). https://doi.org/10.3389/feduc.2022.955572
24. Nasir, J., Norman, U., Bruno, B., Dillenbourg, P.: When positive perception of the robot has no effect on learning. In: 2020 29th IEEE International Conference on Robot and Human Interactive Communication (RO-MAN), pp. 313–320. IEEE (2020). https://doi.org/10.1109/RO-MAN47096.2020.9223343
25. Pareto, L., Barendregt, W., Serholt, S., Ekström, S., Kiesewetter, S.: Augmenting game-based learning with a robot tutee. In: 13th European Conference on Games Based Learning (ECGBL 2019), pp. 560–568. Academic Conferences Ltd (2019)
26. Williams, A.B., Baert, K., Williams, A.: Culturally responsive social robotics instruction for middle school girls. In: ACM/IEEE International Conference on Human-Robot Interaction, pp. 323–324. IEEE Computer Society (2017). https://doi.org/10.1145/3029798.3038427
27. Hmelo-Silver, C.E.: Problem-based learning: what and how do students learn? Educ Psychol Rev. **16** (2004). https://doi.org/10.1023/B:EDPR.0000034022.16470.f3
28. Roscoe, R.D., Chi, M.T.H.: Understanding tutor learning: Knowledge-building and knowledge-telling in peer tutors' explanations and questions. Rev. Educ. Res. **77**, 534–574 (2007). https://doi.org/10.3102/0034654307309920
29. Lave, J., Wenger, E.: Situated learning. Cambridge University Press (1991). https://doi.org/10.1017/CBO9780511815355

30. Alcorn, A.M., et al.: Educators' views on using humanoid robots with autistic learners in special education settings in England. Front. Robot AI **6** (2019). https://doi.org/10.3389/frobt.2019.00107
31. Mostajo, S.T., Legaspi, O.M., Camarse, M.G., Salva, R.A.: Exploring the potentials of robotics in supporting children with autism spectrum disorder. IAFOR J. Educ.: Inclusive Educ. **9** (2021). https://doi.org/10.22492/ije.9.1.05
32. Newton, D.P., Newton, L.D.: Humanoid robots as teachers and a proposed code of practice. Front. Educ. (Lausanne) **4** (2019). https://doi.org/10.3389/feduc.2019.00125

Exploring 3D Printing as an Assistive Technology for Learners with Autism Spectrum Disorder: A Comprehensive Review and Analysis of Scientific Studies

Borislava Kostova[1(✉)], Galya Georgieva-Tsaneva[1], Ivan Chavdarov[2], and Snezhana Kostova[1]

[1] Institute of Robotics, Bulgarian Academy of Science, Sofia, Bulgaria
borislava.kst@gmail.com

[2] Faculty of Mathematics and Informatics, University of Sofia, "St. Kliment Ohridski" Institute of Robotics, Sofia, Bulgaria
http://ir.bas.bg/

Abstract. Autism Spectrum Disorder (ASD) is a broad neurodevelopmental condition affecting many young learners. Educational efforts are made to meet their needs, overcome deficits and increase their well-being in classroom and everyday activities. The aim of this paper is to review the existing literature regarding the impact of 3D-printing activities and 3D-printed educational models on the learning, engagement, and social integration of children and adolescents with autism. Over 100 relevant articles from Google Scholar and Science Direct are reviewed, with 37 selected for an in-depth analysis. Among them, 13 fully met the study criteria. Best practices in this field are identified in order to analyze challenges and propose solutions for optimizing the application of 3D printing technology in special education. The features and findings of those investigations are illustrated in two tables, including factors such as the type of assistive technology and software, research methodology and target groups, lesson design specifics, observed outcomes, and social needs addressed. Protocols for the design of special education lessons are also reviewed and discussed.

Keywords: 3D printing · Autism Spectrum Disorder · Special education

1 Introduction

Autism Spectrum Disorder (ASD) is a neurodevelopmental condition characterized by persistent difficulties in social interaction, communication (both verbal and non-verbal), and behavioral flexibility [1]. These traits often affect how learners with ASD engage with educational content and their peers, necessitating tailored instructional strategies. Assistive technologies (ATs) are widely applied in both educational and therapeutic contexts to support these students' academic development and everyday functioning [2, 3].

D. Vasić and E. Brajković (Eds.): MoStart 2025, CCIS 2609, pp. 27–51, 2026.
https://doi.org/10.1007/978-3-032-02801-3_3

Among the growing range of assistive tools, 3D printing is increasingly recognized for its educational and therapeutic potential [4–6]. It enables the creation of personalized, tangible objects that can be adapted to a learner's sensory, cognitive, and emotional needs. Research highlights the benefits of 3D-printed models in enhancing understanding of abstract concepts, developing fine motor skills, supporting communication [7]. Some studies report that such educational activities boost learner motivation [2, 8–10].

In addition, 3D printing offers opportunities for creativity and self-expression in structured environments that align with the cognitive preferences of many students with ASD [11, 12].

Educational institutions worldwide are gradually adopting 3D printing in STEM/STEAM curricula, recognizing its potential to enhance hands-on learning and digital literacy. However, its targeted use as assistive technology in special education, particularly when aligned with frameworks such as Universal Design for Learning (UDL) [17], remains underexplored in systematized academic reviews [5, 13]. The number of scientific articles on this topic is also limited. Given the nature of special education, more emphasis should be posed to establishing a protocol for technology interventions tailored to the needs of students with ASD. While some studies document individual interventions, there is a lack of comprehensive synthesis evaluating 3D printing's effects on learners with ASD across domains such as engagement, skill acquisition, and social integration [6, 14].

This literature review aims to address this gap by examining the implementation of 3D printing as assistive technology in the education of children and adolescents with ASD. The review is based on a systematic search across major databases, resulting in a focused analysis of 13 empirical and pilot studies that met defined inclusion criteria. This study offers tables with technological solutions and an analysis of applicable educational protocols.

The objectives of this review are to: (1) assess the impact of 3D-printed educational materials on learning and participation; (2) identify best practices in using 3D printing for ASD learners; (3) explore the practical challenges of applying 3D printing in special education; and (4) analyze relevant lesson planning protocols and tools.

The study is guided by the following research questions:

Q1: Can 3D printing be considered an assistive technology (AT) for students on the autism spectrum?

Q2: Does interaction with 3D printing improve engagement, satisfaction, and social skills in ASD learners?

Q3: Can 3D printing enhance creativity among students with ASD?

Q4: What types of 3D printers and software are suitable for children and adolescents with autism?

Q5: What challenges arise when integrating 3D printing into ASD education?

Q6: What instructional protocols support the successful application of 3D printing in special education?

Individuals with ASD often exhibit strong preferences for repetitive activities and specialized interests [16]. Intelligence levels vary, and individuals with high-functioning autism (HFA) or Asperger syndrome tend to excel in STEM disciplines due to their exceptional pattern recognition, organization skills, and attention to detail [15, 16].

Studies have confirmed that individuals with ASD possess cognitive strengths, such as step-by-step task completion, exceptional memory, and advanced analytical abilities [3, 16]. These skills make them well-suited for careers in science and technology. According to a study [17], despite their strong technical abilities, many individuals with ASD face barriers to entering the workforce, primarily due to difficulties with communication, challenges with interdisciplinary thinking, teamwork, and problem-solving. 3D printing technology has the potential to help students with ASD overcome learning barriers by providing personalized, hands-on learning experiences.

While existing literature has explored various assistive technologies for individuals with ASD – such as social robots, AR/VR, or communication apps – there is currently a lack of systematic reviews that focus exclusively on the application of 3D printing as an assistive tool in education. Furthermore, most previous studies examine isolated benefits or technical aspects without synthesizing practical applications, pedagogical frameworks, and challenges in implementation. This study addresses this gap by analyzing the scientific literature specifically related to 3D printing in the context of ASD education, and identifying both best practices and implementation protocols.

2 Method

This study aims to provide a systematic review of the proposed research questions. A comprehensive analysis of the existing literature was conducted on the use of 3D printing in special education and integrated classrooms. Multiple databases were reviewed, including Google Scholar and Research gate. Combinations of terms such as "ASD", "autis", "spectrum", "special education", "3D modelling", "3D printing", "CAD software", "STEM", "STEAM" were searched. The search for these keywords yielded 669 results. A time range of 2014 to 2024 was then set, which reduced the number of results to 523. From these results, 250 scientific articles were available for review via Google Scholar and Science Direct. Subsequently, the time range was increased to 24 years (2024–2000) to include frequently cited pivotal articles in the research of autism spectrum disorder [15, 16], protocols for designing special educational activities targeting to the needs of people with this condition [17] as well as the research on a software tool for automated 3D modelling of assistive devices [18]. Based on the review of these articles, new keywords were searched such as "Universal design of learning", "UDL", "Asperger's", "High functioning autism", "HFA".

The following types of articles were excluded: a) scientific papers that do not use 3D printing in education; b) Articles that do not include children with special needs; c) articles in which the word 3D does not refer to the topic of the study, for example 3D virtual learning technology; d) Articles in which 3D printing is not used for educational purposes. This reduced the number of articles, relevant to the research, to 80. Subsequently, 43 of these articles were excluded from the literature review because they did not provide information regarding the posed research questions. The remaining 37 articles formed the basis of the present literature review. The methodology and results presented in 13 of them were identified as good practices for the inclusion of 3D printing technology in the education of students with ASD. The review of these 13 articles is systematized in Table 1 according to the following criteria: (1) Type of experiment, (2) Participants,

(3) Response prompt, (4) Research design, (5) Dependent variable (measures) and Independent variable (intervention), (7) Country, (8) Institution, (9) Results/Outcomes, (10) Challenges.

The literature review process is illustrated on Fig. 1 and consists of:

1. Keyword Search in databases (Google Scholar, ScienceDirect) using terms like "ASD," "autism," "3D printing," "special education," etc.
2. Filtering by Publication Year: First from 2014–2024, then extended to 2000–2024 to include key prior studies
3. Initial Screening: Removal of irrelevant or non-educational articles
4. In-depth Review: 37 articles selected for deeper evaluation
5. Final Inclusion: 13 studies selected based on relevance, target group (ASD), educational context, and measurable outcomes
6. Data Extraction: Structured tables summarizing methodology, participants, results, and challenges
7. Thematic Analysis: Identification of key benefits, limitations, and protocols from selected studies

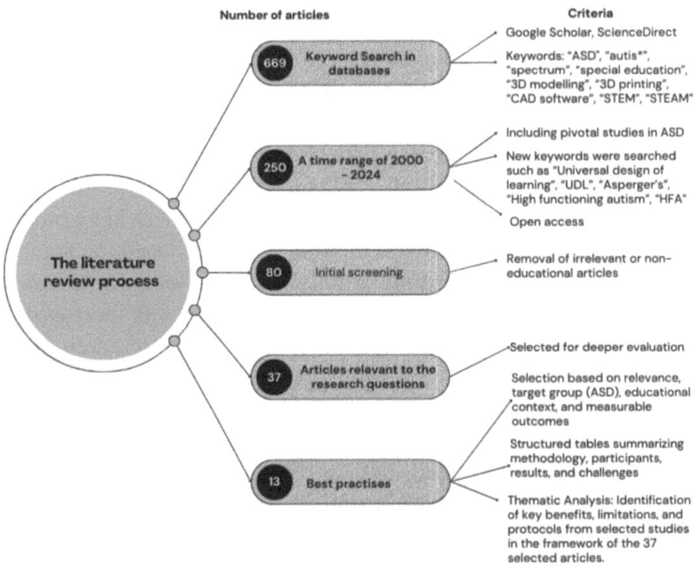

Fig. 1. The literature review process

3 Results

After searching for studies that met the inclusion criteria, the researchers identified 2 pilot [2, 18], 9 empirical and 2 longitudinal studies of which 1 single-case studies [18], 11 group studies and 1 review paper [13]. This is illustrated in Fig. 2.

In the examined studies participated a total sum of 281 students, aged 5–21 years old, 13 parents and 9 teachers. The gender of the students is not specified in any of the studies. All studies provided information about the cognitive, social, academic and/or motor skill functioning of the participants and their improvement as a dependent variable to the instruction.

Four studies were set in special education classrooms and an equal number occurred in integrated education class where students with ASD diagnosis study alongside their neurotypical peers. The review sought to include any study discipline area, interventions in educational activities in the following classes were represented in the referenced studies: digital skills, product development, physical education, STEM/STEAM, writing, comprehension,

Most ($n = 11$) of the analyzed studies developed interventions to assess the effectiveness of the activities on the targeted skills of each participant. Eleven of the studies employed single-case research designs, while two utilized multiple-probe designs (Fig. 3).

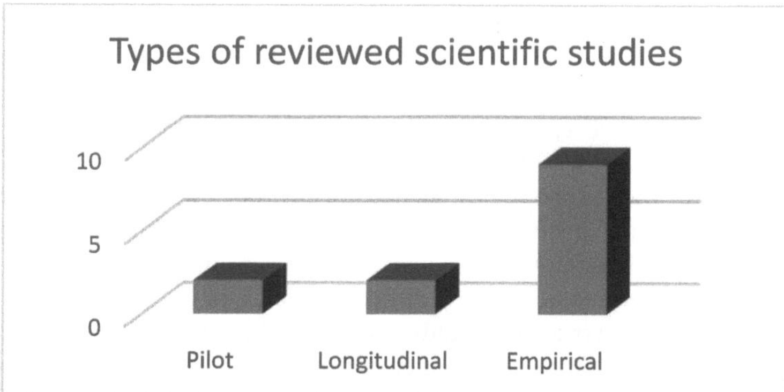

Fig. 2. Types of reviewed scientific studies

3.1 Study Results

The main features of the studies included in the analysis are presented in Table 1 and the features of the 3D printing technology used, in Table 2, in Appendix.

Q1: Can 3D Printing be Considered an Assistive Technology for Students on the Spectrum?

According to the World Health Organisation [19], "assistive products include devices, equipment, instruments or software from 6 functional domains: mobility, vision, hearing, communication, cognition and self-care. Examples of assistive products are physical products such as wheelchairs, spectacles and hearing aids, and digital products such as software and apps". 3D printing is known to take part in the development of traditional assistive devices such as rehabilitation aids, writing aids [9] or braille boards [20] but it is

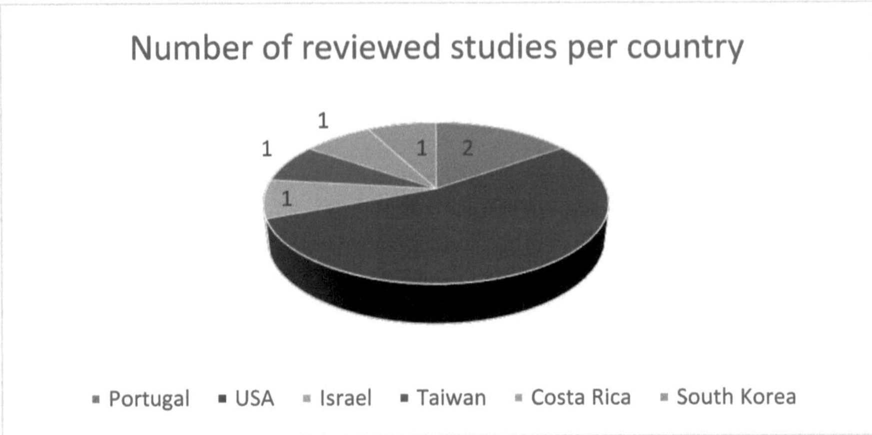

Fig. 3. Number of reviewed studies per country

also increasingly considered by itself as an assistive digital tool offering improvements in social skills and self-realization [2, 8, 9, 14, 20, 21]. Therefore, 3D printing meets the criteria for assistive technology because it personalizes the learning process and addresses specific needs of students – similar to the way communication applications or adapted learning materials facilitate learning.

The existing knowledge about ATs, such as social robots, widely used in educational activities for people with special needs, shows that this group of users generally benefits from these ATs in several ways. They assist in performing physical tasks, monitor personal needs, help overcome sensory difficulties (e.g., physical and cognitive challenges), are activated by voice commands, reduce the burden of management, and are co-created with users [5]. Using the framework of Alboul, L. et al., 2023 [5] we have found cases of using 3D printing in assistance to performing physical tasks linked to fine and gross motor skills [9, 18]. Students on the spectrum have also taken part in the design and prototyping of their 3D modelled and printed educational tools in the cases of [2, 7, 12]. 3D printed toys, tools and robots, in the case of [23] have the benefit of simple, customizable as well as novel design, and individuals with specific needs find that appealing as "it does not create feelings of anxiety and discomfort when interacting with it".

3D printing can assist the individual's specific physical needs with the creation of personalized tools. Pen grips like [24] are popular tools for improving fine motor skills in writing and drawing, as discussed in [9] and [18]. 3D printing can cover the rest of the types of assistance listed above and in [5] in a synergic system together with other assistive programs and applications like alarms, reminders, instructions, voice recording and playback, text-to-speech processing and vice versa, assistants with Artificial Intelligence, etc., already successfully applied in the daily lives of people with ASD.

In the existing literature, ATs are being distinguished in low-tech and mid to high tech [4] relative to the level of technological advancement incorporated into the assistive product. 3D printing falls into the first low-tech variety because of its relative affordability [25] and mainstream use. ATs such as AI-powered modeling tools, VR/AR-enhanced design interfaces, and automated guidance systems could further facilitate 3D printing's positive effects on learning on the spectrum [26].

Q2: Does Interaction with 3D Printing Improve Engagement, Satisfaction, and Social Skills in ASD Learners?
All 13 studies in this review demonstrated positive student outcomes and highlight the role of 3D printing in facilitating communication through personalized assistive devices [2, 6–8]. Studies indicate that 3D printing-related educational activities, whether through direct participation in the printing process or through the use of 3D-printed models, enhance motivation and self-regulation skills [22], improve self-control [8], self-worth [27] and sustain student engagement [21] on a regular basis [27]. The number of studies reviewed, in which the different positive outcomes have been registered, is illustrated in Fig. 4.

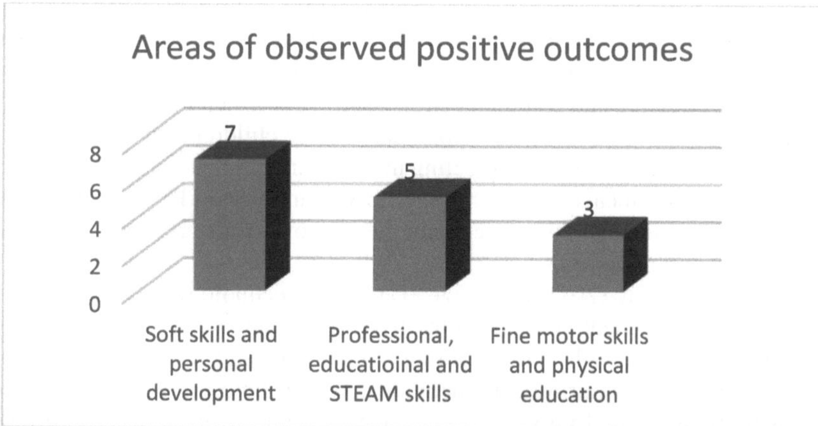

Fig. 4. Areas of positive outcomes registered in the reviewed scientific studies.

Social interaction is often a key area of difficulty for children with ASD, and researchers have explored how 3D printing technology can serve as a facilitator of collaboration and communication. Ref. [4] analyzed how AT, including interactive 3D-printed products, can enhance social engagement and teamwork among ASD students. Their findings indicate that hands-on 3D printing activities encourage cooperative play, shared problem-solving, and structured interactions, leading to improved peer communication and relationship-building. Beyond direct interaction, customized 3D learning aids can be used to support alternative communication methods, allowing non-verbal or minimally verbal ASD students to express themselves through physical models and symbols. The integration of interactive 3D-printed tools in collaborative classroom settings can therefore significantly contribute to the social development and inclusivity of children with ASD.

3D printing provides opportunities for project-based learning, shifting the focus from verbal instructions to practical, skills-based engagement, which has been found to be beneficial for ASD learners [3], who often learn better through action than through abstract explanations. Using 3D technology promotes communication and social interaction skills [2, 8], allowing students to express themselves, get an impulse to share what they've learned [27], resolve problems, recognize their strengths [21], and engage meaningfully with peers [8, 18, 21, 22] contributing to an overall sense of social inclusion, belonging, and community [28]. 3D printing technology also offers a possibility to create unique and personalised tactile patterns which is an important feature for sensory-attentive people on the spectrum.

Existing scientific research supports the notion that 3D printing technology stimulates interest in STEM disciplines among students with high-functioning ASD [6]. This interest can translate into skill development that aligns with labor market demands, ultimately increasing the likelihood of successful professional and social integration.

On the other hand, the study by [7] argues that students with ASD don't improve their STEAM career interest and motivation for science with their participation in such project based activities, as much as their neurotypical peers, because they are more likely to already have high interest in this field in order to participate. The findings of Martin, W.B. et al., 2020 are consistent with the "limited resource theory" of Rachel Cohen-Rottenberg [30] which states that autistic deficit is a cause of missing resource ("information processing and communication issue" [31] which limits the performance in other areas. Dimitrova et al. [30] report that autistic children can start overcoming deficits in social interaction when interacting in environments that induce positive states. Arguably, such environment could be the participation in a project based on their favorite school subject or lesson and this can explain the improvements in the domain of social skills reported by all reviewed studies.

Simpson & Taliaferro (2021) [9] utilize 3D printing technology to create customized assistive devices for students with ASD in physical education classes. In this case, the authors found increased willingness among students to engage with their peers and higher satisfaction levels during class activities. While Simpson et al. [9] focused on physical activity and found improved engagement, Sandoval P. et al. [8] showed that in educational activities, 3D models stimulated enhanced student satisfaction, social inclusion, and communication development. This suggests that the technology is flexible and brings benefits in a variety of contexts – from sports to academic pursuits.

A study by Buehler et al. (2016) [6] in the United States explored 3D printing applications for students with cognitive, motor, and visual impairments. Their findings indicated that 3D printing not only fosters an interest in STEM subjects but also allows for the rapid and cost-effective development of customized educational tools. Likewise, research by Chen, Lin, & Mao (2018) [29] in Taiwan demonstrated significant improvements in fine motor skills, hand-eye coordination, and learning motivation in children with cerebral palsy and autism through the use of 3D-printed educational devices.

According to literature review, all studies analyzed support the idea that participation in 3D printing-related activities increases motivation and social engagement in students with ASD, with more research needed to highlight the long-term effects.

In the current state of research, the generalizability of these findings remains limited. Most studies involve small sample sizes and short-term interventions, which requires caution when extrapolating the results to a broader population of learners. Some studies rely on single-case designs [6], involving only one student, while others involve small groups. This discrepancy highlights the need for further large-scale research.

Q3: Can 3D Printing Enhance Creativity Among Students with ASD?
Creative thinking is often considered an area of deficit in individuals with ASD, despite the fact that some prominent figures within this group have made globally recognized innovative contributions [2]. In [32], it is concluded that children with ASD demonstrate distinctive verbal creativity, as measured by the novel metaphor generation task. Their figural creativity is not lower compared to their neurotypical peers and they scored higher in "innovation" i.e. mixing elements during a "non-existent object" drawing task. The study involved 40 students on the spectrum and 39 neurotypical peers.

Marzanna Farnicka and Margarida Pocinho (2021) [2] in Portugal, explore the potential of 3D printing technology to develop creativity among individuals with ASD. Their experimental study involved 40 participants with ASD engaging in structured activities centered on creative 3D modeling, idea development, and 3D printing production. The results demonstrated successful engagement in imaginative processes, positive emotional experiences among students and their families, improved communication, increased motivation, and a newfound perspective on the capabilities of individuals with ASD [2]. These findings suggest that 3D printing activities can stimulate creativity in students with ASD by combining both a technological and an artistic component, effectively leveraging their strengths in systematization and step-by-step task execution while fostering innovative thinking.

Three of the reviewed articles referenced the term "maker movement" [2, 6, 7], in order to describe a type of lesson design focused on creating a physical or digital object and investigated the impact of such activity on the neurotypical students and their peers with ASD. 3D printing is an element of all these investigations. Two of these studies [6, 7] concluded on the unique cognitive benefits for students with ASD deriving both from the "maker" lesson design and its tool – 3D printing technology. Given that creative expression often poses challenges for individuals on the spectrum, structured activities—such as 3D design and prototyping – provide an organized and predictable framework for developing imaginative problem-solving skills. Unlike traditional creative tasks, which may lack defined procedural structures, 3D printing requires both technical precision and conceptual exploration, making it a suitable medium for fostering creativity in ASD learners.

One of the primary challenges identified in the research by Farnicka & Pocinho (2021) [2] is the difficulty in establishing reliable methods for assessing creative thinking and measuring changes in creativity before and after engaging in 3D printing activities. Another obstacle is the subjective nature of interpreting creative expressions in individuals with ASD, as their thought processes and artistic outputs may differ significantly from neurotypical expectations [35].

Future research should focus on developing standardized tools for evaluating creative development in ASD learners and identifying additional methods for enhancing their engagement in design and prototyping tasks. Additionally, further exploration is needed to assess the long-term impact of 3D printing-based creativity programs on social skills.

Q4: What Types of 3D Printers are Suitable for Use by Children and Adolescents with Autism?
The reviewed empirical studies utilize various types of 3D printers. Marzanna Farnicka and Margarida Pocinho (2021) [2] highlight the importance of safety conditions, emphasizing the need to choose a printer with all heating elements covered. For educational activities involving individuals with ASD, the need to use entirely non-toxic materials [3, 16] is also highlighted, along with ensuring the printed models are sufficiently durable to reduce the likelihood of frustration, distraction [22], and the need to repeat the experiment.

The reviewed scientific literature indicates that the 3D modeling software TinkerCAD is particularly popular for educational activities aimed at individuals with ASD (see Table 2 in Appendix). Although the authors prefer this software for its user-friendliness, most studies report challenges such as the time required for training and familiarization with the program, both for students and teachers [17] and support staff, leading to feelings of helplessness and frustration [33], distraction, and decreased engagement [29]. Another issue is the lack of an easy way to adapt the software to the specific and individual needs of participants with ASD [22, 33].

These studies emphasize the need for personalized, adaptive, and automated approaches to integrating 3D printing into the educational environment to enhance the technology's effectiveness for students with ASD. While the technology shows great potential, challenges such as accessibility, the complexity of 3D modeling software, and the need for ongoing support must be addressed to fully realize its potential in special education [28]. There is a need for specialized software [16] with appropriate design and various options that can be updated to accommodate the changing interests and needs of students [34].

Each individual on the spectrum has very different and specific interface requirements and that these requirements can vary according to their specific physical or cognitive abilities [36]. The authors review the available specialist interface toolkits: the Grid2 software "provides access through switch, touchscreen, eye-gaze, head-pointer and mouse / keyboard" while the author's novel Virtual Sculpting program is a computer-aided technology allowing for the creation of sculptural artefacts. The study points out the need for additional personalization and involvement of specialist catering for the individual's personal needs, for example speech therapist.

Several scientific studies suggest future developments in 3D printing technology for individuals with ASD through integration with assistive programs and applications. These could support students by providing alarms, reminders, guidance, voice recording and playback, text-to-speech and speech-to-text conversion, artificial intelligence assistants, and other tools that have already been successfully implemented in the daily lives of people with ASD. Chen, Lin, and Mao (2018) [29] and Van Bergeijk, Ranaldo, and Shtayermman (2008) [3] report challenges related to the high cost of the traditional assistive devices and the learning curve difficulties in the first stages of new technology integration.

Q5: What Challenges Arise when Integrating 3D Printing into ASD Education?
Despite its numerous advantages, there are significant challenges regarding the widespread implementation of 3D printing in special education as well as neurotypical

classroom. Ref. [10] point out that, despite the popularity of the 3D printing technology, the adoption rate in schools is still low. The main obstacles include the complexity of 3D modeling software and difficulty in manipulating the interface [14], the need for teacher training, time constraints [10, 18] as well as the initial costs associated with acquiring 3D printing equipment [9, 29]. Overcoming these barriers requires the development of more accessible software interfaces. 3D modelling tools focused on automation and ease of use such as the "rings" program developed by [37] offer a glimpse of the possibilities that the technology offers while delivering instant gratification and sparking motivation. Another user friendly software tool is GripFab developed by [18]. Teacher training programs, and adaptive learning strategies that integrate artificial intelligence (AI) and AT can also be included in future 3D printing and modelling tools.

From a practical perspective, these factors suggest the need for institutional support – for schools to allocate resources for equipment and staff training, or for partnerships (e.g. with universities or libraries) to share 3D printers.

Q6: What Instructional Protocols Support the Successful Application of 3D Printing in Special Education?

A major challenge in creating activities for students with ASD is finding ways to accommodate their unique cognitive and behavioral traits. Existing scientific research highlights the importance of creating structured, supportive environments using evidence-based instructional models like Universal Design for Learning (UDL). UDL's effectiveness is supported by empirical evidence [33], making it a valuable framework for providing clear, visually-structured instructions and individualized teaching methods [26, 29, 33]. Similarly, the Handlungsspielraum methodology [35] emphasizes lesson customization by incorporating essential elements for ASD learners, such as visual aids, personalized approaches, and mentoring systems. 3D modelling and printing is naturally consistent with the principles of Universal Design for Learning (UDL) because personalisation is one of its core benefits and so learning is easily adapted to individual cognitive styles [33].

Existing research points out that for neurodivergent students, having a bad mood day can significantly affect their participation and they might "refuse to talk, fail to complete work, and/or remain completely disengaged from the instructor and their design partner" [14]. In order to overcome this challenge, the authors came up with a reward system using the course materials or 3D printed small toys.

In the reviewed scientific studies, it is suggested that students on the spectrum are encouraged to follow a portfolio-based presentation when sharing their 3D printed work with their peers, focusing on visualizing achievements rather than verbal presentations [3, 17, 26]. AT including reminder alarms and structured task management tools, have also proven beneficial for supporting ASD learners in educational settings [3]. Reducing sensory distractions and offering non-verbal communication options, such as written or illustrated responses, further enhance student comfort and engagement [21].

ASDesign is a protocol for the development of assistive technology and smart products to support children on the spectrum [4]. The objective is to create user-centered, adaptable solutions to address the sensory, cognitive, and motor needs of user, promoting independence and engagement.

Although all reviewed studies report positive results from the integration of 3D printing in the education of children with autism, they also present a number of limitations and challenges to be taken into account. Some participants show difficulties in mastering 3D modeling software, which leads to dissatisfaction, refusal to participate or loss of motivation [6, 29], and [14]. In some cases, the printed models do not meet the students' expectations, especially in the absence of sufficient durability or accuracy, which leads to disappointment and refusal to repeat the activity [8, 14]. The supporting personnel often lack prior training, which leads to inadequate use of technology [9, 18]. Some studies do not report significant improvements in creativity, pointing out the difficulty in assessing creativity in the context of autism [2]. In terms of methodological approach, most of the reviewed studies are short-term and involve small samples, which limits the generalizability of the results.

There are software tools available to automate and ease the development of 3D printed assistive devices such as GripFab developed by [18] and the "rings" program in AutoCAD environment developed by [37]. Both programs enable the user to select a basic model and personalise it from a variety of options presented through dialogue windows. The GripFab is developed specifically as a hand grip tool while the "rings" program is currently developed for creation of souvenirs but could be modified to suit this need as well. While GripFab, using OpenSCAD software presents an option for only one grip style without further decorative customization, the "rings" program, using VisualLisp in AutoCAD, provides such dialogue windows while not specifically developed for AT.

The topic of personalization of assistive devices is discussed in [8, 18] but the studies don't mention the possibility to customize the style or decoration of the AT in order to meet the individual interests of a person with ASD (e.g. by modelling a favourite character onto the hand grip) or to choose from a variety of writing tools to be incorporated in the 3D model (pen, pencil, brush, highlighter of different sizes). It is observed that different stages of fine motor skills development require different flexibility of material used for the hand grip – a more flexible one is required with the advancement of skill. An automated 3D modelling tool such as GripFab described in [18] isn't offering the user an option to choose such parameters and is focused on one grip style without further customization.

4 Discussion

The studies reviewed consistently point to improvements in social skills and engagement of students with ASD. However, it is important to recognize that these outcomes are not uniform across participants. For instance, improvements in communication or social skills appear more frequently among students involved in collaborative or project-based 3D printing activities. Improvements in interest and motivation in the field of study is observed in some investigations but other find that this outcome is more significant for neurotypical students. Physical education applications of 3D printing primarily support engagement and confidence, while STEM-focused interventions tend to enhance motor coordination and technological literacy. These variations underscore the importance of context-specific implementation and individualized lesson planning.

The findings from the reviewed studies indicate that 3D printing serves as an effective assistive technology for children and adolescents on the spectrum both as a production and customization tool and as AT by itself offering collaborative learning environments and social wellbeing benefits. The integration of 3D printing as an educational task demonstrates significant positive effects on student engagement and motivation. Participation in 3D printing activities fosters self-regulation, problem-solving, presentation, communication skills and creativity. The reviewed studies highlight how 3D-printed models enhance comprehension by providing tangible, visual aids that reduce cognitive load. For students with ASD, who often face challenges with abstract thinking and verbal communication, 3D printed tactile resources offer an accessible means of interacting with complex concepts. Furthermore, the ability to customize educational materials allows for the alignment of learning activities with students' personal interests, increasing intrinsic motivation and sustained attention during lessons.

When compared with Farnicka & Pocinho (2021) [2], our findings confirm that 3D printing enhances both creativity and emotional engagement. Similar to Chen et al. (2018) [29], we observed consistent improvements in fine motor skills and motivation. Simpson & Taliaferro (2021) [9] demonstrated increased peer interaction during physical activities, aligning with results from Buehler et al. (2016) [18] who documented interest in STEM and skill-building, though they also noted frustrations related to print failures. Our synthesis also echoes Sandoval Poveda & Hernández Montoya (2021) [8] in highlighting the role of 3D printing in improving social inclusion and emotional regulation. These comparisons validate the observed benefits and emphasize the relevance of individualized instructional design.

Future research opportunities focused on the integration of 3D printing in special education include the development of accessible interface toolkits and protocols for such lesson designs. This includes adapting the ASDesign, Universal Design for Learning (UDL) to 3D modeling and prototyping activities. One such application could be the integration between ASDesign and the AutoCAD program for automated modelling of small objects developed by [37] or Gripfab developed by [18]. Elements of ASDesign can be integrated within such software tools such as adaptability, user design input, integrating sensorial design features and patterns, focusing on learning through play and basic ASD needs and deficits, as well as integration with other assistive technologies. It is likely that for students on the low to mid areas of the spectrum, 3D printed tools are given to improve social and motor skills with the help of supporting adults. For students on the high functioning end of the spectrum, an option to learn 3D modelling and printing could be presented through a user friendly program which automatically creates predetermined set of 3D models with different options which the user navigates with dialogue windows. This activity aims to increase their technological literacy and professional skills.

Although several studies address the role of 3D printing in special education, few offer an integrated view that combines educational methodologies, assistive design, and empirical outcomes for learners with ASD. In particular, research is fragmented, with limited attention to long-term effectiveness, challenges faced by educators, and lesson design protocols. This review contributes to the field by consolidating evidence across twelve studies, highlighting real-life applications, and offering a structured synthesis of current practices, which can inform future educational and technological initiatives.

As a summary, the key elements that should be present in an educational activity for students with ASD that incorporates 3D printing technology are:

- An appropriate learning environment and an adapted curriculum developed using the UDL system (or another system for inclusive education);
- A sufficient number of teaching and support staff who are familiar in advance with the individual needs of the students, as well as with the operation of 3D printing technology;
- Appropriate 3D modeling and printing software that offers automation options, an adapted interface, and compatibility with assistive applications and technologies;
- Focusing the activity on the individual interests of the students;
- A focus on project-based work rather than verbal presentations;
- A suitable 3D printer with enclosed heating elements;
- The use of non-toxic materials such as filament.

A limitation of this literature review is the relatively high number of pilot or short term studies included. In general, this represents a gap in the existing scientific investigation of the effect of 3D printing as an assistive technology for people on the spectrum. To address the methodological limitations identified in existing studies, we recommend that future research develop a comprehensive protocol for the integrating 3D printing into special education. This protocol should include a detailed description of the methodology, utilize validated instruments for measuring social and communication skills, involves a larger sample size in experimental studies, uses control and experimental groups, and employ longitudinal approaches to accurately capture the changes attributable to the intervention.

An additional opportunity for future research presents in activities fostering employability skills for young adults on the higher functional end of the spectrum. 3D modelling and printing could be an entry point technology for those individuals and it could be worthwhile investigating the technology's effect on their attitudes.

The results obtained show that 3D printing acts as a catalyst for a number of skills, as it provides a multi-sensory, hands-on experience. It is noteworthy that all studies report positive results in improving social skills, while one study indicates no observable improvement in science-related motivation. It could be worthwhile investigating further the "limited resource theory" of autism and exploring the improvement of soft skills stemming from the participation of a student with ASD in a project-based activity of their interest. Future research should also include critical analyses that highlight the shortcomings or limitations in the use of this technology. Additionally, more quantitative data is needed to accurately capture and assess the scope of the observed improvements.

5 Conclusion

In conclusion, the results of the review show that 3D printing can be considered as an assistive technology for students with autism (Q1), as it facilitates learning through adapted materials and improves key skills. Improvements in engagement, satisfaction and social skills (Q2), as well as fostering creativity (Q3) were observed in a structured approach. For educators, the results suggest that integrating 3D printers into the classroom can be a valuable tool for engaging students with ASD, especially when lessons are aligned with UDL principles. For technology professionals, there is a need to develop more accessible software and safe hardware solutions (Q4) to overcome limitations in usability.

Studies unanimously report increased student motivation and participation, yet significant barriers to implementation exist – software complexity, cost, and need for support (Q5).

A recommendation for future research is to focus on the development of employability skills and career orientation among high-functioning youth with ASD, as well as on their attitudes toward and readiness to use technologies such as 3D printing in the context of future employment.

The reviewed articles lack data from long-term interventions (exceeding one year). Future studies should examine the extent to which the observed positive effects are sustained over time and translated into lasting, transferable skills. Studies among older students and youth with ASD would be useful to determine whether 3D printing can support the acquisition of work skills and the transition to employment. A recommendation for such studies is to start with small 3D printing projects closely related to the interests of students with ASD, gradually increasing the complexity. Providing visual instructions and examples (according to UDL principles) can be key to observing improvements.

Several studies compare the reactions of students with and without autism when working with 3D technologies, finding similar levels of interest, but emphasizing that for students with ASD, the positives (self-confidence, social interaction) are more significant and sustainable. This suggests that while 3D printing is a valuable educational tool for all students, it can act as an effective assistive technology for those with ASD, addressing their specific needs.

Acknowledgments. This work was supported by the Bulgarian National Science Fund contract KP-06-COST/14 16.11.2022, "Application of innovative assistive technologies in the process of social inclusion of people with autism spectrum disorders and/or intellectual disabilities".

Appendix

Table 1. A summary of the selected articles covering the research criteria

Indicators	Description
Authors, Year	Martin, W.B., Yu, J., Wei, X., Vidiksis, R., Patten, K.K. and Riccio, A., 2020
Type of experiment	Empirical
Participants	N = 109 students of which 30 with ASD (18 of them participated in the makers program)
Age of participants	10–14 years old
Response prompt	Observations and interviews; social interaction analysis, a pre/post survey
Research design	Students with ASD were in both experimental and pilot groups. Experimental group participated in idea generation workshop that finalized with the 3D modelling and printing of a project
Dependent variable (measures)	Social skills, science, technology, and engineering self-efficacy and career interest, engineering process literacy
Independent variable (intervention)	Maker program called Inventing, Designing, and Engineering for All Students (IDEA)
Country	USA
Institution	autism-inclusion middle school in New York City
Results/Outcomes	Improved communication, project, presentation skills and engineering process literacy in students with ASD No significant improvement in career interest was observed
Challenges	
Authors, Year	Meaghan McLeod Mozingo, Krzysztof J. Rechowicz, **2023** [21]
Type of experiment	Empirical
Participants	–
Age of participants	Children and adolescents with ASD
Response prompt	Qualitative observations
Research design	–
Dependent variable (measures)	Skill development through STEM and games
Independent variable (intervention)	–
Country	USA

(continued)

Table 1. (*continued*)

Indicators	Description
Authors, Year	Martin, W.B., Yu, J., Wei, X., Vidiksis, R., Patten, K.K. and Riccio, A., 2020
Institution	Old Dominion University, Norfolk, Virginia
Results/Outcomes	Increased participation, self-confidence and skill identification among participants, with positive feedback from parents
Challenges	Challenges in providing specialized support and delivering specific activities for children's diverse needs
Authors, Year	Yu-Lun Chen, Kavitha Murthi, Wendy Martin, Regan Vidiksis, Ariana Riccio, Kristie Patten, **2022** [22]
Type of experiment	Empirical, qualitative research focused on perceptions
Participants	N = 26 (17 with autism, 9 without autism), 13 parents, and 9 teachers
Age of participants	Students aged 11 to 14 years
Response prompt	Semi-structured interviews/focus groups and program diary, over a period of 2 years
Research design	Students participate in engineering design cycle
Dependent variable (measures)	Positive student experience and engagement, skills acquisition, development of interest in STEM and related careers, social relationships and community, and self-determination
Independent variable (intervention)	IDEAS Maker Program
Country	USA
Institution	New York: 3 public schools including students with autism
Results/Outcomes	Increased motivation and skills in areas of interest, such as 3D printing. Development of social relationships, self-regulation, problem solving, and self-advocacy
Challenges	Limitations: represents the high-functioning end of the autism spectrum
Authors, Year	Marzanna Farnicka, Margarida Pocinho, **2021** [2]
Type of experiment	Pilot
Participants	N = 40 (20 – experimental group, diagnosed with ASD; 20 – control group
Age of participants	5–16 years old
Response prompt	Guilford Creativity Test, Semi-Structured Interview, 3D Product Evaluation – of 'novelty' and 'appropriateness' on the Likert scale from 0 to 3), and Observation Grids, Satisfaction questionnaires (on the Likert scale from 1 to 5 to Parents/Teacher and ASD Technicians. The measurement was planned to conduct three times: at the beginning, after six months and after a year

(*continued*)

Table 1. *(continued)*

Authors, Year	Marzanna Farnicka, Margarida Pocinho, **2021** [2]
Research design	Help children in small groups to develop an idea of a product, build it in a 3D modelling software appropriate for children and then print it on a 3D printer
Dependent variable (measures)	Satisfaction in learning, communication skills and creativity
Independent variable (intervention)	3D printing used in educational intervention
Country	Portugal
Institution	Center for Autism and Social Inclusion
Results/Outcomes	Improved communication skills
Challenges	Challenges in assessing creativity through traditional methods; adaptation to 3D technology is needed for participants with ASD
Authors, Year	Pocinho, M., Garcês, S., Diaz, N. and Farnicka, M. **(2017)** [12]
Type of experiment	Longitudinal
Participants	Children in economic disadvantage situations measured by their need of school social support
Age of participants	4–6 years old
Response prompt	Questionnaire to parents, semi-structured interview with them
Research design	Help children in small groups to develop an idea of a product, build it in a 3D modelling software appropriate for children and then print it on a 3D printer
Dependent variable (measures)	Creativity, 3D printing and modelling, technology skills, academic achievement and personal development
Independent variable (intervention)	Framework based on multiple intelligence theory and creativity
Country	Portugal
Institution	Private kindergarden where 3D printing activities were held once a month for 8 months
Results/Outcomes	The project showed possibilities of using 3D technology not only as a tool to improve the development of different skills but also as a communication tool
Challenges	–
Authors, Year	A. Chloe Simpson, Andrea Ruth Taliaferro, **2021** [9]
Type of experiment	Empirical
Participants	–
Age of participants	Students with ASD
Response prompt	Observations
Research design	–
Dependent variable (measures)	Participation of students with specific needs in PE class

(continued)

Table 1. (*continued*)

Authors, Year	A. Chloe Simpson, Andrea Ruth Taliaferro, **2021** [9]
Independent variable (intervention)	3D printed assistive technology
Country	USA
Institution	–
Results/Outcomes	Increased participation and engagement in physical education activities
Challenges	High cost and lack of teacher training
Authors, Year	Sandoval Poveda, A. and Hernández Montoya, D., **2021** [8]
Type of experiment	Empirical
Participants	10
Age of participants	Adolescents with ASD, high school and middle school
Response prompt	Observation: Content analysis of photos and recordings
Research design	–
Dependent variable (measures)	Technological knowledge, positive emotions, social skills
Independent variable (intervention)	Digital fabrication workshops
Country	Costa Rica
Institution	San Jose
Results/Outcomes	Improving social skills such as self-control, communication, positive emotions and teamwork
Challenges	High level of frustration and need for personalized and individual interaction
Authors, Year	Kasirer, A., Adi-Japha, E., & Mashal, N. **(2020)** [32]
Type of experiment	Empirical
Participants	40 children with ASD and 39 peers with typical development
Age of participants	11–15 years old
Response prompt	A sentence completion questionnaire was used to test creative verbal generation; a task of drawing non-existent objects was used to assess figural abilities
Research design	
Dependent variable (measures)	Verbal and figural creativity
Independent variable (intervention)	"the contribution of executive functions to the creative performance"
Country	Israel
Institution	The children with TD were recruited from elementary schools and junior high schools. The participants with ASD were recruited from integrated classes within elementary schools and junior high schools

(*continued*)

Table 1. (*continued*)

Authors, Year	Kasirer, A., Adi-Japha, E., & Mashal, N. **(2020)** [32]
Results/Outcomes	The research points to a unique creative cognition profile among children with ASD
Challenges	–
Authors, Year	Chen, S.H., Lin, C.Y. and Mao, Q.C., **2018.** [29]
Type of experiment	Empirical
Participants	3 children diagnosed with cerebral palsy and ASD
Age of participants	Primary school
Response prompt	Classroom observations
Research design	Design and user test of coin insertion system produced with 3D printing
Dependent variable (measures)	Fine motor skills and social interaction of children with ASD
Independent variable (intervention)	Development of a 3D printed educational device
Country	Taiwan
Institution	National Tainan University, National Chiayi University
Results/Outcomes	Improving fine motor skills, hand-eye coordination, and motivation to learn in children with cerebral palsy and autism
Challenges	High cost of traditional assistive devices, initial difficulties in adapting to the coin insertion system
Authors, Year	Easley, William, et al., **2017** [14]
Type of experiment	Empirical (2 academic semesters (12 weeks each)
Participants	A multisite case study. One site – young adults with intellectual disabilities (ID)
Age of participants	Integrated Postsecondary Course (IPS)
Response prompt	field notes, reviewing student assignments
Research design	Observations during hands-on educational activities with 3D printer and 3D modelling software
Dependent variable (measures)	Computer and digital skills, communication skills
Independent variable (intervention)	–
Country	USA
Institution	Integrated Post-Secondary Classroom (IPS)
Results/Outcomes	Introducing digital skills, Improved presentation skills
Challenges	Navigating mood swings and difficulties in using the software, dissapointment with print fails
Authors, Year	Buehler, E., Comrie, N., Hofmann, M., McDonald, S. and Hurst, A., **2016** [6]
Type of experiment	Empirical

(*continued*)

Table 1. (*continued*)

Authors, Year	Buehler, E., Comrie, N., Hofmann, M., McDonald, S. and Hurst, A., **2016** [6]
Participants	N (6) class observations (with between 3 and 13 students), N (13) interviews with staff, instructors, and therapists. Students with cognitive, motor and visual disabilities
Age of participants	Middle- and high school-aged children
Response prompt	Long-term classroom observations and staff interviews
Research design	Observations during hands-on educational activities with 3D printer and 3D modelling software
Dependent variable (measures)	–
Independent variable (intervention)	3D printing technology for students with special needs
Country	USA
Institution	A special education school serving students with cognitive disabilities and multiple disabilities; a school serving students with visual impairments; and the technology services department of a national organization working with the blind
Results/Outcomes	1. Increased interest in STEM disciplines; 2. The opportunity to create personalized educational tools at a lower cost; 3. Interest in the use of 3D printing in special education and therapy
Challenges	1. Slow learning, leading to frustration, distraction, and decreased interest 2.Difficulty understanding printer capabilities 3. For students with visual impairments: texture and durability are important 4. Need for accessible software (specific design and interface for people with special needs)
Authors, Year	Wonjin, Jo, et al., **2016**
Type of experiment	Empirical
Participants	–
Age of participants	–
Response prompt	Classroom observations and Satisfaction survey
Research design	Observations during hands-on educational activities with 3D printer and 3D modelling software
Dependent variable (measures)	Vocabulary and comprehension skills
Independent variable (intervention)	Development of tactile instructional maps
Country	South Korea
Institution	Seoul National School for the Blind

(*continued*)

Table 1. (*continued*)

Authors, Year	Wonjin, Jo, et al., **2016**
Results/Outcomes	Students highly valued the 3D objects, since using them improved their memorization, understanding and imagination
Challenges	Difficulties in design and cost; length of time for fabrication; and limited materials for building diverse 3D objects
Authors, Year	Buehler, E., Hurst, A. and Hofmann, M., **2014** [18]
Type of experiment	–
Participants	1 student with limited hand motor ability
Age of participants	–
Response prompt	–
Research design	Classroom observations
Dependent variable (measures)	Fine motor skills
Independent variable (intervention)	–
Country	USA
Institution	N/A
Results/Outcomes	Improved hand writing
Challenges	Time constraints and inability of assistive staff to dedicate time to train with 3D printing

Table 2. A summary of the selected articles covering the research criteria on 3D printing and modelling technology

Indicators	Description
Authors, Year	Meaghan McLeod Mozingo, Krzysztof J. Rechowicz, **2023** [21]
Materials used	–
Software used	–
Authors, Year	Yu Lun Chen, Kavitha Murthi, Wendy Martin, Regan Vidiksis, Aria-na Riccio, Kristie Patten, **2022** [22]
Materials used	–
Software used	TinkerCad
Authors, Year	Marzanna Farnicka, Margarida Pocinho, **2021**
Materials used	Flash Forge Creator - a printer where all heating elements are covered for safety reasons 3D non-toxic biodegradable thermoplastic that is easy to print and durable

(*continued*)

Table 2. (*continued*)

Indicators	Description
Software used	TinkerCAD - free, intuitive online 3D modeling software that allows you to work with 2D and 3D objects
Authors, Year	A. Chloe Simpson, Andrea Ruth Taliaferro, **2021** [9]
Materials used	Dremel Digilab 3D45
Software used	TinkerCAD Thingiverse
Authors, Year	Sandoval Poveda, A. and Hernández Montoya, D., **2021** [8]
Materials used	–
Software used	Scratch programming, mBlock programming
Authors, Year	Chen, S.H., Lin, C.Y. and Mao, Q.C., **2018** [29]
Materials used	Polylactic acid (PLA), produced by combining corn starch and sugarcane derivatives, was used in this study because it is biodegradable and does not release toxic substances when printed at a temperature of around 190 degrees
Software used	TinkerCAD
Authors, Year	Buehler, E., Comrie, N., Hofmann, M., McDonald, S. and Hurst, A., **2016.** [6]
Materials used	MakerBot Replicator 2X (Site A and C), Material: ABS or PLA plastic, 2 color; ZPrinter® 450 (Site B), Resin composite powder, multicolor Cubex Duo (Site C), ABS or PLA plastic, 2 color
Software used	TinkerCAD (its suitability for novice users is emphasized); use of ready-made samples from Thingiverse

References

1. Knight, V.F., Sartini, E.: A comprehensive literature review of comprehension strategies in core content areas for students with autism spectrum disorder. J. Autism Dev. Disord. **45**, 1213–1229 (2015). https://doi.org/10.1002/pits.21994
2. Farnicka, M., Pocinho, M.: 3D technology as a tool to improve the well-being of children and adolescents with autism spectrum disorder. In: Polskie Forum Psychologiczne, vol. 26, No. 2, pp. 153–170. Uniwersytet Kazimierza Wielkiego w Bydgoszczy (2021)
3. Van Bergeijk, E., Ranaldo, M., Shtayermman, O.: Teaching STEM to students with autism spectrum disorders. STEM Educ. **81**, 97 (2008)
4. Cañete, R., Peralta, M.E.: ASDesign: a user-centered method for the design of assistive technology that helps children with autism spectrum disorders be more independent in their daily routines. Sustainability **14**(1), 516 (2022). https://doi.org/10.3390/su14010516
5. Alboul, L., Dimitrova, M., Lekova, A., Kaburlasos, V.G., Mitrouchev, P.: Emerging technologies for assistive robotics: current challenges and perspectives. Front. Robot. AI **10**, 1288360 (2023). https://doi.org/10.3389/frobt.2023.1288360
6. Buehler, E., Comrie, N., Hofmann, M., McDonald, S., Hurst, A.: Investigating the implications of 3D printing in special education. ACM Trans. Access. Comput. **8**(3), 1–28 (2016). https://doi.org/10.1145/2870640

7. Martin, W.B., Yu, J., Wei, X., Vidiksis, R., Patten, K.K., Riccio, A.: Promoting science, technology, and engineering self-efficacy and knowledge for all with an autism inclusion maker program. In: Frontiers in Education, vol. 5, p. 75. Frontiers Media SA (2020)
8. Sandoval Poveda, A., Hernández Montoya, D.: Digital fabrication and theater: developing social skills in young adults with autism spectrum disorder. Front. Psychol. **12**, 615786 (2021). https://doi.org/10.3389/fpsyg.2021.615786
9. Simpson, A.C., Taliaferro, A.R.: Designing inclusion: using 3D printing to maximize adapted physical education participation. Teach. Except. Child. **54**(1), 26–35 (2021). https://doi.org/10.1177/00400599211010191
10. Branko, A., Šorgo, A., Helm, C., Weinhandl, R., Lang, V.: Exploring factors affecting elementary school teachers' adoption of 3D printers in teaching. TechTrends **67**(6), 990–1006 (2023). https://doi.org/10.1007/s11528-023-00909-y
11. Gallardo-Echenique, E.E., de Oliveira, J.M., Marqués-Molias, L., Esteve-Mon, F., Wang, Y., Baker, R.: Digital competence in the knowledge society. MERLOT J. Online Learn. Teach. **11**(1) (2015)
12. Pocinho, M., Garcês, S., Diaz, N., Farnicka, M.: 3D technology for children in disadvantage situations Tecnologia 3D para crianças desfavorecidas (2017). https://doi.org/10.17979/reipe.2017.0.13.3063
13. Ford, S., Minshall, T.: Invited review article: where and how 3D printing is used in teaching and education. Addit. Manuf. **25**, 131–150 (2019). https://doi.org/10.1016/j.addma.2018.10.028
14. Easley, W., Buehler, E., Hurst, A., Salib, G.: Fabricating engagement: Benefits and challenges of using 3D printing to engage underrepresented students in STEM learning. In: 2017 ASEE Annual Conference & Exposition (2017). https://doi.org/10.18260/1-2--28347
15. Baron-Cohen, S.: Is Asperger syndrome/high-functioning autism necessarily a disability? Dev. Psychopathol. **12**(3), 489–500 (2000). https://doi.org/10.1017/S0954579400003126
16. Baron-Cohen, S.: Autism: the empathizing–systemizing (E-S) theory. Ann. N. Y. Acad. Sci. **1156**(1), 68–80 (2009). https://doi.org/10.1111/j.1749-6632.2009.04467
17. Basham, J.D., Marino, M.T.: Understanding STEM education and supporting students through universal design for learning. Teach. Except. Child. **45**(4), 8–15 (2013). https://doi.org/10.1177/004005991304500401
18. Buehler, E., Hurst, A. and Hofmann, M.: Coming to grips: 3D printing for accessibility. In: Proceedings of the 16th international ACM SIGACCESS Conference on Computers & accessibility, pp. 291–292 (2014). https://doi.org/10.1145/2661334.2661345
19. World Health Organization Homepage. https://www.who.int/europe/health-topics/assistive-technology. Accessed 31 March 2025
20. Jang, J., et al.: Introduction of 3D printing technology in the classroom for visually impaired students. J. Visual Impair. Blind. **110**(2), 115–121 (2016). https://doi.org/10.1177/0145482X1611000205
21. Mozingo, M.M., Rechowicz, K.J.: Promoting skills in children and teens with autism spectrum disorder through play and STEAM (2023)
22. Chen, Y.-L., Murthi, K., Martin, W., Vidiksis, R., Riccio, A., Patten, K.: Experiences of students, teachers, and parents participating in an inclusive, school-based informal engineering education program. J. Autism Dev. Disord. 1–12 (2021). https://doi.org/10.1007/s10803-021-05230-2
23. Lekova, A., Chavdarov, I., Naydenov, B., Krastev, A., Kostova, S.: Brain-inspired IoT controlled walking robot big-foot. Adv. Sci. Technol. Eng. Syst. J. **4**(3), 220–226 (2019). https://doi.org/10.25046/aj040329
24. Thingiverse.com Homepage, Lefthanded Pink/Thumb Adapted Ball Pen By Flavoredcorn. https://www.thingiverse.com/thing:4612932. Accessed 31 March 2025
25. Gallup, N., Pearce, J.M.: The economics of classroom 3-D printing of open-source digital designs of learning aids. Designs **4**, 50 (2020). https://doi.org/10.3390/designs4040050

26. Davis, K.E.B.: The need for STEM education in special education curriculum and instruction. STEM Education: Strategies for Teaching Learners with Special Needs, 1–20 (2014)
27. Berry, R.Q., Bull, G., Browning, C., Thomas, C.D., Starkweather, G., Aylor, J.: Use of digital fabrication to incorporate engineering design principles in elementary mathematics education, Contemp. Issues Technol. Teach. Educ. **10**, 167–172 (2010). http://www.editlib.org/p/35289
28. Kouo, J.L., Hogan, A.E., Morton, S., Gregorio, J.: Supporting students with an autism spectrum disorder in engineering: K-12 and beyond. J. Sci. Educ. Stud. Disabil. **24**(1), n1 (2021). https://doi.org/10.14448/jsesd.13.0011
29. Chen, S.H., Lin, C.Y., Mao, Q.C.: Effects of 3D printing interactive technology on special education for children with different disabilities. In: Proceeding of the Asian Conference on Education 2018 (pp. 333–340) (2018)
30. Dimitrova, M., Vegt, N., Barakova, E.: Designing a system of interactive robots for training collaborative skills to autistic children. In: 2012 15th International Conference on Interactive Collaborative Learning (ICL), pp. 1–8. IEEE (2012)
31. Rachel Cohen-Rottenberg "Unwarranted conclusions and the potential for harm: my reply to Simon Baron-Cohen" (2011). www.autismandempathy.com
32. Kasirer, A., Adi-Japha, E., Mashal, N.: Verbal and figural creativity in children with autism spectrum disorder and typical development. Front. Psychol. **11**, 559238 (2020). https://doi.org/10.3389/fpsyg.2020.559238
33. Capp, M.J.: The effectiveness of universal design for learning: a meta-analysis of literature between 2013 and 2016. Int. J. Incl. Educ. **21**(8), 791–807 (2017). https://doi.org/10.1080/13603116.2017.1325074
34. Morze, N., Varchenko-Trotsenko, L., Tiutiunnyk, A.: Introduction of steam education with the use of 3D technologies: modelling, scanning, and printing. ISSN: 2414-0325 (n.d.). https://doi.org/10.28925/2414-0325.2016.2.t5159
35. Magkafa, D., Newbutt, N., Palmer, M.: Implementing co-design practices for the development of a museum interface for autistic children. In: Brooks, A.L., Brahman, S., Kapralos, B., Nakajima, A., Tyerman, J., Jain, L.C. (eds.) Recent Advances in Technologies for Inclusive Well-Being. ISRL, vol. 196, pp. 421–443. Springer, Cham (2021). https://doi.org/10.1007/978-3-030-59608-8_22
36. Mcloughlin, L., et al.: Virtual sculpting and 3D printing for young people with disabilities. IEEE Comput. Graphics Appl. **36**(1), 22–28 (2016). https://doi.org/10.1109/MCG.2016.1
37. Chavdarov, I., Kostova, B., Georgieva-Tsaneva, G.: Application development in AutoCAD environment for modeling 3D printed souvenirs targeting STEAM education. In: 2024 International Conference on Software, Telecommunications and Computer Networks (SoftCOM), pp. 1–6. IEEE (2024). https://doi.org/10.23919/SoftCOM62040.2024.10721881

CS Unplugged: Fostering Computational Thinking in Early Childhood

Monika Mladenović[1], Divna Krpan[1(✉)], Jasna Dragičević[2], and Goran Zaharija[1]

[1] Faculty of Science, University of Split, Split, Croatia
divna.krpan@pmfst.hr

[2] School for Design, Graphics, and Sustainable Construction, Split, Croatia

Abstract. Digital literacy is considered the fourth analytical skill that students today should possess, and many initiatives promote its development in children from an early age. It is important to emphasize that the focus should be on using technology and understanding the basic concepts of computational thinking (CT). There is a lack of research on teaching CT in kindergarten, partially due to the absence of age-appropriate technology interfaces that would enable children to engage in more complex projects. On the other hand, CS unplugged teaching methods for fundamental computer science concepts have already been proven successful, even in kindergarten. This paper describes research designed based on Papert's experiments, focusing on using the "turtle" as a real-world object in teaching sequence, branching, and loop algorithms. The research was conducted in three kindergarten groups involving 34 children aged 3 to 6.

Keywords: CS Unplugged · Computational Thinking · Kindergarten · Computer Science · Algorithm

1 Introduction

In today's digital age, computational thinking (CT) is considered the fourth analytical skill [1]. Therefore, CT should be incorporated into formal education, even from kindergarten. Seymour Papert introduced CT in 1980, emphasizing the constructionist approach to education with social and affective dimensions combined with technical content [2]. Papert stressed the importance of access to computers for acquiring CT skills in children, but indicated that some processes can be also executed by humans, even without the aid of a computer [3].

The modern wave of CT was initiated by Wing's seminal essay in 2006, promoting the benefits of thinking like a computer scientist across various professions [1]. Wing and Papert suggest that competencies acquired through computational thinking can be transferred to other disciplines. Lodi and Martini [4] indicate that CT should be observed in its proper context – the Computer Science (CS). However, it means more than being able to make a computer program [1]. CS, with its programming languages, provides a means to make abstract concepts executable and thus more tangible for other disciplines. Computer programming is often used to teach and practice CT in schools [5].

D. Vasić and E. Brajković (Eds.): MoStart 2025, CCIS 2609, pp. 52–66, 2026.
https://doi.org/10.1007/978-3-032-02801-3_4

1.1 CS Unplugged: An Approach for Young Learners

Although educators embraced the importance of CT and emphasized developing CT skills in children early on, the crucial point isn't just exposing children to technology but ensuring they grasp the fundamental CT ideas so they can become not just digitally literate but technologically or digitally fluent [6, 7]. Consequently, technology tools should not focus on introducing basic CT concepts to children because it can even distract learners, especially at an early age. Hence, some authors suggest that short initial introductory programming activities can be perceived as negative and recommend an unplugged approach [8]. The CS Unplugged approach aims to teach computer science (CS) concepts and computational thinking without digital tools [9]. The term originated from a compilation of activities shared online in various formats since the early 1990s. It peaked in 1999 with a free online book [10], and its revised version was published in 2005 [11]. The CS Unplugged website (https://csunplugged.org) provides many fun activities based on learning by doing, and no computers or other electronic devices are required. Also, teachers with less experience find teaching programming intimidating, especially when confronting challenging topics. The "unplugged" approach can assist in covering relatively complex subjects quickly by employing simple items (paper, string, pencils, etc.), eliminating the need to install and use complex software [12]. Hence, it provides a positive experience for both students and teachers.

According to [13], the positive impact of CS unplugged activities on learning outcomes, CT skills, CS concepts, collaboration, creativity, confidence, attitudes, and motivation was addressed in 22 of 55 examined studies. Teachers adopting the unplugged approach also report positive results, contributing to a more meaningful and engaging exploration of computer science for both students and educators [9]. The activities are described as engaging and used to increase interest in the CS field [14–16]. *Unplugged programming* is defined as teaching programming concepts without a computer device and is often executed through physical activity or using different tangible objects [17].

The CS unplugged teaching method has already proven successful in teaching fundamental computer science (CS) concepts, and it is incorporated into many worldwide CS curricula [9]. Moreover, many initiatives from the last decade for promoting computer science (CS) and CT for young students also designed CS unplugged curriculums for educators and students [18, 19]. The method benefits those with limited access to technology, enabling learning without computers or other devices because it offers a wide range of activities as an alternative to text-based and robotic tools [20]. In academic studies, the number of research related to CS unplugged methods from 2017 is growing, but only a few are related to the preschool or kindergarten age [5, 13].

Some researchers believe it is essential that preschool children are exposed to digital tools and programming activities [21]. Educational technology advancements, including graphical blocks on screen or tangible objects (physical manipulatives), allow young children to input commands without knowledge of syntax or any reading skills [22]. This tangible input approach makes programming accessible to young learners who don't know how to use a keyboard and mouse. A study conducted by Bers in 2014 reports that young children (4–6 years old) were able to use a hybrid/graphical computer language (CHERP) to program a robotic vehicle that they built themselves, and they were able to acquire some CT abilities [23]. Another study by Fessakis et al. [24] showed that while working with Logo, young children (5–6 years old) developed social skills, problem-solving abilities, and mathematical concepts.

A research overview by Lye and Koh [25] of studies conducted with children aged 5 to 14 shows that adopting CT through programming is possible. Palmér [26] conducted a study with children aged 3 to 5 where programming was used to facilitate their spatial thinking abilities. The research intervention indicated potential in teaching children spatial thinking through methodical involvement in programming activities. There are reports that CS-unplugged activities positively influenced students' understanding and planning performances [27].

Jean Piaget's theory of cognitive development suggests that children move through four different stages of learning. Piaget's stages are: sensorimotor stage (from birth to 2 years), preoperational stage (ages 2 to 7), concrete operational stage (ages 7 to 11), and formal operational stage (ages 12 and up) [28]. During the preoperational stage, children begin to think symbolically (for example, a child can use an object to represent something else), and they are getting better with language and thinking but still think in very concrete terms.

1.2 Research Context and Objectives

The studies above show that teaching CT to kindergarten children through computer programming and technical devices is possible. However, this paper focuses on teaching CT through unplugged CS activities without using any devices.

Research on CT and using digital (and non-digital) tools at the kindergarten level is scarce [29]. Battal et al. [13] conducted a literature review of studies published between 2010 and 2019 in multiple databases to analyze implementations of CS unplugged and identified 55 studies (17 journal articles and 38 conference papers). However, only two studies were about CS unplugged activities with kindergarten children. Although this paper is not about literature review, we have selected one of those databases ("Association for Computing Machinery (ACM) Digital Library") and checked for publications similar to our paper and published in the last five years. The query included keywords: "unplugged," "preschool OR kindergarten," and "Computer Science" OR "Computational Thinking." After filtering only "Research Article," "Journals," and "Proceedings," we have identified a total of 34 articles (6 journal articles + 28 conference papers) in the ACM database. However, none of those articles was related to the topic. Most were about older students (from elementary school to university), focused on teachers (surveys), literature reviews, or using some device or application. There is insufficient information on which activities and strategies are adopted during kindergarten educational practice [26].

This paper explores the potential of CS Unplugged as a way to teach CT concepts in early childhood education, examining how practical and effective it is and considering its impact on broader digital literacy education. Through this study, we aim to contribute valuable insights to discussions about teaching methods that suit young learners' unique needs and developmental stages in the digital era. The study was based on the results of the pilot study [30] involving CS unplugged activities for kindergarteners [30]. Our activities were based on Seymour Papert's idea [2], a cornerstone for CT as we know it today, which Wing revived, formalized, and broadened in 2006 [1].

Several studies on a similar topic [31–33] have primarily focused on the technical aspects of activities, dealing with techniques, tools, and strategies for implementing computational thinking concepts as part of the curriculum. Instead of exploring how children adopt presented concepts and simultaneously develop CT skills.

Therefore, this research attempts to fill the gaps in the research literature. The following research questions are formulated:

1. To what extent do kindergarten children understand the algorithmic structure of sequence?
2. To what extent do kindergarten children understand the selection algorithm?
3. To what extent do kindergarten children understand the repeating algorithm?
4. What behavior patterns do children develop based on the learning environment created by simulating the micro-world of the Logo programming language?

2 Methodology

The research was conducted in 2023 in the form of workshops held at two local kindergartens and at the Faculty of Science. In all the activities, 34 children aged from 3 to 6 years old participated. In the Croatian educational system, children aged 3–6 belong to the kindergarten group. Data was gathered using qualitative research methods, including participant observation in the kindergarten during CS unplugged activities, and quantitative methods by counting students' advancing through activities. The activities were based on a pilot study [30] found in Papert's experiments with children, resulting in Logo programming language [34]. The study was conducted in two phases. In the first phase, preliminary data captured the natural and spontaneous reactions of the children. Building upon the analysis of the first phase, we proceeded to the second phase, incorporating structured observations that centered on particular activities and the corresponding reactions of the children. Video cameras were used to record these activities, facilitating subsequent analysis and data collection.

2.1 Participants

A total of 34 kindergarten-age children were included in all the activities conducted during the research. One of the groups, K1, consisted of children from a standard kindergarten setting, while the other groups, K2 and K3, comprised children identified as "gifted." It is important to note that gifted children were identified independently by pedagogy and psychology experts through standardized testing conducted within the children's respective kindergartens. The authors of this paper were not directly involved in the testing process; instead, they were provided with the categorized outcomes, allowing for an unbiased approach to the research analysis. Since the K1 group was not tested, it was labeled "mixed," and others with gifted children were labeled "advanced." Table 1 shows the distribution by age and kindergarten group.

Among all children, there were 18 boys and 16 girls, whereas in K1, there were five boys and seven girls; in K2, six boys and four girls; and in K3, seven boys and five girls. The research consisted of two members. The first author, a faculty professor specializing in didactics of informatics, was a nonparticipating observer responsible for

Table 1. Distribution by age and kindergarten group.

Age (years)	3–4	5–6	Total
K1 – mixed group	4	8	12
K2 – advanced group	1	9	10
K3 – advanced group	4	8	12
Total	9	25	34

observing and documenting the conducted activities. The third author was a final-year student specializing in informatics education and had the role of a participating observer who was conducting activities.

The research was conducted in kindergartens K1 and K3, while the K3 group came to the Faculty of Science, where we conducted activities. The sessions were conducted on 16th March 2023 for K1, 28th March 2023 for K2, and 14th April 2023 for the K3 group. Every session lasted for two hours, including mini breaks during sessions. Before all sessions, we gathered informed consent from children's caregivers. The identity of every child is hidden and protected.

2.2 Research Context

Based on the pilot study results, we designed several unplugged (physical) activities [30]. The activities were based on Papert's experiments and Logo programming language. In our setup, one child acted as a "turtle robot" and the other as a "programmer." The "turtle" had to walk following the path represented by the papers on the floor. Figure 1 shows such examples.

Fig. 1. Path for the "turtle" for sequencing (left) and selection (right) algorithms.

The idea is that children can create a "program" using three instructions: "forward," "left turn," and "right turn," presented with the arrows as Fig. 2 shows.

The "programmer" had to create the "program" using instructions, which would lead the "turtle" from the beginning to the end of the path. Afterward, the "turtle" would "execute" the program by following those instructions. In the case of an error, the "programmer" should "fix" the instructions. Figure 3 shows an example of the activity.

We implemented selection, repeat, and selection algorithms. Programs based on the selection algorithms were "executing" in a given sequence of instructions. After several

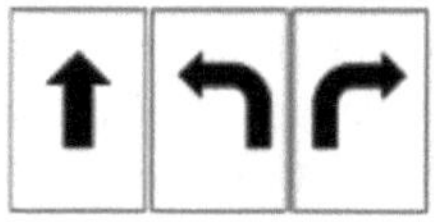

Fig. 2. Instructions for forward left, and right turns.

Fig. 3. An example of the unplugged activity.

examples with the sequence, we introduced a repeat algorithm by pointing out that some instructions are repeating. For the selection algorithm, we introduced conditional behavior with the colors; we explained that for a given color, the "turtle" makes a given action. Table 2 shows the activities examples.

Table 2. Activities examples.

Path	Algorithm	Instructions
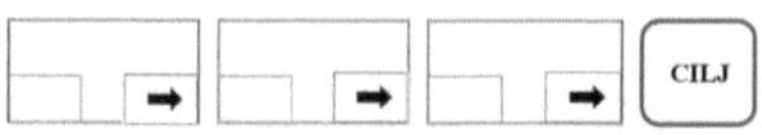	Sequencing	• forward • right turn • left turn
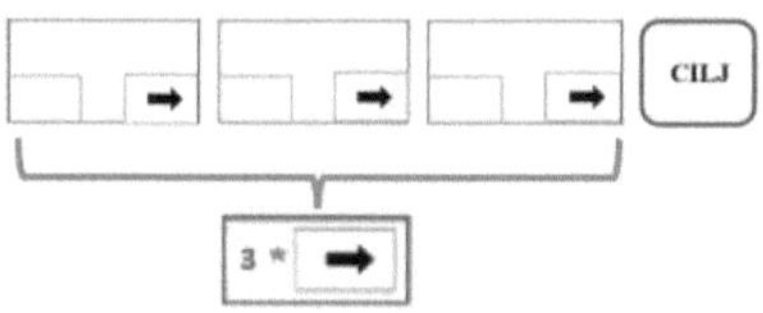	Repeat	• all the instructions above • repeat
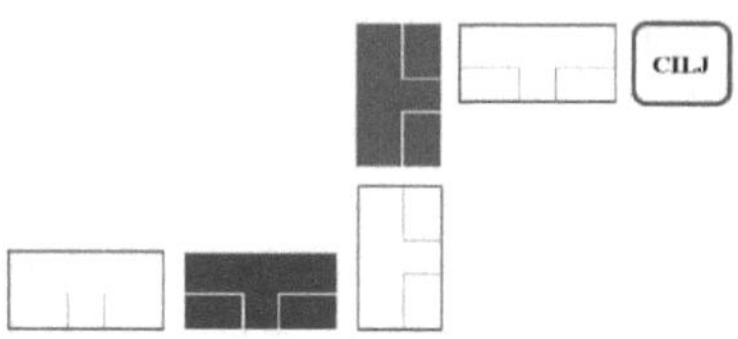	Selection	• All the instructions above • Selection instructions: – Blue - turn around – Green - touch your knees – Red - clap

The data was collected by structured observations, focusing on specific activities and children's reactions. We used video cameras to record the activities to collect data, allowing for later analysis. During the data analysis, where it was possible, we quantified children's behavior for quantitative analysis.

3 Results

We gathered data by structured observation. We defined three types of finishing the task: success, success with difficulties, and quitting. We categorized participants by the age groups 3–4 and 5–6 years old and their kindergartens. We also categorized them by the type of kindergarten: mixed or advanced group. For the quantitative analysis, we used non-parametric Mann-Whitney and chi-square tests. In the following sections, we present the results.

3.1 Sequencing Algorithm

Out of 34 participants, 17 children aged 5–6 learned how to move based on given rules using three basic instructions: "forward," "left turn," and "right turn." Two children from group K1, one aged 3–4 and the other 5–6, took a step back when they made a mistake following the "programmers" instructions. But, after being reminded of the rule about using instructions, they corrected themselves with some help and successfully guided their robot to the goal. Fig. 4 shows the results.

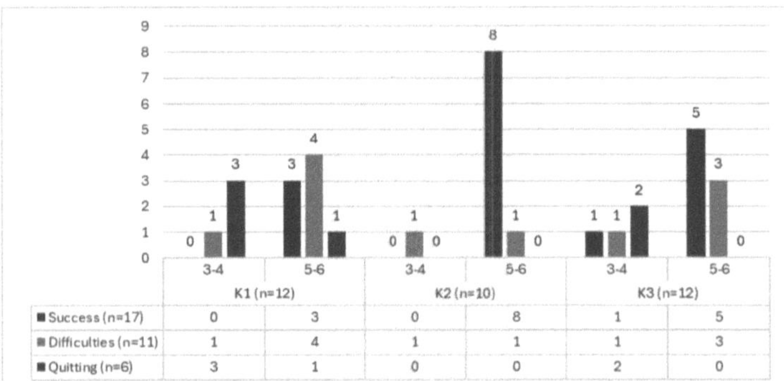

Fig. 4. Descriptives for sequencing algorithm

For the quantitative analysis, first, we conducted the Mann-Whitney test to see if there was a difference between the "advanced" K2 ($n = 10$) and K3 ($n = 12$) groups. The result did not show statistical differences between groups ($U = 40.0$, $p = 0.203$). Therefore, K2 and K3 groups we can treat as one "advanced" group, while K1 is a mixed group.

Further, we conducted the Mann-Whitney test to determine the differences in children's results between age groups. The results showed statistically significant differences

(U = 34.500, p = 0.001) between younger (3–4 years old) and older (5–6 years old) groups. The older group achieved better results than the younger ones, which is expected. Figure 5 shows results for the sequencing algorithm by age group.

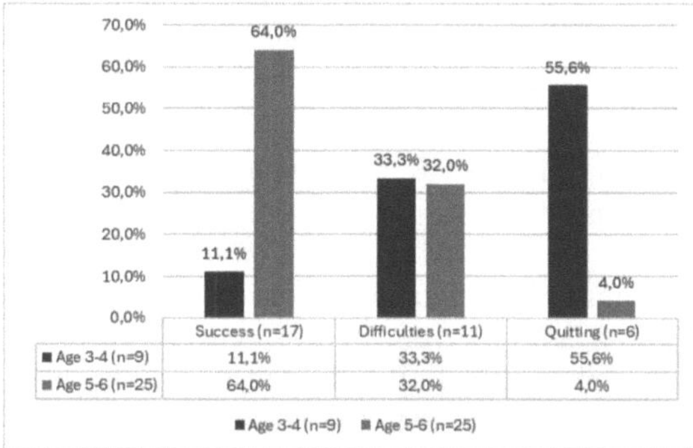

Fig. 5. Results for sequencing algorithm by age groups

Additionally, we conducted a chi-square ($\chi 2$) test to explore differences between the two groups. Chi-square did not show statistically significant differences ($\chi 2 = 5.401$, df = 2, p = 0.067) between the groups, although the p-value is near 0.05. When variable age is included as a layer variable, there were no statistically significant differences for age groups 3–4 ($\chi 2 = 1.440$, df = 2, p = 0.487), 5–6 ($\chi 2 = 4.607$, df = 2, p = 0.100) by "mixed" and "advanced" groups. Figure 6 shows results for the sequencing algorithm by groups.

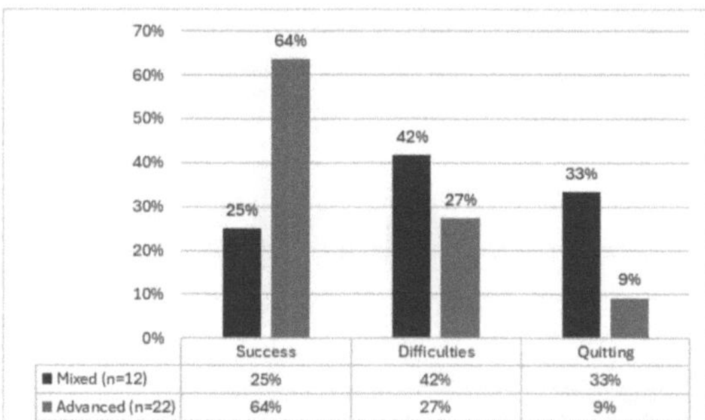

Fig. 6. Results for sequencing algorithm by groups

The analysis showed interesting differences among the kindergarten groups. Combining the "advanced" K2 and K3 groups revealed no significant differences. Therefore, we treated them as one "advanced" group, while K1 remained a mixed group. It was noticed that older kids (5–6 years old) performed better than younger ones (3–4 years old), as expected. However, no significant differences were found when comparing the "mixed" and "advanced" groups, indicating consistent results across different types of kindergartens. Considering that the "advanced" group was recognized as gifted, the results suggest that age is the most dominant factor for sequencing algorithms at kindergarten age. The inclusion of age as a factor in between-groups analysis emphasized that, within specific age groups, there were no notable differences even though one group was made up of gifted children, confirming the reliability of our findings.

3.2 Repeat Algorithm

In this section, we focus on the activities involving the repeat algorithm, which introduces the idea of repeating the same set of actions, adding complexity to children's understanding of computational thinking. Based on the previous findings, elementary school children had the most problems and misconceptions about repeat algorithms [35, 36].

The findings of the pilot study [30] indicated that younger children particularly struggle with maintaining concentration. Therefore, this time, we introduced a repeat algorithm earlier than in a previous study, approximately 10 min from the beginning of the workshop, to minimize the effect of lack of concentration on the results.

By observing, we noted that children aged 5–6 years from all groups (n = 12) could recognize the repeating pattern successfully. Meanwhile, four children of this age group and four younger ones aged 3–4 experienced difficulties. Initially, they did not notice the repeating pattern, but after seeing the two children's successful attempts, they understood the benefit of applying the repetition algorithm. They realized that representing a sequence with only three available commands is more efficient by showing one command and a number indicating how many times to repeat it. Figure 7 shows the results.

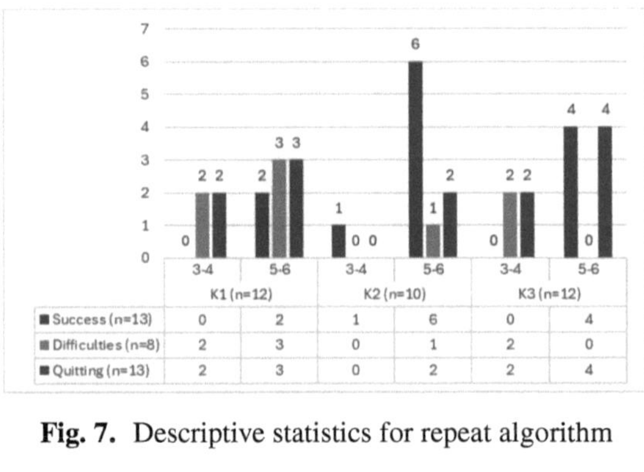

Fig. 7. Descriptive statistics for repeat algorithm

Further, we conducted the Mann-Whitney test to determine the differences in children's results between age groups. The results did not show statistically significant differences ($U = 81.000$, $p = 0.231$) between younger (3–4 years old) and older (5–6 years old) groups. The older group achieved slightly better results compared to the younger ones. Figure 8 shows results for the sequencing algorithm by age group.

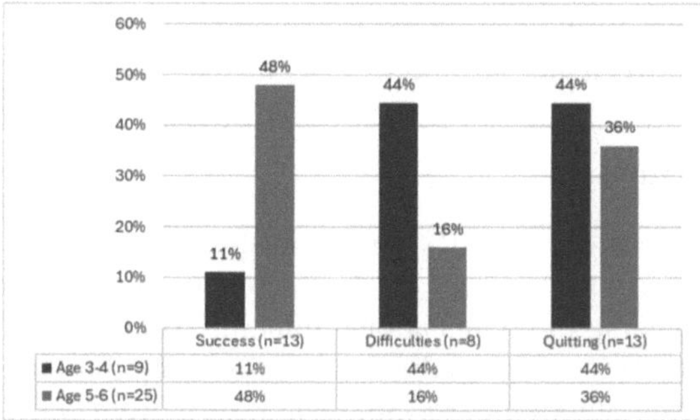

Fig. 8. Results for sequencing algorithm by age groups

We again conducted the Mann-Whitney test to see if there was a difference between "advanced" K2 ($n = 10$) and K3 ($n = 12$) groups, and the result again showed that there were no statistical differences between groups ($U = 37.0$, $p = 0.140$). Therefore, K2 and K3 groups we can treat as one "advanced" group, while K1 is a mixed group. We conducted a chi-square ($\chi 2$) test to compare the two groups. Chi-square did not show statistically significant differences ($\chi 2 = 4.90$, $df = 2$, $p = 0.086$) between the groups. Figure 9 shows the results by group. For further testing, we included layer variable age, but there were no statistically significant differences for age groups 3–4 ($\chi 2 = 9.000$, $df = 2$, $p = 0.638$), 5–6 ($\chi 2 = 4.703$, $df = 2$, $p = 0.095$). Figure 9 shows results for repeat algorithm by groups.

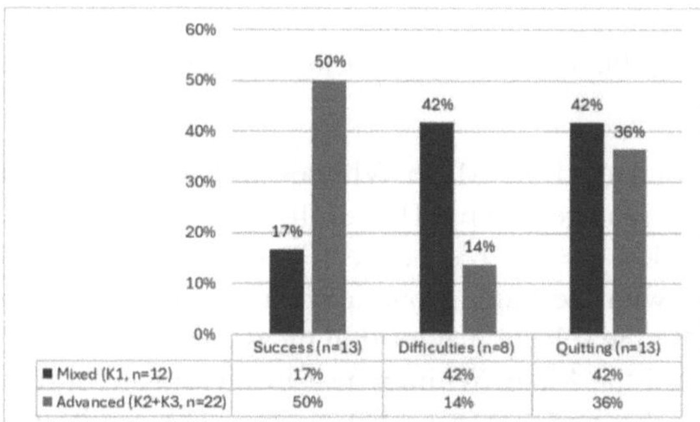

Fig. 9. Results for sequencing algorithm by groups

The results of the activities related to the repeat algorithm in kindergarten revealed interesting findings. Children aged 5–6 from all groups demonstrated a good understanding of repeating patterns, but some encountered initial difficulties, especially in the 3–4 age group. Notably, an equal number of children ($n = 13$) both succeeded and quit the activities related to the repeat algorithm. Given that the repeat algorithm is recognized as the most abstract and challenging among the three basic algorithms (sequencing, selecting, and repeating) [35, 36], the observed difficulties are not surprising. The abstract nature of the algorithm likely contributed to the absence of significant differences in their achievements between the "advanced" and "mixed" groups.

3.3 Selection Algorithm

In this section, we focus on activities involving the selection algorithm. The selection algorithm introduces the concept of actions based on colors, adding complexity to children's understanding of computational thinking. Building on previous findings, elementary school children exhibited the fewest misconceptions and achieved the best results for the selection algorithm [35, 36]. The results from activities related to the selection algorithm align with the mentioned findings, as all participants succeeded (n = 7) with or without difficulties (n = 17) in all activities. Figure 10 illustrates the results by kindergarten and age.

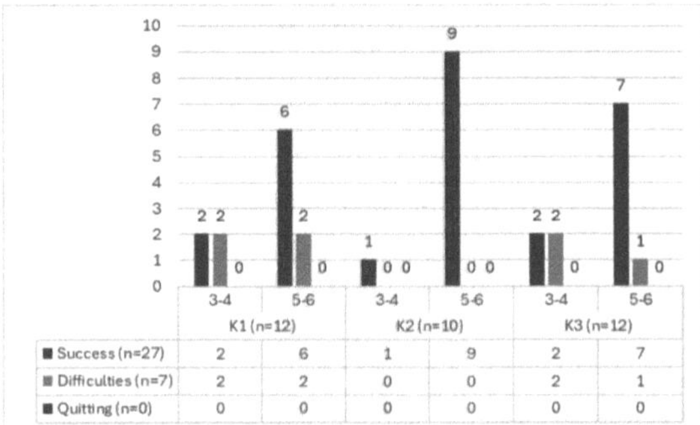

Fig. 10. Results for sequencing algorithm by groups

As before, we conducted the Mann-Whitney test to determine the differences in children's results between age groups. The results did not reveal statistically significant differences ($U = 76.000$, $p = 0.163$) between younger (3–4 years old) and older (5–6 years old) groups, with the older group achieving slightly better results. Figure 11 displays the results for the selection algorithm by age group.

We also conducted the Mann-Whitney test to investigate differences between the 'advanced' K2 (n = 10) and K3 (n = 12) groups. The result showed no statistical differences between groups ($U = 45.0$, $p = 0.346$). Therefore, we can treat K2 and K3 groups as one 'advanced' group, while K1 remains a mixed group. A chi-square ($\chi 2$) test was further conducted to compare the two groups, showing no statistically significant differences ($\chi 2 = 1.843$, $df = 1$, $p = 0.175$) between groups.

For additional analysis, we included age as a layer variable. When layered by age, the results revealed no statistically significant differences for age groups 3–4 ($\chi 2 = 0.90$, $df = 1$, $p = 0.764$) and 5–6 ($\chi 2 = 1.883$, $df = 1$, $p = 0.170$). Figure 12 displays the results for the selection algorithm by groups.

In summary, our investigation into activities focused on the selection algorithm highlights the capabilities of children in comprehending the algorithm. The introduction of

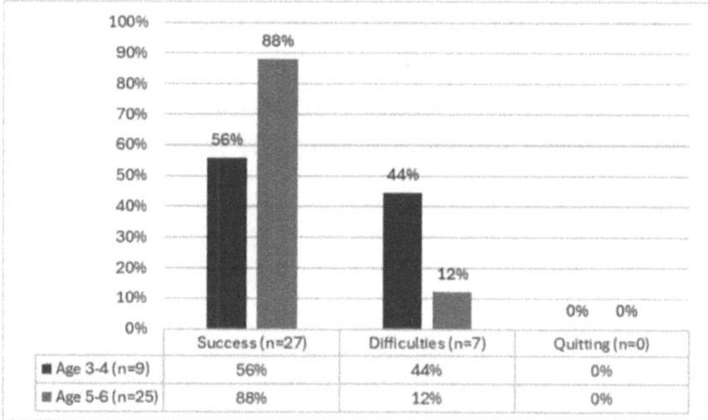

Fig. 11. Results for selection algorithm by age groups

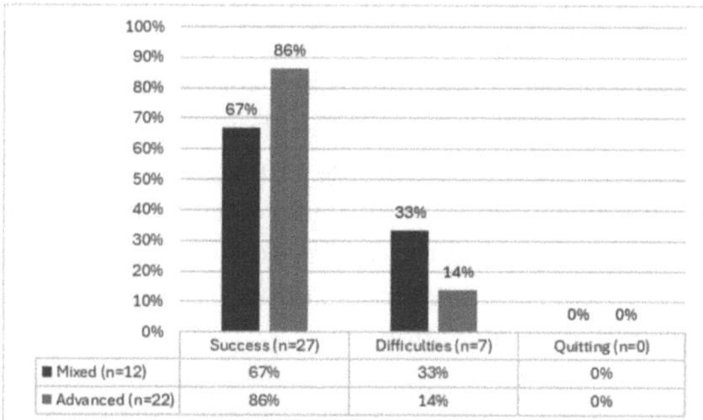

Fig. 12. Results for sequencing algorithm by groups

color-based actions added complexity, yet all participants, regardless of age or kindergarten type, successfully navigated the challenges. Statistical analyses revealed no significant differences between age groups or kindergarten types, affirming the universality of children's achievements with the selection algorithm. However, the small sample size in our study reduces the statistical power and increases uncertainty in the results. While the risk of Type I error (false positive) is controlled by the significance threshold, the small sample size makes it harder to detect true differences (increasing the risk of Type II error).

4 Limitations of the Study

While our study provides valuable insights into the effectiveness of CS Unplugged activities for early childhood education, it is essential to acknowledge certain limitations. First and foremost, our sample size, while representative, may have limitations in generalizability due to the specific demographics of the participating kindergartens. Additionally, the study primarily focused on three fundamental algorithms, potentially overlooking the broader spectrum of computational thinking skills. The reliance on qualitative and quantitative methods may offer a comprehensive understanding, yet the complexity of children's cognitive development demands a more nuanced exploration. Moreover, the short duration of the study and the confined timeframe for each activity may not fully capture the long-term impact or sustained engagement of children in CS Unplugged practices. These limitations require cautious interpretation and encourage future research to delve deeper into diverse demographics, a broader array of computational thinking skills, and extended study durations.

5 Conclusion

Our study dealt with the efficacy of CS Unplugged activities in fostering crucial computational thinking skills among preschool children. Based on the pilot study [30], we designed CS unplugged activities for kindergarten children, focusing on three fundamental algorithms—sequencing, repeating, and selection—in early childhood education. The consistent success across both 'mixed' and 'advanced' groups suggests that age, rather than prior cognitive recognition, plays a pivotal role in children's proficiency in these activities. Mastering fundamental algorithms, including sequencing, repeating, and selecting, indicates a promising development in their computational thinking abilities. However, it is imperative to recognize that our exploration was limited to specific algorithms and may not fully encapsulate the broader spectrum of computational thinking skills. Future research should expand the scope, considering a more extensive range of activities and skills to provide a comprehensive understanding of computational thinking development in early childhood education.

5.1 Selection and Participation of Children

The study was performed according to the ethics and research standards procedures that were in place when conducting research. Since we have already conducted several workshops in local kindergartens, they invited us to conduct the activities described in this paper. The managers of kindergartens handled consent by sending home the children's parents' consent forms. The children were free to participate in or quit activities if they wished to. Participant anonymity was rigorously maintained, as data analysis and reporting were conducted without reference to personal identifiers. This ensured that it was impossible to identify any participant by the data presented in the paper.

References

1. Wing, J.M.: Computational thinking. Commun. ACM **49**, 33–35 (2006). https://doi.org/10.1145/1118178.1118215
2. Papert, S.: Mindstorms: children, computers, and powerful ideas. Basic Book Inc, New York, NY, USA (1980)
3. Bull, G., Garofalo, J., Hguyen, N.R.: Thinking about computational thinking: origins of computational thinking in educational computing. J. Dig. Learn. Teach. Educ. **36**, 6–18 (2020). https://doi.org/10.1080/21532974.2019.1694381
4. Lodi, M., Martini, S.: Computational thinking, between papert and wing. Sci. Educ. **30**, 883–908 (2021). https://doi.org/10.1007/s11191-021-00202-5

5. Montuori, C., Gambarota, F., Altoé, G., Arfé, B.: The cognitive effects of computational thinking: a systematic review and meta-analytic study. Comput. Educ. **210**, 104961 (2024). https://doi.org/10.1016/j.compedu.2023.104961
6. Papert, S., Resnick, M.: Technological fluency and the representation of knowledge. Proposal to the National Science Foundation. MIT Media Laboratory, Cambridge, MA (1995)
7. Wang, Q., Myers, M.D., Sundaram, D.: Digital Natives und Digital Immigrants: Entwicklung eines Modells digitaler Gewandtheit. Wirtschaftsinf. **55**, 409–420 (2013). https://doi.org/10.1007/s11576-013-0390-2
8. Lonati, V., Malchiodi, D., Monga, M., Morpurgo, A.: Is coding the way to go? In: Brodnik, A., Vahrenhold, J. (eds.) Informatics in Schools. Curricula, Competences, and Competitions, pp. 165–174. Springer, Cham (2015). https://doi.org/10.1007/978-3-319-25396-1_15
9. Bell, T., Vahrenhold, J.: CS Unplugged—how is it used, and does it work? In: Böckenhauer, H.-J., Komm, D., Unger, W. (eds.) Adventures Between Lower Bounds and Higher Altitudes: Essays Dedicated to Juraj Hromkovič on the Occasion of His 60th Birthday, pp. 497–521. Springer, Cham (2018). https://doi.org/10.1007/978-3-319-98355-4_29
10. Bell, T., Witten, I.H., Fellows, M.: Computer Science Unplugged . . . off-line activities and games for all ages. "Computer Science Unplugged" (1998)
11. Bell, T., Witten, I.H., Fellows, M., Adams, R., McKenzie, J.: Computer Science Unplugged: an enrichment and extension programme for primary-aged children. University of Canterbury, Computer Science and Software Engineering (2005)
12. Gutiérrez, J.M., Sanders, I.D.: Computer science education in Peru: a new kind of monster? ACM SIGCSE Bull. **41**, 86–89 (2009)
13. Battal, A., Afacan Adanır, G., Gülbahar, Y.: Computer science unplugged: a systematic literature review. J. Educ. Technol. Syst. **50**, 24–47 (2021). https://doi.org/10.1177/00472395211018801
14. Rodriguez, B., Rader, C., Camp, T.: Using student performance to assess cs unplugged activities in a classroom environment. In: Proceedings of the 2016 ACM Conference on Innovation and Technology in Computer Science Education, pp. 95–100. Association for Computing Machinery, New York, NY, USA (2016). https://doi.org/10.1145/2899415.2899465
15. Rodriguez, B., Kennicutt, S., Rader, C., Camp, T.: Assessing computational thinking in CS unplugged activities. In: Proceedings of the 2017 ACM SIGCSE Technical Symposium on Computer Science Education, pp. 501–506. ACM, Seattle Washington USA (2017). https://doi.org/10.1145/3017680.3017779
16. Lin, Y., Liao, H., Weng, S., Dong, W.: Comparing the effects of plugged-in and unplugged activities on computational thinking development in young children. Educ. Inf. Technol. **29**, 9541–9574 (2023). https://doi.org/10.1007/s10639-023-12181-x
17. Faber, H., Wierdsma, M., Doornbos, R.P., van der Ven, J.S., de Vette, K.: Teaching computational thinking to primary school students via unplugged programming lessons. J. Eur. Teach. Educ. Network **12**, 13–24 (2017)
18. Bell, T., Witten, I., Fellows, M.: CS Unplugged. https://www.csunplugged.org/en/. Accessed 23 Jan 2024
19. CODE: CS Fundamentals Unplugged. https://code.org/curriculum/unplugged. Accessed 23 Jan 2024
20. Waite, J.: Pedagogy in teaching computer science in schools: a literature review. Queen Mary University of London and King's College London (2017)
21. Bers, M.U.: Coding as a playground: programming and computational thinking in the early childhood classroom. Routledge, London (2020)
22. Ching, Y.-H., Hsu, Y.-C., Baldwin, S.: Developing computational thinking with educational technologies for young learners. TechTrends **62**, 563–573 (2018). https://doi.org/10.1007/s11528-018-0292-7

23. Bers, M.U., Flannery, L., Kazakoff, E.R., Sullivan, A.: Computational thinking and tinkering: exploration of an early childhood robotics curriculum. Comput. Educ. **72**, 145–157 (2014). https://doi.org/10.1016/j.compedu.2013.10.020
24. Fessakis, G., Gouli, E., Mavroudi, E.: Problem solving by 5–6 years old kindergarten children in a computer programming environment: a case study. Comput. Educ. **63**, 87–97 (2013). https://doi.org/10.1016/j.compedu.2012.11.016
25. Lye, S.Y., Koh, J.H.L.: Review on teaching and learning of computational thinking through programming: what is next for K-12? Comput. Hum. Behav. **41**, 51–61 (2014). https://doi.org/10.1016/j.chb.2014.09.012
26. Palmér, H.: Programming in preschool-with a focus on learning mathematics. Int. Res. Early Childhood Educ. **8**, 75–87 (2017)
27. Cakiroglu, U., Mumcu, S., Atabay, M., Aydin, M.: Understanding problem-solving processes of preschool children in CS unplugged activities. Int. J. Comput. Sci. Educ. Schools **5**, 35–53 (2022). https://doi.org/10.21585/ijcses.v5i3.133
28. Lefa, B.: The Piaget theory of cognitive development: an educational implications. Educ. Psychol. **1**, 1–8 (2014)
29. Howland, K., Good, J., Robertson, J., Manches, A.: Editorial — special issue on computational thinking and coding in childhood. Int. J. Child-Comput. Interact. **19**, 93–95 (2019). https://doi.org/10.1016/j.ijcci.2018.11.001
30. Mladenović, M., Repušić, M., Ozretić, M.: CS unplugged activities for teaching basic programming concepts to kindergarten children. In: ICERI2023 Proceedings, pp. 7674–7682. IATED (2023)
31. Burleson, W.S., et al.: Active learning environments with robotic tangibles: children's physical and virtual spatial programming experiences. IEEE Trans. Learn. Technol. **11**, 96–106 (2018). https://doi.org/10.1109/TLT.2017.2724031
32. Jung, S.E., Won, E.: Systematic review of research trends in robotics education for young children. Sustainability **10** (2018). https://doi.org/10.3390/su10040905
33. Serholt, S.: Breakdowns in children's interactions with a robotic tutor: a longitudinal study. Comput. Hum. Behav. **81**, 250–264 (2018). https://doi.org/10.1016/j.chb.2017.12.030
34. Feurzeig, W.: Toward a culture of creativity: a personal perspective on logo's early years and ongoing potential. Int. J. Comput. Math. Learn. **15**, 257–265 (2010). https://doi.org/10.1007/s10758-010-9168-4
35. Mladenović, M., Žanko, Ž., Granić, A.: Mediated transfer: from text to blocks and back. Int. J. Child-Comput. Interact. 100279 (2021). https://doi.org/10.1016/j.ijcci.2021.100279
36. Žanko, Ž, Mladenović, M., Krpan, D.: Mediated transfer: impact on programming misconceptions. J. Comput. Educ. **10**, 1–26 (2023). https://doi.org/10.1007/s40692-022-00225-z

AI-Driven Customization of Adaptive Learning Content: Lessons from Applying LLMs in Personalized Education

Antun Matija Filipović(✉), Ivana Fastić-Pajk, Hrvoje Puljiz, and Ivan Šabić

Croatian Academic and Research Network – CARNET, Zagreb, Croatia
antun.matija.filipovic@carnet.hr

Abstract. The rise of Artificial Intelligence (AI) and Large Language Models (LLMs) has created new opportunities for intelligent educational systems, particularly in customizing and personalizing learning content. This paper explores strategies, methodologies, and lessons learned in developing adaptive educational content using LLMs within Moodle, a widely used Learning Management System (LMS). Drawing on CARNET's large-scale educational transformation initiatives, the paper demonstrates how LLMs dynamically adapt learning materials to meet specific user needs, knowledge gaps, and learning styles. By leveraging AI-driven content that responds to student performance during assessments, LLMs generate tailored learning materials and personalized pathways. The process includes training and fine-tuning LLMs on domain-specific knowledge, developing content templates, and integrating them into the LMS. This enables differentiated learning experiences unique to each user's progress. Key challenges, including technical complexities, human factors, and cross-stakeholder collaboration, are also discussed. Practical insights are provided on content relevance, system integration, user adoption, and the role of intelligent tutoring systems (ITS) in supporting adaptive learning at scale. This paper offers a roadmap for institutions to incorporate LLMs and AI-driven customization into their learning ecosystems.

Keywords: Adaptive Learning · Custom Learning Content · Intelligent Tutoring

1 Foundations of AI-Driven Adaptive Learning

1.1 Context of Adaptive Learning

Adaptive learning can be described as a personalized educational approach where learning materials, assessments, and instructional paths are dynamically adjusted to meet the specific needs, abilities, and preferences of individual learners. Unlike traditional learning models, adaptive learning systems tailor content delivery in real-time based on user interactions, performance, and feedback. This methodology aims to maximize learning efficiency, engagement, and knowledge retention.

The concept of adaptive learning is not entirely new, as elements of personalization have existed in traditional face-to-face education through differentiated instruction. However, technological advancements, particularly in AI and LLMs, have significantly enhanced the feasibility, scalability, and precision of adaptive learning systems.

D. Vasić and E. Brajković (Eds.): MoStart 2025, CCIS 2609, pp. 67–81, 2026.
https://doi.org/10.1007/978-3-032-02801-3_5

Modern adaptive learning platforms can process vast amounts of user data to generate individualized content, predict student needs, and offer customized interventions [1].

Key drivers for the adoption of adaptive learning include the demand for personalized learning experiences, the availability of digital learning environments such as LMS, and the rapid evolution of AI capabilities. By utilizing AI and LLMs, educational institutions can overcome traditional barriers like limited instructor capacity and provide scalable, personalized support for large numbers of students [2].

Adaptive learning is grounded in cognitive science principles, particularly theories related to mastery learning, spaced repetition, and formative assessment. These principles emphasize the importance of revisiting key concepts, continuously assessing student knowledge, and adjusting learning paths to fill knowledge gaps. This pedagogical foundation ensures that learners acquire a deeper understanding of the subject matter and achieve mastery before progressing to more complex topics.

In educational settings, adaptive learning is implemented through various technologies, including LMS, ITS, and personalized e-learning platforms. Platforms such as Moodle enable the integration of adaptive learning by offering plugins and extensions that incorporate AI-driven decision-making and LLM-based content generation. These platforms track student progress, identify areas for improvement, and offer real-time feedback and personalized recommendations.

The context for adaptive learning continues to evolve as new technologies and AI models become more sophisticated. LLMs have expanded the capabilities of adaptive learning by automating content creation, generating personalized assessments, and delivering natural language feedback. This technological shift has broadened the scope and impact of adaptive learning, making it accessible to educational institutions worldwide [3].

The COVID-19 pandemic accelerated the adoption of digital learning tools and highlighted the importance of adaptive learning. As educators and institutions sought to maintain instructional continuity, many turned to adaptive learning platforms to address the diverse needs of remote learners. The ongoing shift toward hybrid and online learning further positioned adaptive learning as a critical component of modern education [4].

The context of adaptive learning is defined by its focus on personalized instruction, its reliance on AI and LLM-driven technologies, and its goal to enhance learning outcomes for diverse learner populations. As educational institutions strive to offer more flexible, inclusive, and personalized learning experiences, adaptive learning will remain a fundamental approach in shaping the future of education.

1.2 Role of AI and LLMs

AI and LLMs play a vital role in transforming adaptive learning by enabling personalized, responsive, and scalable educational experiences. AI powers decision-making, content adaptation, and real-time personalization, while LLMs facilitate natural language processing, dynamic content creation, and human-like interactions. Together, they provide a robust foundation for adaptive learning systems [5].

AI drives adaptive learning by using predictive analytics and machine learning to assess user performance, identify knowledge gaps, and customize learning paths. It enables continuous formative assessments, ensuring timely intervention and support for learners. AI-driven learning analytics optimize educational outcomes by refining content delivery in real-time, promoting mastery learning, and increasing student engagement.

LLMs enhance adaptive learning by generating tailored content, assessments, and feedback. Unlike pre-designed materials, LLMs create personalized learning materials, quizzes, and explanations on demand. By responding to learner needs, LLMs provide contextualized feedback, guiding students through complex concepts. Their multilingual capabilities enable inclusive access for diverse learner populations, further broadening the scope of adaptive learning [6].

The combined synergy of AI and LLMs allows for large-scale, automated personalization in ITS and LMS platforms. AI handles decision-making, while LLMs offer context-aware, interactive, and personalized feedback. This fusion supports responsive learning pathways, human-like tutoring, and greater scalability. Institutions can deploy adaptive learning solutions to large groups of students with minimal human intervention, as seen in Massive Open Online Courses (MOOCs) and similar large-scale learning environments [7].

The role of AI and LLMs will continue to grow, driving innovations in ITS, adaptive content delivery, and personalized education. As these technologies evolve, they promise more engaging, inclusive, and effective learning experiences for students worldwide.

1.3 ITS and LMS Overview

Intelligent Tutoring Systems (ITS) and Learning Management Systems (LMS) are the foundational technologies enabling adaptive learning. While LMS provide the framework for delivering, managing, and tracking learning activities, ITS focus on individualizing the learning experience through advanced AI capabilities [8].

Together, they create a comprehensive ecosystem for personalized education. This cross-section is the exact place where new possibilities for creating and testing models for further educational advancement can be found.

LMS are designed to support the administration of learning content at scale. Platforms like Moodle allow educators to organize courses, track student progress, and manage assessments. Their modular design enables integration with AI tools and plugins, facilitating data collection and analysis for adaptive learning. LMS serve as the backbone for content delivery, ensuring accessibility and seamless interaction across diverse user groups, including traditional educational institutions such as schools, colleges, universities, and institutes, as well as companies, non-profit organizations, government agencies, professional training services, certification authorities, and independent educators or freelance trainers.

LMS platforms are evolving from content delivery tools to hubs for innovation. Integrating AI enables personalized learning and predictive analytics, while emerging technologies like Augmented Reality (AR) and Virtual Reality (VR), gamification, and generative AI drive immersive and adaptive educational experiences.

ITS complement LMS by offering advanced personalization features. Using AI-driven analytics, ITS analyze learner behaviors and adapt instructional strategies to address individual needs. ITS systems simulate one-on-one tutoring by providing immediate feedback, tailored content, and adaptive challenges based on student performance. These systems use algorithms to predict learning outcomes and suggest targeted interventions, improving efficiency and retention [9].

The integration of ITS with LMS leverages the strengths of both. ITS enhance LMS functionality by providing adaptive pathways, intelligent feedback, and real-time content customization. This synergy transforms traditional LMS into adaptive learning platforms capable of catering to diverse learner profiles. For instance, an ITS can dynamically adjust Moodle course content based on real-time data, creating a highly personalized experience.

The combined use of ITS and LMS empowers institutions to scale personalized learning while maintaining quality and consistency. As educational technology evolves, this integration will remain central to creating flexible, accessible, and effective learning environments.

The integration of ITS and LMS marks a significant step in advancing adaptive education. ITS enhance LMS functionality with real-time feedback and personalized pathways, transforming traditional platforms into adaptive ecosystems. Emerging opportunities lie in refining predictive algorithms for deeper learner insights and expanding scalability through cloud-based ITS. This synergy also opens possibilities for integrating emerging technologies like conversational AI and immersive simulations, further enhancing engagement and accessibility in diverse educational contexts.

2 Design and Methodology

2.1 Content Design Approach and Integration with LMS

The first version of the educational content for the project was developed in-house by the project team to meet the specific needs of the initiative. The primary objective was to create a structured learning experience that dynamically adapts to participant performance. Moodle (version 4.5.2 LTS) was selected as the Learning Management System (LMS) due to its flexibility, scalability, and integration capabilities with AI-driven educational enhancements, which will enable future enhancements.

The initial phase of content development involved designing a default set of educational materials with predefined learning outcomes. These learning objectives were carefully structured to establish a baseline for participant progress. Knowledge reinforcement questions, quizzes, and assessments were incorporated to evaluate learning retention and comprehension. Based on the results from these assessments, additional tailored content was created and integrated into the default curriculum.

During the first iteration of content deployment, the materials were manually integrated into Moodle. This approach enabled easy initial deployment and close monitoring of participant engagement and learning effectiveness. The insights gained from this phase informed the development of a refined second version of the content, incorporating participant feedback and observed learning patterns.

The second version introduced enhancements in content structure and delivery, incorporating data-driven refinements based on performance analytics. Additionally, OpenAI's GPT-4o model was used for partial testing of the content adaptation process.

This allowed an initial assessment of AI-generated content recommendations and their alignment with predefined learning goals.

This structured content development approach ensures that the educational materials evolve in response to learner needs, improving knowledge retention and engagement. The planned, future integration of AI-enhanced learning pathways within Moodle provides a foundation for future iterations of the materials that will further optimize personalized educational experiences.

2.2 Training, Fine-Tuning and Custom Templates Development

The third and current version of the educational materials has been extensively tested using OpenAI's models, including GPT-4o, GPT-4o mini, GPT-o1, and GPT-o3-mini. The goal was to analyze how different models interpret and enhance adaptive learning content, ensuring the highest level of customization and effectiveness. The content was refined by leveraging AI-driven insights to better align with learner needs and improve knowledge retention.

Throughout the testing phase, AI-generated recommendations were evaluated for accuracy, coherence, and pedagogical relevance. Fine-tuning adjustments were made to optimize the delivery of personalized educational materials, improving the contextual relevance of generated explanations, feedback, and assessment items. This process facilitated the development of structured custom templates that streamline content adaptation based on individual learner performance.

Custom templates were developed to automate the generation of quizzes, learning reinforcements, and supplementary content tailored to participants' demonstrated knowledge levels. These templates are structured to integrate seamlessly into Moodle, enabling dynamic updates to learning pathways. The structured design allows content modules to evolve in real-time based on participant performance, fostering a responsive and adaptive learning experience.

The AI-assisted educational content creation process continues to evolve through iterative training and fine-tuning. The application of multiple AI models ensures content diversity and adaptability, allowing for continuous improvements in content personalization and instructional quality. This ongoing refinement process contributes to the scalability and effectiveness of adaptive learning methodologies within the LMS framework.

2.3 Content Validation and Testing

The fourth version of the educational materials introduces dynamically generated content, including both lessons and quizzes, tailored to each participant's individual learning trajectory. This approach allows for the automatic generation of supplementary materials based on performance in default learning pathways, creating an adaptive and personalized experience.

The implementation of dynamic content opens new possibilities for precise knowledge recognition, benefiting both educators and learners. By identifying specific areas where participants struggle, the system generates targeted instructional materials to reinforce understanding. This approach enhances the learning process by ensuring that each student receives the necessary resources to address their unique challenges.

The development of the fourth version involves testing in-house custom-trained large language models to further improve the personalization of generated content. The whole process of development and testing of the materials is conducted on various computers using Windows 11 and macOS Sequoia operating systems.

Current testing is being conducted using Ollama, Cortex, and LM Studio for handling various models. These include GGUF-formatted models: QwQ 32B Q3_K_L, Phi 4 Q6_K, DeepSeek R1 Distill Qwen 7B Q8_0 and Qwen2.5 7B Instruct 1M Q8_0, Granite 3.2 8B Instruct Q8_0, and DeepSeek R1 Distill LLaMA 8B Q8_0, as well as MLX-formatted models: Mistral Nemo Instruct 2407 4bit and LLaMA 3.2 Instruct 4bit (1B and 3B). These tests aim to determine the most suitable base model for further refinement.

Once testing is complete, a single model will be selected as the foundation for a customized training process based on insights gained from this project. The selected model will serve as the core for additional training using knowledge accumulated from other ongoing institutional projects. This iterative approach ensures that the learning materials continuously evolve to align with best practices and real-world educational needs.

To maintain quality and accuracy, the validation of dynamically generated content is conducted through supervised processes. The same AI model used for generation is also involved in evaluating the content, learning from feedback to improve its future outputs. This ensures that AI-generated materials remain pedagogically sound, contextually appropriate, and aligned with defined learning outcomes.

2.4 Pedagogical Alignment and Validation Framework

Ensuring the pedagogical validity of AI-generated content is essential to maintaining instructional quality within adaptive learning environments. The validation approach used in this project integrates structured prompt engineering, expert human review, and iterative improvement based on learner data.

The process begins with carefully designed prompts that include embedded pedagogical constraints. These prompts specify content format, difficulty level, and alignment with learning objectives. This reduces variability in model output and provides initial guidance for the generation process.

Once content is generated, it undergoes human-in-the-loop review. Subject-matter experts (currently) and instructional designers (forthcoming) evaluate the material for relevance, accuracy, cognitive alignment, and clarity. Rubrics are used to ensure consistency across reviewers and to align outputs with educational frameworks such as Bloom's Taxonomy and constructive alignment principles.

Learner performance data, such as quiz results and engagement metrics are used to identify problematic content. Items flagged due to low comprehension or poor performance are either revised or regenerated. Such approach creates a feedback loop that continuously improves the quality of adaptive materials, ensuring that dynamically generated content remains pedagogically grounded while allowing for rapid personalization and scalable deployment.

3 Implementation and Challenges

3.1 Customization Process and Adaptive Pathways

The customization process in adaptive learning is complex and time-intensive, especially when aiming for full individualization. It involves analyzing learner data, generating dynamic content, and continuously refining learning pathways to respond to each learner's profile, preferences, and prior knowledge.

Every learner follows a unique trajectory, which requires the system to interpret interactions and deliver personalized adjustments. This approach is more intricate than standardized models but offers greater relevance and effectiveness.

Adaptive pathways play a central role in enabling learner-centered education. Unlike fixed instructional sequences, they adjust content in real time based on performance, allowing learners to progress at their own pace while reinforcing weaker areas. This reduces cognitive overload and increases retention.

One of the key strengths of adaptive pathways is their ability to accommodate varying levels of prior knowledge. Learners are guided toward appropriate content rather than forced through uniform material, leading to higher motivation and engagement.

On an institutional level, adaptive pathways offer both scalability and flexibility. They support ongoing refinement based on aggregated learner data, which helps improve both content and delivery over time. Although implementation requires an initial investment in time and resources, the long-term benefits in efficiency and learning outcomes make it a sustainable strategy. As AI technologies continue to advance, this approach will likely become more accessible and streamlined.

3.2 Knowledge Pathways and Feedback

The transition from static, linear learning pathways to dynamic, adaptive knowledge pathways has proven essential in optimizing learning outcomes. By continuously analyzing usage data, learner feedback, and project execution insights, it has become evident that flexible knowledge pathways offer significant advantages. Unlike rigid, predefined curricula, dynamic pathways allow learners to engage with content that aligns with their evolving skill levels and knowledge gaps, ensuring a more personalized and effective learning experience.

Investing in adaptive knowledge pathways now provides long-term benefits by making the learning system more scalable, sustainable, and responsive to individual learner needs. While designing such pathways requires significant time and effort, the ability to automatically adjust content based on learner interactions results in higher engagement and retention.

The flexibility of dynamic pathways also ensures that institutions can update and refine their curricula without overhauling the entire educational structure, making content updates more efficient and manageable, which is something that is often overlooked and taken for granted.

Feedback from learners plays a critical role in shaping and refining adaptive learning environments. However, beyond simple user-reported feedback, the evaluation of key factors such as initial knowledge levels, individual aspirations, and user profiles, including background, experience, affinities, and learning styles is equally important. Gathering and analyzing this data allows institutions to create more effective and tailored learning pathways that accommodate different types of learners, from beginners to advanced users, acknowledging, and respecting their specializations.

A structured feedback loop is necessary to continuously improve educational content. AI-powered analytics can assess learner performance, detect engagement patterns, and suggest personalized interventions based on real-time data. Combining qualitative feedback with data-driven insights ensures that adaptive learning remains both user-centric and pedagogically effective, leading to long-term improvements in content delivery and knowledge retention.

3.3 System Integration, User Adoption and Collaboration

The successful implementation of adaptive learning solutions requires the collaboration of a diverse group of experts, including project experts, AI specialists, instructional designers, educators, and software engineers.

Given the complexity and uniqueness of the project, interdisciplinary cooperation is crucial in ensuring smooth integration and effective content delivery. The ability to merge technical expertise with pedagogical strategies allows for the development of dynamic, engaging, and personalized learning environments.

Currently, dynamic content generation is being conducted in an experimental environment that utilizes a broad range of tools, backed by custom Python-based solutions. These tools enable the real-time adaptation of educational materials, enhancing responsiveness to learner progress.

However, at this stage, integration into Moodle still requires a combination of automated processes and manual adjustments. While this approach is effective in delivering personalized learning experiences, it remains resource-intensive and requires continuous refinement.

The long-term vision for system integration involves developing a dedicated Moodle plugin that will allow educators to configure content settings and seamlessly access institution-specific LLMs via API. This would eliminate the need for extensive infrastructure and development expertise, making adaptive learning more accessible to educators without technical backgrounds. The plugin would also facilitate automated content generation, reducing manual intervention while maintaining high levels of personalization.

Despite ongoing advancements in automation, some level of manual post-educational content refinement will remain essential. This process allows educators to incorporate project-specific insights and tailor materials based on real-world feedback. The combination of AI-driven automation and human expertise ensures that learning experiences remain relevant, high-quality, and continuously evolving. By balancing between automation and manual refinement, institutions can maximize the benefits of adaptive learning while maintaining educational consistency and contextual relevance.

3.4 Replication Roadmap and Institutional Adaptation

The implementation approach used in this project is adaptable for institutions aiming to introduce AI-driven adaptive learning. It follows a modular, iterative framework suitable for varying levels of technical capacity and institutional readiness.

The process begins by defining the scope and identifying learning outcomes. Once a target curriculum area is selected, content templates are created, including instructional segments, assessments, and feedback components, all structured for reuse and adaptation.

Moodle serves as the LMS backbone due to its plugin support and API accessibility. AI models are selected based on domain requirements, and supporting tools are chosen to enable local model deployment during the prototyping phase.

Structured prompts and custom templates guide content generation, which is refined through testing, expert validation, and learner feedback. As the system evolves, automation is gradually introduced to support real-time adaptation.

Institutions with sufficient development capacity may create a dedicated Moodle plugin to manage content generation and API access to local or external LLMs. This allows non-technical educators to use adaptive features through a user-friendly interface.

The following summarizes the core implementation steps taken during the project, presented as a generalizable sequence that can guide similar initiatives in other institutional contexts:

- **Define goals:** Define learning goals and select pilot content area.
- **Design templates:** Design modular content templates.
- **Deploy LMS:** Deploy Moodle and configure it for integration (plugin or API).
- **Select models:** Select and test LLMs using structured prompts.
- **Validate content:** Validate content with reviews and learner performance data.
- **Adapt delivery:** Introduce adaptive pathways using AI-generated content.
- **Automate workflows:** Gradually automate generation and delivery processes.
- **Integrate interfaces:** Build an educator-facing plugin for full integration.

4 Insights and Best Practices

4.1 Practical Insights and Initiative

For CARNET, the development and implementation of adaptive learning through LLM-driven customization have yielded significant insights into both the potential and challenges of such an approach. A key takeaway from this project is the complexity of developing fully individualized learning pathways. Unlike traditional instructional methods, adaptive learning requires an ongoing process of content development, refinement, and AI integration, which demands extensive collaboration across multiple disciplines.

One of the primary challenges in executing such a project is balancing automation with human oversight. While AI provides scalability and personalization, continuous supervision is required to validate generated content, assess learning outcomes, and fine-tune adaptive pathways. The iterative nature of content refinement basically means that a fully operational system is never static. Instead of being static, it must be regularly updated based on learner data, AI advancements, and evolving educational standards.

The necessity of real-time updates and improvements introduces logistical obstacles in maintaining the accuracy and relevance of the educational materials.

Additionally, ensuring that AI-generated content aligns with educational standards requires constant validation. While AI models can generate well-structured content, human oversight is needed to verify its pedagogical effectiveness. The complexity increases when considering diverse learner backgrounds, different educational systems, and varying instructional needs. Ensuring inclusivity and accessibility within adaptive learning requires robust mechanisms for adjusting the material to accommodate different learning paces and preferences.

The initiative also highlighted the importance of cross-functional teamwork. Bringing together experts in project management, AI, instructional design, educational psychology, and software development is essential for ensuring that content remains pedagogically sound while being technologically possible and efficient. Additionally, institutional training for educators is critical for the long-term sustainability of AI-assisted adaptive learning frameworks. Providing educators with sufficient knowledge and skills to utilize AI-enhanced learning tools effectively ensures that adaptive learning systems reach their full potential.

4.2 LLM Content Creation

Designing educational content for adaptive learning requires a shift in perspective, as content must be structured with future AI integration in mind. Rather than static, predefined materials, the focus must be on modular, flexible content that can be dynamically adapted to individual learners. This necessitates designing lessons, quizzes, and supplementary materials that can be easily segmented, restructured and expanded based on student progress.

LLM training for educational purposes follows a structured approach, beginning with base model selection and data fine-tuning. The process involves curating domain-specific data, training the model on real-world learning scenarios, and continuously refining it based on user interactions. Custom tweaking ensures that LLM-generated content aligns with internal instructional goals and adheres to pedagogical best practices. Lessons learned from project execution indicate that maintaining an iterative feedback loop between content developers and AI engineers becomes a requirement and that it significantly improves LLM-generated outputs.

Additionally, real-time adaptation capabilities must be embedded into the LLM workflow. By integrating AI-generated insights into the content design process, learning materials can evolve dynamically, ensuring that instructional strategies remain aligned with learner needs. This approach allows organizations to future-proof their educational content by ensuring that materials remain relevant and adaptable as AI capabilities continue to advance, opening new opportunities.

One of the main challenges in this approach is ensuring that AI-generated content maintains pedagogical integrity. AI models rely on pre-existing datasets, which may not always, or at least in enough quantity align with institutional goals or specific educational frameworks. Therefore, an essential aspect of LLM-driven content creation is continuously refining datasets, retraining models, and incorporating human feedback to improve content quality. This practically requires a hybrid approach, where AI-generated materials serve as a foundation but are further curated and refined by human experts.

Another critical consideration is how AI-generated content integrates into existing instructional workflows. While AI can generate learning materials, educators must still oversee their application to ensure alignment with curriculum goals. By embedding AI tools into content management systems and LMS platforms, institutions can streamline the integration process and reduce the manual workload required for adapting content.

4.3 Results, Impact and Best Practices

The implementation of AI-driven adaptive learning has demonstrated measurable improvements in learner engagement, knowledge retention, and overall educational efficiency. Personalized learning pathways have allowed participants to progress at their own pace, leading to higher satisfaction rates and improved outcomes compared to traditional linear learning models. The ability to dynamically adjust content in response to learner performance has reduced cognitive overload, ensuring a more effective knowledge acquisition process.

Beyond individual learning benefits, the adoption of adaptive learning has had a significant impact on organizational culture. The shift towards AI-assisted education has encouraged a more data-driven, innovation-focused mindset, fostering collaboration between technical and educational experts. Additionally, the integration of LLM-driven learning has streamlined content development processes, reducing redundancy and improving efficiency in educational material production.

From a best practices perspective, launching an adaptive learning initiative requires a well-defined knowledge base and a multidisciplinary team. Essential roles include project experts, AI specialists, instructional designers, content developers, data analysts, and developers. Organizations must also prioritize training educators on AI-assisted learning tools to ensure seamless adoption and long-term sustainability.

Furthermore, a structured implementation strategy is key to maximizing the benefits of adaptive learning. This involves setting clear learning objectives, defining assessment criteria, and developing mechanisms for continuous improvement. AI-driven education should not replace traditional teaching methods but rather enhance them by providing additional insights and tools for personalized learning.

Institutions looking to implement adaptive learning should also consider the technological infrastructure required to support AI-driven education. Cloud-based AI models, API integrations, and scalable LMS solutions provide the necessary foundation for expanding adaptive learning capabilities. By investing in these technologies, organizations can ensure long-term success and adaptability.

Failing to embrace innovations in education can result in significant missed opportunities. Traditional learning models often struggle with engagement and knowledge retention, while adaptive learning offers a scalable, personalized alternative that caters to diverse learning needs. Institutions that do not invest in AI-driven educational strategies risk falling behind in terms of efficiency, learner outcomes, and overall competitiveness in the evolving landscape of digital education.

By establishing best practices that focus on interdisciplinary collaboration, continuous refinement, and strategic implementation, organizations can leverage AI and LLM technologies to create impactful, future-proof educational models. Adaptive learning is not merely an enhancement to existing systems but a fundamental shift towards a more responsive, personalized, and effective educational experience with many additional organizational benefits, ranging from culture shifts, discovery and mitigation of risks to identification of new project potentials.

4.4 Generalizable Lessons for Institutions

The design and implementation of LLM-driven adaptive learning content revealed several lessons that can support similar efforts in other institutions. These insights go beyond the context of this project and highlight key factors for sustainable and scalable adoption.

Modular content design is essential. Reusable templates aligned with clear learning goals allow for flexible adaptation and efficient iteration. Starting with semi-automated workflows helps build confidence and operational stability before scaling.

Human oversight remains necessary. While AI enables rapid content generation, expert review ensures alignment with pedagogy and context. Strong results come from collaboration between educators, instructional designers, AI specialists, and LMS administrators.

Effective implementation also requires organizational readiness. Institutions should evaluate their infrastructure, educator support systems, training needs, and data privacy policies. Technical performance alone is not enough to ensure adoption.

Treating adaptive learning as an evolving, collaborative process rather than a one-time deployment helps maintain quality, relevance, and learner impact over time.

5 Conclusion and Future Directions

5.1 Key Findings and Implications

This paper has explored the implementation of AI-driven customization in adaptive learning, leveraging LLMs to personalize educational content dynamically. Several key findings and their implications have emerged from this study.

Enhanced Personalization: Adaptive learning pathways enabled by AI and LLMs provide a highly individualized learning experience, addressing specific knowledge gaps and optimizing educational outcomes.

Scalability and Efficiency: AI-driven learning models reduce the workload on educators by automating content generation, assessment customization, and feedback processes, allowing institutions to scale personalized learning without a proportional increase in manual effort.

Continuous Improvement: The iterative approach to content development ensures that learning materials evolve based on learner performance, AI-driven analytics, and educator insights, leading to a continuously improving educational system.

Interdisciplinary Collaboration: Effective implementation of adaptive learning systems requires collaboration between project and AI experts, instructional designers, software developers, and educators to ensure both pedagogical integrity and technological feasibility.

Challenges of AI Implementation: Despite its benefits, AI-driven education poses challenges related to data privacy, content validation, and technical integration, necessitating ongoing research and oversight to optimize its implementation.

These findings have significant implications for educational institutions, regulators, and technology developers. Institutions that adopt AI-driven adaptive learning models will benefit from improved learner engagement, greater retention rates, and enhanced learning efficiency. However, to maximize these benefits, stakeholders must invest in robust AI governance frameworks, educator training, and infrastructure development.

5.2 Trends, Ethics and Privacy

The landscape of AI-driven adaptive learning is rapidly evolving, with several trends shaping the future of educational technology.

Advancements in ITS: Intelligent Tutoring Systems are expected to become more sophisticated, incorporating real-time conversational AI, multimodal learning (text, video, AR/VR), and deeper personalization through advanced predictive analytics. [10].

Integration of Generative AI: The use of generative AI models in education will continue to expand, providing real-time content generation, personalized assessments, and AI-driven tutoring systems capable of adapting to different learning styles. [11].

Ethical AI in Education: Ensuring fairness and inclusivity in AI-generated content is a growing concern. Bias mitigation strategies, transparent AI model training, and human oversight are essential to prevent discriminatory or misleading educational materials. [12].

Data Privacy and Security: With AI processing vast amounts of learner data, institutions must implement strict privacy regulations, ensuring compliance with global standards such as GDPR and FERPA. The responsible handling of student data is critical to maintaining trust and regulatory compliance. [13].

Autonomy and Human-AI Collaboration: AI is not designed to replace educators but to enhance their capabilities. The future of AI-driven education lies in hybrid models where AI supports instructors by providing insights, automating repetitive tasks, and improving engagement strategies. [14].

Educational institutions implementing AI-driven learning must establish clear ethical guidelines and data protection policies, ensuring that technology serves as a tool for equitable and effective learning rather than a barrier or risk to privacy.

5.3 Final Reflections

The use of AI and LLMs in adaptive learning represents a significant shift in how education is designed and delivered. Moving from static, linear curricula to dynamic, personalized pathways can improve learner engagement, knowledge retention, and instructional efficiency. However, successful implementation depends on balancing automation with human oversight to maintain pedagogical quality.

Future research should focus on improving the quality of AI-generated content, minimizing bias in educational models, and enhancing the integration of adaptive systems with existing LMS platforms.

AI-driven customization is more than an incremental upgrade; it signals a broader change in educational methodology. Institutions that adopt these technologies will be better equipped to offer accessible, high-quality learning that responds to the diverse needs of modern learners.

This paper has outlined strategies, challenges, and best practices for implementing LLM-based adaptive learning. The insights presented provide a foundation for further research and institutional development. Continued innovation, collaboration, and responsible use of AI can support the long-term transformation of education.

Disclosure of Interests. The authors have no competing interests to declare that are relevant to the content of this article.

References

1. Restack: Large language models for adaptive learning. https://www.restack.io/p/adaptive-learning-systems-ai-answer-large-language-models-cat-ai. Accessed 17 Dec 2024
2. Maity, S., Deroy, A.: Generative AI and its impact on personalized intelligent tutoring systems. https://arxiv.org/abs/2410.10650. Accessed 17 Dec 2024
3. Wilichowski, T., Cobo, C.: How the pandemic could change how we teach our children. https://www.weforum.org/stories/2021/01/adaptive-learning-system-policymakers-education-technology-digital. Accessed 17 Dec 2024
4. Gligorea, I., Cioca, M., Oancea, R., Gorski, A.-T., Gorski, H., Tudorache, P.: Adaptive learning using artificial intelligence in e-learning: a literature review. Educ. Sci. **13**(12), 1216 (2023). https://doi.org/10.3390/educsci13121216. Accessed 17 Dec 2024
5. Molinari, A., Sandri, S.: Evolution of LMS design and implementation in the age of AI and large language models. In: Davide Taibi, D., Schicchi, D., Temperini, M., Limongelli, C., Casalino, G. (eds.) AIxEDU - 2nd International Workshop on Artificial Intelligence Systems in Education 2024, AIxIA, vol. 3879, CEUR-WS, Bolzano (2024), https://ceur-ws.org/Vol-3879/AIxEDU2024_paper_35.pdf. Accessed 21 Dec 2024
6. Jaldi, C.D., Ilkou, E., Schroeder N., Shimizu, C.: Education in the era of neurosymbolic AI, web semantics: science, services and agents on the world wide web. J. Web Semant. 100857 (2024). https://doi.org/10.1016/j.websem.2024.100857. Accessed 2 Jan 2024
7. Zapata-Rivera, D., Torre, I., Lee, C.-S., Sarasa-Cabezuelo, A., Ghergulescu, I., Libbrecht, P.: Editorial: generative AI in education. Front. Artific. Intell. **7**, 1532896 (2024). https://doi.org/10.3389/frai.2024.1532896. Accessed 2 Jan 2025
8. Fetaji, B.: Investigating the role of artificial intelligence in education: trends and applications. In: 8th International Congress Towards Sustainable Development – TSD 2024 Book of Abstracts, pp. 41–42. Mother Teresa University, Skopje (2024). https://conference.unt.edu.mk/wp-content/uploads/2024/12/Book-Of-Abstracts-TSD-2024-20-December-2024.pdf. Accessed 10 Jan 2024
9. Aleksandrovna, S. A.: Influence of artificial intelligence on student autonomy in ESP course on the case of Fergana State University. In: 6th Traditional International Scientific and Practical Conference Professional Development of the Personality of the XXI Century in the System of Continuous Education: Problems and Ways of Their Solution (2024). http://ilmiyanjumanlar.uz/uploads/conferences/0065/65_i_20241211_133459_3.12.pdf. Accessed 11 Jan 2024
10. Park University: AI in education: the rise of intelligent tutoring systems. https://www.park.edu/blog/ai-in-education-the-rise-of-intelligent-tutoring-systems/. Accessed 20 Feb 2024

11. AI for Education: guide to integrating generative AI for deeper literacy learning. https://www.aiforeducation.io/ai-resources/guide-to-integrating-generative-ai-for-deeper-literacy-learning. Accessed 22 Feb 2024
12. Barnes, E., Hutson, J.: Navigating the ethical terrain of AI in higher education: Strategies for mitigating bias and promoting fairness. Forum Educ. Stud. **2**(2), 1229 (2024). https://doi.org/10.59400/fes.v2i2.1229. Accessed 22 Feb 2024
13. Sharma, R.: Data privacy in education through FERPA and GDPR adherence. https://www.hurix.com/blogs/data-privacy-in-education-through-ferpa-and-gdpr-adherence/. Accessed 23 Feb 2024
14. Ó Murchú, D.: The integration of artificial intelligence in education and EdTech: ethical challenges, teacher-student AI competences, and the psychological dynamics of human-AI collaboration in the workplace. https://ai4edu.eu/2025/01/23/the-integration-of-artificial-intelligence-in-education-and-edtech-ethical-challenges-teacher-student-ai-competences-and-the-psychological-dynamics-of-human-ai-collaboration-in-the-workplace/. Accessed 1 March 2024

Robot Applications in Theoretical and Practical University Education

Viktorio Malisa[1] and Boris Crnokić[2(✉)]

[1] Förderung der Automation und Robotik (F-AR), Schweizertalstr. 5/1/1, 1130 Wien, Austria
viktorio.malisa@f-ar.at

[2] Faculty of Mechanical Engineering, Computing and Electrical Engineering, University of Mostar, Matice hrvatske b.b., 8800 Mostar, Bosnia and Herzegovina
boris.crnokic@fsre.sum.ba

Abstract. This paper compares two approaches to robotics education that are characterized by a strong practical orientation and a focus on theoretical knowledge transfer. The aim of the study is to analyze the effects of these different teaching methods on students' skills and to shed light on the associated challenges. In addition, the rapid development of robotics and increasing digitalization will be analysed as factors that place new demands on academic education. The study examines the integration of robotics into the curricula of institutions of higher education, contrasting and comparing the pedagogical methods of the University of Applied Sciences, where industry-specific, hands-on training is provided, and the University of Mostar, where robotics is included in more general computer science and engineering curricula. The paper establishes the strengths and weaknesses of both approaches, namely in curriculum development, lab facilities, industry partnerships, and projects. Technological progress is taking place at a rapid pace, meaning that curricula need to be continuously adapted, innovative teaching methods developed and teaching materials regularly updated. In the field of robotics, this poses significant challenges for both universities of applied sciences with their practice-oriented education and universities with their strong scientific focus, as both teaching staff and the entire university organization are under increasing pressure. The study also addresses the ethical dimensions of robotics and AI, advocating ethical standards in robotics studies to foster socially responsible innovation. The paper also recommends a mixed methodology that combines industry engagement with AI-based research, exposing students to practical experience and forward-thinking innovation.

Keywords: Robotics Education · Experiential Learning · Industry Collaboration · Interdisciplinary Learning

1 Introduction

1.1 Background and Context

Robots are used in all industries, from agriculture to manufacturing, the service sector, medicine and space exploration. Their presence can be observed in all environments around the world and includes activities such as diving, swimming, driving, walking,

D. Vasić and E. Brajković (Eds.): MoStart 2025, CCIS 2609, pp. 82–105, 2026.
https://doi.org/10.1007/978-3-032-02801-3_6

flying and even exploring other planets (e.g., NASA's Perseverance rover on Mars). Latest advances in artificial intelligence (AI) and machine learning have further enhanced their capabilities, enabling adaptive decision-making in real-time scenarios. Consequently, the increasing presence of robots in all educational institutions has become a ubiquitous phenomenon, from early childhood education in the form of toys to robot cells in higher education laboratories. The spectrum of robot types ranges from industrial robots and service robots to, more recently, humanoid robots. New categories, such as soft robots and biohybrid systems, further blur the line between biological and mechanical systems.

The technical courses focus on the automation of processes, design and calculation of the kinematics and dynamics of robots and new types of constructions, but also on Human-Robot Interaction (HRI), and sustainable robotics design. Cutting-edge topics like digital twins, swarm robotics, and ethical AI integration are increasingly incorporated into curricula. Social scientists deal with the social effects of the use of robots, in particular the changes in the workplace and the consequences for employees and society, including algorithmic bias in automation, the future of work in the gig economy, and regulatory frameworks for AI accountability.

Ensuring safety in robotics laboratories, in student exercises and projects and in research is of essential importance due to the rise of AI-driven systems and human-robot collaboration. New standards, ISO 10218-2:2025 for industrial robot applications and robot cells included collaborative applications, and risk assessment processes (e.g., failure mode effects analysis) are now integral components of safety training. Communicating the tasks and implementation of safety measures in teaching and research is a challenge and requires careful preparation. There should be interdisciplinary collaboration between policymakers, ethicists, and engineers to convey safety measures, as well as cybersecurity modules for addressing vulnerabilities in connected robotic systems. The old technical specification ISO TS 15066 has been integrated into the new robot standard ISO 10218-2:2025. It is important to emphasize that the term "collaborative robot" is not used in new norms ISO 10218-1:2025 and ISO 10218-2:2025. Only the application can be developed, verified, and validated as a collaborative application. In addition, the term "collaborative operation" is not used in this document [1]. Robotic applications have integrated manual and automatic operation as standard [2].

Mechatronics, automation technology and smart engineering are interdisciplinary sciences that combine the disciplines of mechanics, electrical engineering and computer science, now intersecting with data science, cybersecurity, and sustainable engineering. Examples of these disciplines include an airplane, a car, a production line or a robot, smart manufacturing systems (Industry 4.0), autonomous vehicles, and wearable exoskeletons for healthcare. This article deals with the integration of robotics into the curricula of universities of applied sciences and universities, emphasizing the need for agile educational models that adapt to rapid technological changes and ethical challenges.

1.2 Objectives

The major purpose of the current paper is to compare and contrast two very different approaches to robotics learning, with focus placed on how theoretical knowledge is embedded and utilized in higher learning curricula. Specifically, the research will:

- Compare and contrast the industry-specific, practice-based strategy of the University of Applied Sciences with the inter-disciplinary, research-based strategy pursued by the University of Mostar. This includes curriculum development, laboratory facilities, and industry partnerships.
- Assess the effectiveness of hands-on learning and project-based learning in the field of robotics studies, particularly in the case of collaborative robots, AI systems, and industrial automation. The study will highlight the relevance of internships, team projects, and independent research in preparing students to join the labor market.
- Analyze how ethical issues, such as AI bias, robot-human interaction, and job replacement, are addressed in robotics research. The study will also explore how ethical frameworks and values related to sustainability are embedded in robotics curricula.
- Discuss the role played by industry partnerships in learning robotics, with particular focus on how projects based on real-world applications, internships, and trips to trade fairs help instill practical knowledge and career readiness in students. The study will also explore industry-academia collaboration challenges and benefits.
- According to the comparative analysis, the study will prescribe a mixed methodology combining the best practices from the methods used by both institutions. The methodology will provide students with practical experience as well as forward-thinking innovation, preparing them to address the challenges of an accelerating technological world.

Through these objectives, the paper is to contribute to more inclusive and adaptable robotics learning paradigms that more adequately prepare students to address the demands of a changing, technology-driven economy. The research is also to provide insight into balancing theory and practical application within learning institutions and how to address the ethical and social implications of robotics and automation.

2 Theoretical Foundations and Literature Review

The integration of robotics into higher education curricula necessitates a thorough review of pedagogical frameworks, technological advancements, and ethical considerations. This section synthesizes recent literature to contextualize the theoretical and practical approaches analyzed in this study, emphasizing CDIO (Conceive-Design-Implement-Operate) frameworks, experiential learning, ethical AI integration, and industry-academia collaboration.

The CDIO framework is widely accepted as an effective engineering education model, particularly in robotics. Crawley et al. note that CDIO provides a systematic means to learn by projects, which is most appropriate to the inter-disciplinary field of robotics. The framework enables students to experience the entire cycle of a project, from design to operation, bridging the gap between theory and practice. This is particularly relevant in learning robotics, where exposure to practice is critical in learning by doing [3]. Kolb's theory of experiential learning and Dewey's "learning by doing" concept also justify the incorporation of practical training into robotics studies. The learning cycle of Kolb—concrete experience, reflective observation, abstract conceptualization, and active experimentation—is the theoretical basis on which robotics lab and problem-based learning environments are built. The active involvement in real-world activities by

Dewey establishes the importance of practical exposure to robotics studies, particularly to foster problem-solving and innovation skills [4, 5]. As robotics is increasingly based on artificial intelligence (AI), ethical dimensions have become a part of robotics research. Bostrom presents the ethical dimensions of AI and automation, namely job replacement, algorithmic bias, and safety. These are echoed in the IEEE standards on autonomous and intelligent systems, where transparency, accountability, and ethical decision-making in robotic systems are presented as key requirements [6, 7]. The incorporation of ethical frameworks into robotics curricula is required to train engineers to address the social aspects of their work. Brundage and the IEEE Autonomous and Intelligent Systems initiative recognize the requirement to embed ethical thinking into robotic system design and deployment, particularly in applications involving healthcare and manufacturing, where there is extensive interaction between humans and machines [7, 8].

The use of robotics in teaching and learning has been researched actively [9], and the use of collaborative applications and AI systems have been specifically of interest [10]. Alam and Mohanty present the Integrated Constructive Robotics in Education (ICRE) model, which is centred on the transformative learning aspect of robotics in teaching and learning in the field of STEM [11]. In the same context, some research practically shows through application what this means. Crnokić et al. research highlights the use of project-based learning through LEGO Mindstorms and 3D printing to develop critical thinking and innovation in learners [12]. Industry collaboration is another important aspect in robotics education. Yuan et al. outline the benefit of including industry projects in robotics curricula, particularly in preparing students to join the job market. Their study names the internships and capstone projects as contributing to exposing students to real-world experience in automation, robotics programming, and system integration [13]. Robotics is inherently an inter-disciplinary field, involving mechanical engineering, electrical engineering, computer science, and data science. Han et al. explore the construction of a robotics teaching system grounded on the CDIO framework, with emphasis on the need for inter-disciplinary collaboration in teaching robotics. Their work highlights the importance of integrating theoretical knowledge and practical skills, particularly in robot kinematics, dynamics, and control [14]. Eguchi also examines the ways robotics may be employed to increase inclusivity and access to learning in the area of STEM. She addresses, in her work, the importance of creating inclusive and variable robotics curricula to suit diverse learning needs, particularly through the use of modular robotics sets [15, 16]. Despite the advancements in robotics teaching, there are challenges. Garcia and Rossiter cite the speeding-up pace of technological advancements as one significant challenge, namely keeping curricula abreast with developments in AI and machine learning. They underscore the need for agile teaching models that can adapt to emerging technologies and industry trends [17].

3 University of Applied Sciences

Universities of applied sciences were not established in Austria until the mid 1990s. In contrast to universities, universities of applied sciences focus on the practical training of students. Degrees at universities of applied sciences in Austria are aligned with university degrees, allowing students to transfer between the two educational institutions. Doctoral studies are generally offered at universities.

This study is dedicated to the analysis of the curriculum and study organization of the mechatronics/robotics course after the changeover from the diploma course to the new Bachelor's/Master's courses as part of the Bologna reform in 2005. The description focuses on the core area of robotics and does not take into account the fundamentals of mechanics, electronics and electrical engineering, information technology, economics and soft skills required for the course.

3.1 Bachelor's Degree Program in Mechatronics/Robotics

As part of the Bachelor's degree course in Mechatronics/Robotics with a focus on robotics, an annual admission of 60 students is planned in order to meet the high demands of the course. The continuous and targeted acquisition of suitable technical equipment for the laboratories is therefore essential. Due to rapid technological developments, equipment, machines and software become obsolete very quickly, which is why close cooperation with industry is crucial for the acquisition of laboratory equipment. As part of the implementation of the degree course, robots for teaching were successively acquired in cooperation with companies from German-speaking countries. The number of robots increased continuously, starting with two robots in the first semester, until a total of 25 different robots, a large number of end effectors, necessary sensors and safety elements were available in the fifth semester. The use of standard aluminum profiles facilitates the assembly of underframes and necessary fastenings when expanding robot applications.

As part of the robotics training, a special laboratory has been set up in which various aspects of this technology are examined. These include the control system, the frame, the manipulator, the end effector, the manual control panel and the safety laser sensor. An emergency stop on the wall serves as an additional safety measure. The laboratory regulations contain specific guidelines, such as a ban on bringing food and drink into the laboratory and the requirement that work on the robot must always be carried out by at least one person.

Table 1. Extract from the Bachelor of Mechatronics/Robotics curricula

Title of the Course	ECTS	Semester
Fundamentals of Robotics	3	1
Industrial Robotics I	3	2
Robots: programming and simulation	3	3
Robotics Lab I	3	3
Robotics Lab II	3	4
End effectors	3	4
Robot design	3	4
Internship with project report	27	5
Bachelor thesis	18	6

Robotics 1st and 2nd Semester. Setting up a robotics laboratory that enables safe teaching poses a significant challenge. Initially, a maximum group size of twelve students per instructor was set. Two robots from different manufacturers were installed in the lab, which are programmed using manufacturer-specific programming languages. A PC workstation with simulation software for each robot was set up for each student. One robot has a payload of 3 kg and a reach of 650 mm, while the second robot has a payload of 5 kg and a reach of 800 mm (Fig. 1).

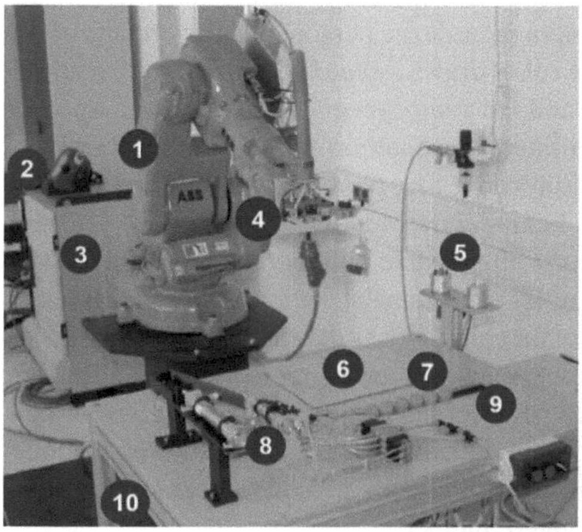

Legend:
1. Robot
2. Hand-held programming device
3. Robot controller
4. Multifunctional gripper
5. Interchangeable pen holder
6. Paper sheet for drawing exercises
7. Work object plastic rollers
8. Chute with pneumatic cylinders
9. Conveyor belt for plastic rolls
10. Frame made of aluminium profiles

Fig. 1. Robotic Training Cell

As part of the "Fundamentals of Robotics" course (see Table 1), the Machinery Directive as well as specific robot standards and behavior in the robot laboratory are taught in the lecture in the lecture hall and in the practical exercises in the robot laboratory. The first steps with the robot are aimed at moving manually in the robot's coordinate systems and measuring and precisely positioning the TCP (Tool Center Point), saving the start and end of the path and tracing the path on a sheet of paper. Before starting the robot exercises, all students receive a set of laboratory rules, which are discussed and signed by the students. It is essential that no more than three students are in front of the robot at any one time, with the student holding the hand-held programming device and practicing on the robot standing in front of the robot. Another student stands to the left and the second student to the right. This means that six students can be positioned, three in front of each robot, while the other students carry out the tasks at the PC workstation in simulations.

The student practicing on the robot must never stand in the robot's working area and must always be able to take a step back to avoid the robot in case of danger. The robot's axes of rotation can entangle hanging items of clothing and pull people towards them and injure them, which is why clothing must be worn close to the body and long hair tied up in the robot laboratory or when working on projects. As part of the course, lecture notes and examination tasks on robot exercises and safety in handling robots are stored in case of an inspection by the labor inspectorate.

Team Projects in the 3rd and 4th Semester. As part of Robotics Lab I and II, three students work in a team on a project on a robot cell, which they then present and document in a project report. Students who have successfully completed the safety examinations and robotics lab exercises in the 1st and 2nd semesters can take part in the team projects. The team can choose from a list of approx. 40 different projects. A place and a suitable robot will be allocated for the chosen project. Concept, construction, assembly, control, etc. are divided among the students. In the next semester, a new team must be formed and the role of team leader must be taken on by another student.

One example of a team project is the development of a system consisting of a robot, a camera, a pen and a sheet of paper. The camera records the person, the movements of the robot are generated from the image and the robot draws a sketch of the person on an A3 sheet of paper. The robot signs the picture and the visitor receives the drawing. Another project is a punch robot, which will be exhibited at a small art fair "Cocktailrobotik" in the run-up to Christmas. This is an industrial robot that pours visitors mulled wine or punch in three flavors of their choice from behind a moose.

Practical team projects provide students with valuable collaborative experience and develop their communication skills as they learn to present ideas clearly and interact effectively with others. They develop important teamwork skills such as assigning tasks, finding solutions together, compromising, working as a team member and team leader, and dealing constructively with differences of opinion. The exchange of different perspectives often leads to more creative and comprehensive solutions. In addition, students acquire organizational skills by planning projects efficiently together, meeting deadlines and using and managing resources in a targeted manner.

Internship 5th Semester. In the fifth semester of the Mechatronics/Robotics course, students complete a work placement in a company. Before the internship begins, the project is submitted to the office, checked and approved. An internship in the fifth semester has many advantages over an internship in the sixth semester. Since all other degree programs throughout Austria have the internship in the sixth semester, it is much easier for mechatronics/robotics students to find an internship in the fifth semester. It is also better for the companies, as they get an intern in both the fifth and sixth semester. In addition, students bring valuable practical experience with them, which they share with their colleagues and which flows into the lectures of the sixth semester. Students also get used to learning again and the majority decide to study for a Master's degree.

Individual Projects in Semester 6. Individual practical projects promote students' independence and personal responsibility. They learn to manage their time effectively, set priorities and plan and carry out projects independently. By working intensively on a specific topic, they can deepen their specialist knowledge and strengthen their analytical and critical skills by independently identifying problems and developing solutions. In addition, individual projects enable targeted self-reflection so that students can better recognize their strengths and weaknesses and develop both personally and professionally. Individual projects in the Bachelor's degree course include projects on simulation, optimizing a production line, ergonomic analysis of a workplace, creating or optimizing control programs for a robot cell, testing new sensors, etc.

3.2 Master's Degree Program in Mechatronics/Robotics

The Master's degree course focuses on service robotics and mobile robotics in industry. A special feature of the course is the subject "Research Institutes I and II" (see Table 2), in which researchers from various institutes report on ongoing research projects and discuss the results with the students.

Table 2. Extract from curricula Master Mechatronics/Robotics

Title of the Course	ECTS	Semester
Service robotics	3	1
Industrial robotics	3	1
Robotics laboratory	3	1
Mobile Robots	3	2
Research institutes I	1,5	2
Teleoperators	1,5	3
Micro and nano automation	1,5	3
Research Institutes II	1,5	3
Master thesis	27	4

The Master's thesis is carried out in a research institute or a company. The topic of the Master's thesis is approved by the degree program, supervised in the company by a member of staff with a university degree and assessed by a professor at the University of Applied Sciences.

Joint Bachelor-Master Projects. As part of the Master's degree course, larger projects are carried out in cooperation with Bachelor's students, with the Master's students taking on the role of team leader. An example of such a project would be a fully automated robot bar with three integrated industrial robots, a shuttle system and four ordering stations where cocktails of choice and beer can be ordered. The drinks are automatically delivered to the location where the order was placed, see Fig. 2.

The combination of Bachelor's and Master's students makes it possible to complete larger projects in one semester, such as the complete robot bar shown here. The project was set up and presented by the students at the Automatica robot trade fair in Munich. The project was published in all the media and was highly appreciated by the partner companies who made their machines available. For the degree program, it is an opportunity to showcase the students' achievements and raise awareness via the media. A Master's student leading a larger project with a Bachelor's team brings several benefits for the course and for all students involved. As a team leader, the Master's student further develops their leadership skills and gains valuable practical experience. This is an excellent opportunity to prepare for future professional challenges. The Bachelor's students also benefit from the experience and knowledge of the Master's student. The Master's student can mentor them and provide valuable insights and advice. This mentoring relationship promotes the exchange of knowledge and supports the academic development of Bachelor students.

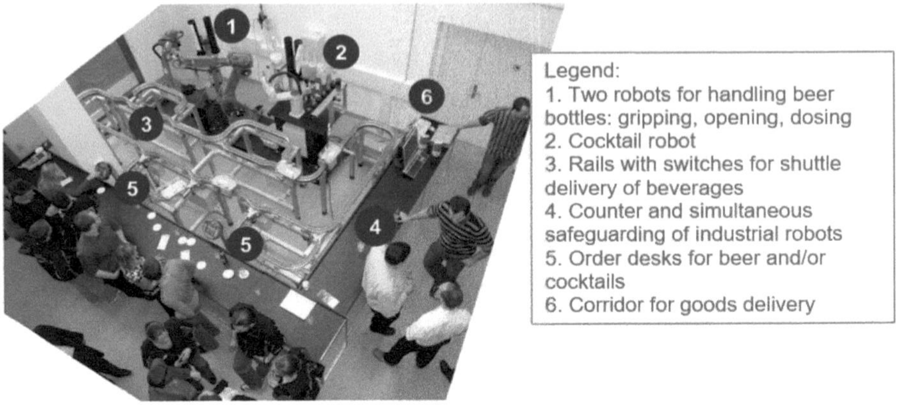

Fig. 2. Fully Automatic Robotic Bar [18]

3.3 Activities Outside the Curriculum

By learning together and participating in exercises, students network easily and intensively within the cohort, which will benefit them later in their careers. This horizontal networking is intensified through group exercises and team projects. Vertical networking during the course of study across the year groups means that students should come into contact with the other 4 year groups before and 4 year groups after. To support this networking, joint excursions to companies, the Robotics Day course event, visits to trade fairs and participation in conferences such as the Mechatronics Platform are organized.

Excursions to the Companies. As part of the degree course, there is one excursion per semester to companies in the surrounding area, with the exception of the work placement and the Master's thesis. The excursion is selected to match the topic of a course, e.g. sensor technology, automation technology, mechatronic systems. However, the excursion has a specific format: it is agreed with the company to give an overview of the industry in a 45-min lecture and then to present its own products or production. This is followed by a guided tour of the production hall in small groups. After the tour, everyone meets again for a discussion in the lecture hall. Excursions to industry are particularly valuable for students as they offer a practical insight into the world of work and combine theoretical knowledge with practical experience. They also promote networking with experts, increase motivation through practical application examples, help with career orientation and promote important social skills such as teamwork.

Trade Fair Visits. Outside of the curriculum, study-related trade fairs such as the Automatica robot trade fair in Munich and Smart Automation in Linz are organized on a voluntary basis. The trade fair visits also have a specific format. As the trade fairs usually take place every two years, students from several semesters travel to the excursions together. A route through the exhibition halls is planned in advance to match the courses of the respective semester. Appointments for demonstrations are arranged with certain exhibitors. The morning is reserved for the agreed demonstrations, the afternoon is free for the students.

Visiting trade fairs such as Automatica, where all the world's robot manufacturers are represented and present their innovations, offers students many advantages during their studies. On the one hand, they have the opportunity to make valuable contacts, exchange ideas with experts and explore potential career paths. In addition, many companies present internship and entry-level offers so that students can apply directly and receive valuable application tips. In addition, trade fairs offer access to current industry developments and innovations that expand students' specialist knowledge. Interaction with companies also strengthens soft skills such as communication skills and professional appearance. In addition, students can experience the application of theoretical knowledge in practice, which promotes understanding and motivation for their studies. Finally, trade fairs make it possible to directly compare different companies and their corporate cultures, which facilitates career orientation.

Robotics Day. On Robotics Day, the students present their outstanding projects, which they developed in teamwork during the third and fourth Bachelor semester. All students from the entire University of Applied Sciences and pupils from all over Austria are invited to visit the exhibition. Media representatives will also be invited and press releases will be distributed. Visitors will have the opportunity to take part in workshops and presentations and ask the teams about their projects. Students have the opportunity to present themselves and their projects to a wide audience and gain valuable experience. They can also exchange ideas with Master's students.

Conference of the Mechatronics Platform. The Mechatronics Platform Austria is an association of mechatronics-oriented university of applied sciences degree programs in Austria, which are particularly concerned with promoting mechatronics, using synergies in the areas of education, research and development and securing Austria as a production location through innovative mechatronic products. Students, graduates, teachers and the economy benefit equally from the intensive cooperation between the degree programs. The event program on the current focus topic is compiled from specialist lectures by lecturers and companies. The event will be accompanied by a suitable exhibition of selected companies. In addition, the three best Bachelor's and Master's theses in the field of mechatronics from Austrian UAS degree programs will be awarded prizes. In addition to the authors of the theses, the best graduate career will also be honored [19].

Participating in the Mechatronics Platform conference is a valuable opportunity for students to further their education, network with students and graduates from other universities of applied sciences and broaden their overall career prospects. Attending the conference can have a positive impact on students' motivation and inspiration, thus boosting their enthusiasm for their studies and future careers. In addition, students whose projects have been submitted for an award receive a certificate that they can add to their CV. This can draw the attention of potential employers to the students' commitment and skills.

4 University of Mostar

The University of Mostar does not offer a separate degree in robotics. Instead, it integrates robotics into a number of different engineering and computer science studies and provides students with a complete approach to learning and applying robotics in theoretical and practical contexts. To put it differently, robotics is part of a number of study programs in different faculties so that students can learn about different aspects of robotics in specialized courses. Table 3 provides an overview of these courses with the most important features of each course.

These courses are included in more broad fields such as mechanical engineering, electrical engineering, computer science, and information technology, because robotics is interdisciplinary in nature. It offers a multi-disciplinary platform for students with

Table 3. Robotics-oriented Courses at the University of Mostar

Study Program/Courses	Objectives	Learning Outcomes	Practical Component
Master's Program in Mechanical Engineering/Robotics	Identify basic robot configurations and applications in industry. Understand robot components, peripheral devices, and integration of AI in robotic systems. Develop skills in modelling, planning, and control robotic systems	Analyse and solve forward and inverse kinematics problems for robotic manipulators. Apply mathematical modelling and simulations in robotics design. Develop practical skills in collaborative robotics and industrial applications	Hands-on projects with collaborative applications using robots (UR5e). Mathematical modelling and simulation in virtual environments. Real-world applications developed in partnership with industry. Includes discussions on safety, job displacement, and AI integration
Master's Program in Electrical Engineering/Fundamentals of Robotics	Provide foundational knowledge in robotic architectures and control theories. Introduce students to AI integration in robotics	Identify different physical structures of robots and their control mechanisms. Understand kinematics and dynamics of robotic manipulators. Apply offline and online programming techniques	Hands-on exercises with robotic arms and mobile robots. Industrial automation simulations. Development of AI-driven robotic control algorithms. Safety measures in autonomous robotic systems

(*continued*)

Table 3. (*continued*)

Study Program/Courses	Objectives	Learning Outcomes	Practical Component
Bachelor's Program in Computer Science/Programming of Robotic Systems	Introduce robotic programming environments and applications. Develop problem-solving skills through robotic simulation	Program mobile and industrial robots using various programming environments. Apply control techniques in real-time robotic applications. Utilize robotic vision for object detection and manipulation	Focuses on programming and debugging robotic systems. Robotics-based projects integrating AI and vision systems. Addressing algorithmic bias in AI-driven robotic decision-making
Master's Program in Computer Science/Robotics in Education	Introduce robotics as a tool for STEM education. Enable students to design and implement robotics-based learning modules	Develop robotic curricula and teaching methodologies. Apply constructivist learning principles through robotics	Applying robotics concepts in educational settings by use of LEGO Mindstorms, Robotino, and other educational robotics kits Hands-on projects on designing robotics-based learning experiences. Promotes inclusivity in STEM education
PhD Program in Information and Communication Technologies/Advanced Applications of Robotic Systems in Education	Develop expertise in robotics research and innovative educational applications	Integrate robotics with AI for smart learning environments. Develop interactive human-robot collaboration models for education	Development of AI-powered tutoring robots. Advanced simulations in virtual reality environments. Focuses on innovative real-world applications. Investigates privacy and bias issues in AI-based tutoring systems

varying backgrounds in informatics and engineering to be exposed to robotics. However, lack of a dedicated robotics program could limit in-depth research and specialization.

4.1 Student Projects

University robotics courses in Mostar emphasize practical application and collaboration with industry, with a particular focus on collaborative applications, artificial intelligence-driven systems, and industrial automation techniques. Of the many student projects that are being implemented in such a paradigm, only a few will be presented here as illustrative examples. Spanning from collaborative robots in industrial automation to AI-driven vision systems and high-precision inspection robotics, these student projects reflect the transformative potential of robotics in industries today. They also reveal areas that need to be improved, such as better material selection, AI model training, and more stringent safety testing. Integration of robotics in various industrial and educational applications has increasingly been essential in modern technological environments. The projects in this section encompass a wide variety of robotic applications, ranging from STEM educational and automation in medicine to manufacturing in industry. Each project demonstrates a strong application of CDIO methodology in ensuring that students move from theoretical knowledge to real-life problem-solving. Overall, these projects as a whole stress the imperative nature of robotics in shaping the future in various industries. They also stress the necessity of interdisciplinarity in learning, whereby engineering, computer science, and ethics must come together to design solutions that not only have technological depth, but social responsibility and sustainability as well.

Robotics and Fundamentals of Robotics

- **The Collaborative Application a Robot UR5e in the Sorting and Packaging of Plastic Bags:** One of the more practical and industry-oriented student projects was automating packaging and sorting plastic bags using a UR5e robot. The primary objective was to test whether robotic automation can be applied to a traditionally labour-based manufacturing process. The project encompassed a holistic approach, ranging from reviewing the existing manual packaging and sorting operation to designing a robotic solution and then implementing it using a robotic arm and a specially designed gripper. The practical application in this project was in how students could design and refine a gripper to manipulate plastic materials, which are lightweight and slippery. Programming a UR5e robot to make repeatable, high-precision movements required a great deal of mathematical modelling and fine-tuning motion parameters to get optimal efficiency. Moreover, testing in a real-world production setting provided insight into real-world operational problems, such as compensation for variations in bag size and material properties. This project demonstrates the importance of robotic flexibility in industrial automation. Through hands-on experience, students achieved a clear understanding of human-robot collaboration in manufacturing, particularly in terms of reducing labour tasks without affecting safety and efficiency. The results showed that the UR5e had a high potential to increase productivity and consistency in packaging, although there was a necessity for further developments in gripping mechanics and motion planning to make it applicable to a wider industry. Figure 3 shows a newly developed and customized gripper for plastic bags, as well as a robot performing bag stacking operations in a laboratory environment.

Fig. 3. Robot Performing Bag Stacking Operations with Customized Gripper

- **The Use of a Human-Robot Application in Detecting and Manipulating Objects of Different Colors and Shapes:** With manufacturing increasingly AI-driven, detection and object recognition have emerged as a priority for automation. This project involved closing the gap between robotic vision and AI-driven decision-making by enabling a UR5e robot to recognize and manipulate objects by colour and shape. Students made use of a Robotiq 2F-140 gripper and a Robotiq wrist camera to provide object recognition and developed customized machine learning algorithms for sorting applications. Technical complexity in this project involved calibrating the vision system to correctly identify and classify objects across various environments. By applying computer vision algorithms in OpenCV and using Python, students optimized image processing techniques to filter out noises and enhance accuracy. Once the objects had been classified, algorithms for moving the robot were fine-tuned to attain best grasping and placing to ensure effectiveness in manipulation. Apart from technical deployment, this project raised critical ethical issues in automation. With more use of robotic vision, AI bias, data privacy, and algorithmic transparency come into focus. The success with this project showed that AI vision could be applied to robotic automation and demonstrated the worth in real-time flexibility and ethical responsibility in autonomous decision-making. With continued advancements, such types of systems could be applied in logistics, assembly lines, and quality assurance environments, further solidifying AI's role in industrial robotics.
- **Proposals for Enhancing the Manipulator for Non-Destructive Testing of Welded Joints in Nuclear Fusion Reactor Doors:** High-precision robotics for non-destructive testing in nuclear engineering was investigated in this project with a particular emphasis on developing a more effective robotic manipulator to inspect welded joints in fusion reactor doors. Unlike typical robotic application in manufacturing, NDT in nuclear applications demands absolute precision, flexibility, and strict adherence to safety regulations. Student tackled a key engineering challenge: increasing maneuverability and reliability in a robotic inspection system for application in cramped, high-radiation environments. He redesigned critical components in the robotic system, including cable management and actuating mechanisms, to

achieve more precise articulation and longer lifespan. Through simulation testing, he tested mechanical stress points, potential failure modes, and energy efficiency, which allowed him to refine design before actual application. One of the key contributions of this project was to investigate alternative gripping technologies and force-feedback mechanisms that significantly enhanced the manipulator's ability to perform sensitive inspection tasks without compromising structural integrity in reactor components. In addition, student also researched radiation-resistant materials to improve robustness in harsh environments.

Programming of Robotic Systems and Robotics in Education

- **Developing a STEM Classroom: Python-Based EV3 Robotic System for Transporting 3D-Printed Boxes:** The STEM educational method relies heavily on hands-on experience and experimentation, and such a project best embodies that philosophy. Created as part of the "Programming of Robotic Systems" course, the project entailed utilizing LEGO MINDSTORMS EV3 and EV3 MicroPython firmware to design a robotic system to transport 3D-printed boxes. The integration of robotics and 3D printing offered students a cross-curricular learning experience that combined software programming, mechanical design, and automation principles. One of the project's strongest practical aspects was continuity from conception to completion. The students began by envisioning a transport mechanism that could automatically identify, grasp, and move small 3D-printed objects. This led them to write Python-based algorithms to operate it, taking into consideration real-world factors such as path planning, collision detection, and error handling. Through iterative testing, students refined the motion accuracy and object manipulation capability of the robot to ensure that the final product performed as it was meant to. The educational value brought about by the project was enormous, in that it helped bridge theory and problem-solving in real life. It showed how robotics can be applied to enhance practical learning experience, especially in STEM areas in which programming, automation, and engineering take a central place. The success in the project demonstrates the potential for educational transformation using robotics, giving students technical innovation and critical thinking skills. Figure 4 shows robotic arm and a conveyor belt, remote controlled car and students working in a team.
- **Automating Pharmaceutical Dispensing: The Role of Robotics in a Virtual Pharmacy:** Pharmaceutical automation has come to be a central topic in robotics, and in this project, the potential application in pharmacy automation using robotic systems was explored. In a DobotLab simulation platform, a pharmacy was designed by students in which a robot replaces human labor in picking and delivering medications. While there was no actual robotic arm, a simulation was implemented to mimic real pharmacy processes with emphasis on object detection, motion planning for robots, and customer interaction workflows. One of the more intriguing aspects in this project was the real-time adaptability of the robotic system. The robot was commanded to grab four different medications, scan them with simulated computer vision software, and dispense them to the pretend customer. One very innovative aspect was how the system could handle medication substitutions, detecting when a customer

Fig. 4. Students Working on Robotic System for Transporting 3D-Printed Boxes

requested a substitution and ensuring to dispense the right item. Although this project was conducted in a virtual setting, it was very much a reflection of real-world pharmacy automation issues like inventory management, human-robot collaboration, and reducing errors. The project also emphasized the value of robotics in health care, particularly in terms of increasing efficiency, accuracy, and safety in pharmaceutical settings. Moreover, it provided students with a preview into the ethical dimensions of automation in health care, with focus on robust error detection, patient safety features, and regulation compliance in putting such a system in real pharmacies. Figure 5 shows a simulated robotic pharmacy environment and a part of programming code created in the Blockly environment.

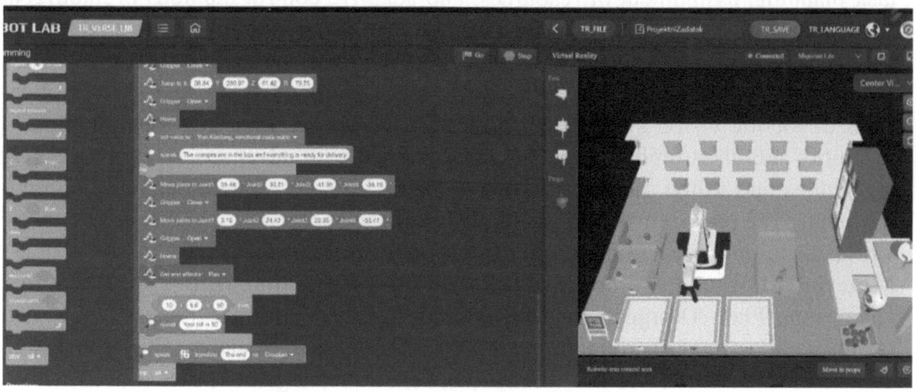

Fig. 5. Simulated Robotic Pharmacy Environment

- **Collaborative Applications for CNC Machine Tending:** The CNC machining automation represents a massive step forward in manufacturing efficiency and precision, and in this project, collaborative robots were utilized as machine tenders. Using simulation software from RoboDK, students designed a multi-robot system with three

KUKA LBR IIWA 7 R800 collaborative robots, each with a specific task in the CNC machining operation. One real-world application of this project was to mimic a fully automated CNC production line and show how robotic systems can be applied to increase efficiency, reduce human workload, and improve production consistency. One challenge that may have been greatest for students was to adjust synchronization between the three robots such that material transfer was smooth and production bottlenecks were avoided. Through multiple runs in RoboDK, students tweaked timing in the system such that transitions from one step to another were smooth. Apart from technical deployment, the project also raised vital questions about automation's future in manufacturing. Through integration of collaborative robots into traditionally human-oriented processes, students explored economic and ethical aspects of automation in the workplace. The project showed how robots could enhance workplace efficiency and safety and indicated the need to retrain workers to work with and maintain robotic systems rather than being replaced by them.

4.2 Student Internships at University

As a part of different study programs, students are required to do mandatory internships for different durations, from 1 to 3 months. The internship can be in an industrial company, or it can be in terms of University projects. Some of the projects that have been carried out by students during internships in industrial companies have been covered in the previous section, and below are a few examples of internships that have been carried out or being carried out by students at the University:

- **AI Optimization in Robotic Assembly and Disassembly:** The project involved a study of how decision-making can be optimized using artificial intelligence in robotic assembly and disassembly. The students conducted a detailed study of AI-based task planning, assignment of resources, and adaptive control methods in intelligent manufacturing settings. The practical part included simulations of AI-assisted robotic decision-making and testing it in human-robot application settings.
- **Computer Vision for Robotics Assembly and Disassembly:** Focusing on applications of robotic vision systems to part detection, localization, and manipulation in assembly and disassembly tasks. Students worked with advanced visual processing algorithms and tested them in real-world scenarios with simulations and lab environments. The project involved integrating AI-based perception systems into robotic workcells to improve automation reliability and flexibility.
- **Material Flow and Resource Optimization with Collaborative Applicatons:** Using ema Plant Designer, students will design and optimize material flow and resource utilization in a production system with collaborative robots. They will design 2D and 3D production and storage layouts, determined logistics process bottlenecks, and will propose how to improve efficiency with collaborative robots. Economic and logistics benefits will be compared using simulations.
- **Simulation and Evaluation of Human-Robot Interaction in Assembly Processes:** This project will simulate human-robot collaboration in assembly processes using ema Work Designer, incorporating ergonomic and safety analyses with EAWS and NIOSH methods. The students will maximize task assignment between human workers and

collaborative robots to improve productivity and worker safety and health. The project will provide valuable insights into ergonomic and effective robotic workplace design.

CDIO and principles of experiential learning are embedded in each internship, with active involvement by students in using theoretical principles in real-life applications. Ethical concerns like workforce automation and human safety constitute integral elements in these projects.

4.3 Student Visits to Industrial Companies: Practical Insights into Robotic Applications

For practical exposure, students conduct visits to industry companies where they observe applications of robotics in manufacturing in real-world settings. Specifically, visits to industry companies such as Alloy Wheels d.o.o. and ThermoFLUX d.o.o. in Jajce are immensely valuable learning activities. Visits like this provide students with practical exposure to robotics applications in manufacturing processes, bridging the gap between industry practices and theoretical concepts.

Alloy Wheels d.o.o. is involved in the production of passenger car wheels made from aluminium, ranging from 14″ to 22″ and compatible with multiple car models. The plant is fully automated and highly energy-efficient, with minimal environmental footprint. When students visit Alloy Wheels, they are able to observe the full application of robotics in every stage of wheel production. Raw materials are melted, and robots are used for precision casting into molds to create wheels, ensuring consistency and quality. Robotic systems perform complicated tasks to serve CNC machining machines, ensuring high accuracy in wheels' form and detailing. Robotic systems perform sorting and rigorous quality checks, utilizing advanced sensors and vision systems to scan for defects. Robots are also used in the final steps of painting because they apply coats of paint evenly, increasing durability and aesthetic appeal while maintaining environmental standards. From these observations, students are able to gain insights into the full application of robotics in manufacturing, with a focus on efficiency, accuracy, and the role of automation in modern manufacturing environments (Fig. 6).

ThermoFLUX d.o.o. is a leading producer of stoves and pellet boilers. The emphasis is placed on the development of technology, and advanced CNC machines are employed in the processes of cutting, bending, and welding. In their visits to ThermoFLUX, students have the opportunity to learn how robotic technologies employed in the process of welding bring accuracy and reliability to assembling components of boilers, enhancing the quality and efficiency of production. They can also learn how the practical application of sophisticated CNC machines to bend and cut sheets of metal mirrors the application of automation to realize high standards in manufacturing. Through these, students have the opportunity to understand how robotics is critical in welding processes, how automation is important in manufacturing, and how technological innovation is critical to maintaining competitive advantage.

Fig. 6. Student Visits to Industrial Companies

5 Comparative Analysis of Robotics Programs at the University of Applied Sciences and the University of Mostar

The chapter will present a systematic comparison of the robotics studies taught by the University of Applied Sciences and the University of Mostar. As the two institutions have contrasting pedagogical styles towards their studies, one being practice-based and emphasizing applied learning and the other incorporating robotics into other computer and engineering studies, a systematic comparison will best highlight their strengths and weaknesses as well as the key differences. Table 4 shows a comparison in the most important categories.

The University of Applied Sciences and the University of Mostar represent two distinct but complementary robotics education models. The first is highly industry-oriented, with a strong hands-on experience, formal robotics curricula, and compulsory internships. The model ensures that students are highly qualified to be employed directly in manufacturing, system integration, and industrial automation. Yet, its practical emphasis limits potential for advanced research and cross-disciplinary innovation. The University of Mostar, on the other hand, is broader and research-integrated, and robotics is incorporated into all engineering disciplines. This equips students with a solid foundation in AI, automation, and cross-disciplinary applications, and supports innovation in AI-based robotics. Yet, the lack of a distinct robotics major and minimal industry-mandatory training may pose challenges to preparing students to work in industry.

Both institutions have a practical learning focus, enabling students to get hands-on experience in automation, robot control, and programming. They implement new technologies, including AI and machine learning, in alignment with industry trends. However, the disciplined, application-based system of the University of Applied Sciences is more appropriate to the development of industry-specific experts, while the inter-disciplinary system of the University of Mostar is more suitable to research and

Table 4. Comparison of Robotics Programs at the University of Applied Sciences and the University of Mostar

Feature	University of Applied Sciences	University of Mostar
Overview of Robotics Education Approaches	Focus on applied learning and hands-on training. Students gain direct experience with industrial robots through practice-based teaching	Robotics is integrated into various engineering programs (mechanical, electrical, computer science), with a mix of theoretical and applied learning
Curriculum Structure and Course Content	Structured robotics degree programs with core subjects like robot control, automation, AI, and human-robot interaction. Heavy emphasis on lab work and industry projects	No dedicated robotics degree, but courses like Fundamentals of Robotics, Programming of Robotic Systems, and Robotics in Education exist within different programs. Focus on interdisciplinary applications
Laboratory and Practical Training Facilities	Well-equipped robotics labs with industrial robotic arms (ABB, KUKA, UR), automated production lines, and VR-based simulation tools	Collaborative applications lab, simulation-based training using RoboDK, MATLAB, and Python. Hands-on work with UR5e, LEGO Mindstorms, and AI-driven robotic vision systems
Internships, Industry Collaborations, and Research Opportunities	Mandatory internships (1–2 semesters) in partner industries. Students work on real-world automation projects under industry mentorship	Internships are mandatory and can be completed in industrial settings or university-based research projects. Collaboration with companies
Team and Individual Student Projects	Industry-driven capstone projects, often developed in partnership with local manufacturing companies. Focus on real-world applications like robotic welding, AI-driven automation, and robot integration	University research and student-driven projects with a mix of theoretical and experimental approaches. Examples include AI-based robotic vision systems, collaborative applications, and STEM robotics projects

development in intelligent automation. In CDIO terms, the University of Applied Sciences puts greater emphasis on the Implement and Operate phases, with an emphasis on real-world implementation, while the University of Mostar puts greater emphasis on the Conceive and Design phases, with an emphasis on AI-supported conception. Similarly, experiential learning theory is more action-based at the University of Applied Sciences, while the University of Mostar encompasses reflective observation and research-based learning. Ethical considerations in automation are also handled differently; the former deals with safety and compliance in industrial robots, while the latter addresses AI bias, human-robot interaction, and the societal implications of automation.

Ultimately, a mixed methodology, combining formal industry engagement with AI-driven research, could potentially deliver the most comprehensive robotics training, offering students practical experience and futures-focused innovation. Although primarily focused on STEM education, the approaches discussed also hold potential for non-STEM disciplines, such as design, media, or social sciences, by promoting creativity, problem-solving, and hands-on collaboration.

The comparison between the two educational approaches is based on qualitative analysis of program structure, types of student projects, and participant feedback. While the study does not use quantitative metrics, observations of student performance and engagement were used to inform conclusions. This study is limited by its qualitative nature and the absence of quantitative metrics for comparison. The findings are based on observations and institutional documentation, which may carry a degree of subjectivity. Further research should include empirical data and multi-institutional analysis to validate the results. Student learning outcomes were informally assessed through quality of completed projects, level of engagement, and tutor observations. Future work could benefit from more structured assessment methodologies to measure educational impact.

6 Conclusion

Studies at universities of applied sciences are practice-oriented. The combination of team and individual projects enables students to develop a wide range of skills that are useful in both academic and professional environments. Team projects promote social and cooperative skills, while individual projects strengthen individual skills and independence. Both types of projects are therefore essential for a comprehensive academic education.

As part of the Mechatronics/Robotics degree course, in addition to the compulsory work placement and Master's thesis, projects are also carried out in industry, which gives lecturers good contact with companies and allows students to find out which projects are currently being worked on in industry. The project reports from the work placement and the Master's thesis allow the courses to be updated and the curriculum to be adapted based on feedback from the company supervisors. All students benefit from the work placement in the fifth semester, as they can share their experiences from the projects in the companies in further courses in the sixth semester.

Figure 7 summarizes the type of cooperation between companies and the degree program.

The comparison between the University of Applied Sciences and the University of Mostar brings out the strengths and weaknesses in how the two institutions tackle

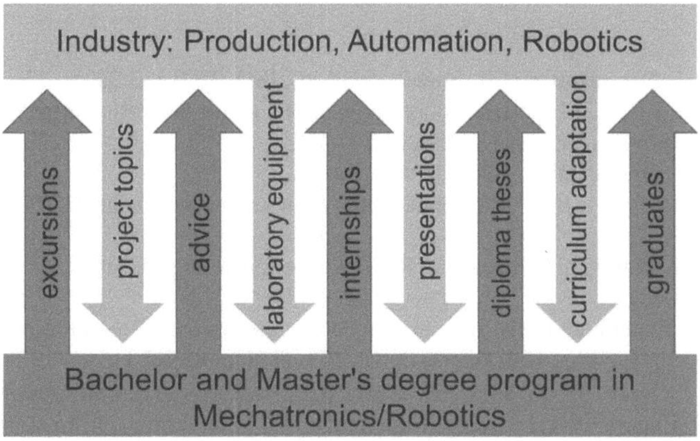

Fig. 7. Cooperation between the Mechatronics/Robotics degree program and industry [20]

robotics studies. The industry-specific training in formal robotics studies, compulsory internships, and highly advanced laboratory facilities are the strengths of the University of Applied Sciences. This system ensures that the graduates are highly competent to work straight away in manufacturing, system integration, and industrial automation. But the focus on practical application may limit potential for advanced research and inter-disciplinary innovation. Alternatively, the University of Mostar integrates robotics into broader computer science and engineering curricula, offering a more inter-disciplinary curriculum. This model gives students a solid foundation in AI, automation, and cross-disciplinary applications, and encourages innovation in robotics based on AI. However, the lack of an explicit robotics curriculum and minimal industry-requisite training may hamper students' preparation in specific industrial jobs.

Both institutions, despite their differing pedagogical approaches, share the same aim to prepare students with the requirements of a tech-based workforce. They implement emerging technologies, including AI and machine learning, as per industry requirements. Ultimately, a methodology that combines formal industry engagement with AI-driven research will best deliver the most comprehensive robotics training. This methodology would give students practical experience and innovative, forward-looking thinking, preparing them to navigate the complexities of an ever-changing technological landscape. By combining the strengths of both approaches, schools can implement a more comprehensive and dynamic robotics curriculum that is better suited to meet the diverse needs of students and industry.

Overall, the secret to robotics education in the future is to balance theoretical knowledge with practical application, and the ethical and social aspects of automation. With robotics transforming industries and reshaping the labor market, institutions have to be agile and responsive to trends. By fostering industry-academia partnerships, and by adopting inter-disciplinary approaches, universities can train their graduates to be technically competent as well as ethically sensitive and socially responsible. This will enable them to contribute to robotics and automation development in a socially responsible fashion.

References

1. International Organization for Standardization, ISO 10218–2:2025 - Robotics—Safety requirements—Part 2: Industrial robot applications and robot cells. https://www.iso.org/standard/73934.html. Accessed 13 Mar 2025
2. International Organization for Standardization, ISO 10218–1:2025 - Robotics—Safety requirements—Part 1: Industrial robots. https://www.iso.org/standard/73933.html. Accessed 13 Mar 2025
3. Crawley, E., Malmqvist, J., Stlund, S.: Rethinking engineering education: the CDIO approach. Springer (2007)
4. Kolb, D.A.: Experiential learning: experience as the source of learning and development, David A. Kolb, Prentice-Hall International, Hemel Hempstead, Herts., 1984. No. of pages: xiii + 256. J. Organ. Behav. **8**(4), 359–360 (1984). https://www.researchgate.net/publication/235701029_Experiential_Learning_Experience_As_The_Source_Of_Learning_And_Development. Accessed 11 Mar 2025
5. Dewey, J.: Experience and education/by John Dewey (1997). http://search.library.leeds.ac.uk/iii/encore/record/C__Rb2241460__Sexperienceandeducation__Orightresult__X5?lang=eng&suite=cobalt. Accessed 11 Mar 2025
6. Bostrom, N.: Nick Bostrom - Superintelligence_ Paths, Dangers, Strategies (2014, Oxford University Press).pdf (2016). https://global.oup.com/academic/product/superintelligence-9780198739838. Accessed 11 Mar 2025
7. IEEE SA - Autonomous and Intelligent Systems (AIS). https://standards.ieee.org/initiatives/autonomous-intelligence-systems/. Accessed 5 Mar 2025
8. Brundage, M.: Taking superintelligence seriously: Superintelligence: paths, dangers, strategies by Nick Bostrom (Oxford University Press, 2014) (2015). https://doi.org/10.1016/j.futures.2015.07.009
9. Crnokic, B., Grubisic, M., Volaric, T., Crnokić, B., Grubišić, M., Volarić, T.: Different applications of mobile robots in education. Int. J. Integr. Technol. Educ. **6**(3), 15–28 (2017). https://doi.org/10.5121/ijite.2017.6302
10. Volarić, T., Crnokić, B.: Artificial intelligence in education and robotics. Pressum, Mostar (2022)
11. Alam, A., Mohanty, A.: Integrated constructive robotics in education (ICRE) model: a paradigmatic framework for transformative learning in educational ecosystem. Cogent Educ. **11**(1) (2024). https://doi.org/10.1080/2331186X.2024.2324487
12. Crnokić, B., Pehar, F., Spajić, J., Bagarić, I.: Stem classroom: Creating a phyton application for an EV3 brick robotic system used to transport 3D printed boxes. Ann. DAAAM Proc. Int. DAAAM Symp. **31**(1), 88 (2020). https://doi.org/10.2507/31ST.DAAAM.PROCEEDINGS.012
13. Yuan, X., Wan, J., An, D., Lu, J., Yuan, P.: Multi-method integrated experimental teaching reform of a programming course based on the OBE-CDIO model under the background of engineering education. Sci. Reports 2024 141 **14**(1), 1–17 (2024). https://doi.org/10.1038/s41598-024-67667-6
14. Han, T., Luo, L., Zhou, G., Lin, B.: Construction of robot practice teaching system based on CDIO model, no. Emim, pp. 1498–1502 (2016). https://doi.org/10.2991/emim-16.2016.304
15. Eguchi, A.: Bringing robotics in classrooms. In: Robotics in STEM Education, pp. 3–31. Springer, Cham (2017)
16. Eguchi, A.: Theories and practices behind educational robotics for all, pp. 68–106 (2021). https://doi.org/10.4018/978-1-7998-6717-3.CH003:
17. Garcia, P., Rossiter, M.: Digital storytelling as narrative pedagogy. Society for Information Technology & Teacher Education International Conference., pp. 1091–1097 (2010). http://www.editlib.org/p/33500/. Accessed 11 Mar 2025

18. Malisa, V.: Jahrzent Mechatronik/Robotik. F-AR Förderung der Automation und Robotik, paco Medienwerkstatt, Vienna (2013)
19. Mechatronik Plattform, Mechatronik Plattform – FH-Studiengänge der Automatisierungstechnik Österreichs. https://www.mechatronik-plattform.at/. Accessed 25 Feb 2025
20. Viktorio Malisa, Aufbau eines neuen Studienganges am Beispiel Mechatronik/Robotik, Konf. AALE 2009. TFH Berlin (2009)

Remote Laboratory for FPGA-Based Education: A Brief Review

Sebastian Karl Mladen Haupt(✉), Marina Prvan, Josip Musić, and Ante Kristić

Faculty of Electrical Engineering, Mechanical Engineering and Naval Architecture (FESB), University of Split, R. Boskovica 32, 21000 Split, Croatia
{shaupt00,mprvan,jmusic,akristic}@fesb.hr

Abstract. The Covid-19 pandemic caused a situation in which both educators and students had to adapt as soon as possible, and a new educational context known as distance learning has become a daily routine for teaching all courses. However, some courses were easily adapted to the new type of learning, while for some courses it was very difficult to provide an efficient online teaching concept. This was especially true for engineering courses such as digital systems design, which requires working in laboratories and performing live demonstrations on digital systems and Field Programmable Gate Arrays (FPGA) boards. One of the biggest problems was that the students did not have access to the boards as they were physically located in the labs. It is not easy for students to buy the equipment for their learning purposes, as the boards are specialized and costly. The idea of this paper is to provide an overview of how researchers in the current state-of-the-art have approached this problem and how they applied distance learning methods to implement systems for students to access remote FPGA boards. Several methods for remote lab implementations were found and described and contrasted by comparing their advantages and disadvantages. Finally, a conclusion is drawn, taking into account potential directions that could be further explored as future work, not only as a tool for practical emergency situations, but also as an additional for in-person teaching.

Keywords: Remote laboratory · Distance learning · Field Programmable Gate Array (FPGA)

1 Introduction

Teaching digital systems design is one of the most important courses in educating future electronics engineering experts. In addition to traditional challenges in designing and modifying a course to keep up with technology developments, teachers are constantly looking to provide new paradigms and perspectives on the learning process [1–3]. One of them is programming physical circuits with Field Programmable Gate Arrays (FPGA), and mostly off-the-shelf solutions are available, whereas students can use hardware description language (HDL) and

D. Vasić and E. Brajković (Eds.): MoStart 2025, CCIS 2609, pp. 106–123, 2026.
https://doi.org/10.1007/978-3-032-02801-3_7

reconfigure the existing hardware to meet the requirements. This is referred to in the literature as the "touch-and-feel" approach to digital system design [1], or the "learning-by-doing" methodology [4].

Hence, the course is very practical and the set-up of the teaching laboratory with physical FPGA equipment is inevitable. It is demanding for students to have hands-on experience with this type of teaching, especially in conditions such as the Covid-19 pandemic, where face-to-face communication is not possible [5]. Remote laboratries were imposed as a necessary tool or platform for distance teaching at that time, not only as an alternative to hands-on experience [5–7] but also to allow students to access the laboratory at any time at their own pace, regardless of the lab availability schedule [8]. There are several learning theories that support this form of teaching and help to understand how students learn in a remote electronic lab setting. It is important to note that it is not possible to fit this type of learning in a single theory, but rather to consider it as a combination of several classical theories, like behaviorism and constructivism [9]. While working on remote FPGA devices in a virtual lab, students apply behavioral learning theory through trial and error, using feedback from the system, and repeating only successful actions. Students are more relaxed than when working in front of a teacher, so they may be more motivated and interested in trying various hands-on tests and experiments with the equipment. The constructivism theory implies that the student actively constructs his knowledge through research and prior experiences, without being guided by the teacher. In this context, ensuring only remote access to a virtual lab for students should be sufficient for the pedagogical frame of learning theories to be accomplished.

Another advantage of the remote lab is its cost effectiveness, as students can access the same FPGA, supporting larger class sizes at lower cost [10,11]. Physical damage to the equipment is also avoided while working remotely instead of handling the physical FPGA devices. However, it is not an easy task to design a remote lab for students and provide them remote access to FPGA boards. Many solutions exist for remote web-based FPGA labs, dealing with the architecture, communication interface, user access administration, and other main functionalities. For example, in [11], a remote FPGA hardware experience for students is provided, improving their motivation and understanding of digital systems. A mechanism for the creation and upload of the FPGA configuration bitstream files is proposed, and students are provided with a visualization of the desired functionality on the FPGA board with an associated web camera. In [10], the authors have previously demonstrated a facility for a remote FPGA education laboratory. The goal is to associate a single computer as a workstation connected to several FPGAs. It can be accessed remotely, and students can power on and power off the boards, reconfigure and debug the programmed designs, and gain access to input/output devices or the status of the LED diodes. However, while the authors report mostly positive feedback, some negative comments are received from students about the lack of visual feedback from the lab. In addition, the virtual nature of accessing the physical devices gave them the impression that they lacked real hands-on experience.

The authors in [12] provide a list of the most famous remote laboratories established all over the world and propose their design for a low-cost and scalable FPGA remote access lab. The student first compiles and simulates the HDL code with a web-based edition of the dedicated software. Then they log in to the server to upload the FPGA bitmap to the board. Students can interface with the hardware switches, buttons, and signals of the light-emitting diode (LED) displays to visualize and validate the desired functionality. A similar approach is given in [13], where the monitoring of the FPGA boards is accomplished through cameras showing the state of the boards (blinking LEDs or the information on an integrated display), and an additional input/output board is connected to each FPGA to handle the input user signals. There are also similar remote solutions that rely on the integration of more expensive commercial and licensed tools such as LabVIEW (Laboratory Virtual Instrument Engineering Workbench), as shown in [14,15]. However, the intention is the same for every attempt at remote laboratory design, as it always tends to incorporate the advantages and minimize the disadvantages of the existing approaches.

The overview of system architectures and the comparison of the available tools for the design of remote laboratories would be of great interest to researchers in this field. There are few state-of-the-art reviews for this purpose [16–19]. Although the former papers originated almost ten years ago and focused on the current trends in remote labs at that time, the crucial paradigms and design guidelines are still of great interest, revealing the implementation challenges that are still novel and actual. However, as technology trends are rapidly changing, we believe that incorporating the standard remote laboratory design features into the most recent context is essential. In addition, remote education of engineers in Science, Technology, Engineering, and Mathematics (STEM) has become a de facto standard in the digital age today [20–22].

Therefore, it is important to achieve a remote laboratory platform for students, and the goal of this work is to provide an overview of the existing remote laboratory-based solutions. The focus is on the application in teaching digital system design courses, specifically digital circuit design using FPGAs. The methods are evaluated by highlighting their advantages, disadvantages, and the challenges that should be addressed. Finally, the contribution of this paper would be in providing an entry point for anyone wanting to create a remote laboratory. In the hope of providing the reader with some ground knowledge that points them in the direction they should take to implement a remote laboratory that is appropriate for their needs.

The paper is organized as follows. In Section 2, a methodology is provided on the search and selection procedure for the paper and inclusion criteria. Next, the results of the survey are presented in Section 3, with a description of the reviewed methods for the remote laboratory implementations for FPGA development. In Section 4, the methods are evaluated by summarizing their advantages and disadvantages. Finally, Section 5 concludes the paper, followed by the references used.

2 Methodology

2.1 Paper Search Procedure

To find different methods and approaches in the construction of remote laboratories, the existing papers from the last six years were examined. Most of the data used in this research were found using Google Scholar. In addition, academic databases such as IEEE Xplore, ACM Digital Library, and Web of Science (WoS) were used to expand the selection of papers. Entering search terms relevant to the topic and refining the results by date and relevance established a solid baseline for this paper.

Multiple search terms were used in this step, all containing the common phrase 'remote laboratory.' This phrase was placed in quotation marks to ensure that only papers explicitly including it were retrieved. To further refine the results, additional keywords were appended, forming four search string combinations: 'remote laboratory,' 'remote laboratory' AND FPGA, 'remote laboratory' AND Artificial Intelligence (AI), and 'remote laboratory' AND robotics.

The idea behind the first search string was to find papers that had conducted some form of experiment with students to evaluate the effectiveness of remote labs. The courses were of less importance at this moment since the student's interactions with the remote lab should be somewhat similar regardless of subject, and as such no additional keyword was used to get more results. Apart from finding out if remote labs have a place in traditional education, all the different findings can be used to avoid mistakes early on. The second search string was used to find papers specifically related to FPGA boards, since they are the main focus of this paper. The goal is to determine which methods are the most widely used for remote labs and to reflect on the pros and cons.

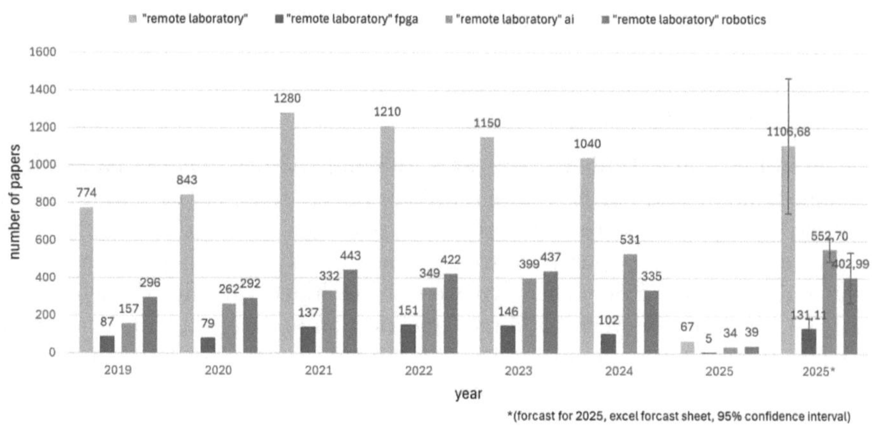

Fig. 1. The papers distribution by year from Google Scholar.

Finally, two more strings were used to assess the popularity of remote laboratories and identify the current main areas of focus. The results are shown in Fig. 1. It includes the number of papers found for each search string, categorized by year, starting from 2019. When observing all the results, a noticeable jump can be seen in 2021 which would correspond to the Covid-19 pandemic. Later, as the pandemic ended, there was a drop in the number of papers, which is expected. Papers mentioning AI stand out as the only ones to increase even after the Covid-19 pandemic, likely due to the recent boom in AI. Remote laboratories for robotics have been consistently popular, even before the pandemic, only being surpassed by AI in 2024. However, it's important to consider that robotics is a broad field, often encompassing areas like FPGAs and micro-controllers, etc. Also shown in Fig. 1 is an extrapolation for the year 2025 based on the years since 2019. It was generated using the Excel Forecast Sheet tool with the default confidence interval of 95%.

Table 1. The number of selected papers from different academic databases.

Database	Pre-selection	Selection of the most relevant papers	Selection based on topic (FPGA remote lab implementation)		Selection after removing duplicates
Google Scholar	705	40	22	18	18
IEEE Xplore	153	40	12	28	12
Other (ACM, WoS)	-	-	-	17	2
Total	-	-	-	-	32

2.2 Selected Papers

As shown in Fig. 1 and Table 1, there were 705 and 153 pre-selected papers from the Google Scholar and IEEE Xplore database on the topic of the remote FPGA laboratory. The papers were then sorted by relevance and the full texts of the most relevant (top 40 papers) were examined. Next, 18 papers from Google Scholar and 28 papers from IEEE Xplore were included that fitted the research subject, i.e. the ones answering a direct question on how to implement a remote FPGA lab. In total 30 papers were included in the review after removing duplicates. An additional quick ad hoc search was performed from other databases (ACM and WoS), resulting in 17 papers considered, of which 15 were duplicates. Finally, the review consists of 32 papers in total.

The remote FPGA lab implementations described in the selected papers were then divided into different methods. These methods are as follows: Direct Connections (DC) [2,5,14,23–27], Web Server Connections (WSC) [12,13,28–46], and Layered Access Systems (LAS) [8,47,48]. The description of the methods in the next section follows the order of the methods listed in Table 2.

Table 2. Distribution of the selected papers by the method used.

Method	Name	References	The number of papers
1	Direct Connections	[2,5,14,23–27]	8
2	Web Server Connections	[12,13,28–46]	21
3	Layered Access Systems	[8,47,48]	3

3 Methods for Remote FPGA Lab Implementations

3.1 Method 1 Direct Connections

Different trends can be noticed when going through the selected papers, and these have much in common. One of them is a setup in which users establish a direct connection to remote hardware [2,5,23–26]. What is meant by a direct connection is that there is no intermediary between the user and the hardware that oversees the connection. This hardware can be viewed as a closed system that has everything needed to use one FPGA board. Apart from the FPGA, the hardware needed for these methods usually consists of a camera and an endpoint that enable the use of the FPGA board over a remote connection. This endpoint (Fig. 2) is achieved in several different ways.

A straightforward approach for connecting with the FPGA is to use a Remote Desktop Application (RDA) such as *Windows remote desktop*, *AnyDesk*, etc. that would be setup on "on-site" personal computers (PC). One example [5] combines a PC, a mobile device, and a micro-controller to access the FPGA. The micro-controller is important for interfacing with the FPGA as its pins can be connected to the GPIO (general-purpose input/output) pins of the FPGA. This means that any pin of the micro-controller can be interpreted as an input or output for the FPGA. The PC is accessed using the *AnyDesk* remote desktop tool and is used to configure both the FPGA and the micro-controller. After having done so, the FPGA can be tested using a mobile application thanks to the connected micro-controller. The application presents the user with an interface and any command that is input by the user is then sent to the micro-controller, which sends it to the FPGA. Another advantage of the micro-controller is that the user can connect a second micro-controller on his end and then send real-time sensor data over the remote connection to the FPGA inputs.

Other examples [23,24] make use of an RPi (Raspberry Pi) as a substitute for a PC where the RPi can be used as a HAT (Hardware Attached on Top) for the FPGA. The configuration is set up in a way that the FPGA can be programmed and interfaced with over the RPi.

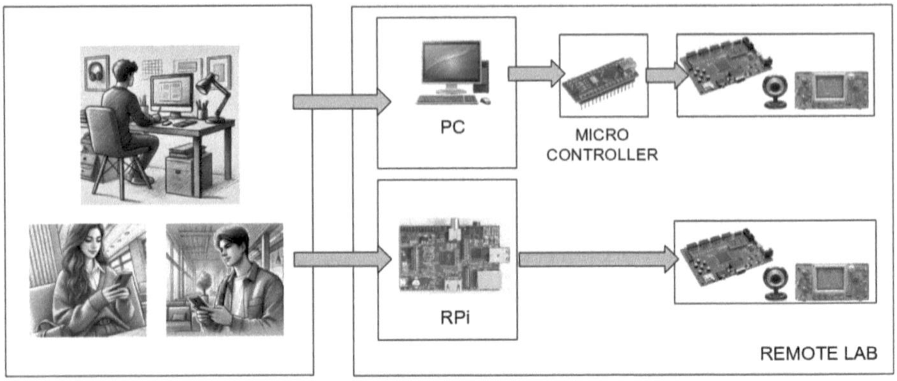

Fig. 2. Students establish a direct connection with the hardware setup.

In [23], remote access is established using a mobile application with a simple user interface (Fig. 3a) and no video feed. To achieve remote access functionality, the user module is embedded into a remote FPGA framework using a pre-made Python script. The module created by the script wires inputs and outputs of the FPGA to input/output managers that provide the user with all the needed functions, like activating a switch or observing LEDs. To transfer or receive all the needed information to or from the RPi a UART (Universal Asynchronous Receiver-Transmitter) connection is created using the GPIO pins. The input/output managers decode/code binary values that are received/transferred from/to the RPi over the UART connection.

The work in [24] is similar to [23], with the main difference being that the user connects to the RPi using an RDA. Once again, the FPGA and RPi communicate over the GPIO pins except that this time a camera is available for observation. The author also designed an enclosure (Fig. 3b) to house all the necessary parts with the option of using a screen for on-site purposes.

Every laboratory has only a set number of PCs that must be available for on-site lab exercises and when using PCs to connect to the FPGA as in [5], they cannot be used for anything else in the meantime. Additionally, every PC can be assigned to only one remote student at a time, and someone would have to be present to power up/down all the workstations. To address these limitations, a schedule would have to be established and students would have very limited access to the workstations. Although RDA implementations have several limitations, they are simple to set up and provide the user with a close-to-on-site experience. The user would have all the standard tools at hand, the same ones as he/she would be using during lab exercises, which is good for accessibility. Students who cannot set up the necessary work environment on their PC would only need the RDA. When the FPGA is accessed using another device similar to an RPi, all PCs remain free for other uses, such as on-site courses, alleviating the very limiting schedule. However, connecting over an RPi leads to a new

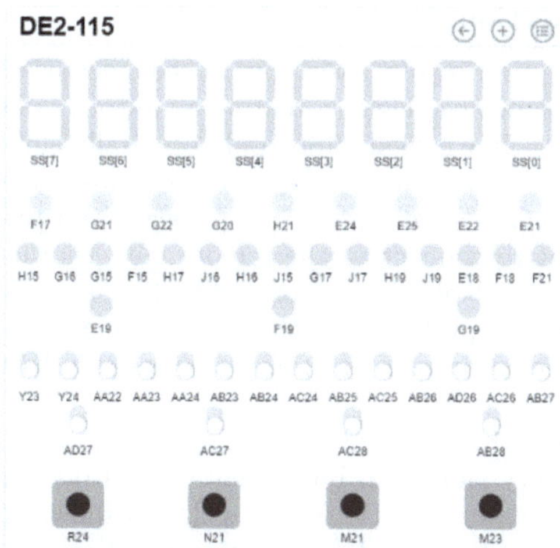

(a) Mobile application user interface [24].

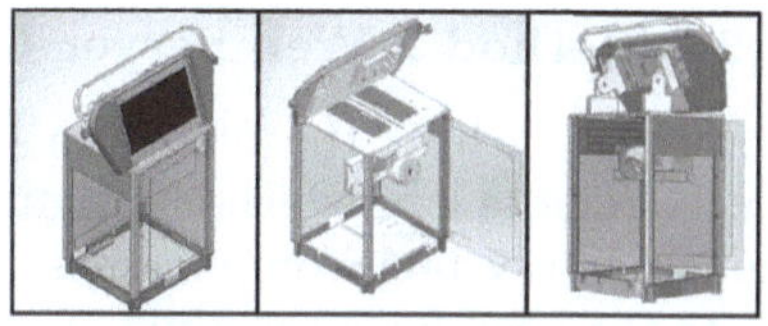

(b) An encloser for housing the parts needed for connection [23].

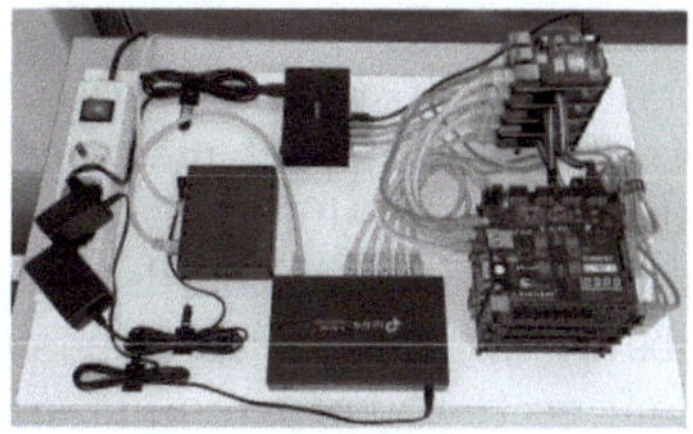

(c) Equipment setup combining FPGA and an RPi [29].

Fig. 3. User interface and equipment.

potential problem, namely accessibility. Now that the student does not have access to the remote PC, the student will have to set up a local workstation with the needed IDE (Integrated Development Environment), which in some cases may have high system requirements. Following all these problems, we can conclude that this method does not scale well with a larger number of students and courses.

Deciding on which approach to use depends heavily on the desired functionality. If a close-to-on-site experience is desired, then [5] is appropriate. However, if the schedule is a problem, then solutions like [24] or [23] might have to be used.

All examples so far used standard programming tools, but another option is available when using LabVIEW [2,14,27]. The approach in [2] uses an RDA for remote access, but instead of running tools like *vivado* or *ISE design suite*, a LabVIEW setup is implemented. This setup enables the programming and monitoring of the FPGA. All the hardware needed for the lab is connected to the PC and set up such that it can be accessed using LabVIEW. In this case, the user has access to a Spartan 3 Xilinx FPGA, a camera, an oscilloscope, and multiple other expansion cards and modules. On the other hand [14] shows the use of LabVIEW's Web server functionality that eliminates the need for an RDA, allowing the user to access the user interface using a web browser.

Although LabVIEW presents an interesting alternative, its significant differences lie in the user interface as well as in the number of tools available. However, it introduces significant inconveniences, as it is based on specific hardware and proprietary licensed software. Not all FPGA boards are compatible with LabVIEW's tools. That is why the Spartan 3 Xilinx FPGA is used in [2].

3.2 Method 2 Web Server Connections

Solutions such as the one from [5] require on-site assistance to connect users to the remote lab, which is a significant inconvenience. Creating an autonomous remote lab system would increase the up-time considerably and potentially eliminate the need for a schedule. To achieve an autonomous system, it should have the capability to manage all the hardware as well as to start, assign, and terminate new sessions to users who want to connect to the remote lab. Another key factor is user management in the form of a queue or reservation system. A very common approach to solving this problem is to introduce a centralized server (Fig. 4) that manages user connections and every connected FPGA board [8,12,13,28–46].

Individual FPGA boards along with their needed hardware can be viewed as subsystems that are in some cases very similar to implementations from the previous section. For example, a combination of FPGA and a RPi is shown in Fig. 3c. With the addition of a centralized server, all users connect to the same endpoint when accessing the remote lab. If directly interfacing with the FPGA is still handled by every individual subsystem, the server essentially only serves as a bridge between the user and the hardware. In some cases like in [28], the server is implemented to take over functions (other than bridging) so that the subsystems do not require an RPi like the previous examples. In such cases, a subsystem would only consist of an FPGA and other tools (e.g., camera). In [28] the server is made from three sub-servers that include a web-based server, a core server, and a live streaming server. The user connects to the web-based server, the live-streaming server sends live camera feedback to the user, and the core server handles all other tasks in regards to the FPGA.

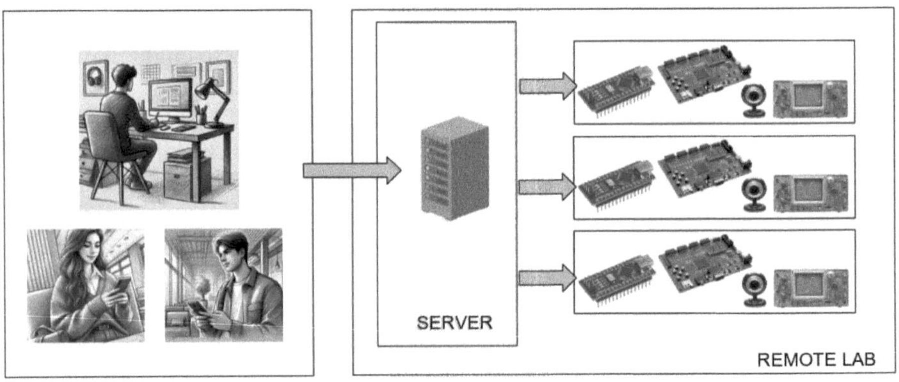

Fig. 4. Web server architecture with and without an RPi (WSC).

Comparing server implementations to direct connection implementations shows that servers mainly fix one problem. By introducing an autonomous solution, the requirements for on-site assistance are significantly reduced, allowing for easier schedule arrangements or even completely removing the need for them. Server implementations also scale better, as less hardware is required when adding a new FPGA board (subsystem).

Depending on the implementation, previously defined drawbacks remain as the student's interaction with the remote lab depends on the user interface. When no IDE is available the students have to set up workstations and using web applications does not provide an on-site experience. Another aspect to take into account is the complexity of implementing a remote lab using a server.

3.3 Method 3 Layered Access Systems

Layered Access Systems [8,47,48] are in many ways similar to WSC implementations. It could be argued that the LAS method is a subset of the WSC method, as both are server-based methods, but the reason why this method is separated into its own sections is due to its few significant changes. These changes stem from the distribution of responsibility to multiple separate systems (servers, Fig. 5). *WebLab-Deusto* [8] presents an extensively developed implementation of LAS. It offers students a full solution so that they don't need an IDE. The workflow is divided into several stages. To begin with, the users have access to an advanced built-in HDL editor and a cloud-based file system, meaning that students do not have to install any coding tools on their local machines. This is a significant advantage over many previously mentioned examples and is comparable to remote desktop approaches when observing accessibility. This represents the first stage of the workflow.

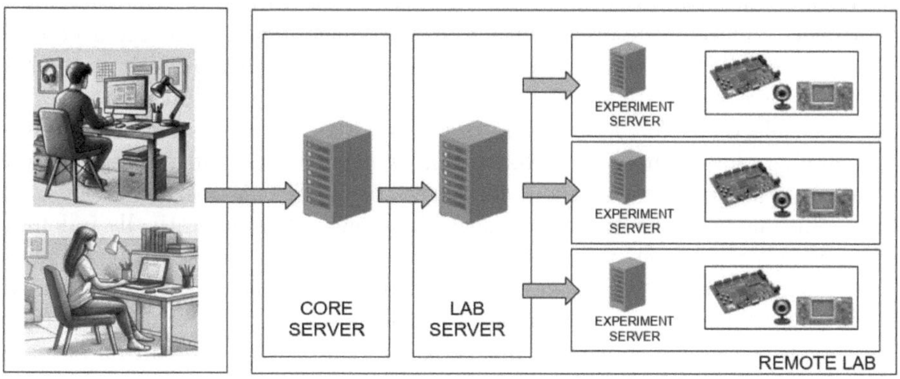

Fig. 5. Remote laboratory structure with LAS (WebLabDeusto).

After coding a project, the student proceeds to the synthesis and implementation stage. This is handled by adding a task to a centralized queue. Every task in the queue gets assigned a Docker instance responsible for the synthesis and implementation. Hence, the number of docker instances corresponds to the number of users in the synthesis stage of their project. All errors and warnings generated during synthesis are shown in a console window, allowing for simple debugging.

Finally, when a bitstream file is generated, the user can move to the final segment, programming the FPGA. Only in this step is the user assigned an FPGA board and if none is available, he is placed in a waiting queue. The user has a live feed of the board and all the peripherals, virtual switches for inputs, as well as a UART terminal. During the first two stages users have unlimited access to their sessions, but during the final stage of programming and testing a short time limit of two minutes is imposed such that every board is used as much as possible. This ensures that every user has access to a board in a timely manner.

The *WebLab-Deusto* implementation offers significant improvements compared to previous implementations. It is highly scalable as the hardware is only accessed when needed, leading to much more efficient up-time for every board. The included editor ensures high accessibility as users don't need to set up a local workstation and along with the debugging console it allows for a standard coding experience. One downside is the limited time access to the actual FPGA. The remote lab setup process could present another challenge as the system is more complex.

4 Evaluation

4.1 Comparison Between Methods

Concerning the advantages and disadvantages of each method, *WebLab-Deusto* offers a very compelling solution with its user management system and accessibility, since every FPGA board is only used when needed to provide high uptime, and users have access to all the tools they need without additional software. One downside of *WebLab-Deusto* is that very little time is allocated for testing, meaning that if more rigorous testing is needed, one will potentially have to wait several times in the queue for access to an FPGA board. On the other hand, solutions with the direct connection approach offer theoretically indefinite testing time per session, with the only limitation being the schedule in place. But this same schedule will most often be very constrained as it is dependent on several factors, leading these methods to be impractical. WSC implementations offer a wide variety of solutions that range in complexity and can be adjusted to specific needs.

Table 3 shows a list of hardware and software needs. Of note is that the table does not mention the actual lab equipment (FPGA, oscilloscope, camera, etc.) as it is the same for every method. Also important is that not all the mentioned hardware is always needed, as depending on the implementation, only some of it may be required. An example of this would be the on-site hardware listed for direct connections, as the RPi can be used as a replacement for the PC.

Table 3. The equipment needed for each method.

Method	Student (home)		On-site (lab)	
	Hardware	Software	Hardware	Software
DC	PC, Mobile device, Micro-controller	RDA/coding tools, Web Browser, Mobile app, Micro-controller software	PC or RPi, Micro-controller	RDA, Hardware specific software or LabVIEW
WSC	PC, Mobile device	Web Browser, Mobile app	Server, RPi or Micro-controller	Hardware specific software
LAS	PC, Mobile device	Web Browser	Server	WebLab-Deusto

Table 4. Simplified comparison between methods.

	Direct connections	Web server connections	Layered Access Systems
Easy lab setup	1	3	4
Schedule	4	2	1
Scaling	5	3	2
User interface	2	3	2
Access time	4	2	3
Accessibility	3	3	1

Finally, Table 4 shows a very simplified comparison between the mentioned methods. The comparison is based on some characteristics that are deemed important. Each characteristic is graded in the range of 1–5 with 1 being positive, 3, neutral, and 5 negative. As every method has a multitude of different implementations, the grading cannot be considered as a precise representation of every implementation, and thus this comparison does not represent the full picture of which method is the best. Not all characteristics of remote laboratories have been taken into account. Some important characteristics that were overlooked are security [41,44,49], user collaboration [44], professor oversight [40], and so on. Virtual laboratories [50] are overlooked as well regardless of whether they could be added as a fourth method as the focus was on using real FPGA hardware.

Some papers included in this review [5,29–31] have verified student satisfaction and the results are all positive, confirming the value of implementing remote laboratories alongside standard laboratory sessions. The summarized findings of the mentioned papers are given in Table 5, where we extracted only the most interesting characteristics studied. Interestingly, most of the students with DC [5] preferred remote lab over simulations, but with WSC [29–31], students did not provide a very high mean grade when asked if remote lab is preferred over traditional. Also, interest in the subject and understanding increase no matter the

Table 5. Summarized results of students' satisfaction surveys.

Ref	Feature studied	Results
[5]	Student performance	Average grade value 8.38 out of 10 with remote lab and 7.89 out of 10 without remote lab (N=32)
	Overall satisfaction	84% of students liked the remote connection to the lab (N=25)
	Understanding	82% of students perceived increased practical skills (N=11)
	Usefulness	70% of students preferred remote lab over simulations (N=32)
[29]	Overall satisfaction	Mean score is 4.31/4.00/4.40 out of 5 (N=32/27/18)
	Usefulness	Mean score is 4.53/4.20/4.70 out of 5 (N=32/27/18)
	Interest in the subject	Mean score is 3.71/3.80/3.90 out of 5 (N=32/27/18)
	Similarity to on-site	Mean score is 4.31/3.90/4.40 out of 5 (N=32/27/18)
	Remote lab better than on-site	Mean score is 2.56/3.00/2.60 out of 5 (N=32/27/18)
[30]	Overall satisfaction	15 students were very satisfied, 33 students were satisfied and 2 students were very dissatisfied (N=50)
	Understanding	43 students perceived full improvement and 7 students perceived partial improvement in learning (N=50)
	Interest in the subject	46 students perceived increased interest for learning (N=50)
[31]	Overall satisfaction	Mean score is 4.0 out of 5 (N=35)
	Understanding	Mean score is 4.0 out of 5 (N=35)
	Remote lab better than on-site	Mean score is 3.90 out of 5 (N=35)

method used. It should be noted that there are few negative feedbacks received from the students [5,30], who had difficulty performing remote laboratory activities due to some technical issues.

Other papers found in the literature [51,52] with similar lab implementations that are not aimed at FPGA development show similar student satisfaction.

4.2 Limitations and Future Work

Although this paper can be used as an entry point for creating a remote laboratory, the reader will still have a lot of options to consider and will have to do more specific research. The described methods often contain different implementations that vary in some way, such as using different hardware or software, leading to a change in the pros and cons. The generalization of different implementations under three methods is the limitation of this paper, and further categorizations of the implementations under the proposed methods could be one way of addressing this limitation.

There are gaps revealed in the current literature that will be addressed in our future work on this topic. First, it is well known that the teacher's role during distance learning is minimal, as the whole educational process is student-centered [53]. Students should be monitored online, with the teacher actively mentoring and overseeing their work in a remote environment. However, the existing literature does not provide specific methods for how teachers can effectively monitor students' progress. Most remote lab implementations focus on how students connect to the physical lab setup and how they can program, simulate, and validate the functionality, rather than addressing the monitoring aspect. We believe that more research should focus on how teachers can mentor students in the remote lab and assist with potential problems. Although some implementations, such as WebLab-Deusto, track student activity through logs, a more direct approach where a supervisor can join a session could offer additional support.

The answer to the question of how easy or difficult it is for teachers to create knowledge assessments or lab exercises with each method is currently missing. A comparison of the effort required by the teacher to set up a specific remote FPGA lab would be valuable. Although the list of advantages and disadvantages is helpful, teachers need a clear understanding of all the necessary steps involved in using each method. In addition, the process of preparing laboratory exercises with a specific method should be addressed. Examples of some lab exercises are mentioned in the papers [8,29,30].

In the literature, it has already been shown that collaborative work between students enhances their learning. Therefore, it should be explored which of the methods enable collaborative work between students. This is mentioned in some papers [5,8,23,33], but it depends on the implementation, so it is not related to the method applied.

5 Conclusion

Based on the papers used for this work, three methods have been described for implementing remote laboratories using FPGA boards. All three methods were explained to finally define a table of pros and cons for all methods. Most implementations have several similarities but end up having different use cases regardless of method, meaning that any method can prove to be useful given the circumstances. In general, a well-designed implementation will take into account time constraints for the schedule, hardware limitations, as well as student accessibility to interact with the remote lab.

The user interface, along with the lab hardware, plays a key role in many implementations, as it determines how students interact with the FPGA. When considering accessibility, it is important to account for the steps required for students to use the remote lab. In some implementations, students must set up a local workstation with the necessary software, while in others they may only need a browser.

A promising implementation is WebLab-Deusto, offering a remarkable user management system allowing for a balanced FPGA time distribution between all users, resulting in very high uptime of the lab hardware. Moreover, while the topic of implementing a remote lab is well worked on, there are still improvements to be made, for example collaboration between students and professors. With this paper, we encourage researchers to fill-in the identified gaps in the current state-of-the-art, and to propose novel methods for developing the remote laboratories for FPGA-based education. Our future goal would be to implement a virtual lab for electronic engineering students attending a digital systems design course. The proposed solution will tend to retain the advantages of the described methods and minimize their perceived disadvantages. The ultimate hybrid approach of the blended learning paradigm will be allowed, combining face-to-face and remote online instructions.

References

1. Ochoa, H.A., Shirvaikar, M.V.: A survey of digital systems curriculum and pedagogy in electrical and computer engineering programs. Faculty Publ. Am. Soc. Eng. Educ. **18** (2019)
2. Balid, W., Abdulwahed, M.: A novel FPGA educational paradigm using the next generation programming languages case of an embedded FPGA system course. In: 2013 IEEE Global Engineering Education Conference (EDUCON), pp. 23-31, Berlin, Germany (2013)
3. Skliarova, I., Sklyarov, V., Sudnitson, A., Kruus, M.: Teaching FPGA-based systems. In: 2014 IEEE Global Engineering Education Conference (EDUCON), pp. 460-469, Istanbul, Turkey (2014)
4. Cifredo-Chacón, M.D.L.Á., Quirós-Olozábal, Á., Guerrero-Rodríguez, J.M.: Computer architecture and FPGAs: a learning-by-doing methodology for digital-native students. Comput. Appl. Eng. Educ. **23**(3), 464-470 (2015)
5. Valencia de Almeida, F., Hayashi, V.T., Arakaki, R., Midorikawa, E., Canovas, S.D.M., Cugnasca, P.S., Corrêa, P.L.P.: Teaching digital electronics during the COVID-19 pandemic via a remote lab. Sensors **22**(18), 6944 (2022)
6. Novas Castellano, N., García Salvador, R.M., Portillo Rodríguez, F., Soler Ortiz, M.J., Fernández Ros, M., Gázquez Parra, J. A., Segura Pardo, F.: FPGAs for Learning Digital Electronics Concepts. In: 16th annual International Conference of Education, Research and Innovation, Seville, Spain (2023)
7. Vorgul, O., Zubkov, O., Svyd, I., Semenets, V.V.: Teaching microcontrollers and FPGAs in quarantine from coronavirus: challenges and prospects. In: II International Scientific and Practical Conference Theoretical and Applied Aspects of Device Development on Microcontrollers and FPGAs (MC and FPGA), pp.14-17, Kharkiv, Ukraine (2020)
8. Hernández-Jayo, U., García-Zubia, J.: Experience of teaching analog and digital electronic using remote laboratories during COVID-19 pandemic. https://kirchernetwork.org/wp-content/uploads/2021/07/DEUSTO-Unai-Hernadez-and-Javier-Garcia-Zubia.pdf Accessed 10 Feb 2025
9. Picciano, A.G.: Theories and frameworks for online education: seeking an integrated model. Online Learn. **21**(3), 166–190 (2021)
10. Rajasekhar, Y., Kritikos, W.V., Schmidt, A.G., Sass, R.: Teaching FPGA system design via a remote laboratory facility. In: 2008 International Conference on Field Programmable Logic and Applications, pp. 687-690, IEEE, Heidelberg, Germany (2008)
11. Morgan, F., Cawley, S., Newell, D.: Remote FPGA lab for enhancing learning of digital systems. ACM Trans. Reconfigurable Technol. Syst. (TRETS) **5**(3), 1–13 (2012)
12. Hoang, T.M., et al.: Implementation of low cost FPGA remote laboratory. ASEAN Eng. J. **5**(1), 56–76 (2015)
13. Reichenbach, M., Schmidt, M., Pfundt, B., Fey, D.: A new virtual hardware laboratory for remote FPGA experiments on real hardware. In: Proceedings of the Int. Conference on e-Learning, e-Business, Enterprise Information Systems, and

e-Government (EEE), p. 1. The Steering Committee of The World Congress in Computer Science, Computer Engineering and Applied Computing (WorldComp), USA (2011)
14. Orduña, P., et al.: Using LabVIEW remote panel in remote laboratories: advantages and disadvantages. In: Proceedings of the 2012 IEEE Global Eng. Education Conference (EDUCON), pp. 1-7, IEEE, Marrakech, Morocco (2012)
15. Monzo, C., Cobo, G., Morán, J.A., Santamaría, E., García-Solórzano, D.: Remote laboratory for online engineering education: the RLAB-UOC-FPGA case study. Electronics **10**(9), 1072 (2021)
16. Maiti, A., Maxwell, A. D., Kist, A.A.: An overview of system architectures for remote laboratories. In: Proceedings of 2013 IEEE International Conference on Teaching, Assessment and Learning for Engineering (TALE), pp. 661-666, Bali, Indonesia (2013)
17. Gomes, L., Bogosyan, S.: Current trends in remote laboratories. IEEE Trans. Industr. Electron. **56**(12), 4744–4756 (2009)
18. Samuelsen, D.A., Graven, O.H.: Remote laboratories in engineering education-an overview of implementation and feasibility. In: LACCEI International Multi-Conference for Engineering. Education and Technology, pp. 1–7. Costa Rica, San Jose (2016)
19. Tawfik, M., et al.: On the design of remote laboratories. In: Proceedings of the 2012 IEEE Global Engineering Education Conference (EDUCON), pp. 1-6, Marrakech, Morocco (2012)
20. Casadesús, M., Llach, J., Matos, V., Pons, M.: REMOTE: first insights into assessing and evaluating remote learning practices in STEM. Procedia Computer Science **232**(2024), 1172–1181 (2024)
21. Hakimi, M., Katebzadah, S., Fazil, A.W.: Comprehensive insights into e-learning in contemporary education: analyzing trends, challenges, and best practices. J. Educ. Teach. Learn. (JETL) **6**(1), 86–105 (2024)
22. Khalid, I. L., Abdullah, M.N.S., Mohd Fadzil, H.: A systematic review: digital learning in STEM education. J. Adv. Res. Appl. Sci. Eng. Technol. **51**(1), 98–115 (2024)
23. Magyari, A., Chen, Y.: FPGA remote laboratory using IoT approaches. Electronics **10**(18), 2229 (2021)
24. Alhammami, M.: FPGA hardware kit for remote training platforms. Discov. Educ. **3**(102) (2024)
25. Flores, A., Raffo, M., Balcazar, M., Yllahuamán, K.: Remote laboratory for teaching digital design using a VPN and embedded system. In: 2021 IEEE XXVIII International Conference on Electronics. Electrical Engineering and Computing (INTERCON), pp. 1–4. Lima, Peru (2021)
26. Abanto, D., Carazas, V., Solis-Lastra, J., Aramburu, C.: Implementation of a web-based interface for remote access to a FPGA board. In: 2022 IEEE Engineering International Research Conference, pp. 1-4, Lima, Peru (2022)
27. Chamunorwa, T., Modran, H.A., Ursuţiu, D., Samoilă, C.: Interactive remote laboratory platform for practical experimentation. In: 2023 6th Experiment@ International Conference, pp. 198-201, Évora, Portugal (2023)
28. Sum, R., Suwansantisuk, W., Kumhom, P.: Remote field-programmable gate array laboratory for signal acquisition and design verification. Int. J. Electr. Comput. Eng. **14**(2), 2344–2360 (2024)
29. Navas-González, R., Oballe-Peinado, Ó., Castellanos-Ramos, J., Rosas Cervantes, D., Sánchez-Durán, J.A.: Practice projects for an FPGA-Based remote laboratory to teach and learn digital electronics. Information **14**(10), 558 (2023)

30. Guerrero-Osuna, H.A., et al.: Developing a cloud and IoT-Integrated remote laboratory to enhance education 4.0: an approach for FPGA-based motor control. Appl. Sci. **14**(22), 10115 (2024)
31. Mayoz, C.A., da Silva Beraldo, A.L., Villar-Martinez, A., Rodriguez-Gil, L., de Souza Seron, W. F. M., Orduña P.: FPGA remote laboratory: experience of a shared laboratory between UPNA and UNIFESP. In: 2020 XIV Technologies Applied to Electronics Teaching Conf. TAEE, pp. 1–8. Porto, Portugal (2020)
32. Kang, L., Luo, C.: Design and implementation of hardware architecture of remote experiment platform based on field programmable gate array. In: 2024 4th International Conference on Electronic Information Engineering and Computer Science (EIECS), pp. 529-532, Yanji, China (2024)
33. Amin, R.A., et al.: FPGARLab: Leveraging FPGA design and verification using intelligent cyber physical system based collaborative remote laboratory. In: 2024 International Congress on Human-Computer Interaction. Optimization and Robotic Applications (HORA), pp. 1–8. Istanbul, Turkey (2024)
34. Lorens, A., Petukhov, G., Romanova, I.: FPGA-Based asynchronous remote laboratory for online learning. In: 2022 International Russian Automation Conference (RusAutoCon), pp. 623-627, Sochi, Russian Federation (2022)
35. Minev, P., Kukenska, V., Varbov, I., Dinev, M.: Systems for remote access to FPGA development boards: review. In: 2022 XXXI International Scientific Conference Electronics (ET), pp. 1-6, Sozopol, Bulgaria (2022)
36. Oballe-Peinado, Ó., Castellanos-Ramos, J., Sánchez-Durán, J.A., Trujillo-León, A.: Remote laboratory for multiple FPGA-Based development platforms. In: 2024 XVI Congreso de Tecnología. Aprendizaje y Enseñanza de la Electrónica (TAEE), pp. 1–5. Malaga, Spain (2024)
37. Wan, H., Liu, K., Lin, J., Gao, X.: A Web-based Remote FPGA Laboratory for Computer Organization Course. In: Proceedings of the 2019 on Great Lakes Symposium on VLSI - GLSVLSI '19 (2019).
38. Hernáiz-Pérez, M., Martín, S.: Development of remote laboratory of the FPGA iceZUM Alhambra. In: 2022 Congreso de Tecnología. Aprendizaje y Enseñanza de la Electrónica, pp. 1–5. Teruel, Spain (2022)
39. Blochwitz, C., et al.: RemEduLa - Remote Education Laboratory for FPGA Design Technology. In: 2022 IEEE International Symposium on Circuits and Systems, pp. 1773-1777, Austin, TX, USA (2022)
40. Cruz, C., et al.: Remote laboratory based on a reconfigurable hardware platform. In: 2024 XVI Congreso de Tecnología. Aprendizaje y Enseñanza de la Electrónica, pp. 1–6. Malaga, Spain (2024)
41. Oballe-Peinado, Ó., Castellanos-Ramos, J., Sánchez-Durán, J. A., Navas-González, R., Daza-Márquez, A., Botín-Córdoba, J., A.: FPGA-Based remote laboratory for digital electronics. In: 2020 XIV Technologies Applied to Electronics Teaching Conference, pp. 1-5, Porto, Portugal (2020)
42. Fujieda, N., Okuchi, A.: A novel remote FPGA lab platform using MCU-based controller board. In: 2023 IEEE International Conference on Teaching. Assessment and Learning for Engineering, pp. 1–6. Auckland, New Zealand (2023)
43. Mateos-Gil, R., De Toro, P.A.R., Madarova, S.: Remote laboratory for system on chip design based on FPGAs. In: 2022 Congreso de Tecnología. Aprendizaje y Enseñanza de la Electrónica, pp. 1–5. Teruel, Spain (2022)
44. Strelets, A.I., Yokhin, M.N., Logvinenko, I.A., Porfireva, S.A.: Multi-user system for remote work with programmable devices. In: 2024 Conference of Young Researchers in Electrical and Electronic Engineering, pp. 83-85, Saint Petersburg, Russian Federation (2024)

45. Mohsen, A.E.R., et al.: Remote FPGA lab for ZYNQ and Virtex-7 Kits. In: 2019 IEEE 62nd International Midwest Symposium on Circuits and Systems, pp. 185-188, Dallas, TX, USA (2019)
46. Al Qassem, L.M., Stouraitis, T., Damiani, E., Elfadel, I.A.M.: A remote FPGA laboratory as a Cloud Microservice. In: 2020 IEEE International Symposium on Circuits and Systems, pp. 1-5, Seville, Spain (2020)
47. Angulo, I., García-Zubía, J., Orduña, P., Rodriguez-Gil, L., Villar, A.: Integral remote laboratory for programmable logic. In: 2019 5th Experiment International Conference, pp. 253–255. Funchal, Portugal (2019)
48. Aitor, V.-M., García-Zubía, J., Angulo, I., Rodríguez-Gil, L.: Toward widespread remote laboratories: evaluating the effectiveness of a replication-based architecture for real-world multiinstitutional usage. IEEE Access **10**, 86298–86317 (2022)
49. Werner, E., Matias, J. C., Daniel Berejuck, M., Saliah-Hassane, H.: Evaluation of blockchain techniques to ensure secure access on remote FPGA laboratories. In: 2021 9th International Symposium on Digital Forensics and Security, pp. 1-6, Elazig, Turkey (2021)
50. Costa, A. S., Silveira, L. D., Reis, A. I.: Live demonstration: pitanga platform for virtual FPGA remote laboratories. In: 2023 IEEE International Symposium on Circuits and Systems, pp. 1-5, Monterey, CA, USA (2023)
51. Soto, J.G., Peña, J.G., Ariza, J.Á., Gil, S.G.: Low-Cost raspberry pi-based remote laboratory for IoT, LoRA and python programming education. In: 2024 XVI Congreso de Tecnología. Aprendizaje y Enseñanza de la Electrónica (TAEE), pp. 1–7. Malaga, Spain (2024)
52. Rejón, C., Martin, S., Robles-Gómez, A.: Easy Development of Industry 4.0 Remote Labs. Electronics **13**(8), 1508 (2024)
53. Kerimbayev, N., Umirzakova, Z., Shadiev, R. et al.: A student-centered approach using modern technologies in distance learning: a systematic review of the literature. Smart Learn. Environ. **10**(61) (2023)

Hands-On Training for Human-Centric Digital Twin in a Learning Factory Environment

Marina Crnjac Žižić[1](✉), Amanda Aljinović Meštrović[1], Boris Crnokić[2], and Ivan Peko[3]

[1] Faculty of Electrical Engineering, Mechanical Engineering and Naval Architecture, University of Split, Split, Croatia
{mcrnjac,amaljino}@fesb.hr

[2] Faculty of Mechanical Engineering, Computing and Electrical Engineering, University of Mostar, Mostar, Bosnia and Herzegovina
boris.crnokic@sum.ba

[3] Faculty of Science, University of Split, Split, Croatia
ivan.peko@fesb.hr

Abstract. The rapid development of market demand and the pursuit of sustainable industrial practices require a change in production and business models. This transformation is being driven by new technologies such as cyber-physical systems (CPS), the Internet of Things (IoT) and cloud computing. Human-centric digital twins (HCDTs) play a crucial role in this transformation as they put people at the heart of digitalization. By integrating human data, ergonomics and real-time interactions, HCDTs not only optimize efficiency, but also improve workplace safety, employee well-being and adaptability. This approach supports the development of flexible, customized and resilient production systems that align with the goals of Industry 4.0 and sustainability. The learning factory environment at the University of Split, Faculty of Electrical Engineering, Mechanical Engineering, and Naval Architecture (FESB), provides an applied education platform that combines academic knowledge with industrial requirements. This program offers students, and industry partners the opportunity to engage in real-world projects focused on the implementation of HCDT. Participants gain hands-on experience using sensors and CPS to collect and analyze data and use modeling and simulation tools to create digital twins. By working in a collaborative environment, students develop critical problem-solving skills while industry partners explore innovative solutions to optimize production processes. This hands-on training provides the participants with the knowledge and technical skills they need to integrate new technologies into engineering and industrial applications, driving innovation and competitiveness in the evolving manufacturing landscape.

Keywords: human-centric digital twins · engineering education innovation · development of hands-on training programs · learning factory · process management · ExCurS project

D. Vasić and E. Brajković (Eds.): MoStart 2025, CCIS 2609, pp. 124–136, 2026.
https://doi.org/10.1007/978-3-032-02801-3_8

1 Introduction

Digital twins (DT) are virtual replicas of physical systems. Digital twins are revolutionizing the industry by bridging the gap between digital and the real world. A Human-Centric Digital Twin (HCDT) is a continuously evolving digital model of a human operator, updated in real-time to improve learning, safety, and efficiency in industrial and educational environments. Unlike traditional digital twins, which primarily focus on machines and processes, HCDTs are oriented towards human-centricity. Their growing importance in engineering education cannot be overstated, as they give students the opportunity to explore, simulate and optimize complex systems in a controlled, risk-free and sustainable environment. By integrating digital twins into the curriculum, future engineers gain hands-on experience with cutting-edge tools, preparing them to develop and manage the sophisticated systems of tomorrow. The approach presented in this paper highlights the urgent need to equip students with the skills required to unlock their potential, serving as a foundational step in advancing sustainable, efficient, and innovative solutions within the rapidly evolving technological landscape. Teaching digital twins in engineering education requires a specific approach to ensure that students gain practical skills and a deep understanding of this transformative technology. The learning factory environment at the University of Split, Faculty of Electrical Engineering, Mechanical Engineering, and Naval Architecture (FESB), provides an applied education platform that combines academic knowledge with industrial requirements. This program offers students, and industry partners the opportunity to engage in real-world projects focused on the implementation of HCDT. By integrating human data, ergonomics and real-time interactions, HCDTs not only optimize efficiency, but also improve workplace safety, employee well-being and adaptability. This approach supports the development of flexible, customized and resilient production systems that align with the goals of Industry 4.0 and Industry 5.0.

2 Learning Factory Environment

The Learning Factory (LF) is a creative and innovative approach to acquiring long-term knowledge. For an environment to be classified as an LF environment, it must fulfill certain requirements. An environment that replicates a real industrial environment as closely as possible and meets the requirements of replicating authentic work processes (both organizationally and technical), producing a real product and integrating a comprehensive didactic concept can be described as a Learning Factory environment [1]. This learning approach focuses on the practical application of theoretical knowledge and thus bridges the gap between learning theory and the understanding of its practical application. The aim of this approach is to give participants (e.g., students and industry employees) the opportunity to directly intervene in production processes, solve real problems and make decisions based on the acquired knowledge. In this way, participants acquire comprehensive professional knowledge and skills tailored to the requirements of industry. This strengthens their self-confidence, improves their problem-solving skills and prepares them for the challenges of the real job market. The positive effects of the LF concept on the skills development of future and current employees have been proven by various studies and practical applications [2, 3]. For example, since the introduction of the LF concept, there has been a significant increase in the number of learning factories worldwide, with growth trends for the future. This underlines that their value is being recognized worldwide. The long-term success of learning factories depends on the integration of new and engaging content into their learning programs. To achieve this, it is important to establish dependencies between research, education, training and knowledge transfer from factory to industry. Figure 1 illustrates these dependencies and highlights the necessary synergy between these aspects to ensure a dynamic and constantly evolving learning environment.

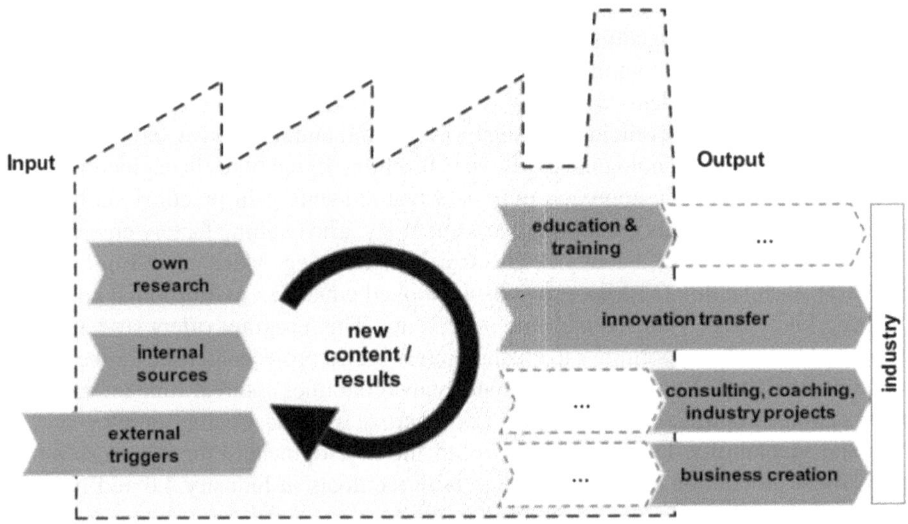

Fig. 1. Dependencies in the learning factories [1]

As a member of an International Association of Learning Factories, the Learning Factory is developing at the Faculty of Electrical Engineering, Mechanical Engineering and Naval Architecture. This LF is being developed and expanded through numerous important research projects, with each project contributing to its further improvement. These projects focus on the integration of advanced technologies, the improvement of production processes and the development of innovative solutions, all of which are actively applied within the framework of collaboration between education and industry. Through this collaboration, these initiatives not only promote academic knowledge and the training of industry personnel but also contribute directly to the creation of new industrial practices and the development of real-world solutions. The main projects that have contributed to and guided the development of this UAA are the following research projects [4]:

- ExCurS - An Excellence based Curriculum for the Improvement of LEAN & Green Management Skills in SME (ExCurS) project focused on lifelong learning and the development of an excellence-based curriculum to improve lean & green management skills in small and medium-sized enterprises. The research presented in this paper

is based on the educational and practical activities carried out as part of the ExCurS project, particularly those focused on application and training related to Digital Twins.
- EU-TEMPUS MAS-PLM – this project focused on product life cycle management (PLM) with sustainable production methods (SP). It aimed to create a framework for the management of products during their life cycle.
- DAAD NIL – this project focused on building a network of innovative learning factories to facilitate the transfer of knowledge between institutions and to intensify the scientific development of learning factory systems.
- EU-LDV LOPEC – this project focused on the development of lifelong learning programs, especially in the field of lean management.
- HRZZ INSENT – the ultimate goal of this project was to develop the Croatian model for innovative intelligent enterprises (HR-ISE model).
- UKF DEPROCIM – this project focused on the development of an integrative procedure for the management of production and service improvement processes.

As part of these projects, LF integrates cutting-edge technologies such as data-driven infrastructure, advanced sensors and actuators, and various software to create digital twins and optimize the entire production process. In this way, the LF at FESB has become an important platform for the integration of theoretical learning and practical application. Furthermore, this LF environment is constantly evolving, with new projects and initiatives contributing to its growth to ensure compliance with industrial requirements.

2.1 Learning Factory at FESB

LF at FESB is divided into five main departments according to functional areas:

1. PC workstations are equipped with various software such as Siemens NX, visTABLE, Tecnomatix and Matlab. This software is used for CAD/CAM purposes, optimization of the entire production process, layout optimization, production simulation, data analysis and visualization, etc.
2. Special areas for training and research on assembly line topics. These areas include two assembly lines where participants study the principles of lean manufacturing, work organization, material flow, assembly line balance and other topics related to assembly line optimization.
3. Space for workshops for students and industry employees.
4. Small machine workshop – for the production of necessary parts for the learning factory.
5. A place where collaboration between humans and robots can be learned, equipped with two robots - Franka Emika Panda and Dobot Magician.

The layout of the LF at the FESB and some of its equipment are shown in Fig. 2.

One of the focal points in the current and future development of this LF is the development of Human-Centric Digital Twins (HCDTs) and their integration into industrial training. To this end, technologies are currently being integrated and developed that enable data acquisition, simulation and real-time monitoring of data. With this goal in mind, the Learning Factory uses a combination of advanced devices and cutting-edge technologies, including Siemens Tecnomatix for simulation and process modeling,

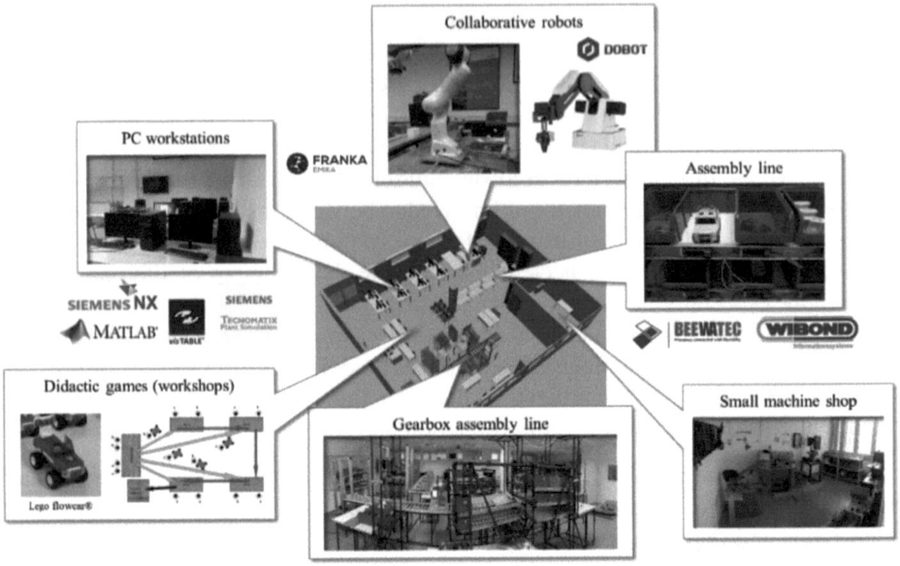

Fig. 2. Layout of the LF at FESB and some of its equipment

which enables the development of a virtual representation of production processes and their optimization. In addition, Arduino sensors and microcontrollers are used for real-time data acquisition, while the Arduino Cloud enables data management and visualization of the collected and analyzed data. These technologies work together to create an interactive learning environment that allows participants to simulate industrial processes, monitor them in real time and improve their hands-on experience and understanding of the use and benefits of Industry 4.0 technologies.

3 Human-Centric Digital Twin (HCDT)

The idea of a Human-Centric Digital Twin (HCDT) is becoming increasingly important in smart manufacturing and digital education. Essentially, an HCDT is a virtual representation of a human operator, created by combining real-time data, artificial intelligence (AI), and cyber-physical systems (CPS). This allows for a more interactive and adaptive experience, improving how people engage with both digital and physical environments. In this chapter, we'll take a closer look at what HCDTs are, their key characteristics, and the features that make them useful. We'll also explore their benefits and drawbacks, particularly in learning factories—hands-on environments where students and professionals develop practical skills in digital transformation.

As Uhlemann et al. [5] explain, a digital twin acts as a virtual counterpart to a physical entity, enabling real-time monitoring and simulation. The human-centric approach expands on this idea by incorporating human behavior, decision-making, and ergonomics, ensuring that technology adapts to people, not the other way around [6].

3.1 Characteristics of Human-Centric Digital Twins (HCDTs)

Human-Centric Digital Twins (HCDTs) stand apart from traditional digital twins due to their focus on the human element within digital environments. Unlike conventional models that primarily simulate machines and processes, HCDTs incorporate real-time human data to enhance learning, productivity, and safety. These advanced systems possess several defining characteristics that make them particularly valuable in industrial and educational settings.

One of the most significant aspects of HCDTs is their ability to capture and analyze human activities, physiological responses, and cognitive load in a digital environment. By monitoring factors such as heart rate, eye movement, stress levels, and decision-making processes, HCDTs create a comprehensive digital profile of the individual. This allows for a deeper understanding of how humans interact with machines and digital systems, enabling tailored interventions to improve efficiency and well-being. A key feature of HCDTs is their ability to synchronize with real-world human actions and system interactions in real-time. Unlike static digital models, these dynamic twins continuously update based on data streams from sensors, wearables, and other input sources. This ensures that the digital representation remains accurate and reflective of the human operator's current state, allowing for immediate adjustments in training, workflow optimization, and safety measures. Artificial intelligence (AI) plays a crucial role in the functionality of HCDTs. Machine learning algorithms analyze collected data to personalize experiences, predict potential errors, and enhance decision-making processes. By recognizing patterns in behavior and performance, AI-driven HCDTs can provide personalized guidance, suggest alternative actions, and even preemptively correct mistakes before they occur. This makes them particularly valuable in high-risk industrial environments and complex learning scenarios where human error can have significant consequences. HCDTs are designed to seamlessly integrate with a range of emerging technologies, including the Internet of Things (IoT), augmented reality (AR), and virtual reality (VR). This interoperability enhances the immersive learning experience by providing interactive and realistic simulations. For example, an HCDT can be connected to an AR headset to overlay real-time data on a user's field of view, offering contextual guidance while performing a task. Similarly, VR environments can simulate real-world scenarios, allowing users to practice skills in a safe and controlled digital space. A distinctive advantage of HCDTs is their ability to provide continuous feedback to users. Through data analysis and AI-driven insights, individuals receive real-time assessments of their performance, allowing them to self-improve and adapt their learning strategies. This feature is especially beneficial in learning factories—industrial training environments where students and professionals gain hands-on experience with digital transformation technologies. By offering instant feedback, HCDTs help learners refine their skills, optimize their workflows, and build confidence in real-world applications [7, 8]. Figure 3 presents human-centric digital twin framework with above discussed components.

The unique characteristics of Human-Centric Digital Twins make them powerful tools for bridging the gap between humans and digital systems. By prioritizing human integration, real-time synchronization, AI-driven adaptation, interoperability with advanced technologies, and continuous feedback, HCDTs offer a dynamic and personalized approach to learning and productivity enhancement. As industries and educational institutions continue to embrace digital transformation, the role of HCDTs will become increasingly vital in ensuring that technology serves and supports human capabilities rather than replacing them.

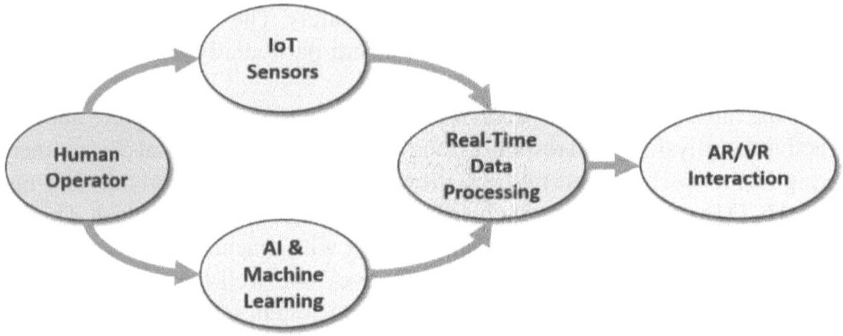

Fig. 3. Human-Centric Digital Twin Framework

3.2 The Role of Human-Centric Digital Twins in Learning Factories

A learning factory is an advanced training environment designed to mimic real-world industrial settings, enabling learners to develop hands-on expertise in Industry 4.0 technologies. These environments provide a bridge between theoretical knowledge and practical application, preparing students and professionals for the evolving demands of smart manufacturing. The integration of Human-Centric Digital Twins (HCDTs) into learning factories introduces a range of innovative features that enhance training effectiveness, improve safety, and personalize the learning experience.

One of the most impactful ways HCDTs transform learning factories is through augmented reality (AR) and virtual reality (VR) simulations. By integrating these technologies with digital twins, learners can engage in highly realistic training scenarios without facing the risks associated with real-world industrial environments. Learning effectiveness depends on a person's ability to process and retain information without becoming overwhelmed. HCDTs leverage AI-driven biometric sensors to monitor cognitive load factors, such as stress, fatigue, and engagement levels [9, 10]. These sensors track real-time physiological responses, including heart rate variability, eye movement, and brain activity, to assess whether a learner is struggling or disengaged. If an individual shows signs of excessive cognitive load, the training system can adjust the difficulty level, introduce breaks, or offer additional guidance, ensuring a more effective and personalized learning experience. Every learner has a unique pace and preferred learning style. HCDTs use AI and real-time performance assessments to tailor training pathways based on individual needs [9, 11]. For instance, if a learner consistently struggles with a particular task, the system can modify the curriculum by offering step-by-step instructions, additional practice modules, or interactive troubleshooting guidance. Modern factories increasingly rely on human-robot collaboration to improve efficiency and productivity. However, ensuring seamless interaction between human operators and industrial robots requires precise coordination. HCDTs facilitate this collaboration by acting as a digital interface between humans and robotic systems. By analyzing movement patterns, predicting human actions, and adjusting robotic responses in real-time, HCDTs help minimize risks, improve safety protocols, and enhance productivity. One of the biggest challenges in workforce training is assessing and validating acquired skills. HCDTs provide an objective, data-driven approach to skill assessment by tracking real-time training performance. These systems can analyze how accurately and efficiently a learner completes a task, compare it against industry benchmarks, and generate personalized competency reports [10, 12, 13].

The integration of Human-Centric Digital Twins (HCDTs) in learning factories represents a significant advancement in Industry 4.0 education and workforce training. By offering immersive simulations, cognitive load monitoring, adaptive learning pathways, human-robot collaboration support, and real-time skill validation, HCDTs create a personalized and highly effective learning environment. As industries continue to embrace digital transformation, learning factories equipped with HCDTs will play a crucial role in preparing the next generation of professionals—ensuring they are skilled, adaptable, and ready for the challenges of the modern industrial landscape, Fig. 4.

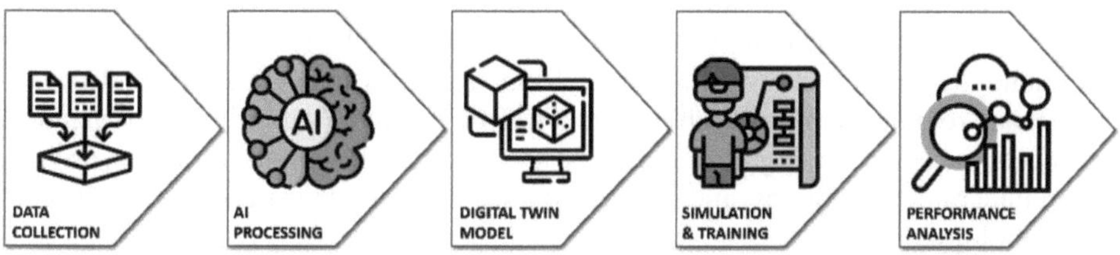

Fig. 4. Workflow of Human-Centric Digital Twin in Learning Factories

3.3 Advantages and Challenges of Human-Centric Digital Twins in Learning Factories

The integration of Human-Centric Digital Twins (HCDTs) in learning factories is transforming how industrial training is delivered. By leveraging real-time data, artificial intelligence, and digital modeling, HCDTs provide a highly interactive, adaptive, and data-driven learning experience. However, while these innovations offer numerous benefits, they also introduce challenges that must be carefully addressed to ensure effective implementation.

Traditional training methods often follow a one-size-fits-all approach, which can lead to inefficiencies and frustration for learners with different skill levels and learning styles. HCDTs personalize the learning experience by continuously analyzing individual performance and adapting training modules accordingly. These digital models provide customized feedback, recommendations, and learning pathways, ensuring that each learner progresses at their own pace. One of the most significant benefits of HCDTs is the ability to simulate high-risk industrial environments without exposing learners to real-world dangers. Through virtual reality (VR) and augmented reality (AR) integrations, trainees can practice handling hazardous equipment, emergency scenarios, and complex manufacturing processes in a controlled digital environment. In traditional training settings, assessing skill acquisition can be time-consuming and subjective. HCDTs address this issue by continuously monitoring and analyzing learner performance in real-time. Metrics such as task completion time, accuracy, and cognitive load help educators refine teaching strategies and provide immediate, data-driven feedback. Artificial intelligence and machine learning algorithms embedded in HCDTs generate valuable insights into learner progress, skill gaps, and overall training effectiveness. This data helps educators, training managers, and industry leaders make informed decisions about curriculum design, workforce readiness, and resource allocation. The ability to access HCDT-based training remotely is particularly valuable in today's fast-changing work environment. Learners can interact with digital twin environments from anywhere, using VR headsets, tablets, or computers. This flexibility makes industrial training more accessible to students, remote workers, and professionals seeking to upskill, reducing geographical and logistical barriers to education [12].

Despite their transformative potential, HCDTs face several challenges that must be addressed to maximize their effectiveness and acceptance [13]. These challenges are shown in Fig. 5.

While Human-Centric Digital Twins (HCDTs) offer game-changing advantages in learning factories, their implementation comes with notable challenges. Personalized training, enhanced safety, real-time performance assessment, data-driven decision-making, and remote learning capabilities make HCDTs valuable tools for modern industrial education. However, organizations must address concerns around cost, data privacy, system integration, AI biases, and user acceptance to ensure the successful adoption of this technology.

As industries continue to evolve with Industry 4.0 advancements, the refinement and accessibility of HCDTs will play a critical role in shaping the future of workforce training. Overcoming these challenges will be key to fully unlocking the potential of digital twins in preparing the next generation of skilled professionals for the smart factories of tomorrow.

4 Hands-On Training for HCDT

The integration of Human-Centric Digital Twins (HCDTs) into industrial education requires a structured approach that combines technological feasibility with practical application. The main motivation for developing such approach is to ensure that students or other participants not only understand the theoretical aspects of digital twins, but also gain practical experience that will improve their problem-solving and decision-making skills in real industrial environments. A well-designed implementation strategy enables students and industry partners to capture, analyze and optimize processes in real time, improving both productivity and ergonomics in the workplace.

To demonstrate this process, an assembly workstation is selected as a case study where Arduino-based sensors, Arduino Cloud and Siemens Tecnomatix are combined to create a dynamic, data-driven learning environment. This approach enables real-time monitoring of human and material movements, which are incorporated into a digital

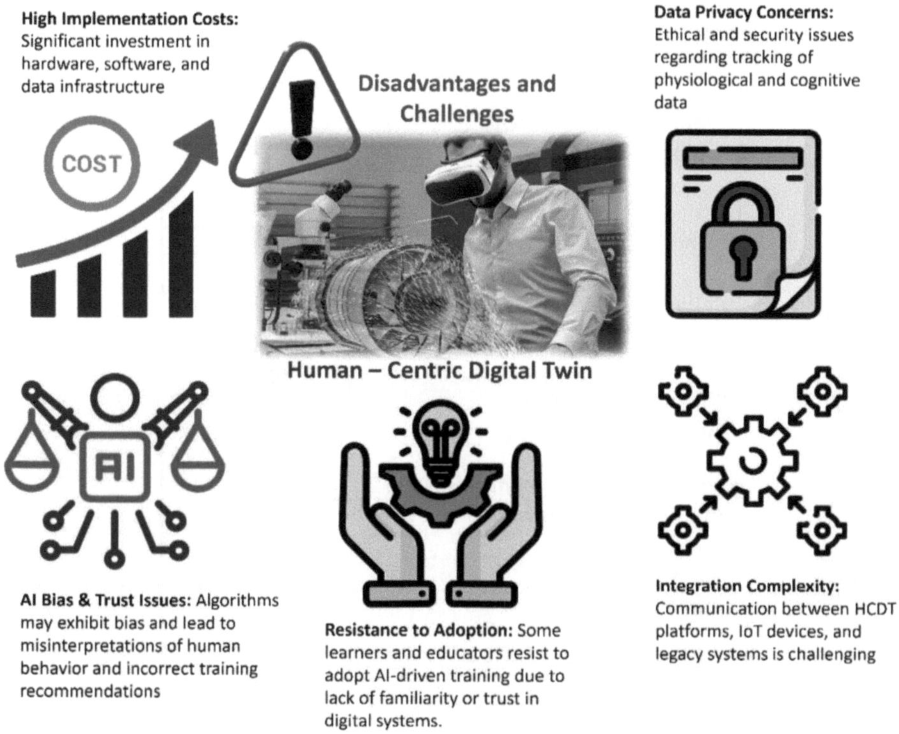

Fig. 5. Disadvantages and challenges of Human-Centric Digital Twin

twin model that simulates and optimizes assembly tasks. Through a structured training program, participants gain hands-on experience with decision regarding necessary equipment, sensor integration, cloud-based data management and digital twin modeling. This provides them essential skills for Industry 4.0 and beyond. The following section outlines the step-by-step methodology for implementing HCDTs in an assembly process to ensure a seamless fusion of digitalization and human-centricity, Fig. 6.

Hands-on training for human-centric digital twin in a learning factory environment begins with a preliminary questionnaire to select suitable technologies and equipment required to create a customized digital twin model for specific process. Participants complete a structured questionnaire to identify the most appropriate equipment for their specific HCDT facility. This questionnaire covers aspects such as the type of sensors needed, compatibility with Arduino and communication protocols, cloud integration requirements and the required inputs and outputs for Tecnomatix simulation. Based on the answers, customized recommendations are given for the selection of suitable hardware, software and connectivity solutions. Once the questionnaire has been completed, the equipment is selected. Participants select Arduino-compatible sensors, actuators and controllers according to their needs. They also select cloud-based platforms for data acquisition and real-time visualization and ensure that the chosen solutions meet the requirements for the integration of the digital twin. In addition, software tools such as

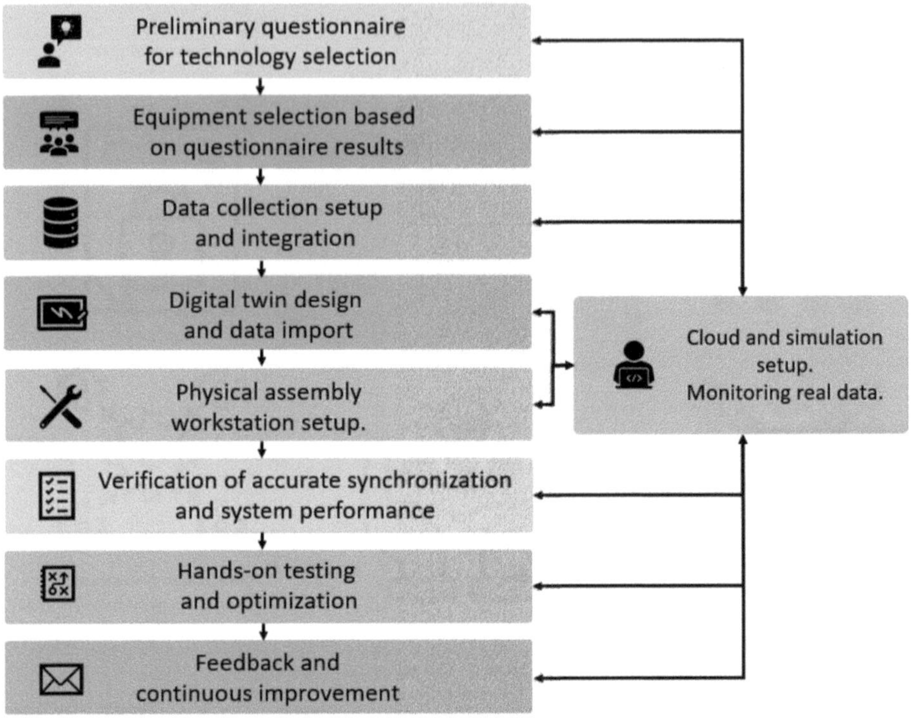

Fig. 6. Procedure for HCDT hands-on training

Siemens Tecnomatix and Arduino IDE are used to enable programming, simulation and real-time data processing. After the selection phase, the data acquisition is set up and integrated. Sensors and actuators are physically connected to Arduino-based systems, and communication protocols such as MQTT are set up to enable real-time data transfer. Cloud connectivity will be configured to enable seamless data acquisition and monitoring to ensure the system can capture and analyze relevant information for further use in digital twin simulations. The functionality of data collection and transmission is tested to verify its reliability. The next step involves digital twin design and data import into Tecnomatix simulation. Siemens Tecnomatix is used to create a virtual assembly process, integrating real-time sensor data into the digital twin environment. The synchronization between real-world process data and the digital representation is ensured. This phase enables a comprehensive comparison between expected and actual process results. Once the digital model has been created, the physical assembly workstation is set up. The selected Arduino devices are used in a real assembly environment and the workstation is integrated into the digital twin simulation to enable bidirectional data exchange. Ergonomic and safety conditions are also evaluated to ensure optimal working conditions for the operators. With the physical and digital environments in place, verification of accurate synchronization and system performance is conducted. Real-time data connections between physical sensors and Tecnomatix are tested to confirm that the digital twin accurately reflects the real-world process. After verification, the participants test and optimize the digital twin system in practice. They conduct experiments to optimize the process parameters, analyze the differences between the digital and physical setups and make necessary adjustments to sensor placement, data acquisition settings or connection configurations. In this phase, the overall efficiency and reliability of the system is improved. The training concludes with feedback and continuous improvement, with participants reflecting on their experiences, evaluating the usability and accuracy of the system and making recommendations for further improvements. Any issues identified with the hardware setup, cloud configurations or digital twin simulations are addressed through iterative changes. Real assembly station at LF is shown in Fig. 7. It is demonstrated how the cloud and the simulation setup enable real-time monitoring of the data. The Arduino Cloud ensures that the sensor data is continuously recorded and visualized, while Tecnomatix validates the accuracy of the digital twin's responses. The monitoring of real-time data helps maintain stable and reliable system operation and enables further development of the HCDT framework for future industrial applications.

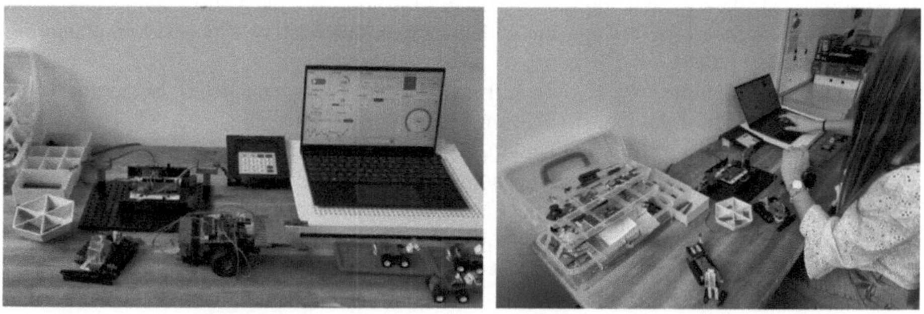

Fig. 7. Assembly station for HCDT hands-on training

This structured approach to hands-on training ensures that participants develop practical skills in the integration of real-time data, the use of cloud-based monitoring and the validation of digital twin simulations. It provides a comprehensive learning experience that enhances their ability to design and implement efficient, human-centric production systems.

5 Conclusion

Teaching digital twins in engineering education requires a deliberate and innovative approach to prepare students for the demands of modern industry. By integrating real-world applications, encouraging hands-on learning, utilizing advanced tools, and fostering interdisciplinary collaboration, educators can ensure that students develop both practical skills and a deep understanding of this transformative technology. Continuous updates to course content, the use of simulations, and professional development for faculty further enhance the learning experience.

Research also underscores the effectiveness of these methods. Studies show that students who use digital twin systems often perform better in critical thinking and academic achievement than their peers. Project-based learning initiatives have proven successful in fostering creativity and interdisciplinary collaboration. In addition, there is evidence that the integration of digital twins significantly increases student motivation and engagement. These findings underscore the importance of using digital twin technologies in education to provide future engineers with tools to compete in the rapidly evolving technological landscape.

Acknowledgments. This research was supported by the EU Erasmus+ "ExCurS" project [grant number 2022-1-ES01-KA220-VET-000086786].

References

1. Abele, E., Metternich, J., Tisch, M., Kreß, A.: Learning factories: Featuring new concepts, guidelines, worldwide best-practice examples, Springer
2. Mladineo, M., Veža, I., Gjeldum, N., Crnjac, M., Bašić, A.: Integration and testing of the RFID-enabled Smart Factory concept within the Learning Factory. Procedia Manufacturing, p. 31, 384–389 (2019)
3. Capetillo, A.T., Ramirez, R.: Evolution from triple helix into penta helix: the case of Nuevo Leon 4.0 and the push for industry 4.0. Int. J. Indust. Eng. Manage
4. Meštrović, A., Crnjac Žižić, M., Crnokić, B., Peko, I., Gjeldum, M.: Learning factory environment for education, science and technology applications. In: 13 International Conference Mechanical Technologies and Structural Materials. Split, Croatia (2024)
5. Uhlemann, T., Lehmann, C., Steinhilper, R.: The digital twin: realizing the cyber-physical production system for industry 4.0. Procedia CIRP **61**, 335–340 (2017)
6. Tao, F., Cheng, J., Qi, Q., Zhang, M., Zhang, H.: Digital twin-driven product de-sign, manufacturing and service with big data. Int. J. Adv. Manufac. Technol. **94**, 3563–3576 (2018)
7. Krupas, M., Kajati, E., Liu, C., Zolotova, I.: Towards a human-centric digital twin for human–machine collaboration: a review on enabling technologies and methods. Sensors **24**(7), 2232 (2024)
8. Peruzzini, M., Bilancia, P., Majić, T., Ostrosi, E., Stjepandić, J.: Human-centric digital twin: a transdisciplinary view. Leveraging Transdisciplinary Engineering in a Changing and Connected World, pp. 923–932 (2023). https://doi.org/10.3233/ATDE230690
9. Brunke, J., Bießmann, F., Fette, M., Stark, R.: Cognitive digital twins: a framework for human-centric AI in manufacturing. Manufac. Let. **31**, 1–6 (2022)
10. Asad, U., Khan, M., Khalid, A., Lughmani, W.A.: Human-Centric Digital Twins in Industry: a comprehensive review of enabling technologies and implementation strategies. Sensors (2023). https://doi.org/10.3390/s23083938
11. Fehling, M., Thees, M., Bähr, S.: Learning factories in the age of digitalization: trends and developments in education for industry 4.0. Procedia Manufac. **55**, 198–204 (2021)
12. Aivaliotis, P., Georgoulias, K., Arkouli, Z., Xant, Z.: Methodology for enabling digital twin using advanced physics-based modelling in predictive maintenance. Procedia CIRP, pp. 81, 417–422 (2019)
13. Grieves, M., Vickers, J.: Digital twin: mitigating unpredictable, undesirable emergent behavior in complex systems. In: Kahlen, J., Flumerfelt, S., Alves, A. (eds.) Transdisciplinary Perspectives on Complex Systems. Springer, Cham (2017). https://doi.org/10.1007/978-3-319-38756-7_4

Ask Not What Math Can Do for AI, Ask What AI Can Do for Math (Education)

Krešimir Rakić[1](✉) and Ivana Međugorac Rakić[2]

[1] Faculty of Mechanical Engineering, Computing and Electrical Engineering, University of Mostar, Matice hrvatske b.b., 88000 Mostar, Bosnia and Herzegovina
kresimir.rakic@fsre.sum.ba

[2] Secondary School of Civil Engineering Juraj Dalmatinac, Kralja Zvonimira 24, 88000 Mostar, Bosnia and Herzegovina
ivana.medugorac.rakic@skole.sum.ba

Abstract. Artificial intelligence in education is bringing significant changes to the way learning and teaching is done, and its application in mathematics teaching opens up numerous opportunities for improving the educational process. There is a clear connection between mathematics and artificial intelligence, as many AI algorithms and technologies base their functionalities on mathematical principles, such as statistics, linear algebra, and optimization theory. This article explores the mathematical foundations that support the development of artificial intelligence, emphasizing how mathematics provides the foundation for understanding and implementing AI technologies. The emphasis of the article will be on the application of artificial intelligence in mathematics teaching, with the aim of improving the experience of students and teachers. AI enables personalized learning, where mathematical models are used to adapt tasks and teaching content to the specific needs of each student. This research will explain how artificial intelligence can help optimize teaching methods, improve learning efficiency, and support the development of metacognitive skills in students. Although the advantages of applying artificial intelligence in education are significant, it is important to consider the challenges and obstacles that may be encountered in implementing this technology in order to fully utilize its potential in mathematics teaching.

Keywords: Artificial Intelligence · Mathematics · Education

1 Introduction

Artificial intelligence (AI) is no longer just a vision of the future but a key component of modern society. Every day, we witness its ability to automate complex tasks, recognize patterns in data, and make decisions based on the analysis of vast amounts of information. Its applications span domains ranging from medical diagnostics and financial analysis to autonomous vehicles and advanced educational systems. However, while AI is often viewed as a technological phenomenon, its core lies in mathematics.

Mathematics is the foundation on which all the key algorithms that enable AI to work are built. From linear algebra, which handles operations on vectors and matrices,

D. Vasić and E. Brajković (Eds.): MoStart 2025, CCIS 2609, pp. 137–150, 2026.
https://doi.org/10.1007/978-3-032-02801-3_9

to differential and integral calculus, which enables model optimization, to probability theory and statistics, which help learn from data – every advance in AI relies on mathematical principles. Without mathematical methods, there would be no neural networks, machine learning (ML) algorithms, or sophisticated models that solve challenges in science, industry, and everyday life today.

However, while mathematics is crucial for the development of AI, we can also ask the opposite question: can AI contribute to the advancement of mathematics, especially in the field of mathematics education? Traditional approaches to teaching mathematics often encounter challenges in understanding abstract concepts and applying theoretical knowledge to real-world problems. However, with the development of AI tools, new opportunities are opening up for interactive learning, visualization of mathematical ideas, and customized teaching methods that meet the individual needs of students.

This paper explores the ways in which AI can become a support for mathematics education, not only as a tool for solving problems but also as a means of fostering deeper understanding and creative thinking. If mathematics enabled the emergence of AI, it is time to ask ourselves how AI can help improve mathematical literacy and modernize teaching methods.

The second chapter provides an overview of mathematicians who have significantly contributed to the establishment of the scientific field of AI and lists the branches of mathematics that provide strong support for modern methods and techniques of AI. The third chapter lists aspects of mathematics education in which AI can significantly improve educational practice, as well as the challenges and issues that the use of AI in mathematics education potentially poses.

2 Mathematical Foundations of Artificial Intelligence

Mathematics is the foundation of AI because it enables precise modelling and analysis of problems related to ML, logic, optimization, and data processing. Without mathematical concepts such as linear algebra, statistics, probability theory, and computational logic, the development of AI would not be possible. The work of numerous mathematicians laid a solid foundation upon which the modern field of AI developed.

2.1 Pioneers of Mathematics in the Development of Artificial Intelligence

One of the first mathematicians whose work significantly influenced AI was George Boole, a British mathematician and philosopher (1815–1864), who developed Boolean algebra, a binary logic system that uses logical operations such as conjunction (AND), disjunction (OR), and negation (NOT). This algebra enabled the development of digital circuits and later logic systems that are the basis of AI. His work enabled the formalization of mathematical logic, which is used today in expert systems and logic programming [1].

Norbert Wiener, an American mathematician and engineer (1894–1964), introduced the concept of cybernetics, a scientific discipline that studies systems that use feedback for regulation and adaptation. Cybernetics was fundamental for the development of robotic systems and adaptive algorithms in AI [2]. Wiener's work enabled the development of models of machines that can learn and adapt based on feedback from the environment.

John von Neumann, a Hungarian-American mathematician and physicist (1903–1957), made key contributions to AI by developing computer architecture and game theory. Von Neumann architecture, which defines the structure of modern computers with memory, processors, and stored programs, became the foundation of the computer systems on which AI algorithms are executed today. His game theory also enabled the mathematical modelling of strategic decisions, which is useful in optimization and autonomous AI systems [3].

Andrey Kolmogorov, a Russian mathematician (1903–1987), whose work in probability theory and statistics enabled the development of probabilistic models of ML. His 1933 axioms of probability theory became standard in data analysis and statistical learning, including Bayesian networks and Markov models, which are now widely used in AI [4].

After him, Kurt Gödel, an Austrian mathematician and logician (1906–1978), proved with his incompleteness theorems in 1931 that in every formal system, there are true statements that cannot be proven within that system. These theorems set philosophical and technical limits to the possibilities of computation and decision-making, which is important for understanding the limitations of AI [5].

Alan Turing, a British mathematician and computer scientist (1912–1954), is considered one of the founders of AI. His 1936 concept of the Turing machine defined a formal model of computation that proved that any algorithm could be executed on an abstract machine [6]. He also proposed the Turing test in 1950, a criterion for assessing whether a machine could exhibit intelligent behaviour equivalent to human behaviour [7]. His research laid the foundation for the later development of AI and ML algorithms.

Claude Shannon, an American mathematician and electrical engineer (1916–2001), laid the foundations of information theory, quantifying the concept of information and developing methods for its efficient encoding and transmission. His work enabled the development of algorithms for data processing, optimizing information transmission, and saving memory resources, which is essential for neural networks and ML [8]. Also, his connection between Boolean algebra and electronic circuits enabled the emergence of digital computers [9].

The development of AI would not have been possible without these mathematicians and their ideas. Their contributions, from logic and information theory to probabilistic models and neural networks, form the foundation of today's intelligent systems. Thanks to mathematics, AI can analyze large amounts of data, learn from experience, and adapt to new situations, which allows it to be widely used in various fields of science and technology.

2.2 Modern Applications of Mathematics in Artificial Intelligence

Various branches of mathematics provide tools for data processing, pattern learning, and decision-making in complex systems. Through theoretical concepts and practical methods, mathematics enables the development of sophisticated AI models that are applied in various fields, from language processing to computer vision. The following are mathematical approaches that significantly shape contemporary AI techniques and contribute to their efficiency and reliability [10].

Linear algebra enables the manipulation and analysis of high-dimensional data, which is essential for many AI algorithms. Techniques such as eigenvalues and eigenvectors are used in Principal Component Analysis (PCA) to reduce the dimensionality of data, thereby reducing model complexity and improving computational efficiency [11]. Singular Value Decomposition (SVD) is also used in Natural Language Processing (NLP) to uncover latent semantic structures in text [12]. In addition, matrix operations are essential in working with deep neural networks, where the weight parameters of the network are represented by matrices, and the propagation of signals through the layers of the model is based on matrix multiplication and the application of activation functions [13]. In computer vision, linear algebra is used for image transformations, such as scaling, rotation, and translation, which enable advanced image processing techniques in AI systems [14].

Differential calculus is essential for function optimization, the basis for training ML models. The gradient descent algorithm uses gradient computation to minimize a loss function, allowing models to learn from data [15]. Integral calculus, on the other hand, is used to calculate areas under curves and probabilities, which are important in many probabilistic models [16]. Differential calculus also plays a key role in computing Jacobians and Hessians, which enable more efficient iterations in optimization algorithms [17]. In fields such as computer vision and neural networks, differential calculus allows for the analysis of changes in image pixels and the calculation of gradients, which are essential for training deep learning models [18].

Probability theory provides a framework for modelling uncertainty and making decisions based on incomplete information. Bayesian networks are used to model probabilistic relationships between variables, enabling prediction and inference in complex systems [19]. Statistical methods, such as regression analysis, allow for the identification of relationships between variables and the prediction of outcomes [20]. Markov chains and hidden Markov models (HMMs) play a key role in modelling sequential data, which is used in speech recognition and time series analysis [21]. Furthermore, Bayes' theorem is applied in classification algorithms such as the Naive Bayes classifier, which is often used in text analysis and spam filtering [22].

Optimization is the core of many AI algorithms, where the goal is to find the best solution within given constraints. Convex optimization allows solving problems where the objective function is convex, which ensures a globally optimal solution [23]. Non-convex optimization deals with more complex problems where the objective function may have multiple local minima, which requires more advanced methods to find the globally optimal solution [24]. Evolutionary algorithms, such as genetic algorithms and swarm optimization methods (eg. Particle Swarm Optimization, PSO), are used to solve problems that do not have exact solutions [25]. In neural networks, optimization plays a key role in fine-tuning hyperparameters, which significantly improves the performance of ML models [26].

Graph theory enables the modelling and analysis of networks and relationships between objects. In AI, graphs are used to represent data structures, such as social networks or neural networks. Graph search algorithms, Breadth-First Search (BFS) and

Depth-First Search (DFS) are used in path planning and social network analysis [27], while Graph Convolutional Neural networks (GCNs) have become key in analyzing data structured as graphs [28]. Applications of graph theory are also seen in anomaly detection in online data, where techniques such as the PageRank algorithm have been applied to fraud detection and web link analysis [29].

Discrete mathematics encompasses the study of discrete structures and is used in algorithms, cryptography and information theory. Set theory and logic are important for ML design, enabling the definition of relations and inference rules [30]. Automata and formal languages are used in NLP and pattern recognition in data [31]. Number theory has applications in cryptography, which is key to security in AI systems [32], while combinatorics helps in optimizing data structures and searching the solution space [33].

Mathematics is an indispensable tool in the development of AI, providing theoretical foundations and practical methods for building efficient and reliable AI systems. Its application covers a wide range of techniques, from linear algebra in neural networks to probability theory in prediction models. Understanding the mathematical fundamentals is essential for progress in this field and the development of more sophisticated AI models.

3 Application of Artificial Intelligence in Modern Mathematics Education

The application of AI in education brings great changes in the way we approach learning and teaching and, in mathematics teaching, opens up new opportunities for improving the experiences of students and teachers. AI offers innovative tools for personalizing learning, improving teaching methodologies and optimizing educational processes. This section explores how AI can improve mathematics teaching and the key challenges associated with its implementation.

3.1 Areas of Application and Comparative Advantages

AI in education, and especially in mathematics teaching, offers a wide range of opportunities for improving educational processes, facilitating access to complex mathematical concepts, and improving the experiences of students and teachers [34]. Different approaches and possibilities for applying AI in mathematics teaching are analyzed, along with the challenges associated with the increasing integration of this technology in modern mathematics education.

Helping in Learning Mathematical Concepts. One of the main ways in which AI can be applied in mathematics teaching is through the personalization of learning. AI-based algorithms can analyze student progress, identify their weaknesses, and offer customized exercises, tasks, and explanations to help students master mathematics more effectively [35]. In addition, AI systems can provide immediate feedback, allowing students to correct errors and improve their understanding. According to Casler-Failing, the use of LEGO robots as an educational tool in mathematics teaching helps students better understand mathematical concepts through practical application and interactive play, which increases their motivation and engagement [36]. Also, AI-based simulations and virtual assistants can further enhance the learning process, allowing students to experiment with different mathematical problems in a safe and stimulating digital environment [37].

Using Robotics to Visualize Mathematical Problems. Robotics in education can play a key role in visualizing mathematical problems. Using robots as a tool to model mathematical concepts, such as geometric shapes, moving objects in space, or calculating space and volume, allows students to better understand abstract mathematical ideas [38]. In addition, the interactive nature of robotics encourages an experimental approach to learning, where students can change variables and immediately see the effects of their changes, further developing their analytical and critical thinking skills [39]. Scientific research such as that by Lopez-Caudana et al. shows that students better understand and retain mathematical information when robots are used to demonstrate mathematical tasks [40]. Furthermore, programming robots to perform mathematical operations can further strengthen logical reasoning skills and encourage interdisciplinary connections between mathematics, computer science, and engineering.

Learning and Practicing Math Problems with AI Assistance. AI is also used to automatically solve problems and provide feedback to students. Students can use tools such as computer-based tutoring systems to help them learn how to solve math problems. These tools use algorithms that can analyze a student's solution, detect errors, and offer corrections or explanations [41]. This approach allows students to learn through their mistakes, which encourages the development of critical thinking and independent learning. In addition, AI can adjust the difficulty of tasks to individual students' needs, gradually increasing the complexity of the problems to challenge them but not discourage them [42]. Furthermore, AI-powered systems can use voice assistants and interactive chatbots to provide students with additional explanations and guided exercises, further enhancing the learning experience [43].

Supporting Teachers in Lesson Planning. AI can also be useful in helping teachers prepare lessons, generate assignments, and tests, and tailor content to the specific needs of students. AI tools can analyze lesson plans and collect data on which mathematical concepts are most difficult for students, which helps teachers plan more effective teaching strategies [44]. In addition, AI systems can automatically grade assignments and provide detailed analysis of student responses, allowing teachers to focus more on individual support for students [45]. AI can also help create dynamic visualizations and interactive materials that make it easier to explain complex mathematical concepts [46]. Furthermore, personalized recommendation systems can suggest additional resources, such as educational videos, simulations, and additional tasks adapted to the pace of each student [47]. Such an approach not only relieves teachers of administrative tasks but also allows them to devote more time to creative and interactive teaching.

Automatic Correction of Assignments and Tests. AI can be used to automatically correct assignments and tests. Based on predefined logic and models, AI systems can identify correct and incorrect answers, assign points, and provide detailed feedback to students on their answers [48]. This process can save teachers time and allow them to focus on more complex educational tasks. In addition to enabling rapid grading, AI can analyze student responses to identify common errors and suggest customized follow-up tasks to improve understanding [49]. Advanced AI systems can also grade not only numerical responses but also more complex response types, such as solving mathematical problems with procedures or short essay responses. Furthermore, AI can provide visualizations of student progress through detailed reports, allowing teachers to better understand their students' strengths and weaknesses [50]. Implementing such systems not only improves the efficiency of grading but also encourages students to deepen their understanding of the material through a personalized feedback process.

Interactive Learning Platforms. AI is enabling the development of advanced interactive platforms that provide students with a dynamic and engaging way to learn mathematical concepts. These platforms often include elements such as virtual assistants, 3D simulations, and integrated tasks, allowing students to explore and solve mathematical problems through play and collaboration [51]. Such an approach can significantly improve understanding of complex mathematical theories and principles. For example, platforms such as Symbolab use AI to break down mathematical problems into logical steps adapted to the student's level, thereby facilitating the learning process. Also, applications such as Khan Academy or DreamBox use algorithms that track student progress and offer customized tasks to help students better master specific mathematical concepts. These interactive platforms not only encourage independent learning, but also allow students to learn at their own pace, providing them with the opportunity to deepen their understanding and application of mathematical knowledge [52].

Support for the Development of Metacognitive Skills. AI can significantly help students develop metacognitive skills, such as self-study and reflection on their learning process. AI-based tools provide recommendations that allow students to analyze their progress, identify weaknesses, and make decisions about further learning strategies, which contributes to the long-term development of independent learning skills [53]. For example, the application of metacognitive strategies can significantly affect successful text comprehension, which is crucial for academic success [54]. In addition, AI systems can provide personalized feedback and adapt content to individual students' needs, thus encouraging the development of their metacognitive awareness [55]. This approach not only improves academic performance but also empowers students to take an active role in their education, developing critical thinking and self-regulation skills.

Adaptive Teaching. Adaptive teaching is one of the most prominent examples of the application of AI in education, where AI uses real-time data about student learning to adjust teaching content and pace. This approach allows teachers to focus on different learning styles, allowing students to progress through the material at a pace that suits them best while maintaining a challenge. The use of AI in adaptive teaching also enables personalized learning, where AI analyzes students' abilities, learning speed, and interests to create a customized learning plan [56]. Such a system can identify areas where a student is struggling and provide additional resources or exercises to improve understanding. Furthermore, AI can provide immediate feedback, allowing students to immediately correct mistakes and improve their knowledge [57]. This adaptability not only improves academic performance but also increases student motivation and engagement, as they feel supported and understand that their learning process is tailored to their individual needs.

The possibilities for applying AI in mathematics education are much broader than those presented in this chapter, including the potential to enhance interdisciplinary learning. However, despite the great potential, there are significant challenges that need to be addressed, such as ethical dilemmas, adaptation of educational methods, and technical barriers, and these issues will be discussed below.

3.2 Challenges and Potential Issues of Using AI in Mathematics Education

Although AI offers numerous advantages, its application in education, especially in the teaching of mathematics, carries certain challenges and issues that should be taken into account.

Technical Limitations and Infrastructure. The application of AI in mathematics education faces challenges related to technical infrastructure. The use of robots and advanced AI tools requires specialized equipment and stable internet access, which can be problematic in less developed educational institutions or areas with limited resources. Maintaining such systems can be expensive, and technical errors or malfunctions can disrupt the teaching process [58]. Furthermore, the lack of technical support can further complicate the integration of AI technologies into the classroom, which can result in uneven quality of education across different schools [59]. These challenges require strategic investments and planning to ensure equal access to technology for all students.

Dependence on Technology. Over-reliance on AI in the classroom can diminish the role of the teacher and reduce personal contact in the educational process. While AI can help personalize teaching, the importance of teacher intervention, emotional support and guidance should not be overlooked. There is a risk that students may become too dependent on technology, which can reduce their ability to solve problems independently without the help of tools [60]. Also, excessive use of technology can lead to a decrease in social skills and interactions among students. Therefore, it is crucial to find a balance between the use of technology and traditional teaching methods to ensure the holistic development of students [61].

Data Collection and Protection. The use of AI in education involves the collection of large amounts of data about students, which can raise concerns about the privacy and security of this data. While AI systems can improve educational outcomes, it is necessary to ensure that student data is protected and used in accordance with ethical guidelines. Inadequate data protection can lead to misuse of information or violation of student privacy [62]. In addition, transparency in the way data is collected and used is essential to build trust among students, parents, and teachers. Educational institutions should establish clear data protection policies and protocols to ensure the ethical use of technology in education [63].

Lack of Teacher Training. One of the key challenges in implementing AI in mathematics education is the lack of adequate teacher training. Although many teachers are interested in integrating AI into their teaching, they are often not sufficiently trained in the proper use of these technologies. Increasing professional development programs that include training in working with AI tools can be crucial for the successful implementation of AI in classrooms. Without adequate training, there is a risk of inadequate or ineffective use of technology, which can negatively impact the quality of teaching [64]. In addition, ongoing support and resources for teachers can help maintain their motivation and competence in using new technologies [65].

Cultural and Social Barriers. The implementation of AI in education can be hampered by cultural and social barriers, including distrust of technology, differences in access to education, and social norms that vary from region to region. In some societies, the use of robots and AI in education may be met with resistance due to fears of replacing teachers or threatening the traditional education system [66]. Economic inequalities can also affect the availability of technology, which can deepen existing educational gaps. For the successful integration of AI into education, it is necessary to take into account local cultural and social contexts and involve the community in the implementation process to ensure the acceptance and effectiveness of the technology [67].

High Implementation Costs. The development, implementation, and maintenance of AI systems can be extremely expensive, which can be a barrier for many educational institutions, especially those with limited budgets. Not all students and teachers are able to use the latest technologies, which can lead to digital inequality [68]. High costs can limit access to quality educational resources and tools, especially in less developed areas. In order to reduce these inequalities, it is necessary to provide financial support and resources for schools with limited resources and to promote the development of accessible and sustainable technologies [69].

Bias in Data and Algorithms. AI systems can be subject to biases due to the data they are trained on. If the student data is not representative of all groups, the AI system can develop biased recommendations or solutions that are not applicable to all students. In the context of mathematics, this can result in misunderstanding and unfair grading [70]. Bias in AI can arise from using data that reflects existing social inequalities and stereotypes. For example, facial recognition algorithms often recognize lighter-skinned individuals better because they are trained on such datasets, which can lead to discrimination. Algorithms can also take over and reinforce existing social inequalities if they are not properly designed or if they use inadequate data, which can result in unfair conclusions or discrimination. It is therefore crucial to ensure that AI systems are developed and implemented in a way that recognizes and minimizes biases, in order to avoid unfair consequences and ensure equity in education [71].

Incorporating AI into mathematics education presents both opportunities and challenges that require careful consideration and strategic planning. While AI has the potential to enhance learning, improve engagement, and provide personalized instruction, its successful implementation depends on addressing technical, financial, and ethical concerns. Ensuring equal access to technology, maintaining a balance between AI and traditional teaching methods, and providing adequate teacher training are essential for maximizing its benefits. Furthermore, transparent data protection policies and sensitivity to cultural and social contexts can foster trust and acceptance of AI in education. By overcoming these challenges, AI can be effectively integrated into mathematics teaching, ultimately enriching the learning experience for students.

4 Conclusion

The use of AI in education, and in particular in mathematics teaching, brings significant opportunities for improving the educational process, but it also raises a number of questions and challenges that require careful consideration.

First, the clear connection between mathematics and AI cannot be overlooked. Many AI systems are based on mathematical models and algorithms that use statistics, linear algebra, probability theory, and optimization. Understanding these mathematical principles is crucial for the design and implementation of effective AI technologies, thus creating a solid foundation for the application of AI in various fields, including mathematics teaching. Through working with AI, students can develop a deeper understanding of these mathematical concepts, as many AI technologies enable visualization and interactive learning.

In the context of mathematics teaching, the application of AI can bring numerous benefits. One of the greatest contributions is the possibility of personalizing instruction. AI tools can tailor tasks and content to students based on their specific needs, abilities, and learning styles, enabling greater engagement and better understanding of mathematical concepts. This personalization also allows students to progress at their own pace, reducing the frustration often caused by a mismatch between the pace of instruction and individual student abilities.

Furthermore, AI can play a key role in analytics and assessments, making it easier for teachers to track student progress and identify areas that require additional attention. Automated assessment systems based on AI can significantly reduce the time spent on administrative tasks, allowing teachers to focus on more interactive work with students. These systems can also help identify patterns in learning, allowing teachers to intervene in a timely manner and provide additional support to struggling students.

However, the application of AI in mathematics education is not without its challenges. One of the main problems mentioned in the literature is technology dependency. While AI can enhance the teaching process, overreliance on technology can diminish the role of the teacher in the classroom, as well as limit students' social skills. While many aspects of education can be automated, teachers still play an indispensable role in providing emotional and social support to students, as well as interpreting educational needs and challenges that are not always apparent through computer systems.

Ensuring equal access to technology across all educational institutions is also a challenge. Given that the development and implementation of AI systems can be expensive, there is concern that schools with limited resources will be left out of this technological advancement. This could lead to an increase in digital and educational inequalities among students, which is especially important in societies with greater economic disparities.

In addition, ethical issues related to data collection and the protection of student privacy are also crucial. AI systems often require the collection of large amounts of data on students, which can raise concerns about the security of that data. Transparency in how data is collected and used, as well as adherence to ethical guidelines, are essential to building trust among students, parents, and teachers.

It is interesting to note that while AI may have great potential for educational reform, technology alone will not be enough without the appropriate preparation of teachers and education systems. Many teachers are not sufficiently trained to work with AI tools, and without ongoing professional support, there is a risk of misuse of the technology. Therefore, it is crucial to invest in teacher training and ensure that they have the necessary knowledge and skills to effectively apply AI in teaching.

Ultimately, the application of AI in mathematics teaching has enormous potential to improve the educational process, but it is important that this potential is realized through a thoughtful and balanced implementation. It is important to take into account the challenges and risks and strive to ensure equal access to technology, professional training for teachers and transparent data protection. Only through this approach can AI truly improve mathematics teaching and provide students with better educational opportunities.

References

1. Roanes-Lozano, E., Laita, L.M., Hernando, A., Roanes-Macías, E.: An algebraic approach to rule based expert systems. Revista de la Real Academia de Ciencias Exactas, Físicas y Naturales. Serie A, Matemáticas **104**(1), 19–40 (2010)
2. Fradkov, A.L., Shepeljavyi, A.I.: The history of cybernetics and artificial intelligence: a view from saint petersburg. Cybern. Phys. **11**(4), 253–263 (2022)
3. Hanley, J.T.: GAMES, game theory and artificial intelligence. J. Defense Anal. Logist. **5**(2), 114–130 (2021)
4. Koski, T., Noble, J.: Bayesian networks: an introduction. Wiley, Chicester (2009)
5. Gelgi, F.: Implications of Gödel's incompleteness theorem on AI vs. Mind. NeuroQuantol. **3**, 186–189 (2004)
6. Van Leeuwen, J., Wiedermann, J.: the turing machine paradigm in contemporary computing. In: Engquist, B., Schmid, W. (eds.) Mathematics Unlimited—2001 and Beyond. Springer, Berlin, Heidelberg (2001)
7. French, R.M.: The turing test: the first 50 years. Trends Cogn. Sci. **4**(3), 115–122 (2000)
8. Upadhyaya, P.: When machine learning meets information theory: some practical applications to data storage, Doctoral Dissertation, Texas A&M University (2020)
9. O'Regan, G.: Boolean algebra and digital computing. In: O'Regan (ed.) The Innovation in Computing Companion: A Compendium of Select, Pivotal Inventions, pp. 57–62. Springer, Berlin, Heidelberg (2018)
10. Meenu, S.: The role of mathematics in artificial intelligence and machine learning. Innovat. Res. Thoughts **10**(3), 60–65 (2024)
11. Hasan, B.M.S., Abdulazeez, A.M.: A review of principal component analysis algorithm for dimensionality reduction. J. Soft Comput. Data Min. **2**(1), 20–30 (2021)
12. Steinberger, J., Ježek, K.: Text summarization and singular value decomposition. In: Yakhno, T. (eds.) Advances in Information Systems. ADVIS 2004. LNCS, vol. 3261. Springer, Berlin, Heidelberg (2004). https://doi.org/10.1007/978-3-540-30198-1_25
13. Nandakumar, K., Ratha, N., Pankanti, S., Halevi, S.: Towards deep neural network training on encrypted data. In: Proceedings of the IEEE/CVF Conference on Computer Vision and Pattern Recognition Workshops (2019)
14. Lohit, S., Turaga, P., Veeraraghavan, A.: Invariant methods in computer vision. In: Ikeuchi, K. (ed.) Computer Vision. Springer, Cham (2021). https://doi.org/10.1007/978-3-030-63416-2_826
15. Andrychowicz, M., et al.: Learning to learn by gradient descent by gradient descent. In: Lee, D, Sugiyama, M., Luxburg, U., Guyon, I., Garnett, R. (eds.) Advances in Neural Information Processing Systems, vol. 29 (2016)

16. Briol, F.X., Oates, C.J., Girolami, M., Osborne, M.A., Sejdinovic, D.: Probabilistic integration. Stat. Sci. **34**(1), 1–22 (2019)
17. Griewank, A.: Complexity of Gradients, jacobians, and hessians. In: Encyclopedia of Optimization, pp. 1–12. Springer Nature Switzerland (2025)
18. Coelho, C., Costa, M.F.P., Ferrás, L. L.: fractional calculus meets neural networks for computer vision: a survey. AI **5**(3), 1391–1426 (2024)
19. Yodo, N., Wang, P., Zhou, Z.: Predictive resilience analysis of complex systems using dynamic bayesian networks. IEEE Trans. Reliab. **66**(3), 761–770 (2017)
20. Harrell, F.E., Jr., Lee, K.L., Califf, R.M., Pryor, D.B., Rosati, R.A.: Regression modelling strategies for improved prognostic prediction. Stat. Med. **3**(2), 143–152 (1984)
21. Rabiner, L.R.: A tutorial on hidden markov models and selected applications in speech recognition. Proc. IEEE **77**(2), 257–286 (1989)
22. Peng, W., Huang, L., Jia, J., Ingram, E.: Enhancing the naive bayes spam filter through intelligent text modification detection. In: 2018 17th IEEE International Conference on Trust, Security and Privacy in Computing and Communications/12th IEEE International Conference on Big Data Science and Engineering, pp. 849–854. IEEE (2018)
23. Bertsimas, D., Popescu, I.: Optimal inequalities in probability theory: a convex optimization approach. SIAM J. Optim. **15**(3), 780–804 (2005)
24. Jin, C., Netrapalli, P., Jordan, M.: What is local optimality in nonconvex-nonconcave minimax optimization?. In: International Conference on Machine Learning, pp. 4880–4889 (2020)
25. Gad, A.G.: Particle swarm optimization algorithm and its applications: a systematic review. Arch. Comput. Meth. Eng. **29**(5), 2531–2561 (2022)
26. Hossain, R., Timmer, D.: Machine learning model optimization with hyper parameter tuning approach. Global J. Comput. Sci. Technol.: D Neural Artific. Intell. **21**(2), 7–13 (2021)
27. Pathak, M.J., Patel, R.L., Rami, S.P.: Comparative analysis of search algorithms. Int. J. Comput. Appl. **179**(50), 40–43 (2018)
28. Bhatti, U.A., Tang, H., Wu, G., Marjan, S., Hussain, A.: Deep learning with graph convolutional networks: an overview and latest applications in computational intelligence. Int. J. Intell. Syst. **2023**(1) (2023)
29. Sangers, A., et al.: Secure multiparty pagerank algorithm for collaborative fraud detection. In: Financial Cryptography and Data Security: 23rd International Conference, pp. 605–623. Springer International Publishing (2019)
30. Hüllermeier, E.: Fuzzy methods in machine learning and data mining: status and prospects. Fuzzy Sets Syst. **156**(3), 387–406 (2005)
31. Kamble, U., Nalawade, S., Mahadik, T., Salunke, Y., Dedgaonkar, S., Shelke, P.: Survey of application of automata theory in natural language processing. In: 2024 ASU International Conference in Emerging Technologies for Sustainability and Intelligent Systems, pp. 1–4. IEEE (2024)
32. Kraft, J., Washington, L.: An introduction to number theory with cryptography. Chapman and Hall, London (2018)
33. Chu, G.: Improving combinatorial optimization. In: Proceedings of 23rd International Joint Conference on Artificial Intelligence, pp. 3116–3120 (2011)
34. Hwang, G.J., Tu, Y.F.: Roles and research trends of artificial intelligence in mathematics education: a bibliometric mapping analysis and systematic review. Mathematics **9**(6), 584 (2021)
35. Sayed, W.S., et al.: AI-based adaptive personalized content presentation and exercises navigation for an effective and engaging e-learning platform. Multimedia Tools Appl. **82**(3), 3303–3333 (2023)
36. Casler-Failing, S.L.: The effects of integrating LEGO robotics into a mathematics curriculum to promote the development of proportional reasoning. Doctoral Thesis, School of Education, University at Albany, State University of New York (2017)

37. Kretzschmar, V., Sailer, A., Wertenauer, M., Seitz, J.: Enhanced educational experiences through personalized and AI-based learning. Int. J. Stud. Educ. **6**(2) (2024)
38. Liu, H., Sheng, J., Zhao, L.: Innovation of teaching tools during robot programming learning to promote middle school students' critical thinking. Sustainability **14**(11), 6625 (2022)
39. Lopez-Caudana, E., Ramirez-Montoya, M.S., Martínez-Pérez, S., Rodríguez-Abitia, G.: Using robotics to enhance active learning in mathematics: a multi-scenario study. Mathematics **8**(12), 2163 (2020)
40. Sáez-López, J.M., Sevillano-García, M.L., Vazquez-Cano, E.: The effect of programming on primary school students' mathematical and scientific understanding: educational use of mBot. Educ. Tech. Res. Dev. **67**(6), 1405–1425 (2019)
41. Arroyo, I., Woolf, B.P., Burelson, W., Muldner, K., Rai, D., Tai, M.: A multimedia adaptive tutoring system for mathematics that addresses cognition, metacognition and affect. Int. J. Artif. Intell. Educ. **24**, 387–426 (2014)
42. Srinivasa, K. G., Kurni, M., Saritha, K.: Harnessing the power of AI to education. In: Learning, Teaching, and Assessment Methods for Contemporary Learners: Pedagogy for the Digital Generation, pp. 311–342. Springer Nature Singapore (2022)
43. Supriyadi, E., Kuncoro, K.S.: Exploring the future of mathematics teaching: insight with chatgpt. union: Jurnal Ilmiah Pendidikan Matematika **11**(2), 305–316 (2023)
44. Moundridou, M., Matzakos, N., Doukakis, S.: Generative AI tools as educators' assistants: designing and implementing inquiry-based lesson plans. Comput. Educ.: Artific. Intell. **7** (2024)
45. Ivy, J., Maiorca, C., Burton, M., Roberts, T., Ivy, K.: Lesson planning and assessment: exploring the integration of AI tools in mathematics teacher preparation. Mathematics Education in Digital Age Proceedings of the 17th ERME Topic Conference MEDA, vol. 4, pp. 207–214 (2024)
46. Liang, H.N., Sedig, K.: Can interactive visualization tools engage and support pre-university students in exploring non-trivial mathematical concepts? Comput. Educ. **54**(4), 972–991 (2010)
47. Atalla, S., et al.: An intelligent recommendation system for automating academic advising based on curriculum analysis and performance modeling. Mathematics **11**(5), 1098 (2023)
48. Mollick, E., Mollick, L.: Assigning AI: seven approaches for students, with prompts. arXiv preprint arXiv:2306.10052 (2023)
49. Owan, V.J., Abang, K.B., Idika, D.O., Etta, E.O., Bassey, B.A.: Exploring the potential of artificial intelligence tools in educational measurement and assessment. Eurasia J. Math. Sci. Technol. Educ. **19**(8), em2307 (2023)
50. Mishra, P.: Revolutionizing education with AI and ML. Internet of Behavior-Based Computational Intelligence for Smart Education Systems, pp. 53–94 (2025)
51. Hwang, W.Y., Hu, S.S.: Analysis of peer learning behaviors using multiple representations in virtual reality and their impacts on geometry problem solving. Comput. Educ. **62**, 308–319 (2013)
52. Pashchenko, O., Skorupska, O., Zhuravel, A.: The role of technology in math education. Collection of Scientific Papers Scientia, pp. 168–176 (2024)
53. Pedro, F., Subosa, M., Rivas, A., Valverde, P.: Artificial intelligence in education: Challenges and opportunities for sustainable development. Working Papers on Education Policy 07, UNESCO Education Sector (2019)
54. Mijušković, M.: Metakognitivne strategije i razumijevanje teksta. Filolog - Časopis za jezik, književnost i kulturu **9**, 105–115 (2014)
55. Chang, D.H., Lin, M.P.C., Hajian, S., Wang, Q.Q.: Educational design principles of using AI Chatbot that supports self-regulated learning in education: goal setting, feedback, and personalization. Sustainability **15**(17), 12921 (2023)

56. Demartini, C.G., Sciascia, L., Bosso, A., Manuri, F.: Artificial intelligence bringing improvements to adaptive learning in education: a case study. Sustainability **16**(3), 1347 (2024)
57. Wang, W.S., Lin, C.J., Lee, H.Y., Huang, Y.M., Wu, T.T.: Enhancing self-regulated learning and higher-order thinking skills in virtual reality: the impact of ChatGPT-integrated feedback aids. Educ. Inform. Technol. 1–27 (2025)
58. Hakimi, M., Shahidzay, A.K., Kohistan, J.: Transforming education with artificial intelligence: potential and obstacles in developing countries. J. Electric. Electron. Eng. **3**(5), 01–09 (2024)
59. Pratiwi, H., Riwanda, A., Hasruddin, H., Sujarwo, S., Syamsudin, A.: Transforming learning or creating dependency? teachers' perspectives and barriers to AI integration in education. J. Pedagogic. Res. 1–16 (2025)
60. Nzoka, F.K.: Artificial intelligence in education: a hindrance or an enabler? Eur. J. Contemp. Educ. E-Learn. **2**(2), 101–108 (2024)
61. Taylor, K. N.: How does Social Media Use Impact Students' Addiction, Interpersonal Skills, and Well-Being? Doctoral Dissertation, Northcentral University San Diego (2020)
62. Huang, L.: Ethics of artificial intelligence in education: student privacy and data protection. Sci. Insights Educ. Front. **16**(2), 2577–2587 (2023)
63. Kaddouri, M., Mhamdi, K., Chniete, I., Marhraoui, M., Khaldi, M., Jmad, S.: Adopting AI in education: technical challenges and ethical constraints. In: Fostering Inclusive Education With AI and Emerging Technologies, pp. 25–72. IGI Global (2025)
64. Umoh, E.: Artificial intelligence and the future of teaching and learning mathematics in a global context: an overview of contemporary research. Available at SSRN 5126695 (2025)
65. Ottenbreit-Leftwich, A.T., Glazewski, K.D., Newby, T.J., Ertmer, P.A.: Teacher value beliefs associated with using technology: addressing professional and student needs. Comput. Educ. **55**(3), 1321–1335 (2010)
66. Viberg, O., et al.: What explains teachers' trust in ai in education across six countries?. Int. J. Artific. Intell. Educ. 1–29 (2024)
67. Li, H.: AI in education: bridging the divide or widening the gap? Exploring equity, opportunities, and challenges in the digital age. Adv. Educ. Human. Soc. Sci. Res. **8**(1), 355 (2023)
68. Ahmed, F.: The digital divide and AI in education: addressing equity and accessibility. J. AI Educ.: Innovat. Opportun. Challen. Future Direct. **1**(2), 12–23 (2024)
69. VatandoustMohammadieh, M., Mohajeri, M.M., Keramati, A., Ahmadabadi, M.N.: AI-powered digital framework for personalized economical quality learning at scale. arXiv preprint arXiv:2412.04483. (2024)
70. Idowu, J.A., Koshiyama, A.S., Treleaven, P.: Investigating algorithmic bias in student progress monitoring. Comput. Educ.: Artific. Intell. **7**, 100267 (2024)
71. Vidyadhari Chinta, S., Wang, Z., Yin, Z., Hoang, N., Gonzalez, M., Le Quy, T., Zhang, W.: FairAIED: navigating fairness, bias, and ethics in educational AI applications. arXiv e-prints, arXiv-2407 (2024)

Exploratory Data Analysis and Prediction of Fuel Prices in FBiH Relative to Oil Price Movements

Hrvoje Ljubić(✉), Tomislav Volarić, and Robert Rozić

University of Mostar, Trg hrvatskih velikana 1, Mostar, Bosnia and Herzegovina
{hrvoje.ljubic,tomislav.volaric,robert.rozic}@fpmoz.sum.ba
https://www.sum.ba/

Abstract. This paper presents an exploratory data analysis and prediction model for fuel prices in the Federation of Bosnia and Herzegovina (FBiH) relative to oil price movements. The study focuses on the Super 98 fuel type and utilizes data collected from the Federal Ministry of Trade of BiH's eOPC application from December 2018 to September 2023. The analysis employs various data visualization techniques and statistical methods to identify trends and correlations. A recurrent neural network, specifically a long-short-term memory (LSTM) model, is constructed to predict future fuel prices based on historical data and the movements of BRENT and WTI oil prices. The results indicate a high correlation between fuel prices in FBiH and BRENT oil prices, with the LSTM model demonstrating high predictive accuracy. This research provides valuable insights for decision makers in the economics and energy sectors and suggests potential future research directions, but also publicly publishes and analyzes an official Ministry dataset over a period of 5 years for 716 gas stations and six fuel types.

Keywords: Exploratory data analysis · Time series forecasting · Deep learning · Fuel prices · Oil prices

1 Introduction

The relationship between fuel prices and oil prices is a critical area of study in economics, particularly for consumers, businesses, and policy makers. Fuel prices are primarily influenced by crude oil prices, but other factors also play an important role. Two dominant oil trading exchanges are the British BRENT (Brent Crude) and the American WTI (West Texas Intermediate). BRENT is the benchmark for the oil market in Europe, Africa, and the Middle East, originating from oil fields in the North Sea, while WTI is the benchmark for the oil market in the USA, sourced from oil fields within the USA. This paper attempts to propose a model capable of predicting future prices in the Federation of Bosnia and Herzegovina (FBiH) in relation to the movements of oil prices.

D. Vasić and E. Brajković (Eds.): MoStart 2025, CCIS 2609, pp. 151–170, 2026.
https://doi.org/10.1007/978-3-032-02801-3_10

This study focuses on the Federation of Bosnia and Herzegovina (FBiH), where fuel prices are subject to various economic and geopolitical pressures. By examining data from December 2018 to September 2023, this paper explores fuel price patterns, focusing on the Super 98 fuel type, across 716 gas stations and multiple fuel types. Utilizing official data from the Federal Ministry of Trade of BiH's eOPC system, the analysis provides a comprehensive view of fuel price trends in the region. The data pipeline includes data aggregation, cleaning, and preparation stages, making it suitable for forecasting models.

In FBiH, from 2018 to 2023, there were 716 active petrol stations using six types of fuel: Super 95, Super 98, Diesel 10ppm, LPG, LUEL BAS 1002, and Diesel 50ppm. For practical reasons and scope of work, only one type of fuel, Super 98, is analyzed in detail. Data for this paper were collected from the official eOPC (electronic price change form) application of the Federal Ministry of Trade of BiH, where all petrol stations within the territory of FBiH enter price and margin changes for petroleum products, and the new price officially applies from the next day at 00:00h.

After changes are made, the administrative staff at the Ministry must verify and approve or reject them. The first fuel price record in the observed dataset is from December 25, 2018, and the last is from September 31, 2023. Besides verification by the Ministry, the application has additional checks that alert users of potential errors and allows form cancellation in case of mistakes, confirming the validity and correctness of the data. It is assumed that a certain amount of time (more than one week) is needed for fuel price changes to be triggered by changes in exchange prices.

This paper is divided into seven sections, including the introduction. The second section is related work, while third section describes the database model, server, web and mobile applications, and the method of exporting and preprocessing data from the official eOPC application. The fourth section provides theoretical background on the methods and techniques used, while the fifth section describes the exploratory data analysis conducted at the canton level and a more detailed analysis of data at the FBiH level. The sixth section describes the construction of a deep learning model, specifically a recurrent neural network, and the seventh section presents conclusions and potential future research directions.

2 Related Work

Forecasting crude oil prices has attracted significant research interest due to the global economic implications of oil price volatility. Oil price prediction is an important task that some researchers were engaged in 20 years ago [3, 8] and even much earlier [9]. In this paper, we investigate the impact of oil price changes on the prices of oil derivatives in FBiH, which is not such a common task, so in this section we will cover papers for both tasks.

In recent years, researchers have applied various machine learning (ML) and hybrid models to improve the accuracy and reliability of crude oil price predictions under complex and volatile conditions. Here we summarize some key approaches.

Authors in [19] proposed a hybrid approach utilizing Long Short-Term Memory (LSTM) networks optimized with the Salp Swarm Algorithm (SSA) incorporating a Disputation Operator (DO) for crude oil price forecasting. The study applied this method to West Texas Intermediate (WTI) oil data, achieving high accuracy in both raw and decomposed data formats. The SSA-DO model showed significant improvement in short-term predictions, emphasizing the importance of advanced optimization techniques to refine the performance of the ML model in volatile markets.

Gupta and Nigam [4] explored Artificial Neural Networks (ANN) for crude oil price prediction, emphasizing the importance of optimal lag selection to enhance prediction accuracy. Using historical data, the ANN model effectively captured the non-linear patterns inherent in oil price fluctuations, outperforming traditional models and highlighting the potential of ANN in managing complex time-series data.

Bildirici et al. introduced a novel hybrid model [5] combining Logistic Smooth Transition Autoregressive Generalized Autoregressive Conditional Heteroskedasticity (LSTARGARCH) and LSTM networks to analyze oil price volatility during the COVID-19 pandemic and the Russia-Saudi Arabia oil price war. Their model successfully handled chaotic and non-linear price patterns, achieving improved predictive accuracy compared to traditional GARCH models, especially during periods of high volatility.

Authors in [6] employed a complex network and LSTM hybrid model to tackle the non-linear characteristics of crude oil prices. This model utilized k-core centrality and visibility graphs to preprocess oil price data, which enhanced the LSTM's ability to predict price trends under complex market conditions. The study demonstrated the robustness and improved accuracy of complex network-enhanced ML models for crude oil price forecasting.

In [7], Zhao et al. applied an LSTM model to predict Brent crude oil prices within the context of a low-carbon economic transition. The model showed effective performance in capturing general price trends, although some deviations occurred during periods of extreme fluctuation. This study highlighted LSTM's applicability in energy markets, providing critical insights for policy-making amid shifting energy dynamics.

These studies indicate that hybrid models combining LSTM with various optimization and preprocessing techniques, such as SSA, GARCH, and complex network analysis, can significantly improve the accuracy of crude oil price forecasts.

The integration of advanced deep learning methods with domain-specific adjustments demonstrates promising results, particularly in managing volatile and non-linear data typical of energy markets. This research field continues to evolve as hybrid and ML models adapt to changing economic conditions, including global energy transitions and geopolitical disruptions.

3 Data Source

3.1 Database

The database manager used by the application is MySQL 8.0. The relational database model is shown in Fig. 1. The initial dataset was exported to a CSV file by executing the following query:

```
SELECT companies.title AS company,
       gas_stations.title AS gas_station,
       articles.shortname AS article, cantons.title AS canton,
       townships.title AS township,
       form_articles.valid_from AS valid_from,
       form_articles.current_price AS price,
       form_articles.current_gain AS gain,
       form_articles.current_gain_percent AS gain_percent,
       gas_stations.open_from, gas_stations.open_to,
       gas_stations.latitude, gas_stations.longitude
FROM form_articles
LEFT JOIN forms ON forms.id = form_articles.form_id
LEFT JOIN gas_stations ON forms.gas_station_id = gas_stations.id
LEFT JOIN townships ON gas_stations.township_id = townships.id
LEFT JOIN companies ON gas_stations.company_id = companies.id
LEFT JOIN articles ON articles.id = form_articles.article_id
LEFT JOIN cantons ON townships.canton_id = cantons.id
WHERE forms.deleted_at IS NULL
  AND forms.status = 'approved'
  AND form_articles.valid_from IS NOT NULL
  AND gas_stations.active = 1
  AND forms.created_at IS NOT NULL
  AND forms.deleted_by_id IS NULL
  AND forms.valid_from IS NOT NULL
GROUP BY form_articles.id
ORDER BY form_articles.valid_from;
```

After executing the displayed SQL query, a CSV file containing exactly 180,808 rows was exported, with each row representing a price change for a type of fuel at a specific petrol station. The data also include information on the municipality, canton, GPS coordinates, margins, and the working hours of the petrol station. Data in this format are not very useful for analysis as prices are not shown for each day, but only changes for one station for one petroleum product for a specific date. For this reason, a Python script was created to record the prices and margins for each station and type of fuel for each day from the first to the last available date in the dataset, resulting in a significantly larger dataset containing 3,751,511 rows. Dataset is available at [2]. This dataset is then sorted by date, and columns that are no longer relevant for analysis and prediction in this paper are removed.

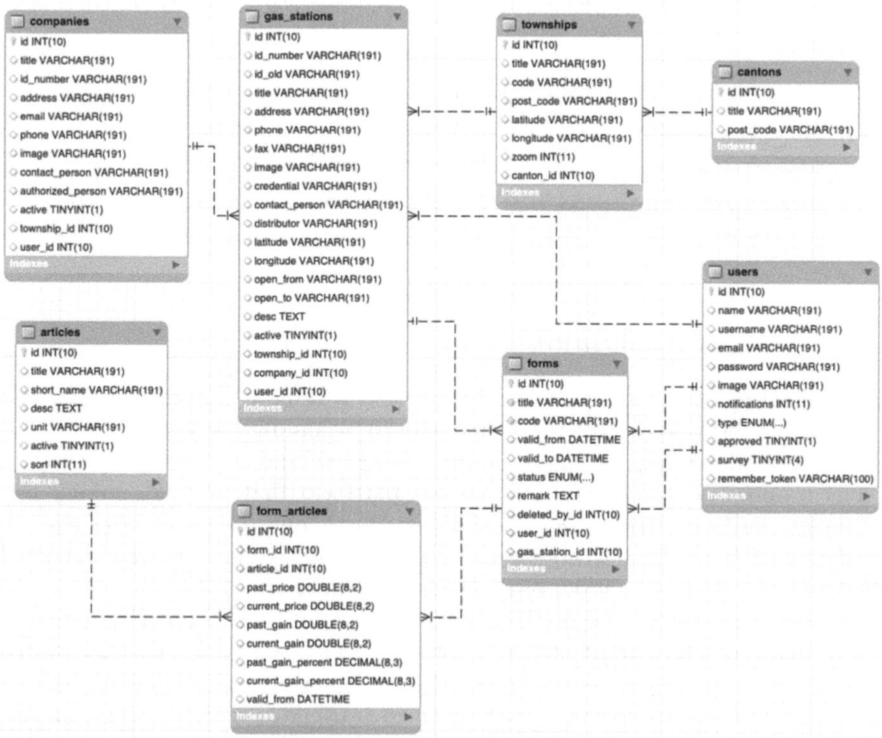

Fig. 1. Relational database model

The new dataset has five columns: (i) type of fuel, (ii) date, (iii) price, (iv) margin, and (v) canton. Since columns (i) and (v) contain only textual values, they need to be converted to categorical variables. Next, prices are grouped by (i) date and (ii) by date and canton, and the average price is calculated through grouping and aggregation. An example of part of the data is shown in Table 1.

As the final step in this preparation, the type of fuel Super 98 is filtered and merged using the Pandas library with three other CSV files by date: WTI and BRENT oil price movements and the EUR/USD exchange rate. All prices are rounded to a maximum of four decimal places. After merging by date, the data are finally exported to two CSV files for analysis and prediction. Using the built-in Pandas functions, it was confirmed that there were no duplicates or missing values for fuel prices, but there were some missing values for BRENT and WTI. So we filled the gaps by taking the arithmetic mean between the last known and the next known values for both exchanges. Now, the file containing the average price per day for the entire FBiH has 1,711 rows, and the file containing average prices by canton has 16,530 rows.

Table 1. Example of the first 5 rows of the final dataset

date	mean_price	wti	brent	eur_usd	canton
2023-08-31	2.8337	83.55	87.29	1.8046	Srednjobosanski kanton
2023-08-31	2.8196	83.55	87.29	1.8046	Tuzlanski kanton
2023-08-31	2.8287	83.55	87.29	1.8046	Unsko-sanski kanton
2023-08-31	2.8340	83.55	87.29	1.8046	Zapadnohercegovački kanton
2023-08-31	2.8395	83.55	87.29	1.8046	Zeničko-dobojski kanton

3.2 Server and Application

The application and database are hosted on a remote Ubuntu 16.04 server on Amazon's AWS LightSail platform, offering scalability, reliability, and cost-efficiency for managing its infrastructure. The backend is developed using the Laravel framework, a powerful PHP-based platform that provides robust tools for routing, authentication, and database management. The user interface (UI) is designed with the Bootstrap framework for responsive layouts and the VueJS framework to deliver dynamic, interactive user experiences (Fig. 2).

The development of the application began in late 2016, focusing on creating a stable and efficient platform tailored to the needs of its users. However, the application underwent extensive testing and iterative development cycles to ensure stability and performance across various usage scenarios. Additionally, a significant amount of time was dedicated to training a large number of users, including petrol station operators and administrative staff. As a result, the application officially went into production with the first dataset in 2018, following the completion of testing and training phases.

In addition to the web-based application used by petrol stations and the Ministry's administration, a complementary mobile application was developed to serve the general public. The mobile application is available for download on Google Play and the App Store, as illustrated in Fig. 3. It enables users to subscribe to specific petrol stations or fuel types and receive real-time push notifications about price changes, enhancing accessibility and user engagement. This integration of web and mobile platforms ensures a comprehensive and user-friendly system for all stakeholders.

4 Theoretical Background

4.1 Data Visualization

In the first part of this research, four common techniques are used in exploratory data analysis: histogram, box plot, violin plot, and scatter plot matrix. A histogram is a graphical representation of the distribution of a dataset consisting of a series of bars, where the height of each bar represents the frequency or number of observations within a specific interval. The histogram helps in identifying the

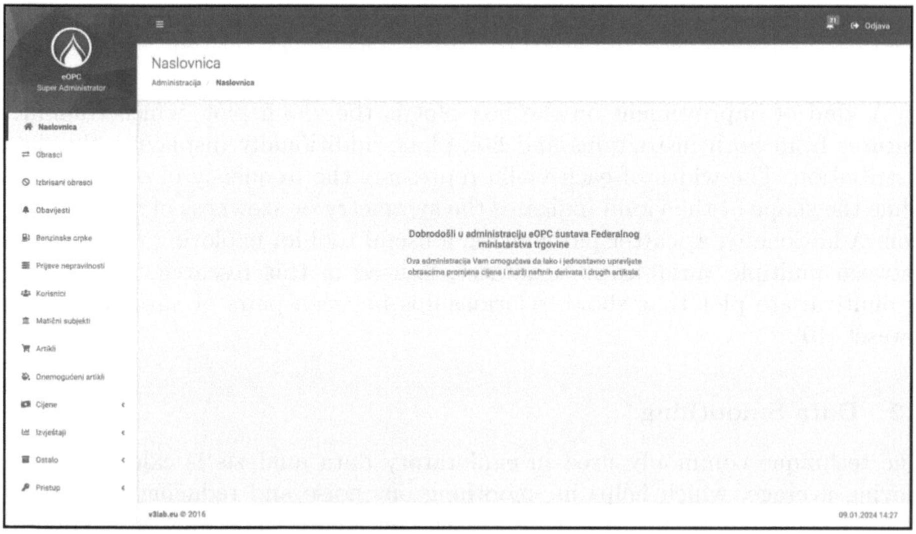

Fig. 2. Administrator application user interface

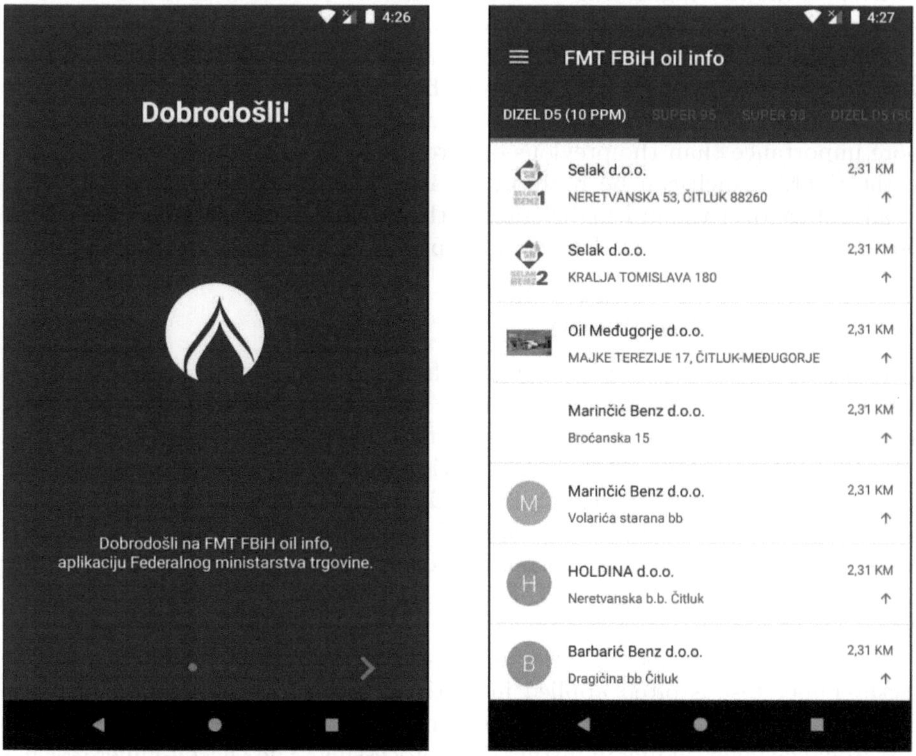

Fig. 3. Two views of the mobile application for citizens

presence of outliers, but a more informative tool in this regard is the box plot. A box plot summarizes key statistical measures of a dataset, including the median, first quartile, third quartile, and all present outliers [1].

A kind of improvement on the box plot is the violin plot, which combines features from both histograms and box plots, additionally displaying the data distribution. The width of each violin represents the frequency of observations, while the shape of the violin indicates the symmetry or skewness of the distribution. Additionally, a scatter plot matrix, a useful tool for exploring relationships between multiple variables in a dataset, is used in this research. It is a type of multivariate plot that shows relationships between pairs of variables in the dataset [10].

4.2 Data Smoothing

One technique commonly used in exploratory data analysis is calculating the moving average, which helps in smoothing out noise and reducing the impact of extreme values within the data, identifying trends. The moving average is calculated by taking the average of a specific number of consecutive data points (window) in a time series.

Besides the moving average, a more advanced technique used for the same purposes is the exponentially weighted moving average (EWMA). The basic idea behind the EWMA method is to create a new representation of the data where the most recent data have more weight, and weights exponentially decrease towards older data. Exponential decay means that each new data point receives more importance than the previous one, resulting in the dataset being "shifted to the right," which can be both an advantage and a disadvantage. However, an advantage over the moving average is that there is no data loss, while in the moving average, the oldest data are lost, precisely half of the defined window.

4.3 Data (Non)Stationarity

A stationary time series is a series whose characteristics remain constant regardless of the time of observation, meaning that the time series does not show trends or seasonality. In deep learning, stationarity is not necessary but is a desirable characteristic for reliable prediction of time-dependent data [11]. Non-stationarity is present in most real-world datasets, and the simplest way to achieve stationarity is by differentiation, i.e., subtracting a value from the previous or future value. If it is subtracted from the first neighbor, it is first-order differentiation, and it can be of higher order depending on the problem and data [12].

To determine whether a series is non-stationary and to what extent, the Dickey-Fuller test is often applied in statistics and exploratory data analysis. Besides stationarity, this test can help determine whether a time series has trends or seasonal changes, aiding in further data processing. The Dickey-Fuller test has a null hypothesis (H0) and an alternative hypothesis (H1). To confirm or reject the hypothesis, the p-value threshold, set to $p = 0.05$ by default, is used. If the value is less than p, it means the observed dataset is stationary, and the null hypothesis is confirmed. If the value is greater, the dataset is non-stationary, and the alternative hypothesis is accepted [13].

4.4 Similarity Measures

In this section, four well-known metrics used later in the work to compare two distributions are briefly described. Pearson's correlation coefficient (PCC) measures the linear relationship between two variables. Values range from -1 to 1, where -1 indicates a complete negative correlation, 1 indicates a complete positive correlation, and 0 indicates the absence of a linear relationship. R-squared (R2) or the coefficient of determination measures the similarity of two data series and ranges from 0 to 1, with 1 indicating complete data overlap. Since values are between 0 and 1, R2 is often interpreted as the percentage accuracy of the regression model. Mean absolute error (MAE) is the average absolute difference between actual and predicted values, providing information on the average size of the error regardless of direction (positive or negative deviation). Mean squared error (MSE) is the average squared difference between actual and predicted values. MSE further emphasizes larger errors due to squaring differences, giving greater weight to larger errors compared to smaller ones. Unlike R2 and PCC, where the goal is to achieve values close to 1, the goal for MAE and MSE is to achieve values as close to 0 as possible.

4.5 Recurrent Neural Networks

Recurrent neural networks (RNNs) are a neural network architecture for sequential data. They have numerous applications, such as natural language processing, sound processing, and working with time-dependent data. The unique feature of these neural networks is their feedback connection, allowing them to remember earlier data, unlike classical feedforward neural networks. Additionally, the inputs and outputs of RNNs can be of variable length. The two most popular versions of RNNs are the long-short term memory (LSTM) network [15] and the gated recurrent unit (GRU) network [16], which address the vanishing and exploding gradient problem present in the basic version [17].

5 Exploratory Data Analysis

The average price of Super 98 for the entire dataset was 2.3542 KM. The lowest average price during the entire period was 1.6479 KM (on May 8, 2020), and the highest was 3.4525 KM (on July 6, 2022). These extreme values and their dates demonstrate the significant impact of global events and geopolitical situations on the prices of oil and petroleum products. During the COVID-19 pandemic (2020), the lowest fuel price was observed, while a few months after the start of 2022, due to various events in Europe and the world, the highest price was reached. The WTI and BRENT exchange values at that time were 24.73 and 24.49, respectively, and 100.31 and 108.54 in their respective units.

Concerning data dispersion measures, it is important to mention that the standard deviation of the average price is 0.388735, and the variance is 0.151115. Variance is the average squared deviation of a data series from its mean, and the standard deviation is the square root of the variance.

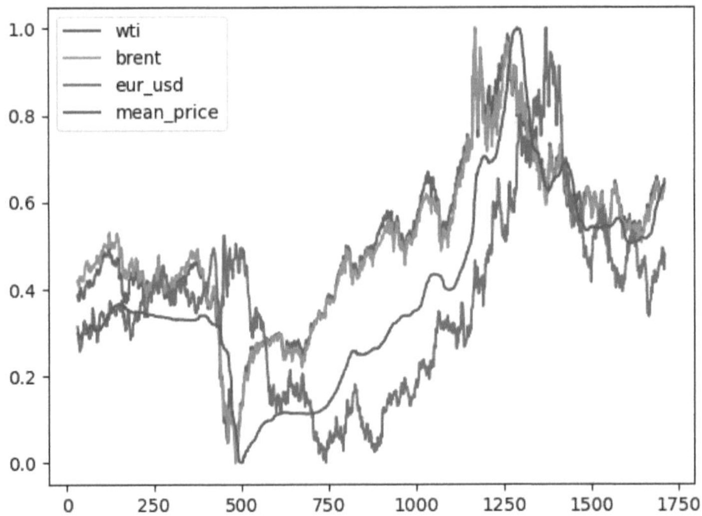

Fig. 4. Graphical representation of average prices WTI, BRENT, and EUR/USD

A graphical comparison of all four features in the dataset is shown in Fig. 4. The graph clearly shows that changes in oil prices (WTI and BRENT features) occur before fuel price changes, and changes in the EUR/USD exchange rate occur significantly later after fuel and oil price changes. From this, it can be concluded that EUR/USD movements do not affect oil prices; therefore, this feature is excluded from further research and analysis.

5.1 Data Shifting

To better perceive the shift between the WTI and BRENT distributions and the average price distribution, a small experiment with data shifting was conducted. In a repetitive loop with steps from 1 to 120 (1 day to 120 d), the average price data were shifted. After the shift, the correlation of each shifted dataset with the original was measured using R2 and PCC metrics. The graph of correlation coefficients is shown in Fig. 5 (Fig. 6).

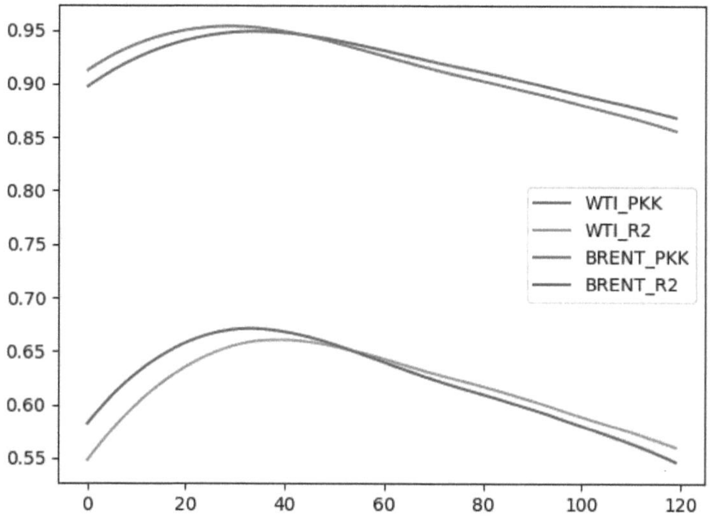

Fig. 5. PCC and R2 in relation to shifted datasets

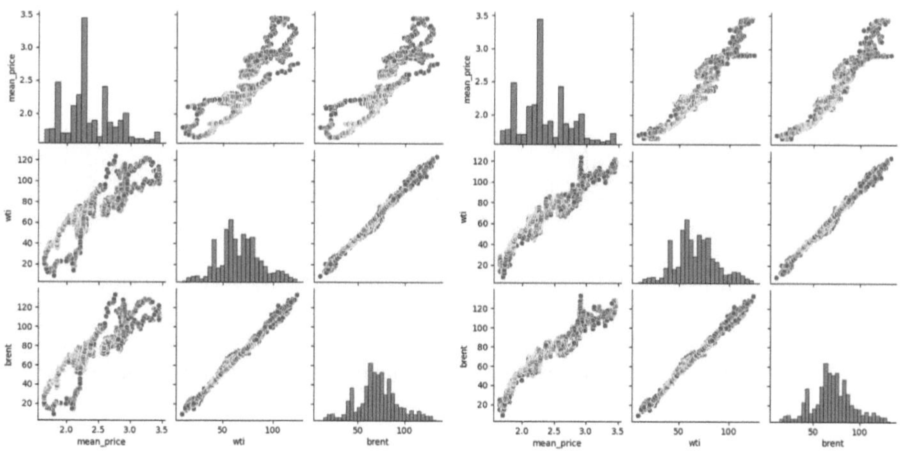

Fig. 6. Scatter plot matrices before and after data shifts

The best coefficients for WTI were 0.94906 and 0.66069 for PCC and R2, respectively, both for a shift of 36 d. For BRENT, these values were best for a shift of 32 d, amounting to 0.95384 and 0.67128. From this, it can also be concluded that fuel price movements in FBiH depend more on the BRENT than on the WTI exchange, considering the response speed of changes and the correlation coefficient values, which makes sense given the geographical characteristics of FBiH. When BRENT and WTI are shifted by 32 and 36 d, respectively, the graph shown in Figure ?? is obtained. However, this dataset will not be used further and serves only to gain additional insights into the data before model construction.

5.2 Visual Features of Data

A histogram of the average price divided into 20 sections is shown in Fig. 8, and a box plot is shown in Fig. 7a . These graphs provide valuable insights into the data distribution but are not sufficient for determining completely accurate data. To this end, the NumPy histogram function can be used to provide these data in a tabular form, and the Pandas describe function can be used to determine the values of the first and last quartiles.

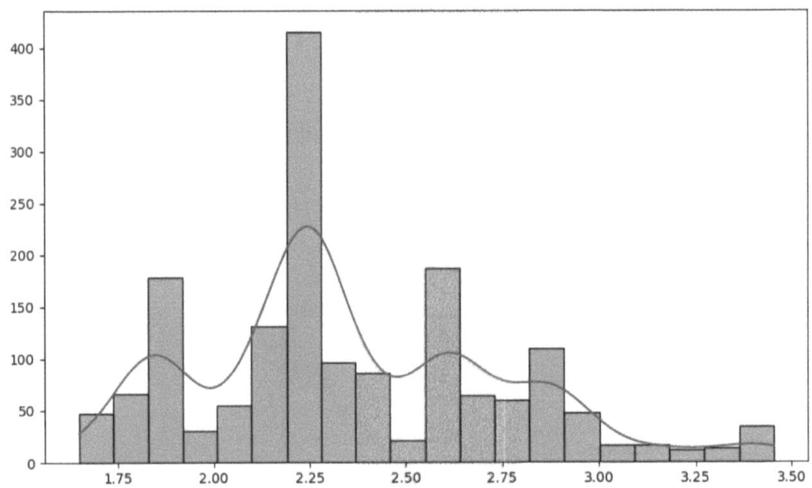

Fig. 7. Visualization of average fuel price data using histogram, box plot, and violin plot

The largest section (the seventh in order) in the shown histogram ranges from 2.18928 KM to 2.27951 KM and contains 426 records. The first quartile starts at 2.1207 KM, and the last at 2.6228 KM. The number of outliers in the box plot is 32.

To gain additional insights into the data, a more complex and informative representation than the previously shown box plot, the violin plot, is used. The violin plot not only displays the data presented in the box plot but also shows data distributions. Since the data in the columns are not in the same intervals, for valid comparison, data scaling is required. The MinMaxScaler from the SciKit-learn package was used for this purpose, which scales the values of all columns

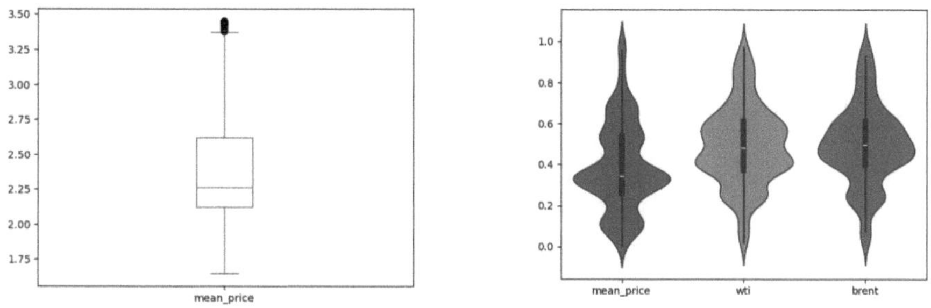

(a) Box plot of average fuel price (b) Violin plot of all features

Fig. 8. Histogram of average fuel price divided into 20 sections

between 0 and 1 proportionally [18]. The violin plot of this dataset is shown in Fig. 7b .

5.3 Stationarity of the Dataset

Since the data are time-dependent, it is useful to examine whether the dataset is stationary. Additionally, examining the autocorrelation, partial autocorrelation, seasonality, and trend of the output variable provides valuable insights into time-dependent data. For this purpose, the dataset was subjected to the Dickey-Fuller

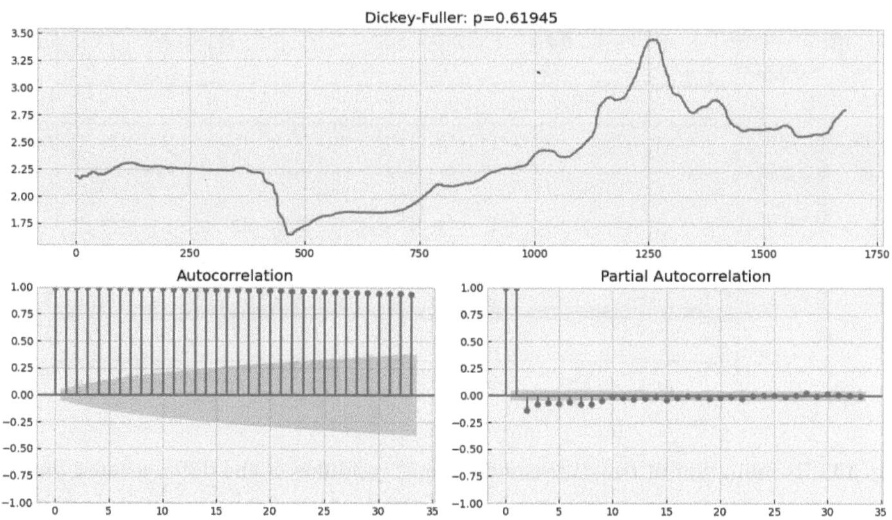

Fig. 9. Dickey-Fuller test for the original dataset

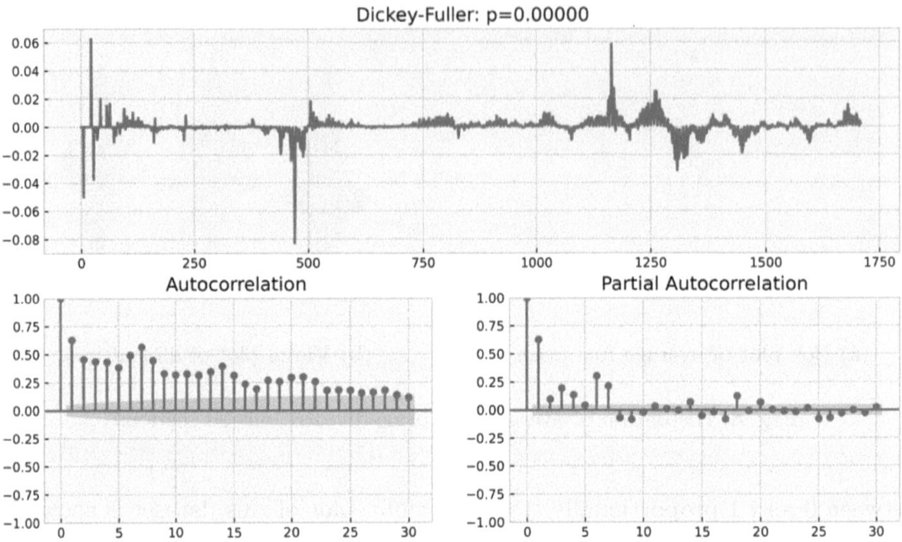

Fig. 10. Dickey-Fuller test for the differentiated dataset

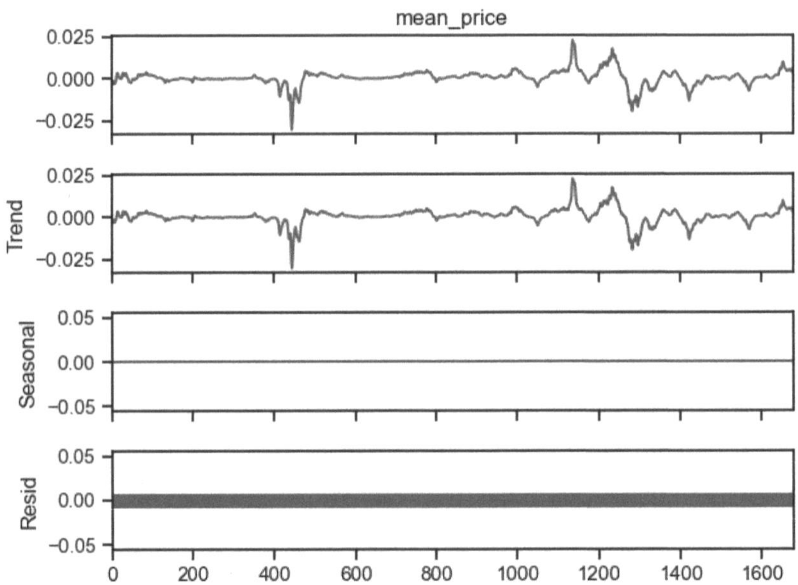

Fig. 11. Examination of trend, seasonality, and residuals of the differentiated dataset

test. All the mentioned aspects can be graphically observed in Fig. 9. The Dickey-Fuller test has a p-value of 0.62, indicating that the null hypothesis is rejected, meaning the dataset is non-stationary.

To achieve stationarity of the dataset, first-order differentiation was performed, followed by five-fold smoothing (MWS=5) with EWMA using a window size of 2. The results of the repeated test are shown in Fig. 10. Now it is evident that p=0, clearly satisfying the conditions for stationarity.

To further confirm the absence of seasonality and trend in the data, the graph in Fig. 11 is examined. The graph shows no visible trend or seasonality, which is further confirmed by the residual graph (subplot number 4 labeled "Resid").

6 Deep Learning Model

6.1 Model Preparation

In this section, the construction and training of an LSTM model for predicting the average fuel price movement in FBiH based on historical data and exchange data from WTI and BRENT are described. For training the model, a stationary differentiated dataset representing daily price changes was used. The goal is to make a prediction for the next week using data from the entire previous month. To prepare the dataset suitable for LSTM, a moving window is used to create sequences of 30 d of historical data as input, and the next 7 d are taken as output. This means a "sequence-to-sequence" model needs to be created. The data are divided into training, validation, and testing sets in a ratio of 70:10:20. The input data are scaled with MinMaxScaler. After experimenting with several different models, a classic LSTM model with one hidden layer was selected. Only the training set was smoothed from both directions with a window size of 2 for 8 times to avoid data shifting to the right. The validation and test sets are in their original form after differentiation.

For tuning hyperparameters, KerasTuner was used, and it was found that the best batch size was 16 from the offered set 1, 2, 4, 16, 32, 64, 128, and the number of units in the first layer was 64 from the offered set 16, 32, 64, 128. The dropout layer was chosen with a coefficient of 0.5 from the offered set 0.1, 0.2, 0.3, 0.4, 0.5. The learning rate was set to 0.001.

Experimenting with a learning rate scheduler, which usually decreases the learning rate according to an algorithm, did not contribute to model improvement, so it was not used for training the final model. This architecture was used to build the final model, which was trained for 500 epochs using the Adam optimization algorithm, and RMSE was used for the loss function.

Additionally, an early stopping mechanism was introduced to stop training in case of overfitting on the validation set, with patience set to 10 and weights restored to the best epoch. This means if the model has a lower loss on the training set than the validation set for 10 consecutive epochs, training stops and the weights from the best epoch are restored. Training stopped, and the weights from the 113th epoch were restored. The activation function in the first layer is the hyperbolic tangent (tanh), and in the output layer, it is a linear function.

ReLU and Leaky ReLU functions, often used in these models, were not the best choice for this problem, as the hyperbolic tangent provided much better results.

6.2 Model Results

Prediction of average fuel price movement using the LSTM model was performed on the last 20% of the dataset, representing the test set. This ensured that the model was evaluated on unseen data, providing a realistic measure of its predictive performance. Once the model was trained and predictions were generated, a cumulative sum at the row level was applied to calculate the net difference in price movement for the entire week. The final value in each row, corresponding to the last column, represented the total sum of all daily differences for that week. These predicted values were then compared to the actual price difference values, as illustrated in Fig. 12.

To translate the predictions into actual fuel price values, the calculated differences were added to the original dataset, shifted back by seven days to align with the time series structure. This adjustment ensured that the predictions were cumulative and consistent with the historical price trends. The final results, showcasing the predicted fuel prices compared to the actual prices, are displayed in Fig. 13.

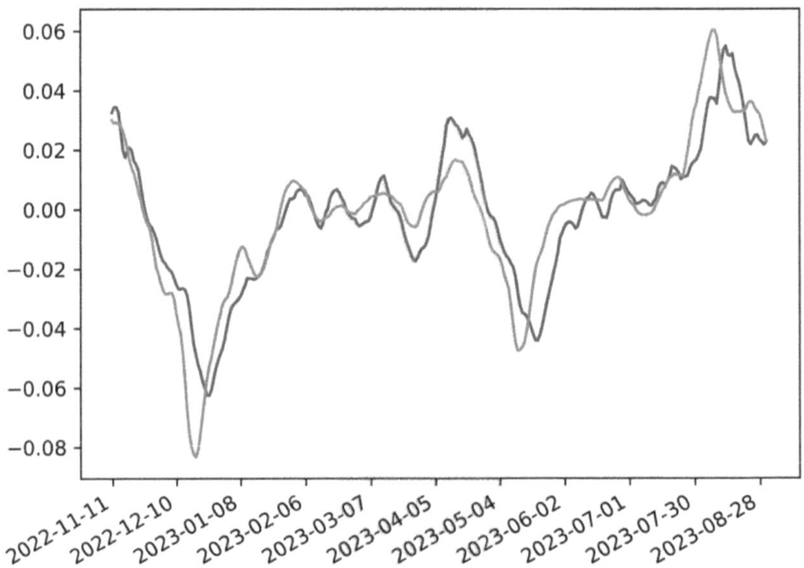

Fig. 12. LSTM model predictions

This process resulted in the creation of two datasets: one representing the differences in daily fuel prices and another with the actual predicted fuel prices. A comparison of the predicted values with the actual values was performed using statistical metrics. The R2 and Pearson correlation coefficients were employed to assess the model's performance. For the prediction differences, the model achieved an R2 value of 0.77470 and a Pearson correlation of 0.88995, indicating strong alignment with observed trends. When comparing the predictions with the original data, the model yielded an R2 value of 0.94406 and a Pearson correlation of 0.97179, demonstrating a high degree of accuracy and reliability in forecasting fuel price movements.

These results highlight the model's capability to effectively capture both short-term variations and long-term trends in fuel price data, making it a valuable tool for decision-making in economic and energy sectors. Further improvements and testing could enhance its applicability across different datasets and prediction scenari os.

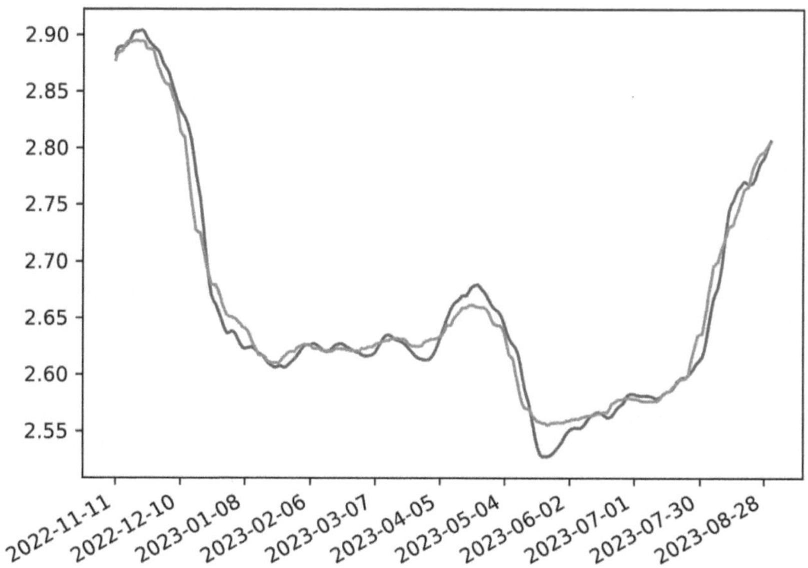

Fig. 13. Model predictions after cumulative sum and addition with the initial value

7 Conclusion and Future Work

The prediction of average fuel prices in FBiH is possible using a deep learning model and utilizing historical data and exchange data. The first phase of the research focused on exploratory data analysis to gain insights into the observed dataset. Data smoothing methods contributed to a better understanding of emerging patterns by reducing noise and extremes, providing a foundation for further analysis and better preconditions for prediction. The second phase involved data differentiation to achieve dataset stationarity, which plays an important role in eliminating trends and seasonal variations, enabling more accurate predictions. After data preparation, the research included building an LSTM model to predict fuel price movements. The LSTM model showed high accuracy in prediction, indicating that fuel price movements largely depend on oil price movements. These results have practical applications in economics, energy, and related sectors, providing relevant information to decision-makers within these sectors for better resource management and consumption optimization.

It appears that changes in fuel prices in BiH take approximately one month to reflect variations in the WTI and BRENT stock exchanges.

The continuation of the research would be aimed at researching the remaining 5 types of fuel, analysis and prediction, but also their mutual relations and influence on each other. Also, as it seems that this dataset could to be a good basis for experimenting with data imputation, which is a very important aspect of time-dependent data, that would be one of the directions of future research. Simple traditional imputations, such as linear or average imputation, are often used, but more advanced solutions, like those using generative adversarial networks (GANs) [30] or transformers [14], which have shown their superiority in natural language processing and time-dependent data (such as [28,29]) in recent years compared to other generative models, can be explored.

This study also suggests the exploration of state-of-the-art time-series models, such as iTransformer [21], SOFTS [20], and PatchTST [22], using the NeuralForecast library [23]. Additionally, slightly older models like Informer [24] and TimeMixer [25], as well as more recent advancements such as RMoK [26] based on KAN networks [27], could provide valuable models and insights.

Acknowledgements. The authors are grateful to the Federal Ministry of Trade of Bosnia and Herzegovina for the permission to publicly publish the dataset and the entire research.

Declarations

Competing Interests. Not Applicable.

Funding Information. Not Applicable.

Author Contribution. Hrvoje Ljubić and Robert Rozić conducted the data analysis and developed deep learning model. Tomislav Volarić conceptualized the study and contributed to the methodology.

Data Availability Statement. Data is publicly available on Kaggle (https://www.kaggle.com/datasets/hljubic/fuel-prices-fbih-2018-2023

Research Involving Human and/or Animals. Not Applicable.

Informed Consent. Not Applicable.

References

1. Li, M., Vigni, V., Durante, C., Cocchi, M.: Exploratory data analysis. In: Data Handling in Science and Technology, vol. 28, Elsevier, pp. 55–126 (2013). https://doi.org/10.1016/B978-0-444-59528-7.00003-X.
2. Ljubić, H.: Fuel Prices (FBiH 2018-2023) [Data set]. Kaggle (2024). https://doi.org/10.34740/KAGGLE/DS/5272270
3. Wang, S., Yu, L., Lai, K.K.: A novel hybrid AI system framework for crude oil price forecasting. Chinese Academy of Sciences Symposium on Data Mining and Knowledge Management. Berlin, Heidelberg: Springer Berlin Heidelberg (2004)
4. Gupta, N., Nigam, S.: Crude oil price prediction using artificial neural network. Procedia Computer Science **170**, 642–647 (2020)
5. Bildirici, M., Bayazit, N.G., Ucan, Y.: Analyzing crude oil prices under the impact of COVID-19 by using LSTARGARCHLSTM. Energies **13**(11), 2980 (2020)
6. Bristone, M., Prasad, R., Abubakar, A.A.: CPPCNDL: crude oil price prediction using complex network and deep learning algorithms. Petroleum **6**(4), 353-361 (2020)
7. Zhao, Y., Hu, B., Wang, S.: Prediction of Brent crude oil price based on LSTM model under the background of low-carbon transition. arXiv preprint arXiv:2409.12376 (2024)
8. Yousefi, S., Weinreich, I., Reinarz, D.: Wavelet-based prediction of oil prices. Chaos, Solitons Fractals **25**(2), 265–275 (2005)
9. Abramson, B., Finizza, A.: Using belief networks to forecast oil prices. Int. J. Forecast. **7**(3), 299–315 (1991)
10. Garner, H., Fernstad, S.J.: Comparative evaluation of the scatter plot matrix and parallel coordinates plot matrix. In: 2022 26th International Conference Information Visualisation (IV), Vienna, Austria: IEEE, pp. 114–122 (2022). https://doi.org/10.1109/IV56949.2022.00027.
11. Hyndman, R.J., Athanasopoulos, G.: Forecasting: Principles and Practice'
12. Liu, Y., Wu, H., Wang, J., Long, M.: Non-stationary transformers: exploring the stationarity in time series forecasting. arXiv, (2023). http://arxiv.org/abs/2205.14415 Accessed 22 Jan 2024
13. Test for Stationarity on Inflation Rates in Nigeria using Augmented Dickey Fuller Test and Phillips-Perron Test
14. Vaswani, A.: Attention is all you need. Adv. Neural Inf. Process. Syst. (2017)
15. Hochreiter, S., Schmidhuber, J.: Long Short-Term Memory. Neural Comput. **9**(8), 1735–1780 (1997). https://doi.org/10.1162/neco.1997.9.8.1735
16. Cho, K., et al.: Learning phrase representations using RNN encoder-decoder for statistical machine translation, arXiv (2014). http://arxiv.org/abs/1406.1078 Accessed 23 Jan 2024
17. Kang, J., Zhang, W.-Q., Liu, W.-W., Liu, J., Johnson, M.T.: Advanced recurrent network-based hybrid acoustic models for low resource speech recognition. EURASIP J. Audio Speech Music Process. **2018**(1), 1–15 (2018). https://doi.org/10.1186/s13636-018-0128-6

18. Müller, A.C., Guido, S.: Introduction to machine learning with Python: a guide for data scientists, 1st edn. O'Reilly, Beijing Boston Farnham Sebastopol Tokyo (2016)
19. Jovanovic, L., et al.: Multi-step crude oil price prediction based on LSTM approach tuned by SALP swarm algorithm with disputation operator. Sustainability **14**(21), 14616 (2022)
20. Han, L., et al.: SOFTS: Efficient Multivariate Time Series Forecasting with Series-Core Fusion. arXiv preprint arXiv:2404.14197 (2024)
21. Liu, Y., et al.: itransformer: Inverted transformers are effective for time series forecasting. arXiv preprint arXiv:2310.06625 (2023)
22. Nie, Y., et al.: A time series is worth 64 words: Long-term forecasting with transformers. arXiv preprint arXiv:2211.14730 (2022)
23. Olivares, K.G., et al.: NeuralForecast: User friendly state-of-the-art neural forecasting models. PyCon Salt Lake City, Utah, US 2022 (2022): 6
24. Zhou, H., et al. Informer: beyond efficient transformer for long sequence time-series forecasting. In: Proceedings of the AAAI conference on artificial intelligence, vol. 35. No. 12 (2021)
25. Wang, S., et al.: Timemixer: Decomposable multiscale mixing for time series forecasting. arXiv preprint arXiv:2405.14616 (2024)
26. Han, X., et al.: KAN4TSF: Are KAN and KAN-based models Effective for Time Series Forecasting?. arXiv preprint arXiv:2408.11306 (2024)
27. Liu, Z., et al.: Kan: Kolmogorov-arnold networks. arXiv preprint arXiv:2404.19756 (2024)
28. Zhang, Y., Yan, J.: Crossformer: transformer utilizing cross-dimension dependency for multivariate time series forecasting. The Eleventh International Conference on Learning Representations (2022)
29. Liu, Yong, et al.: itransformer: inverted transformers are effective for time series forecasting. arXiv preprint arXiv:2310.06625 (2023)
30. Goodfellow, I., et al.: Generative adversarial nets. Advances in Neural Inf. Process. Syst. **27** (2014)

The Role of Artificial Intelligence Tools in Enhancing Organizational Communication Strategy: An Analysis of Their Impact on Targeted Advertising and Public Interaction

Damir Vasilj, Željko Matković(✉), and Nikica Bubalo

University of Mostar, Trg Hrvatskih Velikana 1, Mostar, Bosnia and Herzegovina
damir.vasilj@sum.ba, zeljkomatkovic@hotmail.com

Abstract. With an emphasis on targeted advertising and public communication this study researches the effects of AI tools on communication strategies of organizations. While testing Hypothesis posits that AI enhances targeted advertising through successful data analysis. The principal hypothesis posits that AI technologies augment communication strategies through personalized, timely, and data-driven public engagement. Using a quantitative approach with 51 participants, the study employed descriptive statistics, Kruskal-Wallis tests, and regression analysis. Results show that 73.7% of the variance in AI tool effectiveness is explained by budget readiness, internal communication frequency, and external communication quality. Both hypotheses were confirmed, demonstrating AI's critical role in improving communication strategies and targeted advertising outcomes within organizations.

Keywords: artificial intelligence · organizational communication · communication strategy · targeted advertising · data-driven interaction

1 Introduction

The introduction of AI has transformed most industries, including marketing and communication. AI tools offer new opportunities for organisations to enhance their communication strategies through targeted and data-driven communication with the public. The aim of this paper is to examine how AI tools are affecting the achievement of organisational communication strategies, particularly how they are assisting in advertising targeting, engagement with the public, and the success of general communication.

Previous research has delineated the transformative potential of AI in marketing and communications. Work by Vujnovic et al. (2023) and Kupec et al. (2021) identifies AI's role in transforming communication paradigms and marketing strategy through web personalization and precision messaging [10, 23]. Other scholars, including Stoeckle (2023) and Cheng and Jiang (2022), discuss AI's role in persuasion technology and customer-brand relationships [5, 21]. Additionally, research by Zerfass, Hagelstein, and

D. Vasić and E. Brajković (Eds.): MoStart 2025, CCIS 2609, pp. 171–181, 2026.
https://doi.org/10.1007/978-3-032-02801-3_11

Tench (2020) reveals the gap between perceived and actual AI competencies among communication professionals [24].

The integration of AI into digital transformation strategies is also noted by Nesterenko, Miskiewicz, and Abazov (2023), Zhao (2024), and Senyapar (2024), who emphasize AI's role in optimizing public relations practices and supporting strategic communication [14, 19, 25].

This study is grounded in the following main and supporting hypotheses:

- **Main Hypothesis:** The application of artificial intelligence tools significantly contributes to achieving an organization's communication strategy by enabling personalized, timely, and data-driven interaction with the public, resulting in a better understanding of audience needs and increased trust in the organization.
- **Supporting Hypothesis 1:** AI improves targeted advertising by analysing large amounts of data to accurately identify target audiences.

The hypotheses will be tested by quantitative research and a common questionnaire to obtain data from different organizations. Descriptive statistics, Kruskal-Wallis tests, regression analysis, and correlation analysis will be applied to test the effectiveness of AI tools in enabling communication strategies.

It is expected that a positive relationship exists between the deployment of AI tools and improved communication strategies, the increased perceived efficacy of AI tools among institutions utilizing them heavily, and evidence to demonstrate that specialized advertisement through the use of AI improves communication. The study has the objective to enhance knowledge about AI application within communication as well as provide practitioners and scholars with information on how to leverage AI in strategic communication effectiveness.

2 Literature Review

Researchers have been examining different aspects of AI for communication and marketing, both benefits and problems for modern organizations. Vujnovic, Swiatek, Kruckeberg and Galloway (2023) call attention to the potential for AI to transform learning in public relations, its potential impact on restructuring teaching and learning models in higher education institutions [23].

Similarly, Kupec, Jakubíková, and Kupec (2021) describe synergistic use of web personalization and AI as effective tools for enhancing marketing communications, with a model for use in operational practice in strategic marketing [10]. Stoeckle (2023) is history-focused, describing the development of persuasion technologies and establishing the future role of AI in public relations, advocating for critical examination of AI's impact [21].

In the wake of this line of discussion, Zerfass, Hagelstein, and Tench (2020) present evidence-based findings of cross-country surveys of AI adoption in communication management and unveil the discrepancy between professionals' reported AI capacity and what is possessed [24]. Zytnik and Lequick (2023) take an HR approach by drawing attention to the need for organizational acclimatization to AI tools to make productivity as well as workers' welfare possible [26]. Lim and Valley (2024) stress the application of AI tools, such as ChatGPT, to facilitate campus communication and show how AI is applied in public relations in daily life [11]. Stone et al. (2020) describe strategic decision-making in marketing, referencing that business organizations must adopt AI to retain their leadership role [22]. Cheng and Jiang (2022) examine the impact of AI chatbot advertisements on customer-brand relationships [5]. Nobre (2020) says that automated chatbots in PR and propaganda are usually put in action for a cause [16].

Nesterenko, Miskiewicz, and Abazov (2023) describe the overall role of digitalization in marketing communication, attributing it to AI as the enabler of more accurate and better-performing solutions [14]. Huang and Rust (2021) presented strategic map of AI in marketing according to the classification of AI applications into mechanical, cognitive, and emotional AI for improving marketing activities [9].

Vujnovic, Swiatek, Kruckeberg, and Galloway (2023) discussed the influence of AI on education within public relations and revealed how AI technology can revolutionize the education systems [23].

Stoeckle (2023) gave a historical background of persuasion technology, exploring the future role of AI in public relations campaigns [21]. Cheng and Jiang (2022) discussed the impact of AI chatbots on marketing, hence the significance of personalized interactions to enhance customer-brand relationships [5]. Kupec, Jakubíková, and Kupec (2021) emphasize the importance of web and AI personalization towards achieving maximum maximization of advertisement marketing communications [10]. Stone et al. (2020) examined strategic applications of AI in marketing decision-making with the assertion that it has enormous potential towards the formation of competitive value [22]. Huang and Rust (2021) developed a strategic framework where AI was classified into mechanical, cognitive, and emotional depending on their corresponding roles in planning development and planning implementation [9].

While researching how AI influences enhancing consumer interaction and communication Al-Nsour and Ali (2024) advocated for the fact that AI technologies can enhance customer loyalty for Saudi Arabian organizations by means of customized ways of communication [1]. Similarly, Nkembuh (2024) explored the application of AI for personalization in strategic communications and derived ethical principles on transparency and privacy of data whilst in, and after, analysis [15].

AI in digital transformation is also a hot topic now. Nesterenko, Miskiewicz, and Abazov (2023) addressed the changes in marketing methods with the digitization of the environment [14], while Nesterenko and Olefirenko (2023) studied how AI changed the perspective of modern advertising [13]. According to Osei-Mensah, Asiamah, and Sackey (2023) AI has become one of the major factors in determining the future of strategic communication [17].

And PR practices are also being transformed by AI technologies. Zhao (2024) conducted a systematic review of PR and AI, finding that tools such as ChatGPT are transforming traditional PR strategies [25]. In an Indonesian context, Arief and Gustomo (2020) explored the implications of AI and big data for PR practice and concluded that, although AI can automate some tasks previously handled by communicators, human expertise is still needed to establish genuine relationships with stakeholders [3].

Gayaparsad and Ramlutchman (2024) investigated how AI can transform marketing communications through strategic integration approaches that optimize customer experience with consideration for ethical implications [8]. Senyapar (2024) elaborated on the use of AI in content generation, influencer marketing, and predictive analytics, emphasizing the potential of AI in streamlining communication approaches [19].

The study conducted by Mardhika in 2023 researched AI media monitoring systems and its positive impact on PR practices [12]. Mardhikas research in 2023 stressed that strategic communication management requires human oversight [12]. According to Ardila (2020), AI now helps PR organizations to develop strategic messages and to spread them through specific influencers [2]. The study concluded that PR practitioners must manage the ethical and reputational risks which accompany the productivity benefits provided by AI [2]. The study by Seidenglanz and Baier (2023) expanded on these questions and demonstrated that AI-driven tools like ChatGPT transform PR and communications management by introducing new tasks and roles for professionals who need to define AI technology limits in terms of knowledge and understanding [18].

Fardiah et al. (2024) explored the role of AI in government PR strategies through an electronic-based government (SPBE) study in West Java [7]. AI and chatbots improved communication efficiency and transparency in public services, their study added [7]. Dunan and Mudjiyanto (2020), for example, examined the Indonesian government's PR strategies during the Industrial Revolution 4.0, identifying AI and big data analytics as crucial for improving public information services and implementing automated communication systems [6].

Silviani (2024) addressed the Indonesian PR profession, exploring ethical dilemmas and job challenges due to AI integration [20]. Research urged equilibrium between AI's efficiency and preserving the human element in PR methodology [20]. Bourne (2019) provided a critical lens on how AI is intertwined with neoliberal ideologies in PR, where, in many cases, corporate interests take precedence over ethical concerns and societal impacts [4]. The research cautioned against overwrought optimism in the adoption of AI and urged voices from across the spectrum to be considered in discussions around AI.

3 Methodology

Utilizing a quantitative research design this study research if AI software can be utilized to achieving communication goals of organisations. The study collected and analysed numerical data to develop trends, relationships, and differences between groups. The quantitative method was necessary due to the collected statistical data, objectivity, and the capacity to generalize findings to organizational environments.

Out of 60 people provided with the questionnaire, 51 responded, constituting the sample size. The respondents were drawn from a cross-section of different companies that varied in size, industry segments, and ownership structures (private and public). Convenience sampling was used for ease of selecting the respondents from an accessible pool. A standardized online questionnaire comprising both closed-ended and Likert scale items was used to gather data. The study asked respondents if their company is ready to embrace and use AI technologies, as well as how they feel about AI marketing and PR tools. In this study were used analytical techniques to process and analyse the data:

- IBM SPSS: Used for statistical analysis, including descriptive statistics, correlation analysis, Kruskal-Wallis tests, and regression analysis.
- Questionnaire: The survey was conducted through Microsoft forms, included questions aligned with research hypotheses, focusing on key metrics such as effectiveness, readiness for budget adjustment, and the perceived improvement in communication quality.

Data analysis was a process involving multiple steps:

1. Descriptive statistics included the sample characteristics and fundamental statistical values such as the mean, standard deviation, and response distribution.
2. Pairwise comparison and the Kruskal-Wallis Test: checked differences in perception by organizational groups (e.g., by type and size of ownership) regarding the effectiveness of AI.
3. Regression Analysis: Determined how variables (such as budgeting willingness and enhancing internal communication) affect the effectiveness of AI tools.
4. Visualization: The process of presenting data as graphics to facilitate result understanding and presentation.

By using the above techniques, the study ensured research hypotheses were scientifically and thoroughly tested, and organizational communication strategy contribution by AI was better understood.

4 Results

The effectiveness of paid AI tools in public communication was rated slightly positive (mean = 2.35 on a 1–3 scale), with moderate variability (SD = 0.688). Responses leaned toward higher effectiveness (skewness = −0.594) and showed a broad distribution (kurtosis = −0.705).

Organizational readiness to adjust budgets for AI tools was moderately rated (mean = 2.24) with high consistency (SD = 0.428). The data indicated a lean toward lower budget readiness (skewness = 1.286) with a relatively even distribution (kurtosis = −0.361).

AI tools are sometimes employed for internal communication (mean = 2.00), exhibiting moderate variability (SD = 0.490) and a symmetrical response distribution (skewness = 0.000, kurtosis = 1.509). Participants observed minimal enhancement in the quality of external public communication via AI tools (mean = 1.88, SD = 0.588), exhibiting virtually symmetrical answers (skewness = 0.019) and a uniform distribution (kurtosis = −0.052).

The effectiveness of AI tools in identifying target groups was also moderate (mean = 2.24, SD = 0.428), with responses leaning lower (skewness = 1.286) and an even distribution (kurtosis = −0.361). AI tools' contribution to PR and marketing campaigns' success scored moderately (mean = 2.22, SD = 0.461), with a slight skew toward lower ratings (skewness = 0.767) and a normal response distribution (kurtosis = 0.209).

The frequency of using AI tools for market research was moderate (mean = 2.22, SD = 0.461), showing consistent responses and a trend toward lower use (skewness = 0.767), with a near-normal distribution (kurtosis = 0.209).

The Kruskal-Wallis test was conducted to determine if the frequency of AI tool usage for internal communication (GH3) influences the perceived effectiveness of AI tools in public communication (GH1). The results showed a statistically significant difference among groups ($p = 0.012$), boxplot in Fig. 1 visually supports that finding by showing distinct median values and distributions among the groups.

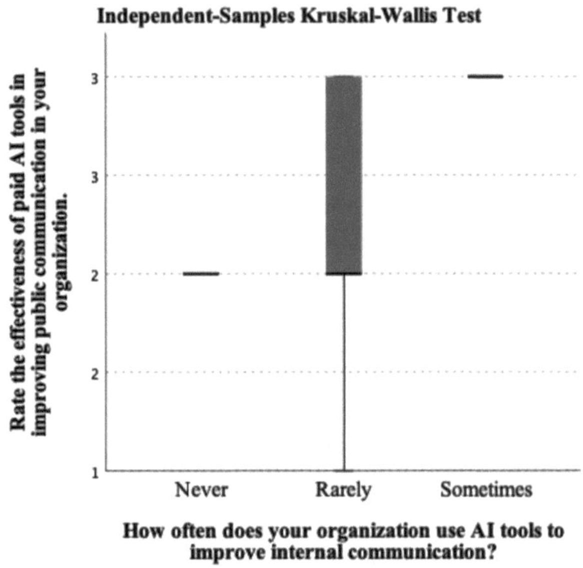

Fig. 1. Kruskal-Wallis test

The largest gap between average ranks (39.50 vs. 17.00) indicates a significant difference in the perception of AI tool effectiveness. Organizations that occasionally utilize AI tools internally assess their efficacy in public communication significantly higher than those that do not employ such tools at all. The disparity between 39.50 (Sometimes) and 25.41 (Rarely) illustrates a notable enhancement in perceived efficacy along with heightened frequency of AI tool utilization. This discovery underscores that even a shift from seldom to occasional usage can significantly influence organizational communication methods.

Although the difference between 25.41 (Rarely) and 17.00 (Never) is smaller, it still suggests that even limited use of AI tools improves perception compared to no use at all. The Fig. 2 effectively presents the pairwise comparisons of the average ranks for how often organizations use AI tools to improve internal communication, specifically comparing the groups Never, Rarely, and Sometimes, providing a clear visualization of how usage frequency influences perceived effectiveness.

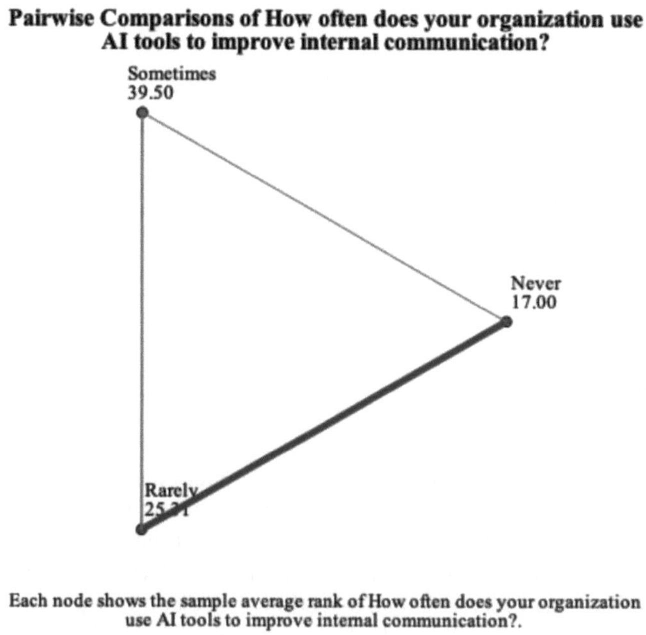

Fig. 2. Pairwise comparison

The regression model exhibited a robust fit, with a R^2 value of 0.737, signifying that 73.7% of the variance in the perceived efficacy of AI technologies in public communication can be explained by the chosen predictors. The Adjusted $R^2 = 0.720$ further supported the model's stability, indicating low shrinkage when applied to the population, as illustrated in Fig. 3.

Model Summary

Model	R	R Square	Adjusted R Square	Std. Error of the Estimate
1	.858[a]	.737	.720	.364

a. Predictors: (Constant), How much would you say AI has improved the quality of your organization's communication with the external public?, How willing is your organization to adjust the budget for AI tools in public relations and marketing activities?, How often does your organization use AI tools to improve internal communication?

Fig. 3. Regression analysis R model

The ANOVA findings supported the model's statistical significance ($F = 43.792$, $p < 0.001$), suggesting that the predictors together explain the efficacy of AI technologies in public communication, as illustrated in Fig. 4.

ANOVA[a]

Model		Sum of Squares	df	Mean Square	F	Sig.
1	Regression	17.416	3	5.805	43.792	<.001[b]
	Residual	6.231	47	.133		
	Total	23.647	50			

a. Dependent Variable: Rate the effectiveness of paid AI tools in improving public communication in your organization.

b. Predictors: (Constant), How much would you say AI has improved the quality of your organization's communication with the external public?, How willing is your organization to adjust the budget for AI tools in public relations and marketing activities?, How often does your organization use AI tools to improve internal communication?

Fig. 4. Anova analysis

5 Discussion

The results of this study provide solid proof of the impact of AI tools on an organization's communication strategy, particularly in public communication and direct marketing. The study largely confirms the main hypothesis that the application of AI tools significantly assists an organization in achieving its communication strategy through personalized, timely, and data-driven interaction with the public. The results reveal a strong correlation between the application of AI tools, budget readiness, and communication effectiveness, in line with earlier research conducted by Kupec et al. in 2021 and Vujnovic et al. in2023 highlighting the transformative power of AI in marketing and communication [10, 23].

Regression analysis revealed that the predictors in the model explained 73.7% of the variance in the effectiveness of AI tools in public communication. This robust finding indicates the large influence of budget preparedness, internal communication practices, and perceived quality of external communication on achieving communication strategy goals. The robust negative influence of budget preparedness (Beta $= -0.851$, $p < 0.001$) signifies that companies not willing to spend budgets on AI tools are bound to struggle in utilizing their full potential in public communication. This finding aligns with Zerfass, Hagelstein, and Tench (2020), whose study identified the mismatch between AI capabilities as seen and believed by communication practitioners [24].

Surprisingly, while applying AI tools in internal communication was found to significantly positively affect the outcome (Beta $= 0.534$, $p < 0.001$), the self-perceived external communication quality enhancement had a negative effect (Beta $= -0.428$, $p < 0.001$). This gap may imply that while internal familiarity with AI tools enhances their deployment outside, their actual application of public communication plans may not necessarily be as great as within. This finding could be a signal of potential conflict between internal methods and external outcomes of communication, which would indicate that routine training and incorporation practices are critical for realizing the total potential of AI [22].

The Kruskal-Wallis test also supported the hypothesis further by indicating a statistically significant difference ($p = 0.012$) between the perceived effectiveness of AI tools by the frequency of their use for internal communication. The findings revealed that organizations which utilized AI tools from time to time internally gave the effectiveness of public communication significantly higher scores compared to those organizations which never or seldom utilized AI tools. This implies that regular but non-redundant use of AI tools can support communication approaches, affirming the necessity to find a balance to AI assimilation in organizational practice [5].

To substantiate Hypothesis 1, where AI was described to boost focused advertising by scouring large data banks to ensure accurate prediction of target audiences, was also authenticated by the good correlation between AI tool effectiveness and targeted advertising outcome. Results pointed out that the ability of AI to analyse information and give feedback on the preferences of the audience maximally maximizes the quality of marketing efforts, resulting in greater engagement and belief in the target audience [9].

The study offers tangible implications for organizations that want to enhance their communications strategy with AI instruments. First, budgetary provision for financial assistance towards AI programs is crucial, such that fiscal readiness has an influence on perceived AI instrument quality. Second, constant intra-firm application of AI instruments should be encouraged to develop organization competence and effectiveness in utilizing such instruments in an extra-firm role. Finally, organizations should be mindful of internal operations' alignment with external communication goals in a way that internal training and AI deployment translate into concrete public communication results.

Although the research is rich in results, it also has certain limitations that should be addressed in future research. The sample was not very large, which might influence the external validity of the results. Second, the research relied on self-reported measures, which can result in response bias. Subsequent research may use a mixed-methods design, with quantitative analysis coupled with qualitative observations to investigate the underlying factors that contribute to perceptions of AI tool effectiveness. Additional research may explore sector-specific effects of AI tools and longitudinal data analysis to identify how continuous use of AI impacts organizational performance over time.

The findings contribute to a bigger picture of AI's role in enhancing organizational communication strategies. The findings support the view that strategic uptake of AI instruments, driven by adequate budgetary means and internal support, can spearhead significant improvement in public communication effectiveness and targeted advertising efficacy.

6 Conclusion

The research provides practical guidance for firms desiring to improve their communication strategy with AI technology. Budget planning for the AI projects matters as preparedness in financial terms directly relates to the value, they see in deploying the tools. The habitual internal use of AI technologies must be fostered to facilitate capacity development and promote confidence in their external use.

Organizations must align internal processes with external communication objectives to enhance internal training and AI utilization, hence generating measurable public communication results.

This work offers significant insights yet presents few challenges for further research. The sample size was limited, perhaps constraining the external validity of the results. The study utilized self-reported data, which may result in response bias.

Future research should employ a mixed-methods approach, integrating quantitative analysis with qualitative data to clarify the reasons behind the perceived effectiveness of AI tools.

Also, in future research should be examined sector-specific effects of AI tools and perform longitudinal assessments to evaluate the enduring influence of AI implementation on organizational performance.

The study contributes to knowledge of the value contribution AI adds to framing the organisational communications strategy. The evidence supports the hypothesis that strategic investment in AI applications enabled by the facilitation of the presence of budgetary means and top-management support can make a dramatic difference to the effectiveness of public communications and the efficiency of targeted advertising.

References

1. Al-Nsour, I.A.A.F., Ali, E.A.H.H.M.: Using artificial intelligence to enhance customer communications at major saudi companies. J. Philanthropy Market. **4**(1), 619–636 (2024)
2. Ardila, M.M.: The rise of intelligent machines: How artificial intelligence is transforming the public relations industry. Unpublished Thesis, University of Southern California, School for Communication and Journalism (2020)
3. Arief, N.N., Gustomo, A.: Analyzing the impact of big data and artificial intelligence on the communications profession: a case study on Public Relations (PR) Practitioners in Indonesia. Int. J. Adv. Sci. Eng. Inform. Technol. **10**(3), 1066–1071 (2020)
4. Bourne, C.: AI cheerleaders: public relations, neoliberalism and artificial intelligence. Public Relat. Inquiry **8**(2), 109–125 (2019)
5. Cheng, Y., Jiang, H.: Customer–brand relationship in the era of artificial intelligence: understanding the role of chatbot marketing efforts. J. Product Brand Manage. **31**(2), 252–264 (2022)
6. Dunan, A., Mudjiyanto, B.: The republic of indonesia government public relations communication strategy in the era of the industrial revolution 4.0. JATI-J. Southeast Asian Stud. **25**(1), 58–78. (2020)
7. Fardiah, D., Darmawan, F., Rinawati, R., Supaat, V.E.M., Hadnansyah, E.: Digital transformation through electronic-based government system performance as public relations strategy. PRofesi Humas **9**(1), 23–48 (2024)
8. Gayaparsad, K., Ramlutchman, N.: the influence of artificial intelligence (AI) in transforming marketing communications: a theoretical review. Expert J. Market. **12**(1) (2024)
9. Huang, M.H., Rust, R.T.: A strategic framework for artificial intelligence in marketing. J. Acad. Mark. Sci. **49**, 30–50 (2021)
10. Kupec, M., Jakubíková, D., Kupec, V.: Web personalization and artificial intelligence as tools for marketing communications. Media Literacy Acad. Res. **4**(2) (2021)
11. Lim, Y.J., Valley, R.G.: Revolutionizing campus communications: the power of ChatGPT in public relations. J. Public Relations Educ. **10**(2), 91–129 (2024)
12. Mardhika, H.: How the introduction of AI (Media Monitoring) tools affects the field of public relations. Jurnal Manajemen Bisnis **10**(2), 555–569 (2023)
13. Nesterenko, V., Olefirenko, O.: The impact of AI development on the development of marketing communications. Market. i menedžment innovacij **14**(1), 169–181 (2023)
14. Nesterenko, V., Miskiewicz, R., Abazov, R.: Marketing communications in the era of digital transformation. Virtual Econ. **6**(1), 57–70 (2023)
15. Nkembuh, N.: Beyond algorithms: a comprehensive analysis of AI-driven personalization in strategic communications. J. Comput. Commun. **12**(10), 112–131 (2024)

16. Nobre, G.: Artificial Intelligence (AI) in communications: Journalism, public relations, advertising, and propaganda. Guilherme Fráguas Nobre, 1–9. (2020)
17. Osei-Mensah, B., Asiamah, E.O., Sackey, R.: Strategic communication and artificial intelligence: reviewing emerging innovations and future directions. Arch. Bus. Res. **11**(1), 85–102 (2023)
18. Seidenglanz, R., Baier, M.: The impact of Artificial intelligence on the professional field of Public Relations/Communications Management: Recent developments and opportunities. Artificial Intelligence in Public Relations and Communications: cases, reflections, and predictions, pp. 14–25 (2023)
19. Senyapar, H.N.D.: Artificial intelligence in marketing communication: a comprehensive exploration of the integration and impact of AI. Technium Soc. Sci. J. **55**, 64 (2024)
20. Silviani, I.: Quo vadis Indonesian public relations profession: dilemma on the rise of AI. Jurnal Studi Komunikasi **8**(1), 053–063 (2024)
21. Stoeckle, T.: If then, or What if? What the history of PR (and of 'persuasion technology') can teach us about the future role of AI in PR. Artificial Intelligence in Public Relations and Communications: cases, reflections, and predictions, vol. 26 (2023)
22. Stone, M., et al.: Artificial intelligence (AI) in strategic marketing decision-making: a research agenda. Bottom Line **33**(2), 183–200 (2020)
23. Vujnovic, M., Swiatek, L., Kruckeberg, D., Galloway, C.: What is AI Teaching Us About Public Relations Education?. Artificial Intelligence in Public Relations and Communications: Cases, Reflections, and Predictions, vol. 137 (2023)
24. Zerfass, A., Hagelstein, J., Tench, R.: Artificial intelligence in communication management: a cross-national study on adoption and knowledge, impact, challenges and risks. J. Commun. Manag. **24**(4), 377–389 (2020)
25. Zhao, X.: A systematic review of public relations research in the context of artificial intelligence. Commun. Hum. Res. **36**, 92–101 (2024)
26. Zytnik, M., Lequick, M.: Getting colleagues comfortable with AI: a human-centered approach to technology in organizations. Artificial Intelligence in Public Relations and Communications: cases, reflections, and predictions, vol. 73 (2023)

AI Technologies in Music Education: Personalized Learning for Elementary School Students

Lidija Vladić Mandarić and Emil Brajković(✉)

University of Mostar, Trg hrvatskih velikana 1, Mostar, Bosnia and Herzegovina
{lidija.vladic.mandaric,emil.brajkovic}@fpmoz.sum.ba
https://www.sum.ba

Abstract. The development of artificial intelligence (AI) is bringing significant changes to music education, particularly through a personalized learning approach at the primary level. This paper explores the application of AI technologies in adapting teaching content to the cognitive and affective characteristics of students. AI enables flexibility in learning, adjusts the pace, and provides systematic real-time feedback. By using AI tools, students have the opportunity for interactive and adaptive learning, while teachers can more effectively monitor their progress through specific case studies that demonstrate the pedagogical impact of AI in primary school music education.

The benefits include increased motivation, the development of creativity, and more precise evaluation of musical competencies. Despite numerous advantages, challenges such as ethical concerns, the potential depersonalization of teaching, and the need for teacher training remain key aspects of AI implementation in education. The research findings confirm that AI can significantly enhance music education if implemented in accordance with pedagogical principles and ethical guidelines.

This topic is significant as it explores how AI can tailor teaching to the individual needs of students, which is one of the key trends in modern education. Additionally, it allows for the exploration of specific AI tools that can assist teachers in educating children.

Keywords: artificial intelligence · music · personalized learning · primary education

1 Introduction

Music education plays a key role in the overall development of a child, fostering creativity, emotional intelligence, and cognitive abilities. Through learning music, students develop auditory, motor, and analytical skills while also acquiring values such as discipline, collaboration, and aesthetic sensitivity. Traditional approaches to music education, although effective, often face challenges such as varying learning paces, limited resources, and the need for individualized instruction.

D. Vasić and E. Brajković (Eds.): MoStart 2025, CCIS 2609, pp. 182–195, 2026.
https://doi.org/10.1007/978-3-032-02801-3_12

The modern development of artificial intelligence brings innovative solutions to the field of education, enabling a personalized learning approach and adapting teaching content to the individual needs of students. AI technologies, such as AIVA (Artificial Intelligence Virtual Artist), Amper Music, Yousician, and others, are increasingly used to analyze students' abilities, generate customized exercises, and provide real-time feedback. In the field of music education, AI allows students to engage in interactive learning, develop creativity, and acquire musical skills flexibly, while helping teachers monitor progress and adjust teaching methods.

The aim of this research is to theoretically analyze the application of AI technologies in primary school music education, with an emphasis on personalized learning. The study examines how AI tools can enhance learning efficiency, increase student motivation, and enable more precise assessment of musical competencies. Through a review of relevant literature, an analysis of existing AI applications, and case studies, the paper will present the potential benefits and challenges of implementing artificial intelligence in primary school music instruction.

2 A Brief Historical Overview of AI Applications in Music Education

The evolution of artificial intelligence in education has unfolded over several decades, with its application in music education becoming particularly significant in the 21st century. Beginning with early intelligent tutoring systems (ITS) developed in the 1960s, such as PLATO (Programmed Logic for Automatic Teaching Operations), AI has gradually enhanced educational processes by enabling content adaptation to students' needs. In its early stages, the development of computer pedagogy focused on simple adaptive systems that analyzed student responses and provided feedback based on predefined rules [1]. However, with advancements in artificial intelligence, particularly in machine learning and sound processing, technologies have become more sophisticated, allowing for advanced performance analysis, personalized teaching, and music composition generation, significantly transforming the paradigms of music education.

As early as the 1980s and 1990 s, with the development of digital technology and the first music software, such as MIDI sequencers and early algorithmic composition systems, researchers began experimenting with the potential applications of AI in music education. Programs like David Cope's *Experiments in Musical Intelligence* and interactive real-time music generation systems laid the groundwork for today's AI technologies, which enable students to analyze and process musical data. Alongside the development of computer-based composition, pedagogical tools started incorporating AI to adapt teaching methods, particularly in music theory instruction and aural skill development [2].

The transition into the 21st century brought exponential advancements in artificial intelligence, with a particular focus on deep learning and large-scale data processing. This progress enabled more sophisticated applications in music education, from digital learning platforms to advanced performance analysis systems. Tools like *SmartMusic* and *Yousician* utilize advanced algorithms to assess rhythm, intonation, and technical performance, providing personalized feedback that allows for individualized learning. These systems not only evaluate performance based on predetermined criteria but also offer suggestions for improvement, simulating the role of a teacher in real time [3] .

At the same time, AI began to support the creative aspects of music education. Generative models such as *AIVA*, *Amper Music*, and Google's *Magenta* project allow students to create their own compositions using algorithms that analyze musical styles and structures. These tools not only expand the possibilities for experimenting with musical ideas but also encourage students to explore new sonic forms, merging traditional compositional techniques with computational music analysis and generation.

In the past decade, the integration of artificial intelligence with other advanced technologies, such as augmented and virtual reality, has opened new horizons in music education. Interactive learning systems enable the simulation of musical ensembles in virtual environments, while platforms like *Soundtrap* facilitate collaborative music creation regardless of students' physical location [4]. These innovations not only enhance accessibility to music education but also redefine how students develop their skills, allowing them to expand their musical competencies through AI and digital technologies [6].

Today, artificial intelligence is not merely a tool for analyzing and teaching music; it has become an active participant in the learning process, enabling new teaching methods that adapt to students' individual needs. Although AI cannot fully replace the pedagogical role of teachers, its implementation in music education creates opportunities for more dynamic and adaptive learning approaches, continuing the evolution of educational paradigms in the digital age.

2.1 E-Learning Systems in Music Education

E-learning represents a modern form of education that relies on electronic technologies to provide access to educational content outside the traditional classroom. This mode of learning encompasses a wide range of methods, including online courses, programs, and educational levels that are fully delivered via the internet. Although often equated with terms such as online learning, computer-assisted learning, and digital education, e-learning involves an interactive process in which students and teachers engage in two-way communication, either in real-time or through asynchronous methods. This allows learning to be adapted to the individual needs of users, significantly increasing the efficiency of the educational process, including in the field of music education [7].

The development of e-learning is closely linked to advancements in information and communication technologies, which have enabled the integration of multimedia elements such as videos, interactive simulations, and virtual classrooms. In the context of music education, such resources allow students to access online lessons, sheet music, interactive practice tools, and virtual ensembles that facilitate remote collaboration. The key advantage of e-learning lies in its flexibility, as it enables students to access educational content regardless of time and location. Additionally, e-learning in music facilitates access to education for individuals who may not be able to participate in live classes regularly, such as musicians pursuing professional development or individuals learning to play an instrument at their own pace. However, despite numerous advantages, e-learning in music education also presents certain challenges, such as limitations in developing performance skills due to the lack of immediate feedback and difficulties in synchronizing online ensembles due to network latency.

The effectiveness of e-learning is often examined through the lens of pedagogy and didactic strategies. E-learning approaches can generally be divided into two main categories: those that focus exclusively on technology and those that combine technological aspects with the goal of enhancing teaching and learning processes [7]. The optimal application of e-learning in music requires carefully designed educational content that includes interactive elements such as digital metronomes, software tools for sound analysis, and applications for developing aural skills. In this context, constructivist approaches to education, which encourage students to engage in exploratory learning and independent problem-solving, have proven particularly effective in e-learning for music, especially through online improvisation and composition workshops.

Ultimately, while e-learning does not replace traditional teaching methods in music education, it significantly complements and enriches them. By integrating modern technological solutions such as notation software, virtual instruments, and online masterclasses, new opportunities arise for improving the quality of music education. However, it is essential to maintain a balance between technological innovations and pedagogical principles to ensure that e-learning remains focused on its primary goal: providing high-quality music education that meets the needs of contemporary society and fosters the artistic development of individuals.

2.2 Key AI Tools and Their Practical Applications in Music Education

The modern educational process is unimaginable without digital technologies, which have redefined teaching and learning methods. The development of computers, the internet, and multimedia systems has enabled a dynamic and interactive approach to educational content, increasing student engagement and enhancing the quality of the learning experience. Digital tools not only expand the audiovisual possibilities for presenting content but also allow for the adaptation of educational materials to the individual needs of students. Information technology has paved the way for new forms of learning, where flexibility and accessibility of knowledge become key aspects of the educational process [8] [9].

A particularly significant advancement is the integration of artificial intelligence into education, especially in the field of music education. The development of intelligent systems enables innovative teaching methods that foster students' creative development and interpretative skills. Algorithms analyze musical performances, provide feedback, and adjust content to individual educational needs. While AI cannot replace the role of a teacher, its application allows for the development of new pedagogical strategies that enhance the analysis of musical structures and facilitate the understanding of compositional techniques. AI tools not only expand teaching possibilities but also transform the learning experience toward greater individualization and engagement.

In this context, AIVA (an AI tool for music analysis), based on deep learning, analyzes musical structures and generates new compositions, allowing students to explore harmonic progressions and arrangements [4]. In educational programs, students can use AIVA to analyze their own compositions or learn about music theory through practical examples [10].

Amper Music facilitates intuitive creation of musical backgrounds adaptable to various styles, while MuseNet (an AI music generation tool) employs deep learning to encourage an understanding of polyphony and orchestration. One of the most well-known examples of artificial intelligence in music is OpenAI's MuseNet project, which uses deep learning to generate original musical compositions in various styles, including jazz and pop music. This tool can combine different instruments and styles, allowing users to explore new musical landscapes. In schools, MuseNet can be used as a tool to foster creativity among music students, enabling them to experiment with different styles and structures [11]. Alongside compositional capabilities, AI tools like Boomy, Ecrett Music, and LANDR enable rapid creation of musical compositions, generation of music tailored to specific needs, and automatic sound mastering [12]. The use of AI tools to create interactive experiences has also become popular. For example, applications like Google Magenta allow users to create visual representations of their musical compositions using machine learning. These applications can be used in schools to encourage collaboration among students through joint music and art creation [13].

AI technology also contributes to the development of performance and listening skills through interactive applications like Yousician and SmartMusic (AI tools for music education), which provide personalized lessons, automatic performance analysis, and real-time feedback. Some educational programs utilize these tools to help students learn to play instruments through interactive lessons that adjust the pace and difficulty according to the student's progress. These tools employ sound recognition technology to assess students' performances and provide real-time feedback. In schools, such tools can significantly enhance the music learning experience by offering a personalized approach for each student.

Melodics specializes in teaching drumming, keyboard, and MIDI controllers, using interactive exercises that adapt to progress, helping students develop a sense of groove, while EarMaster allows for gradual development of pitch, chord, and rhythm recognition skills, which is particularly useful in solfège and music theory. Soundtrap, a digital audio workstation with an AI component, assists students in composing, producing, and editing music while enabling remote collaboration. On the other hand, Soundbeam uses motion sensors to generate sound, providing inclusive opportunities for individuals with disabilities. In some schools and rehabilitation centers, AI is used to develop music therapy programs that assist students with special needs or emotional difficulties. By using algorithms that analyze emotional responses to different types of music, therapists can tailor sessions to better meet individuals' needs [14].

Additionally, AI tools encourage creativity by enabling digital composition and exploration of various compositional techniques. Humtap allows users to sing a melody, which AI then transforms into a complete musical composition, while Orb Producer Suite generates melodies, chords, and arrangements, facilitating the composition process for music producers and composers. Meludia is an interactive platform that uses AI to develop listening and rhythmic skills (Table 1).

Table 1. AI Tools and Their Practical Applications in Music Education

AI tools	Functionality
AIVA	Analyzes musical structures and generates new compositions,
Amper Music	Facilitates intuitive creation of musical backgrounds
OpenAI's MuseNet	Deep learning to generate original musical compositions
LANDR	Rapid creation of musical compositions
Google Magenta	Visual representations of musical compositions
Yousician and SmartMusic	AI tools for music education
Melodics	Teaching drumming, keyboard, and MIDI controllers
EarMaster	development of pitch, chord, and rhythm recognition skills
Soundtrap	Digital audio workstation
Soundbeam	Uses motion sensors to generate sound
Humtap	Allows users to sing a melody
Orb Producer Suite	generates melodies, chords, and arrangements
Meludia	Develop listening and rhythmic skills.

Integrating AI technologies into music education not only facilitates the analysis and creation of music but also enables a personalized learning approach tailored to individual abilities and interests. This not only enhances the teaching process but also fosters creativity through interactive and adaptable learning methods, allowing teachers to plan lessons more effectively and provide customized educational experiences.

2.3 Integration of AI Tools with Traditional Teaching Methods

Despite numerous advantages, AI technologies cannot completely replace teachers and traditional teaching methods; rather, they complement them, allowing for a more effective and adaptable approach to learning. Artificial intelligence brings numerous innovations to the educational process, but its application in music education must be strategic and thoughtful to maintain a balance between technological support and artistic expression.

The key to successfully integrating AI systems into music teaching lies in combining traditional and contemporary approaches through several methodological guidelines. This involves blending digital and practical exercises, where AI tools can serve as valuable resources for analyzing performances, practicing rhythm and intonation, and automatically adapting tasks to the individual abilities of students. However, the role of the teacher remains crucial in shaping the teaching process, providing interpretive guidance, and encouraging creative expression. AI can optimize the technical aspects of practice, while the teacher directs students toward a deeper understanding of music and its emotional experience.

Using AI as an assistant can be applied as a tool for personalizing instruction, such as assigning customized homework, automatically tracking student progress, and providing additional learning materials. This approach allows teachers to better identify student needs and provide individualized support. AI tools can analyze student performances in real-time, suggest corrections, and offer detailed feedback, thereby increasing the effectiveness of teaching [15].

It is essential to balance technology with emotional expression, as this can enhance the technical aspects of musical performance, since music is not solely a technical skill but also an artistic expression [16] . Therefore, it is important that technology does not overshadow the creative aspects of teaching. AI can help develop precision, but interpretation, feeling, and the personal touch of students must remain the focus of pedagogical work. Teachers should use AI as a tool to assist students in honing their skills while simultaneously encouraging the development of their personal style and musical interpretation.

Integrating AI technologies into music education opens up new possibilities for a personalized approach to learning, increasing student motivation, and optimizing teaching processes. However, to ensure quality music education, it is crucial to maintain a balance between technological innovations and pedagogical principles that foster creativity and artistic expression.

3 Personalized Learning with the Help of AI

Personalized learning represents a modern approach to education that tailors instructional content to the individual needs, interests, and abilities of students. Unlike the traditional teaching model, which is based on a uniform curriculum and the same pace of learning for all students, personalized learning allows flexibility in methods and the rhythm of knowledge acquisition. A key role in this approach is played by artificial intelligence, which analyzes student data through advanced algorithms, tracks their progress, and automatically adjusts instructional materials to their individual needs. Machine learning algorithms enable precise identification of a student's strengths and weaknesses and suggest appropriate tasks and real-time feedback [17] [18].

In the context of music education, the application of AI technology further enriches the learning process by adapting the level of difficulty of exercises, suggesting specific corrections in performance, and generating personalized musical examples to help students better understand certain theoretical and performance concepts. One of the most significant advantages of AI in education is its ability to process large amounts of data, allowing for in-depth analysis of student progress. Artificial intelligence systems record student practice sessions, evaluate performance success, and detect areas where additional practice is needed. Additionally, AI can predict the most effective learning methods for individual students and recommend suitable resources.

Today, there are a variety of AI tools that facilitate personalized music learning tailored to individual student needs. Yousician uses AI to analyze performances on instruments like guitar and piano, offering interactive lessons that adapt to the student's pace of progress. SmartMusic assists teachers in assigning customized tasks and uses AI evaluation to monitor the development of performance skills. EarMaster develops ear training and recognition of musical intervals, chords, and rhythmic patterns through customized exercises, while Melodics offers AI-guided lessons in drumming and keyboard playing, adjusting the level of difficulty based on the student's progress [19].

Furthermore, AIVA allows students to explore music composition by analyzing their preferences and styles, while Soundtrap, as a digital audio workstation (DAW), enables experimentation with music production with AI support in shaping arrangements [3]. ChatGPT can be used as an interactive assistant for learning music theory, generating lyrics, and providing explanations of concepts from music education, contributing to a personalized approach in teaching [20].

The application of AI technology in music education brings numerous benefits, including increased student motivation, interactivity in the learning process, and timely and accurate feedback. Providing access to music resources outside the classroom is especially significant for those who cannot afford individual lessons with instructors. However, despite all the advantages, it is essential to maintain a balance between technology and the human factor in education. Teachers remain irreplaceable in the teaching process, and AI tools should serve as support to enhance the learning experience rather than completely replace it. Therefore, it is crucial that the implementation of AI tools in the educational system is thoughtful, considering pedagogical, technical, and ethical aspects, to ensure quality and comprehensive music education for all students.

3.1 Advantages and Challenges of AI Application in Music Education: Ethical and Pedagogical Implications

The development of artificial intelligence brings significant innovations in the field of music education, especially in the elementary school context, where students exhibit diverse learning styles, abilities, and interests. The integration of AI technologies allows for the adaptation of teaching methods, encourages interactivity, and facilitates personalized access to learning music. However, despite numerous advantages, their implementation in the educational system faces certain pedagogical and ethical challenges.

The application of artificial intelligence in music education opens up possibilities for enhancing traditional teaching methods, ensuring more effective and accessible education. Some key advantages include personalized learning, where AI systems can analyze students' abilities and progress and accordingly adjust content, pace, and teaching methods [17] [18]. This enables students to learn at their own pace, reducing frustration and increasing learning efficiency. Interactive learning in this context involves using AI tools, such as reciprocal applications and digital platforms, allowing students to actively participate in musical activities through virtual instruments, listening exercises, and creative composition tasks.

Furthermore, advanced algorithms can analyze student performance in real time, providing precise suggestions for improving intonation, rhythm, and dynamics, enabling more effective learning and faster progress, all while offering timely feedback. Increased motivation and engagement favor gamification in education, or the use of games and interactive elements, which can significantly boost students' interest in music. AI-driven lessons often include rewards, challenges, and personalized goals, encouraging students to practice regularly [21]. Accessibility to education is another advantage, as AI tools enable students to access quality music education and practice even outside formal school settings. This is particularly beneficial in situations where students do not have access to qualified teachers or music schools.

Despite its advantages, the integration of artificial intelligence into the music education process faces a range of challenges encompassing technical, pedagogical, and ethical aspects of applying this technology. A key issue relates to teacher training, as educators must acquire new knowledge and skills to effectively implement AI tools in their teaching. This requires ongoing professional development in digital technologies while simultaneously developing pedagogical strategies that allow for their optimal application in educational contexts. The role of the teacher in this process undergoes significant transformation, with artificial intelligence acting not as a replacement but as a support in teaching. The human element remains crucial in the educational process, particularly concerning the interpretative and emotional aspects of the musical art. In this regard, the quality of pedagogical work should not be compromised by automation but rather enhanced through the integration of technology into existing teaching practices [22].

The application of artificial intelligence in education also raises ethical questions, particularly concerning student privacy and the transparency of algorithms that analyze their abilities and progress. It is essential to ensure compliance with ethical standards, especially regarding the protection of sensitive data and regulations regarding its use. Additionally, while AI systems enable individualized instruction, it is important to prevent the depersonalization of teaching to preserve the dynamic interaction between teachers and students, which is fundamental to the development of creativity and artistic expression [23].

Despite technological advancements, current AI systems still cannot fully understand and interpret the emotional dimension of musical performance, which presents a significant challenge in artistic education. However, artificial intelligence can serve as a valuable tool for enhancing music education, particularly at the elementary school level, where it contributes to the adaptation of teaching content, increases student engagement, and ensures timely feedback. Successful implementation of AI technologies in this area requires a balanced approach that considers pedagogical, technical, and ethical aspects, with the teacher's role remaining irreplaceable while AI acts as a catalyst for innovation and improvement in the music learning process.

The development and application of artificial intelligence in music education raise a wide range of pedagogical and ethical questions, redefining the role of the teacher, the learning process, and the long-term implications for the educational system. While AI brings innovative approaches to personalized learning, evaluating student performances, and creative musical practices, its implementation requires critical reflection on the challenges, limitations, and potential risks to ensure its optimal application in educational contexts.

The introduction of AI tools in music education significantly changes the dynamic of the relationship between teachers and students, with the teacher's role increasingly shifting towards mentorship and artistic guidance. Rather than being the exclusive source of knowledge, the teacher assumes the role of a facilitator who encourages students to engage in creativity, critical thinking, and self-expression through music. AI tools can take on technical tasks, such as analyzing intonation and rhythm, but they cannot replace the emotional support and pedagogical strategies that are essential for the holistic development of students [24].

4 Survey Research

The results of the survey research on the analysis of attitudes toward the implementation of artificial intelligence in music education in primary education raised two key research questions: 1) examining the existence of statistically significant differences in the perception of the role of artificial intelligence and information technologies on the cognitive and social development of children based on age, and 2) exploring whether there is a significant correlation between attitudes about the role of artificial intelligence and information technologies in the cognitive and social development of children and attitudes about the application of artificial intelligence in music education in primary education.

Based on the relevant literature, two research hypotheses were formulated: 1) the existence of differences in attitudes toward the role of artificial intelligence and information technologies in the cognitive and social development of children, depending on the age of participants, with the expectation that younger participants (under 30 years old) would express more positive attitudes compared to older participants; and 2) the existence of a significant positive correlation between attitudes about the role of artificial intelligence and information technologies in the cognitive and social development of children and attitudes about the application of artificial intelligence in music education in primary education [25].

The study involved 44 elementary school teachers from Bosnia and Herzegovina, of whom 29 were women and 15 were men. Participants were categorized by age, work experience, and level of education. Most participants (50%) were under 30 years old, and 66% were employed in urban areas. None of the participants had formal education in the field of AI or information technologies [25].

Various questionnaires were used, including socio-demographic data and attitudes toward AI in education. Participants rated their attitudes toward nine (9) statements about the use of AI in music education on a scale from one (1) to five (5). The survey was distributed online, emphasizing anonymity and voluntary participation. Participants were encouraged to be honest in their responses, with the understanding that there were no right or wrong answers. Deviations from normal data distribution were analyzed, and one-way ANOVA was used to examine differences by age, while Pearson's correlation coefficient (r) was used to assess the relationship between attitudes [25].

The research findings highlighted two key research issues related to the perception of artificial intelligence (AI) in an educational context. First, significant differences in attitudes toward the role of AI in children's development were identified, with younger participants (under 30 years) expressing markedly more positive attitudes compared to participants aged 31 to 50 years. These results suggest that attitudes toward technology may vary depending on demographic factors such as age, reflecting different educational and life experiences [25]. Second, the research revealed a significant positive correlation between attitudes regarding the role of AI in the cognitive and social development of children and attitudes toward its application in music education. Participants who expressed positive beliefs about the potential of AI to enhance children's development also showed a preference for its integration into the music education process. These results emphasize the importance of considering AI as a tool that can not only enrich educational methods but also shape teachers' and educators' attitudes toward new technologies .

Overall, the research highlights the significance of participants' age as an important factor in shaping attitudes toward AI in education and implies the need for further investigation to better understand the connection between perceptions of child development and the application of AI in music teaching. These findings can serve as a foundation for future studies and the development of educational policies that integrate technologies like AI into teaching practices.

5 Conclusion

The introduction of artificial intelligence into music education presents significant opportunities as well as challenges. This paper explored how AI technologies can support personalized learning for elementary school students, highlighting their advantages and limitations, and how teachers can integrate them into the teaching process. By analyzing available AI tools and their potential in music education, several key insights were identified: personalized learning allows students an individualized approach, as AI tools like AIVA, Amper Music, and MuseNet can tailor content to the cognitive and affective characteristics of students, thereby promoting more effective and engaging learning. Although not specifically designed for music, ChatGPT can assist in writing song lyrics, analyzing harmony, understanding music theory, and providing suggestions for compositions or improvisation.

Overall, AI can enhance student motivation and creativity, as interactive tools allow students to explore music in innovative ways, fostering their curiosity and development of creative expression. Naturally, the role of the teacher remains irreplaceable; while AI can provide detailed analyses of performances and personalized feedback, the teacher's critical pedagogical role in interpretation, emotion, and musical expression is essential.

There are technical, economic, and ethical challenges to consider. Unequal access to technology, the need for teacher training, and the protection of student privacy are key issues that must be addressed when implementing AI tools in education. To effectively integrate AI technologies into music education, further exploration of several areas is necessary, such as the ongoing development of AI tools that support musical expression, as future innovations should enable better recognition of the emotional components of performance, not just technical accuracy.

To evaluate the long-term effects of AI tools on music education, research is needed to analyze how AI impacts the development of musical skills and student creativity over extended periods. Teacher training in the use of AI tools remains one of the essential issues, where institutions need to develop educational programs to equip teachers with the competencies for effective application of AI in teaching. Finally, the development of ethical guidelines is crucial for establishing clear standards for the use of AI in education, with particular emphasis on privacy protection and the preservation of the human aspect of learning.

AI technologies represent a significant step in modernizing music education. Their ability to adapt to students' needs and analytically track progress can enhance the teaching process. However, their application must be thoughtful and aligned with pedagogical principles to maintain a balance between technological innovations and traditional teaching methods.

The integration of AI tools in music instruction provides teachers with greater flexibility and improves access to educational resources. By using AI mentors and virtual assistants available 24/7, students can continuously refine their musical skills. As technology advances, AI will play a key role in shaping the future of music education, combining innovation with pedagogical principles to enhance the learning experience and foster the creativity of new generations.

Ultimately, while AI can be a powerful tool in music education, its application should be viewed as support for teachers rather than a replacement for the human factor. With the proper use of AI, along with clear ethical guidelines and quality teacher training, it is possible to create an educational environment that combines the best of technology and the arts, encouraging future generations of musicians to engage in creative expression and lifelong learning.

References

1. Evens, M., Michael, J.: One-on-One Tutoring by Humans and Computers. Psychology Press, New York (2006)
2. Garcia, C.: Algorithmic music david cope and EMI. Computer History Museum (2015). https://computerhistory.org/blog/algorithmic-music-david-cope-and-emi;. Accessed 18 Feb 2025
3. Bell, A.P.: Can Music Learning Be Enhanced by Artificial Intelligence? Oxford University Press (2018)
4. Martinez, A.: AI in Music Education: Personalized Learning Paths. Flourishprosper (2024)
5. Author, F., Author, S., Author, T.: Book title, 2nd edn. Publisher, Location (1999)
6. Yu, L., Ding, J.: Application of music artifical intelligence in preschool music education. IOP Conference Series: Materials Science and Engineering, 750 (2020)
7. Volaric, T., Crnokić, B.: Umjetna inteligencija u obrazovanju i robotici. Pressum, Mostar (2022)
8. Matasić, I., Dumić, S.: Multimedijske tehnologije u obrazovanju. Medijska istraživanja **18**(1), 143–151 (2012)
9. Boni, K.: Suvremena nastavna tehnologija u nastavi glazbene kulture i glazbene umjetnosti (Završni rad). Sveučilište Josipa Jurja Strossmayera u Osijeku, Osijek (2018)
10. Hunt, C.: AI and music: how artificial intelligence is changing the way we learn music. Int. J. Music Educ. J. **105**(3), 41–47 (2019)
11. Kelleher, J.D.: Duboko učenje (prijevod: čubrilo. Gospodarska misao, Mirko), Zagreb (2021)
12. Jurić, L.: 27 najpopularnijih AI alata (2024). https://www.vidilab.com/teme/softverska-tema/7035-27-najpopularnijih-ai-alata. Accessed 19 Feb 2025
13. Magenta – make music and art. https://magenta.tensorflow.org/. Accessed 19 Feb 2025
14. Novosel, D.: Didaktičko oblikovanje multimedijskoga udžbenika u nastavi glazbene kulture (doktorski rad). Zagreb: Filozofski fakultet, 354 str (2017). http://darhiv.ffzg.unizg.hr/8588/1/Novosel%20doktorat%20konacni%20oblik%20nakon%20o brane.pdf; Accessed 15 Feb 2025
15. Podobnik, V., Petric, A., Kusek, M.: Artificial Intelligence for Solving Real-Life Problems. Croatian Oper. Res. Rev. **11**(2), 195–211 (2020)
16. Miller, T. E., Shahriari, A.: World Music: A Global Journey. Routledge (2017)
17. Clow, D.: MOOCs and learning analytics: the current state of play. Int. J. Inf. Educ. Tech. **3**(5), 412–416 (2013)
18. Elliott, D. J., Silverman, M.: Music education: navigating the future, new york – london: routledge (2014)
19. Hofstetter, F. T.: Digital music learning: the role of ai in music education. New York – London: Routledge (2005)
20. Holster, J.: Augmenting music education through AI: practical applications of ChatGPT, music educators journal, June, 36–42 (2024)
21. Bradašić, M.: Suvremena nastavna tehnologija u nastavi Glazbene kulture (Diplomski rad). Sveučilište Josipa Jurja Strossmayera u Osijeku, Osijek (2016)

22. Bekić, I., Tomas, M.: Primjena umjetne inteligencije u obrazovanju: izazovi i mogućnosti. Zbornik radova Filozofskog fakulteta u Zagrebu **38**(1), 89–110 (2021)
23. čotić, D., Vladić Mandarić, L.: Glazbene aktivnosti s djecom od I. do IV. razreda osnovne škole,Suvremena pitanja, god. XIII., br. 27.pp.58–83 (2019)
24. Mislav, K.: Umjetna inteligencija i čovjek: suradnja koja transformira industrije, informacijske tehnologije (2023)
25. Sesar, M.: Umjetna inteligencija u nastavi glazbe primarnog obrazovanja. Diplomski rad, FPMOZ Sveučilište u Mostaru (2024)

Cross-Lingual and Cross-Domain Evaluation of ChatGPT's Translation Performance

Angelina Gašpar[1(✉)] and Marija Knežević[2]

[1] Catholic Faculty of Theology, University of Split, Split, Croatia
angelina.gaspar@kbf-st.hr
[2] Faculty of Humanities and Social Sciences, University of Split, Split, Croatia
marija@ffst.hr

Abstract. The development of large language models, such as ChatGPT, has significantly advanced in machine translation (MT), particularly in multilingual text generation and interpretation. However, assessing the translation quality of these models across diverse languages and domains remains a complex challenge. This study proposes a comprehensive approach to assessing the translation performance of ChatGPT 4o, designed to capture the nuances of its multilingual capabilities. The methodology combines traditional evaluation metrics (e.g., BLEU, METEOR, TER, ChrF, COMET, and BLEURT) with human-centered evaluation methods that prioritize linguistic quality and contextual accuracy. The evaluation spans four languages (English, Italian, French, and Croatian) and covers publicly available domain-specific texts in religion, medicine, economics, and law, comprising a total of 676 sentences. The human evaluation was conducted by two experts specializing in English-French and English-Italian language pairs, as well as 26 English language undergraduates. The assessment was based on several key criteria, including linguistic nuance, grammatical and syntactic precision, terminological consistency, contextual appropriateness, textual coherence and flow, and adherence to punctuation and formatting norms. The research addressed the following questions: Does ChatGPT provide equally accurate translations across all languages? Are there significant differences in translation quality depending on the domain? What are the most common discrepancies or errors when compared to reference translations? What is the relationship between automatic metrics and human judgments? Could ChatGPT potentially outperform a human translator in certain contexts? The analysis highlights the model's strengths and limitations in various linguistic settings and identifies areas for improvement to enhance translation reliability.

Keywords: ChatGPT · multilingual evaluation · translation quality assessment · machine and human evaluation · specialized domains

D. Vasić and E. Brajković (Eds.): MoStart 2025, CCIS 2609, pp. 196–211, 2026.
https://doi.org/10.1007/978-3-032-02801-3_13

1 Introduction

In an increasingly globalized world, the demand for accurate and reliable translation across multiple languages has never been higher. The rapid advancement of large language models (LLMs) like ChatGPT has significantly influenced the field of machine translation offering unprecedented capabilities in generating human-like text across diverse languages [1]. However, a comprehensive evaluation of its translation capabilities across multiple languages is essential to assess its strengths and weaknesses. Recent research has focused on evaluating ChatGPT's translation quality using a variety of evaluation metrics such as BLEU (Bilingual Evaluation Understudy), which measures n-gram overlap between the MT output and a human reference translation not accounting for synonymy or variations in word order; METEOR (Metric for Evaluation of Translation with Explicit Ordering), which considers synonyms, stemming, and reordering in addition to n-gram matching; TER (Translation Edit Rate), which assesses translation quality by quantifying necessary edits (insertions, deletions, substitutions, and shifts), and ChrF (Character n-gram F-score), which evaluates character-level n-gram precision and is particularly effective for morphologically rich languages. Advanced neural metrics like COMET and BLEURT, leveraging pre-trained models and human quality judgments, capture semantic similarity and fluency more effectively.

However, despite these advancements many metrics still struggle to account for cultural nuances, stylistic appropriateness, and fluency, which are essential for natural and accurate translations. They do not distinguish between minor and significant errors, nor do they localize issues in the translation. They rely heavily on reference translations, which can introduce bias if the references are of poor quality or limited in variation. Most importantly, they fail to incorporate human judgment, crucial for assessing subjective factors like context, tone, and audience appropriateness. As language models become more sophisticated, there is a growing need for evaluation frameworks that can accurately reflect the quality of translations in a way that aligns with human judgment. The correlation between automatic metrics and human judgment is influenced by factors such as language pairs and domain or style. For some language pairs significant syntactic or lexical divergence can make surface similarity metrics less reliable. Additionally, automatic metrics may fail to capture domain-specific nuances in highly specialized or creative texts, further impacting their alignment with human evaluations.

Human evaluation of machine translation focuses on assessing the quality of translations in a nuanced and context-aware manner that goes beyond what automatic metrics can achieve. It emphasizes several key aspects including adequacy, which evaluates whether the translation accurately conveys the meaning of the source text without omissions, distortions, or additions. It also considers fluency in terms of grammaticality, readability, and naturalness of the translation in the target language to ensure it sounds native and free of awkward phrasing. Cultural and contextual appropriateness is also assessed, determining if the translation aligns with cultural norms, idiomatic expressions, and the intended tone for the target audience and context. A human evaluator also identifies error severity and localization, pinpointing specific types of errors, such as grammatical, lexical, or semantic issues, and evaluating their impact on overall comprehension and usability. Additionally, it often involves comparative judgments where machine translations are scored alongside reference translations frequently through side-by-side evaluations. Human evaluation captures qualitative aspects of translation that are difficult for automatic metrics to measure providing insights into both the meaning and usability of the output.

ChatGPT often produces fluent and coherent translations, even for complex language pairs. It can handle various text formats including news articles, scientific papers, and creative writing. It can be adapted for specific translation tasks, such as technical, literary, or medical translation. Although it can generate fluent translations for high-resource languages, it may sometimes produce inaccurate or imprecise translations due to the limited training data for under-resourced languages or distant-language-pairs translation [2]. The quality of the generated translations can be influenced by the specific prompt or query. This study explores the current methodologies and metrics used in the evaluation of translation quality, with a particular focus on multilingual contexts.

It addresses the following research questions: Does ChatGPT provide equally accurate translations across all languages? Are there significant differences in translation quality depending on the domain? What are the most common discrepancies or errors when compared to reference translations? What is the relationship between automatic metrics and human judgments? Could ChatGPT potentially outperform a human translator in certain contexts? The objective is to contribute to the development of more robust, transparent, and user-centric evaluation methods to enhance the reliability and effectiveness of machine translation systems.

The main contribution of this paper is both human and machine evaluations of ChatGPT's translation performance across various domains in both highly-developed and under-developed languages.

The next section, Sect. 2, provides a comprehensive review of different approaches to multilingual translation evaluation. Section 3 describes the proposed approach including human and automatic evaluation of ChatGPT-generated translations. The obtained results are discussed in Sect. 4 and conclusions with study limitations and recommendations for enhancing translation quality assessment are given in Sect. 5

2 Related Work

The evaluation of translation quality in multilingual contexts has gained significant attention with the emergence of advanced language models like ChatGPT. This review synthesizes recent research focusing on methodologies, metrics, and findings related to the translation quality of ChatGPT. Leiter et al. [3] emphasized the need for explainable metrics in machine translation proposing frameworks that enhance transparency and trust in evaluation processes. Kocmi and Federmann [4] introduced GEMBA, a GPT-based metric for evaluating translation quality capable of operating with or without a reference translation. The evaluation focuses on zero-shot prompting across multiple GPT versions demonstrating that the method achieves state-of-the-art accuracy with GPT-3.5 and larger models validated against MQM-based human labels for three language pairs (English-German and Russian, and Chinese-English).

Freitag et al. [5] explored challenges in human evaluation of high-quality machine translation systems and the absence of standardized procedures. Using the MQM framework, they conducted the largest MQM study on WMT 2020 shared task outputs. The study highlighted discrepancies between professional and crowd worker evaluations, a preference for human output, and the superior performance of automatic metrics based on pre-trained embeddings over crowd workers. Castilho et al. [6] examined current and emerging methods for defining and measuring translation quality in human and machine translation workflows across research, education, and industry contexts. Drawing on literature from various related fields, they highlighted the need for diverse approaches while addressing persistent challenges that must be resolved to strengthen translation quality assessment in increasingly technology-driven environments.

Guerreiro et al. [7] introduced xCOMET, an open-source learned metric that combines sentence-level evaluation with error span detection. It achieves state-of-the-art performance across sentence-level, system-level, and error span evaluations while also highlighting and categorizing error spans to enhance quality assessment. xCOMET effectively identifies localized critical errors and hallucinations. Using the MQM framework as the gold standard, Agrawal et al. [8] systematically stress-tested the ability of current metrics to identify translations with no errors as marked by humans. The findings reveal that current metrics often over or underestimate translation quality, indicating significant room for improvement in machine translation evaluation.

In addition to machine metrics, human evaluation remains a critical component of translation quality assessment. Banat and Abu Adla [9] explored the effectiveness of GPT-3 in translating specialized religious texts from Arabic to English. The study involved human evaluators who rated the translations based on accuracy, fluency, and overall quality. The results indicated that GPT-3's translations were comparable to those produced by human translators. In another study comparing ChatGPT to professional human translators, GPT-4 was evaluated across six language pairs including high- and low-resource languages such as English-Chinese and English-Hindi. Researchers used the MQM framework highlighting that ChatGPT produces competitive translations particularly in general and colloquial domains, but struggles with domain-specific terminology in fields like biomedicine or ICT. This limitation is attributed to a lack of specialized training data. The study also emphasized ChatGPT's ability to produce natural, idiomatic translations reducing translationese as opposed to traditional systems, Yan et al., [10].

Zhao et al. [11] compared ChatGPT with Google Translate and Huawei Translate across various domains. While ChatGPT excelled in informal and idiomatic expressions achieving high direct assessment (DA) scores in general domains, it fell short in BLEU scores and domain-specific accuracy, terminology in particular. The results suggest that while ChatGPT is robust for general-purpose translation it requires improvement for specialized contexts. Jiao et al. [12] examined the translation performance of ChatGPT-4's and commercial translation products like Google Translate. The findings suggest that ChatGPT-4 performs competitively in high-resource European languages but lags in low-resource or distant languages. Lai et al. [13] reached a similar conclusion after evaluating ChatGPT-4 on seven tasks across 37 languages with varying resource levels. Han et al. [14] provided a comprehensive survey of translation quality assessment methods covering both manual evaluation criteria and automated metrics, which were further categorized into detailed subgroups.

3 Methodology

Two experts in the English-French and English-Italian language pairs collected four domain-specific English texts and their multilingual versions. Source texts in English were used as reference texts to evaluate the quality of ChatGPT-generated translations in French, Italian, and Croatian language. The prompt used in ChatGPT was: "Can you provide localized French, Italian, and Croatian versions of the following English text, please?" The prompt used to obtain the revised English versions was:" Can you provide a revised version of the text while maintaining domain-specific terminology, style, tone and sentence boundaries, please?" Human evaluation of ChatGPT translation quality included two bilingual experts and 26 English language undergraduates.

Two bilingual experts performed a comparative evaluation of ChatGPT-generated translations against human translations across four domains–religion, medicine, economy, and law–while assessing five linguistic aspects. They evaluated language nuance (LN) i.e. the absence of subtleties or idiomatic expressions from the source text; grammar and syntax (G&S) i.e. unusual sentence structures or grammatical constructions not typical of native writing; contextual understanding (CU), i.e. the ability to capture cultural references, or context that a native speaker would naturally grasp; flow and coherence (F&C) i.e. naturalness and logical progression, and finally, punctuation and formatting (P&F) i.e. whether strict adherence to the source text punctuation aligned with conventional usage in the target language. The results were divided into three categories: Outmatch (where ChatGPT surpassed human translation), Exact match (where translations were equally accurate), and Fuzzy match (where necessary adjustments were needed to align with the reference translation). A "No match" category was initially included in the table, but was later removed as ChatGPT successfully translated all sentences across all languages. Experts assessed the quality of ChatGPT-generated translations for English and Croatian consensually to ensure reliability and impartiality. Twenty-six English language undergraduates from the Faculty of Humanities and Social Sciences of the University of Split were tasked with distinguishing between human-written English texts and ChatGPT-edited versions, as well as between human-generated and ChatGPT-generated translations from English to Croatian. They were required to identify the human-written or human-translated texts by applying the criteria established by the experts and to justify their selections with well-reasoned arguments.

3.1 Dataset Description

The dataset consists of 676 sentences in four languages–English (EN), French (FR), Italian (IT), and Croatian (HR)–covering four distinct domains: religion (86 sentences, 511 words) [15], medicine (106 sentences, 514 words) [16], economy (91 sentences, 512 words) [17], and law (55 sentences, 512 words) [18]. Unlike other texts, which have a relatively similar number of sentences, the legal text contains fewer sentences due to the complex sentence structure typical of legal language. The sentence count per language varied, with both English and French having the highest count of 81 sentences each. Italian followed closely with 76 sentences, while Croatian had the fewest, 72 sentences. The English texts and their multilingual versions were obtained from online sources. These texts are excerpts from books or official documents created or verified by human experts. ChatGPT was used to obtain revised English versions across all domains. It also translated human-generated English texts into French, Italian, and Croatian.

3.2 Automatic Evaluation

The preprocessing pipeline for multilingual translation metrics was designed to process text data across four domains (religion, medicine, economy, and law) and four languages (English, Italian, French, and Croatian). It involved several steps to ensure the input data were suitable for translation quality evaluation. First, the raw text was split into sentences using NLTK's *sent_tokenize* to handle multilingual input effectively. The text was then cleaned and normalized by removing unnecessary whitespaces and line breaks with regex. Special characters and diacritics were standardized using Unicode normalization (NFKC). Sentences were tokenized with NLTK's *word_tokenize* producing consistent linguistic units for comparison. Additionally, references and hypotheses were matched in length to ensure fair evaluation across metrics that required sentence alignment. The BLEU metric evaluates translation quality by calculating the precision of n-grams between the hypothesis and reference texts, while also applying a brevity penalty to discourage overly short translations. It produces a score between 0 to 100 with higher values indicating a closer match to the reference. TER measures the number of edits needed to convert a hypothesis into the reference text. A lower score indicates fewer edits, implying higher translation quality. ChrF calculates F-scores at the character level, emphasizing linguistic similarity through character n-grams, with scores also ranging from 0 to 100. METEOR evaluates translation quality by aligning hypotheses and references based on precision, recall, and a harmonic mean. It accounts for synonyms and stemming producing scores between 0 and 1, with higher values indicating better alignment. COMET uses neural models to assess translations providing a holistic view by considering hypotheses, references, and optional source texts. Its scores are continuous, with higher values reflecting better semantic and contextual accuracy. BLEURT, leveraging pre-trained BERT-style models, evaluates semantic similarity between hypothesis and reference sentences. It produces a score where higher values indicate better alignment and translation quality. These metrics were implemented using NLTK, sacrebleu, comet and bleurt Python libraries.

4 Results

To gain a deeper understanding of the overall findings, the following subsections provide a detailed analysis of translation performance across individual domains and languages, using both machine metrics and human evaluations.

4.1 Automatic Evaluation

Machine translation metrics complement each other by evaluating translations from multiple perspectives. BLEU, TER, and ChrF are statistical and focus on n-gram precision/recall while METEOR enhances precision/recall with semantic alignment. COMET and BLEURT use deep learning to evaluate semantic and contextual accuracy offering a nuanced understanding of translation quality. Table 1 presents translation quality metrics comparing human-made translations and ChatGPT-generated translations across different domains and languages as well as human-written English texts and ChatGPT-edited versions.

Table 1. Translation metrics results across different domains and languages.

Domain	Lang	BLEU	TER	ChrF	METEOR	COMET	BLEURT
Religion	EN	80.508970	38.413510	73.836380	0.701320	0.776120	0.522660
Religion	IT	82.215620	44.440780	76.224700	0.196800	-0.790650	-0.434620
Religion	FR	83.276420	30.133860	76.779090	0.196540	-0.867420	-0.440780
Religion	HR	70.343190	44.007860	62.675740	0.515160	0.956940	0.227900
Medicine	EN	76.710930	38.884620	71.485740	0.383220	-0.010510	-0.057130
Medicine	IT	79.040970	40.461580	74.329220	0.495520	0.108410	0.085050
Medicine	FR	83.861860	38.845960	78.372910	0.494150	0.123910	-0.040620
Medicine	HR	76.255880	43.438140	67.034810	0.507710	0.632680	0.084250
Economy	EN	77.684370	51.000000	70.551310	0.673810	0.658500	0.351720
Economy	IT	73.924800	68.528280	63.325130	0.443940	0.351770	-0.012340
Economy	FR	72.220810	64.158080	64.186040	0.471900	0.317050	-0.037950
Economy	HR	68.021010	69.737370	59.665660	0.337830	0.510460	-0.013020
Law	EN	95.212620	6.634910	93.848490	0.946190	0.801770	0.686390
Law	IT	86.238840	40.865210	82.216410	0.619590	0.675800	0.326190
Law	FR	88.179340	51.997120	85.209430	0.789170	0.713820	0.314810
Law	HR	85.623040	59.155500	81.751770	0.781010	0.995840	0.455990

In the case of the religious text, French performed the best with a BLEU score of 83.28, a TER of 30.13, and a ChrF of 76.78, reflecting a high degree of alignment with reference translations. By contrast, Croatian struggled with the religious text, achieving a comparatively lower BLEU score of 70.34 and a ChrF of 62.68. In the case of the medical text, French reached the highest BLEU score of 83.86 and a ChrF of 78.37 while Croatian achieved a lower BLEU score of 76.26 and a ChrF of 67.03. However, the relatively low COMET and BLEURT scores across all languages for this domain highlighted some discrepancies in semantic fluency and adequacy. In the case of the economic text, English performed the best achieving a BLEU score of 77.68 and a METEOR score of 0.67. Croatian showed the weakest performance with a BLEU score of 68.02 and a TER of 69.74 indicating that a significant number of edits are needed for improvement. The translations of the economic text generally exhibited the highest TER values compared to other types of texts, indicating greater difficulty in achieving fluency and alignment. Conversely, the legal text demonstrated the greatest overall performance, particularly in English, which achieved near-perfect scores with a BLEU of 95.21, a TER of 6.63, and a ChrF of 93.85, reflecting the formulaic and structured nature of legal texts. Even Croatian, which typically struggled with other types of texts, performed relatively well in legal domain, achieving a BLEU of 85.62 and a ChrF of 81.75.

As shown in Table 2, when aggregated across all domains, the best results were achieved for English with a BLEU score of 82.53 and a ChrF score of 77.43, suggesting consistently strong similarity between reference texts and ChatGPT-revised versions. Conversely, Croatian underperformed, with a BLEU score of 75.06 and a ChrF of 67.78, indicating persistent challenges across domains. Among the domains, the legal text demonstrated the highest overall translation quality with a BLEU score of 88.81 and a ChrF of 85.75, while the economic text posed the biggest problem, with a BLEU score of 72.96 and a TER of 63.36, indicating its linguistic and semantic complexity.

Table 2. The aggregated translation performance across all domains and languages.

Type	BLEU	TER	ChrF	METEOR	COMET	BLEURT
Economy	72.962748	63.355932	64.432035	0.481870	0.459445	0.072102
Law	88.813460	39.663185	85.756525	0.783990	0.796808	0.445845
Medicine	78.967410	40.407575	72.805670	0.470150	0.213622	0.017888
Religion	79.086050	39.249003	72.378978	0.402455	0.018748	-0.031210
EN	82.529223	33.733260	77.430480	0.676135	0.556470	0.375910
FR	81.884608	46.283755	76.136867	0.487940	0.071840	-0.051135
HR	75.060780	54.084717	67.781995	0.535427	0.773980	0.188780
IT	80.355058	48.573962	74.023865	0.438962	0.086333	-0.008930

The results showed strong translation performance for English and French, especially in structured domains like law, while Croatian consistently faced challenges in achieving high scores across all metrics, particularly in more complex or less-structured domains such as economy and medicine. The translations of the economic text appeared to be the most difficult overall, whereas the translations of the legal text benefited from its formalized and predictable linguistic structures. While BLEU and ChrF scores indicated strong surface-level alignment, lower COMET and BLEURT scores in certain domains and languages pointed to areas for improvement, particularly in achieving semantic richness and fluency.

4.2 Human Evaluation

Student Evaluation of the Quality of ChatGPT-Generated Translations in Croatian: The analysis revealed that students were more successful at distinguishing human translations from ChatGPT-generated ones in the legal and medical domain, while they faced challenges in the religious and economic domains. In the legal domain, 20 out of 26 students (77%) correctly identified the human translation, most probably due to the structured and precise nature of the legal language. Similarly, in the medical domain, 16 students (62%) successfully identified the human translation, emphasizing errors in grammar, syntax, and vocabulary use as the key distinguishing factors. In contrast, the religious domain proved to be the most challenging, with only 4 students (15%) identifying the human translation. This suggests that ChatGPT is relatively adept at handling the stylistic and semantic nuances of religious texts making its translations harder to distinguish from human work. The economic domain also presented challenges, with only 12 students (46%) identifying the human translation. Here, issues such as terminological inconsistency, language nuance, and grammar contributed to the difficulty. These results indicate that the ability to differentiate between human and ChatGPT-generated translations varies significantly by domain. ChatGPT performed well in stylistically nuanced domains like religion, where errors are less apparent, while its limitations in vocabulary use, grammar, and language nuance became more evident in highly structured or technical domains like law and medicine. This highlights the importance of domain-specific considerations in evaluating the quality of machine translations.

Student Evaluation of ChatGPT-Revised English Versions: The results of student evaluations indicated that ChatGPT's ability to generate human-like texts varied across domains. In the religious domain, the majority of students, i.e. fifteen out of 26 (58%) were able to distinguish between the original English text and the ChatGPT-revised version. However, in the medical domain, only 5 students (19%) correctly identified the original text, suggesting that ChatGPT's revisions closely resembled the reference text. It is most probably due to the structured and technical nature of medical writing. In the economic and legal domains, 10 (38%) students recognized the original text, respectively. While ChatGPT could closely imitate economic and legal discourse, there were still certain nuances or inconsistencies that made ChatGPT-generated text distinguishable from reference text. Overall, ChatGPT-revised versions were least detectable in the medical domain, while in religious, economic, and legal domains students were more frequently able to identify differences. Students noted that the primary distinction between human-written and ChatGPT-generated texts was in vocabulary choices, more natural sentence structure, and overall coherence. Human writing appeared more natural, intuitive, and contextually appropriate. Sentences in the ChatGPT version were shorter and, at times, overly structured. There were instances of literal translations and unusual word choices, such as "the formation of children by the media," which seem robotic compared to the more natural "impact of media in forming children." ChatGPT often substituted words with less appropriate synonyms. Although ChatGPT could produce well-structured content, its reliance on rigid phrasing, unnatural vocabulary substitutions, and occasionally awkward expressions made it identifiable. Thus, while ChatGPT demonstrated strong language capabilities, human intuition, nuance, and fluidity remain superior in producing a clear and natural text. Students faced difficulty in identifying the original Croatian text in the religious domain and original English text in the medical domain.

Expert Evaluation: The evaluation of ChatGPT's translations across four languages–English (EN), French (FR), Italian (IT), and Croatian (HR) and four domains–religion, medicine, economy, and law-revealed distinct patterns. ChatGPT performed well in religion, medicine, and economy, whereas it underperformed in law. Its performance varied by language, with French showing the highest and Croatian the lowest accuracy. Across all domains, the number of sentences where ChatGPT outmatched or exactly matched human translation was the highest in religion and medicine. In contrast, law showed the highest number of "fuzzy" matches, indicating difficulties in legal language precision. Table 3 shows domain and language-specific ChatGPT performance.

Domain-specific performance: In the religious domain, ChatGPT's translation accuracy was exceptional, particularly in Italian (100%) and French (95.8%). The English version reached 87.5% accuracy while the Croatian one was slightly less accurate (81%). The high percentage of sentences in which ChatGPT outmatched humans indicated that it could effectively handle religious domain; its phrasing and theological terminology. The slight differences in accuracy across languages indicated that some cultural or linguistic nuances were better captured in Italian and French than other languages. ChatGPT also excelled in medical translations with French, Italian, and Croatian all reaching 100% accuracy when combining outmatch and exact matches. English followed closely behind with 95.7% accuracy. The best results in translation accuracy across all four languages are probably due to the structured nature of medical texts. In the economic domain, ChatGPT generated highly accurate translations with French achieving a perfect (100%) accuracy rate. The accuracy rates for Italian (90.5%) and Croatian (90.9%) followed closely, unlike those for English (85.7%). However, the strong overall performance in this domain highlighted the ChatGPT's competency across all languages. Legal translations were the greatest challenge

Table 3. Domain and language-specific ChatGPT performance (o:outmatch, e:exact match, f:fuzzy match).

D-L	LN				G&S				CU				F&C				P&F			
	o	e	f	#	o	e	f	#	o	e	f	#	o	e	f	#	o	e	f	#
Religion-EN	19	2	3	24	17	4	3	24	19	3	2	24	13	9	2	24	5	17	2	24
Religion-FR	19	4	1	24	18	6	0	24	16	6	2	24	17	7	0	24	4	20	0	24
Religion-IT	19	0	0	19	14	3	2	19	14	2	3	19	15	2	2	19	4	14	0	18
Religion-HR	15	2	4	21	12	6	3	21	10	8	3	21	15	5	1	21	4	16	1	21
Medicine-EN	22	0	1	23	21	2	0	23	19	3	0	22	20	3	0	23	9	14	0	23
Medicine-FR	21	4	0	25	21	4	0	25	21	4	0	25	21	4	0	25	4	21	0	25
Medicine-IT	19	4	0	23	14	9	0	23	18	5	0	23	17	6	0	23	5	18	0	23
Medicine-HR	13	3	0	16	11	8	5	24	10	7	7	24	10	12	2	24	2	22	0	24
Economy-EN	16	2	3	21	14	18	1	33	12	0	0	12	14	0	0	14	2	0	0	2
Economy-FR	19	4	0	23	21	2	0	23	19	4	0	23	21	2	0	23	3	20	0	23
Economy-IT	19	0	2	21	13	7	1	21	19	1	2	22	18	2	2	22	4	17	1	22
Economy-HR	20	0	2	22	19	2	1	22	20	2	0	22	20	2	0	22	2	20	0	22
Law-EN	4	9	0	13	4	8	1	13	1	11	1	13	2	11	0	13	0	12	1	13
Law-FR	9	0	0	9	9	0	0	9	1	0	0	1	9	0	0	9	1	0	1	2
Law-IT	1	4	8	13	4	2	7	13	2	8	3	13	3	6	4	13	0	10	3	13
Law-HR	4	6	3	13	5	5	3	13	1	11	1	13	6	6	1	13	1	12	0	13
Religion	72	8	8	88	61	19	8	88	59	19	10	88	60	23	5	88	17	67	3	87
Medicine	75	11	1	87	67	23	5	95	68	19	7	94	68	25	2	95	20	75	0	95
Economy	74	6	7	87	67	29	3	99	70	7	2	79	73	6	2	81	11	57	1	69
Law	18	19	11	48	22	15	11	48	5	30	5	40	20	23	5	48	2	34	5	41
EN	61	13	7	81	56	32	5	93	51	17	3	71	49	23	2	74	16	43	3	62
FR	68	12	1	81	69	12	0	81	57	14	2	73	68	13	0	81	12	61	1	74
IT	58	8	10	76	45	21	10	76	53	16	8	77	53	16	8	77	13	59	4	76
HR	52	11	9	72	47	21	12	80	41	28	11	80	51	25	4	80	9	70	1	80

for ChatGPT with significant variation in performance across languages. While English (100%) and French (100%) translations were highly accurate, the Italian translation achieved significantly low accuracy rate (38.5%), making it the weakest-performing domain in the study. Croatian performed moderately well at 76.9% accuracy indicating some challenges in legal terminology and syntactic complexity. The difficulty in handling legal language was likely due to its precise, formal structure where even small deviations could lead to significant differences in meaning. These results suggested that legal translations require further refinement, particularly in Italian where a high number of fuzzy matches indicated lower translation quality (Table 4).

Language-Specific Performance: In English, ChatGPT processed 81 sentences with an accuracy of 91.4%. It performed best in structured domains like medicine and religion where it produced 61 outmatch and 13 exact matches. Due to the complexity and specificity of legal language there were fewer exact matches and

Table 4. A heat map displaying ChatGPT's individual values as colours.

D-L	LN			G&S			CU			F&C			P&F		
	o	e	f	o	e	f	o	e	f	o	e	f	o	e	f
Religion-EN	79%	8%	13%	71%	17%	13%	79%	13%	8%	54%	38%	8%	21%	71%	8%
Religion-FR	79%	17%	4%	75%	25%	0%	67%	25%	8%	71%	29%	0%	17%	83%	0%
Religion-IT	100%	0%	0%	74%	16%	11%	74%	11%	16%	79%	11%	11%	22%	78%	0%
Religion-HR	71%	10%	19%	57%	29%	14%	48%	38%	14%	71%	24%	5%	19%	76%	5%
Medicine-EN	96%	0%	4%	91%	9%	0%	86%	14%	0%	87%	13%	0%	39%	61%	0%
Medicine-FR	84%	16%	0%	84%	16%	0%	84%	16%	0%	84%	16%	0%	16%	84%	0%
Medicine-IT	83%	17%	0%	61%	39%	0%	78%	22%	0%	74%	26%	0%	22%	78%	0%
Medicine-HR	81%	19%	0%	46%	33%	21%	42%	29%	29%	42%	50%	8%	8%	92%	0%
Economy-EN	76%	10%	14%	42%	55%	3%	100%	0%	0%	100%	0%	0%	100%	0%	0%
Economy-FR	83%	17%	0%	91%	9%	0%	83%	17%	0%	91%	9%	0%	13%	87%	0%
Economy-IT	90%	0%	10%	62%	33%	5%	86%	5%	9%	82%	9%	9%	18%	77%	5%
Economy-HR	91%	0%	9%	86%	9%	5%	91%	9%	0%	91%	9%	0%	9%	91%	0%
Law-EN	31%	69%	0%	31%	62%	8%	8%	85%	8%	15%	85%	0%	0%	92%	8%
Law-FR	100%	0%	0%	100%	0%	0%	100%	0%	0%	100%	0%	0%	50%	0%	50%
Law-IT	8%	31%	62%	31%	15%	54%	15%	62%	23%	23%	46%	31%	0%	77%	23%
Law-HR	31%	46%	23%	38%	38%	23%	8%	85%	8%	46%	46%	8%	8%	92%	0%
Religion	82%	9%	9%	69%	22%	9%	67%	22%	11%	68%	26%	6%	20%	77%	3%
Medicine	86%	13%	1%	71%	24%	5%	72%	20%	7%	72%	26%	2%	21%	79%	0%
Economy	85%	7%	8%	68%	29%	3%	89%	9%	3%	90%	7%	2%	16%	83%	1%
Law	38%	40%	23%	46%	31%	23%	13%	75%	13%	42%	48%	10%	5%	83%	12%
EN	75%	16%	9%	60%	34%	5%	72%	24%	4%	66%	31%	3%	26%	69%	5%
FR	84%	15%	1%	85%	15%	0%	78%	19%	3%	84%	16%	0%	16%	82%	1%
IT	76%	11%	13%	59%	28%	13%	69%	21%	10%	69%	21%	10%	17%	78%	5%
HR	72%	15%	13%	59%	26%	15%	51%	35%	14%	64%	31%	5%	11%	88%	1%

more fuzzy matches. French translations showed the highest overall accuracy across all domains achieving 98.8% accuracy across 81 sentences. With 68 outmatched and 12 exact translations, ChatGPT performed the best in medical and religious domains. French generated translations closely aligned with human translations thus resulting in the most reliable language for ChatGPT's performance. As far as Italian is concerned, ChatGPT translated 76 sentences with an accuracy of 86.8%. The best performance was observed in the religious and economic domains while legal translations had the highest number of fuzzy matches, most probably due to complex sentence structure and specialized terminology. Croatian translations achieved moderate accuracy of 87.5% across 72 sentences. Medicine was the best domain while legal and economic texts proved more difficult.

ChatGPT provided the highest accuracy in religion and medicine achieving 90–100% accuracy across multiple languages. However, Law proved to be the weakest domain, especially in Italian where translation quality was significantly lower. French was the best-performing language with 98.8% accuracy across all domains. English followed with 91.4% accuracy performing well except in legal translations. Croatian (87.5%) and Italian (86.8%) exhibit more inconsistencies with Italian showing the most difficulty in legal texts.

Table 5 presents one sentence per domain and for each language to illustrate ChatGPT's outperformance compared to human-written sentences.

Table 5. Cross-domain and cross-language examples of ChatGPT outperformance.

Original Sentence	ChatGPT-Generated Sentence
The role of parents is of primary importance.	The role of parents is paramount.
Paroxysms of crying and fussiness often occur at about the same time of day or night and continue for hours for no apparent reason.	Paroxysms of crying and fussiness frequently occur at similar times of day or night and may last for hours without any obvious reason.
Thenceforth, a serious political struggle was altogether out of the question.	From that point onward, meaningful political struggle was no longer feasible.
(3) Any references to the Union in this decision should be understood as including the European Atomic Energy Community.	(3) Any reference to the Union in this Decision should be understood to include the European Atomic Energy Community.
Comment le bien commun est-il protégé et promu?	Comment protéger et promouvoir ce bien commun ?
Le médecin doit être rassurant et doit montrer qu'il comprend à quel point un nourrisson souffrant de coliques peut être stressant pour les parents.	Les médecins doivent également reconnaître combien un nourrisson coliqueux peut être stressant pour les parents.
Le christianisme ne s'est-il pas élevé lui aussi contre la propriété privée, le mariage, l'Etat ?	Le christianisme n'a-t-il pas dénoncé la propriété privée, le mariage, l'État ?
À la date d'entrée en vigueur de l'accord, les mandats de tous les membres des institutions, organes et organismes de l'Union qui ont été nommés,...	À la date d'entrée en vigueur de l'accord, les mandats de tous les membres des institutions, organes et agences de l'Union qui ont été nommés,...
Le complesse sfide che l'educazione contemporanea deve affrontare sono spesso collegate alla diffusa influenza dei media nel nostro mondo.	Le sfide complesse che l'educazione affronta oggi sono spesso legate all'influenza pervasiva dei media nel nostro mondo.
La colica é frequente e determina periodi di pianto senza motivo apparente in un bambino altrimenti sano.	La colica ÃÍ caratterizzata da periodi frequenti e prolungati di pianto senza una ragione apparente in un lattante altrimenti sano.
Data la sua posizione storica, l'aristocrazia francese e inglese era chiamata a scrivere libelli contro la moderna società borghese.	A causa della loro posizione storica, le aristocrazie di Francia e Inghilterra trovarono la loro vocazione nella scrittura di pamphlet contro la società borghese moderna.
Ai termini della dichiarazione relativa all'accordo di recesso e alla dichiarazione politica, nel caso in cui la posizione dell'Unione da adottare in sede di comitato misto riguardi la proroga del periodo di transizione, il Consiglio delibererà conformemente agli orientamenti del Consiglio europeo e ogni eventuale decisione in merito alla proroga del periodo di transizione terrà conto dell'adempimento, da parte del Regno Unito, degli obblighi a norma dell'accordo, compresi i relativi protocolli.	Secondo la dichiarazione relativa all'accordo di recesso e alla dichiarazione politica, quando la posizione dell'Unione da adottare nel Comitato misto riguarda l'estensione del periodo di transizione, il Consiglio agirà conformemente alle linee guida del Consiglio europeo, e qualsiasi decisione sull'estensione del periodo di transizione terrà conto dell'adempimento degli obblighi da parte del Regno Unito ai sensi dell'accordo, compresi i relativi protocolli.
Izlažući djecu onome sto je estetski i moralno najbolje, pomaže im se da razviju svoje mišljenje, razboritost i sposobnost razlikovanja.	Djeca izložena onome što je estetski i moralno izvrsno razvijaju osjećaj za ljepotu, razboritost i vještine razlučivanja.
Nakratko se može pokušati hranjenje hipoalergenom dojenačkom formulom, kako bi se utvrdilo ima li dojenče intoleranciju mlijeka, no treba izbjegavati česte promjene mliječnih formula.	Hipoalergena formula može se kratko isprobati kako bi se utvrdila eventualna intolerancija na proteine kravljeg mlijeka, ali treba izbjegavati česte promjene formule.
Kao što je pop uvijek išao ruku pod ruku s feudalcem, tako isto i popovski socijalizam ide s feudalnim.	Kao što je svećenik uvijek bio uz veleposjednika, tako je klerikalni socijalizam uvijek bio uz feudalni socijalizam.
šest mjeseci prije nego što se članak 5. Protokola o Irskoj/Sjevernoj Irskoj uz Sporazum o povlačenju počne primjenjivati, preispitat će se modaliteti za sudjelovanje država članica na sastancima Zajedničkog odbora i posebnih odbora, uzimajući u obzir novu situaciju koja tako nastane.	šest mjeseci prije nego što članak 5. Protokola o Irskoj i Sjevernoj Irskoj Sporazuma o povlačenju postane primjenjiv, ponovno će se razmotriti načini sudjelovanja država članica na sastancima Zajedničkog odbora i posebnih odbora, uzimajući u obzir novu situaciju.

Regarding ChatGPT's underperformance, the model added the word "Saint" in the French, Italian, and Croatian translations (e.g., Saint Jean-Paul II, Exhortation apostolique Familiaris consortio, n. 76). However, since that was a reference and saints do not write, the translation appeared awkward. Furthermore, in the legal domain ChatGPT produced a literal translation from English and used passive voice, which is not recommended by the EU Joint Practical Guide. In other domains and languages, modifications of synonyms were not justified. However, there were no instances of ChatGPT failing to translate sentences in any language.

5 Conclusion

The relationship between automatic metrics and human judgment indicated that, while BLEU and ChrF scores demonstrated strong surface-level alignment, lower COMET and BLEURT scores in many cases highlighted the need for improvement in semantic richness and fluency. Machine metric scores for English language showed that ChatGPT-revised versions closely aligned with reference texts unlike Croatian ChatGPT-generated versions that underperformed, indicating consistent difficulties across all domains that may be attributed to the limited resources developed for that language. Student evaluations showed that identifying the human-made Croatian translation was most challenging in the religious domain, while identifying the source English text was most challenging in the medical domain. Expert evaluations revealed that ChatGPT achieved the highest accuracy in the religious and medical domains across multiple languages, a result that was supported by machine metrics. However, law was the weakest domain in terms of translation accuracy, especially in Italian where performance dropped significantly. Translations in the economic domain were generally less accurate and more inconsistent, most probably due to the linguistic characteristics and the fact that the text was written in the 19th century. French was the best-performing language across all domains, followed by English, despite some imprecisions in legal translation. Croatian and Italian showed greater inconsistencies, with Italian particularly struggling with legal texts.

ChatGPT outperformed human translators particularly in the medical and religious domains, but in more nuanced domains like law and economics, the human expertise proved to be essential for ensuring accuracy, proper context, and precise wording. These findings emphasized the impact of language structures on translation accuracy and the challenges posed by complex, specialized domains. The limitations of this study include potential biases in evaluating the translation quality of French and Italian, as the assessment was conducted by a single annotator. While it offers a robust solution for many translation needs, ChatGPT remains complementary to human translators, especially for nuanced or domain-specific tasks. Future research will focus on testing more sophisticated metrics that can capture subtle nuances of translation quality, such as cultural appropriateness and style, collecting high-quality multilingual dataset to enhance LLM training, mitigating biases in both training data and models to ensure fair and unbiased translations, and incorporating more human annotators to enhance the accuracy and objectivity of translation evaluations.

Acknowledgments. We thank our colleague Ines šarić-Grgić for her support in conducting automatic evaluations, as well as for her ideas and inspiration which significantly contributed to the quality of this paper.

References

1. Zhu, W., et al .: Multilingual machine translation with large language models: empirical results and analysis. In: Findings of the Association for Computational Linguistics: NAACL 2024. pp. 2765–2781, Mexico City, Mexico. Association for Computational Linguistics. (2024)
2. Peng, K., et al .: Towards making the most of ChatGPT for machine translation. In Findings of the Association for Computational Linguistics: EMNLP. pp. 5622–5633, 2023. Association for Computational Linguistics, Singapore (2023)
3. Leiter, C., Lertvittayakumjorn, P., Fomicheva, M., Zhao, W., Gao, Y., Eger, S.: Towards explainable evaluation metrics for machine translation. J. Mach. Learn. Res., 25, 75:1-75:49. https://arxiv.org/abs/2306.13041 (2023)
4. Kocmi, T., Federmann, C.: Large language models are state-of-the-art evaluators of translation quality. In:European Association for Machine Translation Conferences/Workshops (2023). https://arxiv.org/abs/2302.14520
5. Freitag, M., Foster, G., Grangier, D., Ratnakar, V., Tan, Q., Macherey, W.: Experts, errors, and context: a large-scale study of human evaluation for machine translation. Transactions of the Association for Computational Linguistics 2021; 9 1460–1474 (2021). https://doi.org/10.1162/tacl_a_00437
6. Castilho, S., Doherty, S., Gaspari, F., Moorkens, J.: Approaches to human and machine translation quality assessment. (2018)
7. Guerreiro, N. M., Rei, R., Stigt, D.V., Coheur, L., Colombo, P., André F. T.: Martins: xCOMET: transparent machine translation evaluation through fine-grained error detection. Transactions of the Association for Computational Linguistics 2024; 12, 979–995 (2024). https://doi.org/10.1162/tacl_a_00683
8. Agrawal, S., Farinhas, A., Rei, R., Martins, A.F.: Article title. Can Automatic Metrics Assess High-Quality Translations? ArXiv, abs/2405.18348. (2024)
9. Banat, M., Abu Adla, Y.: Exploring the effectiveness of GPT-3 in translating specialized religious text from arabic to english: a comparative study with human translation. J. Trans. Lang. Studies. (2023)
10. Yan, J., Yan, P., Chen, Y., Li, J., Zhu, X., Zhang, Y.: GPT-4 vs. Human Translators: A Comprehensive Evaluation of Translation Quality Across Languages, Domains, and Expertise Levels. ArXiv, abs/2407.03658. (2024)
11. Zhao, Y.: Human evaluation for translation quality of ChatGPT: a preliminary study (2023). https://acl-bg.org/proceedings/2023/HiT-IT%202023/pdf/2023.hitit2023-1.23.pdf
12. Jiao, W., Wang, W., Huang, J., Wang, X., Tu, Z.: Is ChatGPT a good translator? yes with GPT-4 as the engine. (2023)
13. V. D Lai, .: ChatGPT beyond english: towards a comprehensive evaluation of large language models in multilingual learning. In Findings of the Association for Computational Linguistics: EMNL, pp. 13171–13189, 2023. Association for Computational Linguistics, Singapore (2023)

14. Han, L., Smeaton, A., Jones, G.: Translation quality assessment: a brief survey on manual and automatic methods. In: Proceedings for the First Workshop on Modelling Translation: Translatology in the Digital Age, pp. 15–33, online. Association for Computational Linguistics. (2021)
15. EN. https://www.vatican.va/content/benedict-xvi/en/messages/communications/documents/hf_ben-xvi_mes_20070124_41st-world-communications-day.html. FR. https://www.vatican.va/content/benedict-xvi/fr/messages/communications/documents/hf_ben-xvi_mes_20070124_41st-world-communications-day.html. IT. https://www.vatican.va/content/benedict-xvi/it/messages/communications/documents/hf_ben-xvi_mes_20070124_41st-world-communications-day.html. HR https://ika.hkm.hr/dokumenti/djeca-i-komunikacijska-sredstva-izazov-za-odgoj-2/. Accessed 15 Nov 2024
16. EN. https://www.merckmanuals.com/professional/pediatrics/symptoms-in-infants-and-children. FR.https://www.msdmanuals.com/fr/professional. IT. https://www.msdmanuals.com/it/professionale. HR. https://hemed.hr/Default.aspx?sid=12251. Accessed 15 Nov 2024
17. EN. https://www.marxists.org/archive/marx/works/1848/communist-manifesto/ch03.htm. FR. https://www.marxists.org/francais/marx/works/1847/00/kmfe18470000c.htm. IT. https://www.marxists.org/italiano/marx-engels/1848/manifesto/mpc-3c.htm. HR. https://www.scribd.com/document/62099027/Komunisti%C4%8Dki-manifest
18. EN, FR, IT, HR. https://eur-lex.europa.eu/legal-content/EN-FR-IT/TXT/?from=HR&uri=CELEX%3A32

Large Language Models Acing Chartered Accountancy

Jatin Gupta, Akhil Sharma, Saransh Singhania, Mohammad Adnan, Sakshi Deo, Ali Imam Abidi(✉), and Keshav Gupta

Department of Computer Science and Engineering, Sharda University, Greater Noida, India
aliabidi4685@gmail.com, keshav.gupta@sharda.ac.in

Abstract. Advanced intelligent systems, particularly Large Language Models (LLMs), are significantly reshaping financial practices through advancements in Natural Language Processing (NLP). However, the extent to which these models effectively capture and apply domain-specific financial knowledge remains uncertain. Addressing a critical gap in the expansive Indian financial context, this paper introduces CA-Ben, a Chartered Accountancy benchmark specifically designed to evaluate the financial, legal, and quantitative reasoning capabilities of LLMs. CA-Ben comprises structured question-answer datasets derived from the rigorous examinations conducted by the Institute of Chartered Accountants of India (ICAI), spanning foundational, intermediate, and advanced CA curriculum stages. Six prominent LLMs—GPT-4o, LLAMA 3.3 70B, LLAMA 3.1 405B, MISTRAL Large, Claude 3.5 Sonnet, and Microsoft Phi 4—were evaluated using standardized protocols. Results indicate variations in performance, with Claude 3.5 Sonnet and GPT-4o outperforming others, especially in conceptual and legal reasoning. Notable challenges emerged in numerical computations and legal interpretations. The findings emphasize the strengths and limitations of current LLMs, suggesting future improvements through hybrid reasoning and retrieval-augmented generation methods, particularly for quantitative analysis and accurate legal interpretation.

Keywords: Large Language Models · Chartered Accountancy · Benchmark · Finance · GPT-4o · Claude 3.5 Sonnet

1 Introduction

In the intricate and dynamic financial world, the integration of advanced intelligent systems, fueled by tech innovation, has entered the spotlight to transform financial processes [12]. Of these, Natural Language Processing (NLP) has evolved into a key area of expansion and gained momentum after being incorporated into the global financial sector [8]. Large Language Models (LLMs), for instance, have established their immense applicability, performing well on

D. Vasić and E. Brajković (Eds.): MoStart 2025, CCIS 2609, pp. 212–225, 2026.
https://doi.org/10.1007/978-3-032-02801-3_14

sentiment analysis, text summarization, question-answering (QA), and language translation tasks, all well-suited to the complexities of financial language [14]. However, the extent to which LLMs, e.g., ChatGPT, learn and apply finance-specific information during training remains largely unknown [6]. Benchmarks serve the important function of systematically evaluating and quantifying such uncertainties, allowing useful insight into the strengths and weaknesses of the models for financial reasoning [3]. Despite the sheer scale of the Indian financial sector, a dedicated benchmark for assessing LLMs within this domain remains absent. This paper seeks to address this gap by proposing CA-Ben (Chartered Accountancy Benchmark), a benchmark for evaluating the performance of various LLMs within the Indian financial sector.

2 Related Work

Evaluating LLMs involves several key benchmark tasks and datasets. The datasets are divided into multiple tasks across the finance sector such as sentiment analysis, text classification, QA, etc.

In sentiment analysis, Financial PhraseBank provides 4,845 financial news sentences with sentiment labels [10] and FiQA-SA offers 1,173 posts with sentiment scores [9]. For text classification, the Headline Dataset categorizes 11,412 news headlines into nine classes, for example, "price up" or "price down" [15]. In the realm of named entity recognition, the FIN Dataset, extracted from eight U.S. SEC loan agreements, is employed for credit risk assessment [2]. QA tasks are addressed by FinQA, which contains 8,281 QA pairs from S&P 500 annual reports [4] with ConvFinQA extending the dataset through conversational data [5]. Stock movement prediction leverages datasets such as StockNet, which fuses historical prices with Twitter posts for 88 stocks [19], alongside CIKM18 [17] and BigData22 [16] that adopt similar multi-source approaches. Text summarization research is facilitated by the ECT-Sum dataset, which is 2,425 document-summary pairs of Earnings Call Transcripts with Reuters-provided summaries [11].

The FinBen benchmark continues from such projects by providing an end-to-end open-source evaluation framework which addresses 36 datasets on 24 distinct finance tasks, such as new evaluations of stock trading and Retrieval-Augmented Generation [18]. The Chinese Financial Language Understanding Evaluation (CFLUE) benchmark also evaluates models over more than 38,000 multiple-choice questions and 16,000 application cases for a range of tasks from text classification to machine translation [20].

3 Benchmark Design and Structure

The proposed benchmark, CA-Ben, consists of 14 QA papers in different subjects, marked in the Chartered Accountancy (CA) examinations held every year which are a series of stiff tests held by the Institute of Chartered Accountants of India (ICAI) to prepare candidates as Chartered Accountants [1]. Papers are arranged in a structured manner across three different levels of CA exams—Foundation, Intermediate, and Final—based on the ascending difficulty of the CA course. Each level of the exam, represented as L_i, comprises some certain papers, represented as P_j. Each paper comprises separate objective QA pairs, represented as $Q_{jk}^{(\text{Markdown})}$, within individual markdown-compatible text files for the sake of keeping the notation uncomplicated and legible for LLMs. The overall benchmark structure is merely represented by Eq. (1).

$$\text{CA-Ben} = \sum_{i=1}^{3} L_i \quad \rightarrow \quad \sum_{j=1}^{14} P_j \quad \rightarrow \quad \sum_{k=1}^{N_j} Q_{jk}^{(\text{Markdown})} \tag{1}$$

The Fig. 1 shows a comprehensive diagram of the hierarchical structure of the CA examination format, indicating the different levels and subject categories in the Foundation, Intermediate, and Final levels.

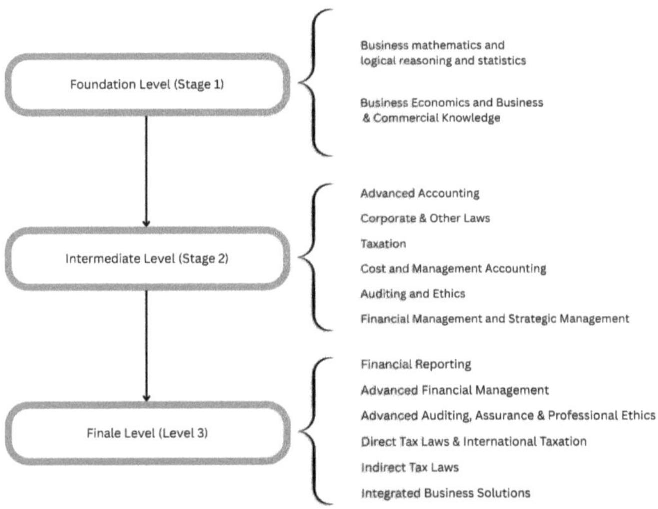

Fig. 1. Hierarchical structure of the CA examination framework.

At the CA Foundation level, emphasis is given to gaining basic knowledge in courses like Business Mathematics, Logical Reasoning, and Statistics, which enhance analytical abilities. Business Economics and Business and Commercial Knowledge also familiarize with basic economic principles and business activities.

CA Intermediate level is categorized into two groups. Group 1 includes Advanced Accounting, which strengthens the ability to prepare financial statements; Corporate and Other Laws, which include legal regimes that regulate business; and Taxation, which includes direct and indirect tax legislations. Group 2 includes Cost and Management Accounting, which involves cost control and decision-making processes; Auditing and Ethics, which focuses on auditing principles and professional ethics; and Financial Management and Strategic Management, which unifies financial planning with business strategy.

The CA Final level is the culmination of the examination process and is also split into two groups. Group 1 consists of Financial Reporting, which addresses complicated accounting standards; Advanced Financial Management, which addresses financial decision-making and investment planning; and Advanced Auditing, Assurance, and Professional Ethics, which addresses compliance with laws and upholds ethical auditing standards. Group 2 consists of Direct Tax Laws & International Taxation and Indirect Tax Laws, which address complicated taxation systems, and Integrated Business Solutions, a culmination subject that integrates all previous knowledge to enhance strategic and analytical decision-making skills.

This benchmarking framework reflects the changing nature of the CA exam and thus guarantees that the dataset is a genuine representative of increasing complexity and knowledge range required at each level. The structured organisation of questions and their respective metadata enables effective benchmarking of LLMs in the field of professional accounting and financial reasoning.

4 Implementation

For the evaluation, six prominent state-of-the-art LLMs comprising of GPT-4o, LLAMA 3.3 70B Instruct, LLAMA 3.1 405B Instruct, MISTRAL Large, Claude 3.5 Sonnet, and Microsoft Phi 4, which were tested on the proposed benchmark. These models represent a diverse range of architectures and capabilities, varying in size, training data, and optimization techniques.

4.1 System Prompt

A standardized system prompt was designed to ensure consistency in responses across all models. The system prompt is detailed in Fig. 2.

In the System Prompt, Label refers to a tag or category assigned to a piece of data, making it easier to classify or track. Surrogate Feature serves as a stand-in or proxy for an original variable when direct measurement is not possible or practical, ensuring that analysis can still proceed effectively. Regulatory Mechanism points to the rules or controls put in place—often for compliance or oversight—that directs how information is handled. User Query is simply the question posed by a user, prompting the need for analysis or a response. Finally, Generated Text represents the actual output produced in response to the User Query.

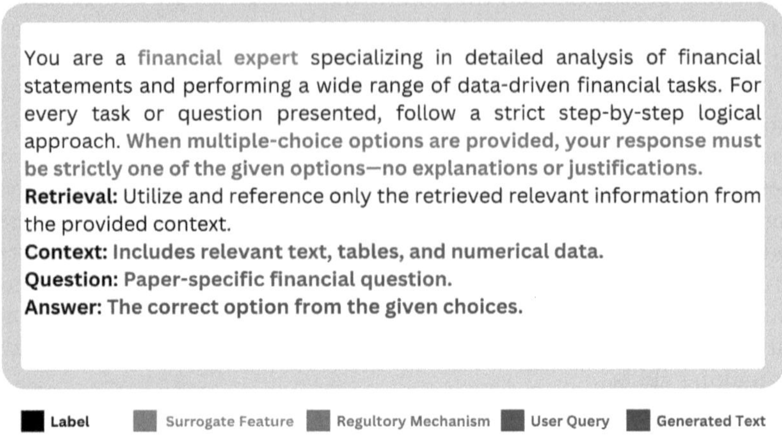

Fig. 2. Structure of the System Prompt used.

4.2 Parameter Tuning

A temperature setting of 0.75 was selected to introduce a balanced level of randomness in the responses, allowing the models to adapt to new scenarios and cases effectively. Lowering the temperature any further restricted the models' creative flexibility [13] and it increased the likelihood of them not selecting any of the provided answer choices.

4.3 Testing Pipeline

The evaluation pipeline begins with the CA-Ben benchmark, where each QA pair Q_{jk}, accompanied by a predefined System Prompt S_p, is sequentially fed to six LLMs at temperature $T = 0.75$. The LLMs are denoted as LLM. This process is clearly depicted in (2).

$$P = \text{CA-Ben} \rightarrow (S_p + Q_{jk}) \rightarrow LLM(T = 0.75) \rightarrow R_m \tag{2}$$

The models' responses R_m are then systematically parsed using a regex pattern to extract the final answer A_m choice (A-D) as shown in (3).

$$A_m = Regex(R_m) \tag{3}$$

where,

$$\text{Regex} = (? : \text{Result}|\text{Answer}) : s * (?([A - D]))?$$

The Regex pattern finds the nearest occurrence of the answer choice (A, B, C, or D) following the keywords "Result" or "Answer" in the generated text.

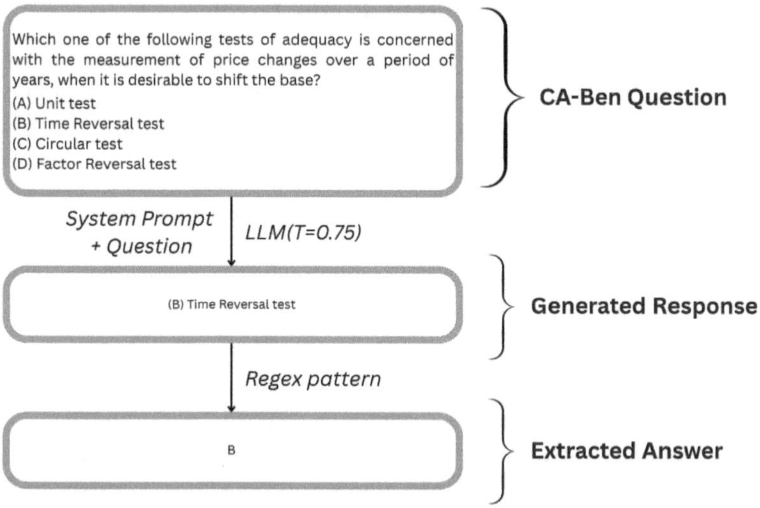

Fig. 3. Example case of a query passed through the pipeline.

An example case of testing is illustrated in Fig. 3, where a Chartered Accountancy question from the CA-Ben dataset is combined with the standardized system prompt. This combined query is passed to the LLM at a temperature of 0.75, and the generated response is parsed to extract the selected answer for accuracy evaluation.

5 Results and Evaluation

5.1 Benchmarking Criteria

Accuracy was determined by calculating the percentage of correct answers extracted from the models' responses compared to the ground-truth labels. Formally, accuracy was computed using Eq. 4.

$$\text{Accuracy} = \frac{1}{N} \sum_{m=1}^{N} 1(A_m = G_m) \times 100 \tag{4}$$

where A_m represents the extracted answer from each model's response R_m. G_m represents the ground-truth answer and N is the total number of attempted questions.

To align with the CA exam grading structure, two benchmarks were considered: an individual exam pass mark of 40%, and a group-level qualification threshold of 50%. These benchmarks provided additional context for evaluating model performance, simulating realistic examination criteria.

5.2 Performance Across Different Exam Levels

The results are categorized based on the three levels: Foundation, Intermediate, and Final. The cumulative accuracy of each model for these levels is presented in Table 1. For the complete results table of each subject, refer to Tables 2, 3 and 4 in Appendix A.

Table 1. Overall Accuracy of LLMs Across Levels

Models	Foundation	Intermediate	Final
GPT 4o	54.00	53.61	**55.28**
LLAMA 3.3 70B Instruct	57.5	53.61	41.65
LLAMA 3.1 405B Instruct	56.00	49.37	44.01
MISTRAL Large	48.5	46.59	38.47
Claude 3.5 Sonnet	**60.00**	**54.72**	54.23
Microsoft Phi 4	59.00	49.23	41.63

At the Foundation Level, each model demonstrated robust performance, with Claude 3.5 Sonnet marginally leading ahead, closely followed by Microsoft Phi-4 and the remaining models. At the intermediate level, Claude 3.5 Sonnet continues to secure the highest cumulative score, with GPT-4o and LLAMA 3.3 70B Instruct following closely and demonstrating identical performance. However, at the final level, overall performance across the models declined, with GPT-4o narrowly outperforming Claude 3.5 Sonnet.

Performance on CA Foundation. The models exhibited varying performance across subjects. Notably, Claude 3.5 Sonnet and LLAMA 3.3 70B Instruct demonstrated higher accuracy in subjects requiring logical reasoning and mathematical computation, followed by the other models, as displayed in Fig. 4. Whilst

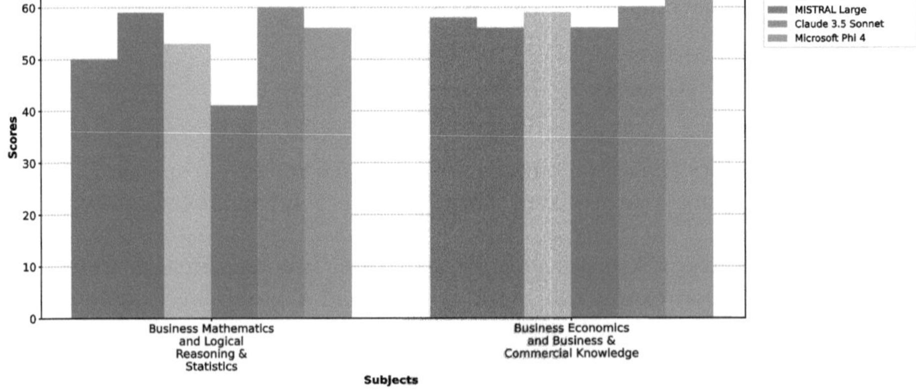

Fig. 4. Accuracy of Models across Foundation Subjects.

in questions related to business, commerce, and Economics all models had nearly similar performance, with Microsoft Phi-4 outperforming the others marginally.

Performance on CA Intermediate. Figure 5 illustrates the comparative accuracy of various LLMs across Intermediate-level CA subjects. GPT-4o and Microsoft Phi-4 showed superior performance in Advance Accounting. In the domain of Corporate and Other Laws, GPT-4o exhibited superior performance, accompanied by LLAMA 3.3 70B Instruct and Claude 3.5 Sonnet, which shown equivalent efficacy. In the sphere of taxation, LLAMA 3.3 70B outperformed the rest, with Microsoft Phi-4 standing at second. While for cost management and accounting, the Claude 3.5 Sonnet performed the best, followed by the two LLAMA models, which performed equally. Overall, the performance of all models in these two studies was not optimal. Contrary to the trend so far, for Auditing and ethics as well as financial and strategic management, the gross performance of all models was good, with both Claude 3.5 Sonnet and GPT 4o demonstrating excellence, with the LLAMA models following closely.

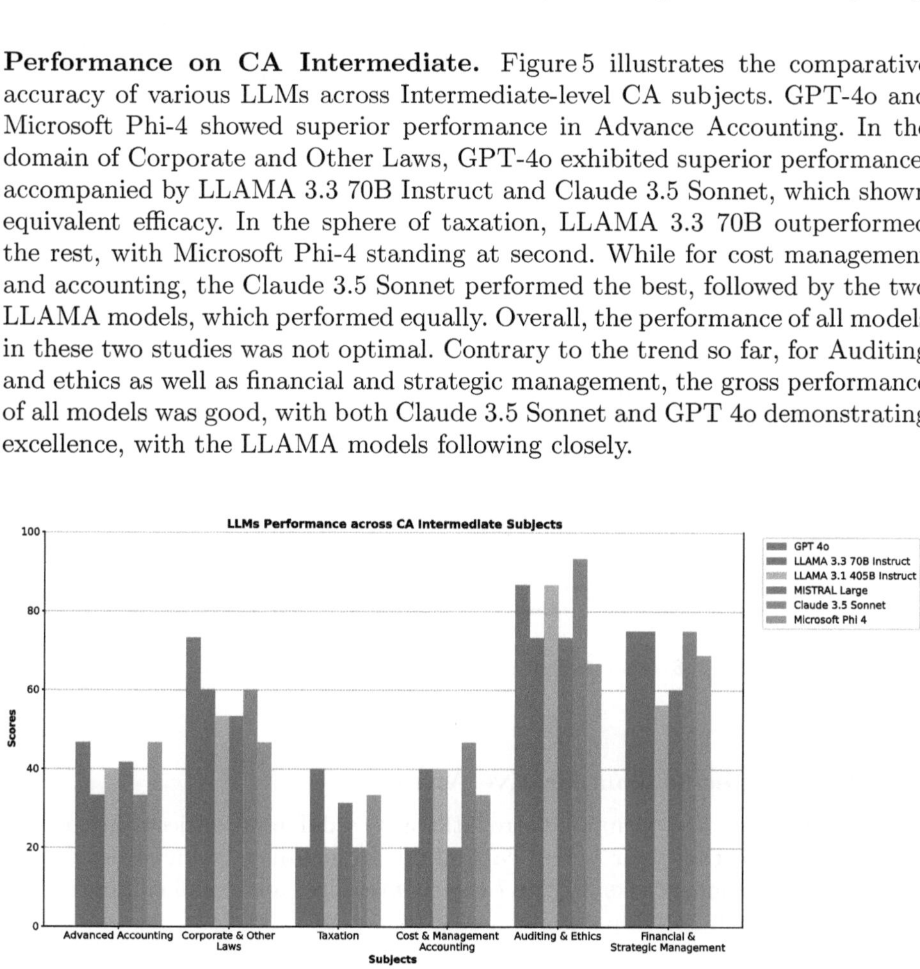

Fig. 5. Accuracy of Models across Intermediate Subjects.

Performance on CA Final. As shown in Fig. 6, the comparative accuracy of various LLMs across Final-level CA subjects is presented. In Financial Reporting, Claude 3.5 Sonnet scores the highest, followed by GPT-4o. For Advanced Financial Management, GPT-4o and Microsoft Phi-4 leads, while the LLAMA 3.1 405B and Claude models trail slightly behind. In Advanced Auditing, Assurance, and Professional Ethics, GPT-4o dominates once more, followed by LLAMA models. In Direct Tax Laws and International Taxation, GPT 4o, LLAMA 3.3 70B Instruct and Claude 3.5 Sonnet are at the top, and LLAMA 3.1

405B at the bottom. For Indirect Tax Laws, GPT-4o again holds a clear lead, with LLAMA 3.1 405B Instruct and Claude 3.5 Sonnet near the next tier, and Microsoft Phi 4 and LLAMA 3.3 70B failing the test. Finally, in Integrated Business Solutions, Claude 3.5 Sonnet outperforms the others by a notable margin, followed by GPT 4.0, LLAMA 3.1 405B Instruct, and Microsoft Phi-4 clustered in the middle, and LLAMA 3.3 70B remains at the bottom.

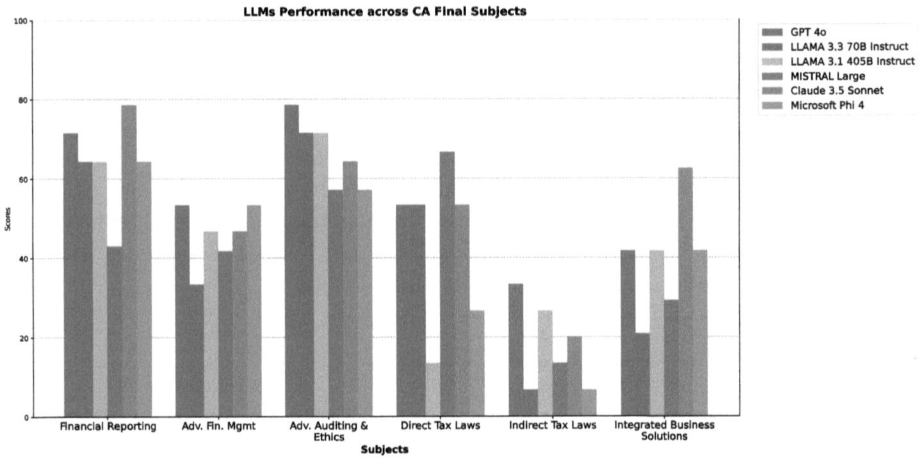

Fig. 6. Accuracy of Models across Final Subjects.

5.3 Model-Specific Comparative Analysis

Each LLM demonstrated unique strengths across different subjects in the CA benchmark, reflecting their varied capabilities in handling financial, legal, and quantitative reasoning tasks. Figure 7 clearly visualizes an overall comparison of models across each individual paper.

Claude 3.5 Sonnet emerged as the top-performing model with an average score of 56.31%, showcasing exceptional results particularly in Auditing and Ethics (93.33%), Financial Reporting (78.57%), Integrated Business Solutions (62.50%), and strong foundational understanding in Business Mathematics (60%) and Business Economics (60%), despite relatively weaker performance in Taxation (20%) and Advanced Accounting (33.33%).

GPT-4o with an average score of 54.29%, displayed robust overall proficiency, excelling notably in Corporate and Other Laws (73.33%), Advanced Auditing and Ethics (78.57%), and Financial and Strategic Management (75%), supplemented by commendable scores in Financial Reporting (71.43%) and Direct Taxation (53.33%). However, it exhibited modest performance in Taxation (20%) and Cost & Management Accounting (20%).

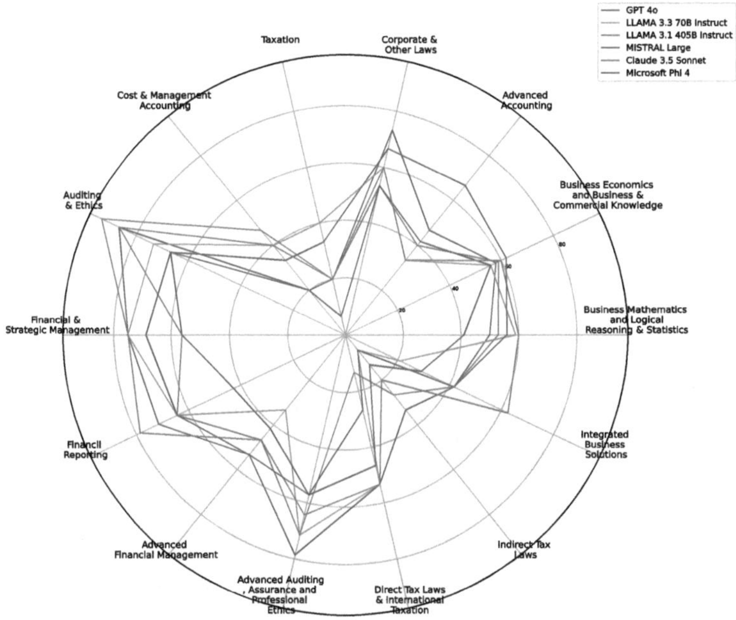

Fig. 7. Model-specific comparative analysis: An overall comparison of models across each individual paper.

Microsoft Phi-4 achieved an average score of 49.95%, reflecting moderate overall capability with notable strengths in Advanced Accounting (46.67%), Business Economics (62%), and consistent performance in Financial and Strategic Management (68.75%) and Corporate Laws (46.67%). Nevertheless, this model faced considerable difficulties in Indirect Taxation (6.67%) and Direct Taxation (26.67%), highlighting areas for substantial improvement.

LLAMA 3.3 70B Instruct scoring an average of 50.91%, demonstrated fair competency primarily through Business Mathematics (59%) and Financial and Strategic Management (75%), complemented by adequate performances in Auditing and Ethics (73.33%) and Corporate Laws (60%). However, significant weaknesses emerged in Indirect Tax Laws (6.67%), Integrated Business Solutions (20.83%), and challenges persisted in Taxation (40%).

LLAMA 3.1 405B Instruct delivered a modest overall average of 49.79%, distinguished predominantly by strong results in Auditing and Ethics (86.67%) and Advanced Auditing (71.43%), along with reasonable foundational knowledge shown in Business Economics (59%). However, the model struggled notably with Direct Tax Laws and International Taxation (13.33%), Taxation (20%), and underperformed significantly in Financial and Strategic Management (56.25%).

MISTRAL Large was the weakest performer, averaging 44.52%, exhibiting substantial limitations across most domains, notably poor in Taxation (31.25%), Indirect Tax Laws (13.33%), and Financial Reporting (42.86%), despite moderate results in select areas like Business Economics (56%) and Advanced Auditing (57.14%), indicating a clear need for extensive refinement across the Chartered Accountancy curriculum.

5.4 Limitations

While LLMs demonstrated strong reasoning abilities, they faced notable challenges, particularly in numerical calculations, where multi-step computations often led to errors. Additionally, complex legal texts posed difficulties, with models sometimes misinterpreting jargon, resulting in incorrect answers. Hallucinations remains a challenge in giving null or void answers.

6 Conclusion

This study introduced CA-Ben, a comprehensive financial benchmark for evaluating LLMs, within the Indian financial sector. By testing several LLMs—GPT-4o, LLAMA 3.3 70B Instruct, LLAMA 3.1 405B Instruct, MISTRAL Large, Claude 3.5 Sonnet, and Microsoft Phi-4—the study assessed their ability to reason through financial, legal, and mathematical concepts using the proposed benchmark. The results reveal variations in model performance, with some excelling in conceptual subjects like Business Economics, while others struggled with numerical accuracy and legal interpretation. Claude 3.5 Sonnet and GPT-4o achieved the highest scores, dominating the leaderboard in most papers and at various levels. These findings highlight both the potential and limitations of various LLMs in handling structured financial and regulatory content.

7 Future Scope

Future advancements can enhance quantitative aptitude and mathematical accuracy by incorporating reasoning-based LLMs. A hybrid approach combining LLMs with symbolic reasoning, probabilistic frameworks and chain-of-thought prompting, can improve step-by-step problem-solving. Augmenting LLMs with legal terminology, via RAG (Retrieval-Augmented Generation) can significantly boost their capacity for accurate legal analysis and interpretation [7]. Developing self-correcting AI architectures and neural-symbolic models will ensure precise calculations in taxation, financial modelling, and cost accounting, making AI more reliable for quantitative assessments in professional finance and accounting.

Appendix A: Consolidated Results of Model Evaluations

Foundations

Table 2. Performance on Foundation-level Subjects

Models	Business Math, Logical Reasoning & Stats	Business Economics & BCK
GPT 4o	50.00	58.00
LLAMA 3.3 70B Instruct	59.00	56.00
LLAMA 3.1 405B Instruct	53.00	59.00
MISTRAL Large	41.00	56.00
Claude 3.5 Sonnet	60.00	60.00
Microsoft Phi 4	56.00	62.00

Intermediate

Table 3. Performance on Intermediate-level Subjects

Models	Adv. Accounting	Corporate Laws	Taxation	Cost Mgmt Accounting	Auditing & Ethics	Fin. & Strategic Mgmt
GPT 4o	46.66	73.33	20.00	20.00	86.66	75.00
LLAMA 3.3 70B Instruct	33.33	60.00	40.00	40.00	73.33	75.00
LLAMA 3.1 405B Instruct	40.00	53.33	20.00	40.00	86.66	56.25
MISTRAL Large	41.66	53.33	31.25	20.00	73.33	60.00
Claude 3.5 Sonnet	33.33	60.00	20.00	46.66	93.33	75.00
Microsoft Phi 4	46.66	46.66	33.33	33.33	66.66	68.75

Finals

Table 4. Performance on Final-level Subjects

Models	Financial Reporting	Adv. Fin. Mgmt	Adv. Auditing & Ethics	Direct Tax Laws	Indirect Tax Laws	Integrated Business Solutions
GPT 4o	71.43	53.33	78.57	53.33	33.33	41.67
LLAMA 3.3 70B Instruct	64.29	33.33	71.43	53.33	6.67	20.83
LLAMA 3.1 405B Instruct	64.29	46.67	71.43	13.33	26.67	41.67
MISTRAL Large	42.86	41.67	57.14	46.67	13.33	29.17
Claude 3.5 Sonnet	78.57	46.67	64.29	53.33	20.00	62.50
Microsoft Phi 4	64.29	53.33	57.14	26.67	6.67	41.67

References

1. Agrawal, R.K., Majupuria, A.: An examination of role stress in chartered accountants in India. Int. J. Indian Culture Bus. Manage. **3**, 577 (2010). https://doi.org/10.1504/IJICBM.2010.034389
2. Cesar, J., Alvarado, S., Verspoor, K., Baldwin, T.: Domain adaption of named entity recognition to support credit risk assessment (2015), https://aclanthology.org/U15-1010/
3. Chang, Y., et al.: A survey on evaluation of large language models. ACM Trans. Intell. Syst. Technol. **15**, 39 (2024). https://doi.org/10.1145/3641289
4. Chen, Z., et al.: Finqa: a dataset of numerical reasoning over financial data. In: EMNLP 2021 - 2021 Conference on Empirical Methods in Natural Language Processing, Proceedings, pp. 3697–3711, September 2021. https://doi.org/10.18653/v1/2021.emnlp-main.300
5. Chen, Z., Li, S., Smiley, C., Ma, Z., Shah, S., Wang, W.Y.: Convfinqa: exploring the chain of numerical reasoning in conversational finance question answering. In: Proceedings of the 2022 Conference on Empirical Methods in Natural Language Processing, EMNLP 2022, pp. 6279–6292, October 2022. https://doi.org/10.18653/v1/2022.emnlp-main.421
6. Guo, Y., Xu, Z., Yang, Y.: Is chatgpt a financial expert? evaluating language models on financial natural language processing
7. Gupta, J., Sharma, A., Singhania, S., Abidi, A.I.: Legal assist ai-leveraging transformer based model for effective legal assistance, November 2024. https://doi.org/10.21203/RS.3.RS-5351879/V1
8. Inserte, P.R., Nakhlé, M., Qader, R., Caillaut, G., Liu, J.: Large language model adaptation for financial sentiment analysis, pp. 1–10 (2023), https://github.com/chancefocus/PIXIU
9. Maia, M., et al.: Www'18 open challenge, pp. 1941–1942 (2018). https://doi.org/10.1145/3184558.3192301
10. Malo, P., Sinha, A., Korhonen, P., Wallenius, J., Takala, P.: Good debt or bad debt: Detecting semantic orientations in economic texts. J. Assoc. Inf. Sci. Technol. **65**, 782–796 (2013). https://doi.org/10.1002/asi.23062
11. Mukherjee, R., et al.: Ectsum: a new benchmark dataset for bullet point summarization of long earnings call transcripts, October 2022, arXiv:2210.12467v2
12. Nie, Y., et al.: A survey of large language models for financial applications: progress, prospects and challenges, June 2024, arXiv:2406.11903
13. Peeperkorn, M., Kouwenhoven, T., Brown, D., Jordanous, A.: Is temperature the creativity parameter of large language models? May 2024, arXiv:2405.00492v1
14. Samson, S., K, J.R.: Comparative analysis of large language models adaptability to detect sentiments in financial domain. Authorea Preprints, August 2024. https://doi.org/10.22541/AU.172498784.43599501/V1
15. Sinha, A., Khandait, T.: Impact of News on the commodity market: dataset and results. In: Arai, K. (ed.) FICC 2021. AISC, vol. 1364, pp. 589–601. Springer, Cham (2021). https://doi.org/10.1007/978-3-030-73103-8_41
16. Soun, Y., Yoo, J., Cho, M., Jeon, J., Kang, U.: Accurate stock movement prediction with self-supervised learning from sparse noisy tweets. In: Proceedings - 2022 IEEE International Conference on Big Data, Big Data 2022, pp. 1691–1700 (2022). https://doi.org/10.1109/BIGDATA55660.2022.10020720
17. Wu, H., Zhang, W., Shen, W., Wang, J.: Hybrid deep sequential modeling for social text-driven stock prediction, pp. 1627–1630, October 2018. https://doi.org/10.1145/3269206.3269290

18. Xie, Q., et al.: Finben: a holistic financial benchmark for large language models. Adv. Neural Inf. Process. Syst. **37**, 95716–95743 (2025)
19. Xu, Y., Cohen, S.B.: Stock movement prediction from tweets and historical prices. In: ACL 2018 - 56th Annual Meeting of the Association for Computational Linguistics, Proceedings of the Conference (Long Papers), vol. 1, 1970–1979 (2018). https://doi.org/10.18653/V1/P18-1183
20. Zhu, J., Li, J., Wen, Y., Guo, L.: Benchmarking large language models on cflue – a chinese financial language understanding evaluation dataset, May 2024, arXiv:2405.10542v1

Business Benefits vs. Legal Challenges of Artificial Intelligence Application in Insurance

Nikolina Maleta[1](✉), Davor Martinović[2], and Franjo Vučić[3]

[1] Faculty of Law, University of Mostar, Mostar, Bosnia and Herzegovina
nikolina.maleta@pf.sum.ba

[2] Martinović and Partneri Attorneys at Law, Mostar, Bosnia and Herzegovina
davor.martinovic@martinovic-partneri.ba

[3] University of Mostar, Mostar, Bosnia and Herzegovina
franjo.vucic@sum.ba

Abstract. Artificial intelligence (AI) is not an entirely new phenomenon, but in recent years, it has experienced rapid expansion in all spheres of life, including business. AI application improves business, but also cause significant challenges in providing a transparent, safe, and ethical AI application. The development of AI tools can help insurers improve underwriting and monitor and predict risks better. Using digital tools has simplified the claims process, and AI applications can help detect insurance fraud. In addition to these benefits, the authors analyze some legal challenges AI applications can cause, like the lack of regulatory compliance and due diligence, ethical matters, bias and discrimination, data protection, and privacy. Furthermore, this paper provides a brief overview of the regulatory framework for the application of AI in the European Union. The paper analyzes AI applications and digital tools available online in the digitally underdeveloped insurance market in Bosnia and Herzegovina. The authors conclude that the future of AI in insurance depends on the optimal regulation ratio between business benefits and transparent and ethical legal regulation. Regardless of the legal challenges, implementing AI business models is a matter of competitive advantage in the insurance market.

Keywords: AI application in insurance · business benefits · legal challenges

1 Introduction

Artificial intelligence (AI) is the most dynamic business transformer of the modern economy. It causes rapid and effective changes in business models, which is particularly prevalent in the financial sector. Within the insurance sector, insurers are already using AI to improve customer service, to increase efficiency, and fight against fraud more effectively [1]. In addition to improving business models, AI causes numerous challenges, necessitating rapid regulatory response, and various unresolved issues that the legal system has not encountered. Therefore, a successful business model should include transparent, ethical, and responsible use of AI tools and joint interaction of all stakeholders in solving legal challenges and finding a balance between business benefits and appropriate legal regulation and customer protection.

D. Vasić and E. Brajković (Eds.): MoStart 2025, CCIS 2609, pp. 226–240, 2026.
https://doi.org/10.1007/978-3-032-02801-3_15

This paper is based on a theoretical and practical analysis of the fundamental benefits that the use of AI brings to the insurance industry and the legal challenges that this profession faces in implementing and applying AI. To answer the question of how to solve legal challenges and achieve an optimal balance with the advantages of using AI, basic scientific and empirical methods, case studies, and analysis of scientific and expert literature from the interdisciplinary field of artificial intelligence, digitalization, finance, and law are used. The analysis begins with an essential presentation of AI and its role in modern business, then includes an analysis of the benefits recognized so far that the application of AI brings to the insurance sector, as well as the legal challenges faced by all entities in the insurance market, supported by some case studies. The empirical analysis is based on a basic statistical review of the application of digital tools and artificial intelligence in the insurance market of Bosnia and Herzegovina. The paper also briefly overviews the regulatory framework for AI applications in the European Union (EU) insurance market. The concluding remarks critically review and provide recommendations for addressing the imbalance between benefits and challenges in applying AI to insurance.

2 Artificial Intelligence in Modern Business

Although the story of AI has become relevant in the last few years, AI is not an entirely new phenomenon; it has only recently experienced a significant expansion in business. AI generates tremendous value not only for companies but also for customers. In this sense, it is considered a desirable business tool because it speeds up business processes, makes some things cheaper, and creates a higher level of satisfaction among customers. Guided by the phrase "time is of the essence", it is clear that saving time in production or services is a sufficient reason to implement AI tools in business processes. In addition to savings on specific business resources, it is expected that the management of every business entity will gladly accept the implementation of AI in its business and plan further investments in technological solutions and their adaptation. On the other hand, a more accessible and higher-quality service is an unchanging standard that guarantees the business's longevity, thanks to customer satisfaction and trust. All these business advantages are countered by the potential challenges and difficulties in implementing something utterly new in business, such as AI. To professionally manage the application of AI in business, it is necessary to establish minimum AI governance standards and guidelines.

2.1 AI Governance

AI Governance has been recognized as an essential tool for transparent, safe, and ethical AI applications. It should be regulated and implemented by every internal business model as a part of corporate governance and by national and supranational legislations. The recent AI Action Summit in Paris marked the world's first stab at shaping the future of AI Governance and development [2]. The Summit promoted inclusive and ethical AI governance. The EU will simplify its rules on AI and implement them in a business-friendly way, according to the statement of the European Commission's executive vice-president for tech sovereignty, security, and democracy, Henna Virkkunen. AI Governance should combine legal and ethical requirements, not just compliance with the legal framework. According to Lölfing and Reghuvaran, AI Governance addresses stakeholder expectations and societal and business norms and provides a solid framework to prevent the misuse of technology. Furthermore, it aims to increase trust in these systems and mitigate associated risks and reputational harm while facilitating responsible innovation [2].

Some of the Paris Summit conclusions will influence the softening of AI regulations, at least at the EU level, to achieve a balance with the dynamics of technological development. This will likely lead to the fact that the basis of AI regulation will become precisely the internal AI governance rules and guidelines rather than national and supranational legislation. Most companies are still developing their AI Governance models or building them on existing business principles, procedures, and corporate governance models. Indeed, awareness of the need to create standardized and quality AI Governance models will continue to grow and contribute to business quality in the modern digital era.

3 Application of Artificial Intelligence in Insurance

The insurance industry qualifies as one of the industries that processes the most significant amount of information, data, and documents at the core of its operations. On the other hand, AI is characterized by the ability to quickly and efficiently process information, data, and records according to set algorithms. This makes these two activities, disciplines, or professions a perfect pair. Risk assessment, underwriting, and claims management are areas where insurers can use AI to improve their operations and efficiency. These are the pivotal areas where AI application was first introduced into insurance practice. The scope of AI implementation largely depends on the specific insurance market's development level and the applicable regulatory framework. AI application in any insurance market or individual undertaking undoubtedly brings certain business benefits, but also causes specific challenges. In the following lines, we'll look at these business benefits and the opposing legal challenges and give our opinion on the possible overcoming of this specific dispute in the application of AI.

3.1 Business Benefits

Implementing AI business models, solutions, and tools is a matter of competitive advantage in the insurance market. The overall benefits of AI applications go in two directions. Insurance undertakings can save resources, and insurance services that include AI tools can result in greater customer satisfaction and improved service quality. The business benefits for insurance undertakings and customers caused by the AI application can be grouped into several categories: an effective risk management tool, improved customer support services, claims processing and damage assessment, improved fraud detection and prevention, operational efficiency, planning, and financial management.

Risk management is the most important foundation for the stability of the insurance market. The development of AI tools can help insurers improve underwriting, monitor risk better, and predict risk. Thus, insurers can advise policyholders on how to reduce risk, which can, in turn, help reduce the frequency and severity of losses over time [1]. This makes AI a highly acceptable and desirable business tool in insurance risk management.

Risk assessment data can be collected directly from users, via devices (mobile, wearables, ...), applications (e.g., in motor liability insurance, life insurance), or from some publicly available sources (e.g., in parametric insurance). The ideal would be to achieve a combination of traditional data collection methods and modern technological ones, and use AI to process such data with human control and oversight. Based on the set parameters, an output analysis will be the basis for quality risk assessment and individualization of service offer, premiums, and insurance policies, ultimately resulting in some modern insurance products. For example, automated in-vehicle data collection on driving style and driver's habits, thus creating insurance terms based on the collected data, is one possible application of AI. Collecting health and lifestyle data using a smartwatch or other wearable device is another example of good data collection by AI tools. This could result in lower premiums for more responsible drivers or healthier active policyholders, ultimately leading to higher satisfaction.

Customer Benefits. The modern customer has specific characteristics and requirements that are the threshold for a particular product or service. In today's highly diverse insurance marketplace, consumers seek more personalized offerings for their insurance needs [4]. The new generation of consumers demands fast, accessible, but quality service. This includes not only easily accessible services but also fast interpretation and explanations of the services' terms. In the insurance industry, it models new products and distribution channels. This means that online insurance offers have become standard among all insurers. The information available on the internet is more easily accessible to modern consumers, and the usual first step in searching for insurance services is to access the insurer's website or use the insurer's mobile application. In particular, digital tools may offer clearer, more accessible information to policyholders about the costs and performance of the products, terms and conditions, benefits, and options, among other details [5].

Consumers also demand the ability to respond to questions asked online quickly. That's what so-called chatbots, or conversational AI, are for. Conversational AI is the set of technologies behind automated messaging and speech-enabled applications that offer human-like interactions between computers and humans [1]. Chatbots, voicebots, or virtual assistants can answer less complex and frequently asked questions, while humans are irreplaceable for all the more complex ones. This is supported by a survey (Eurobarometer) conducted by EIOPA in 2024, according to which only 30% of consumers trust that chatbots offer accurate and complete support in their purchase [6]. On the other side, according to Bandari, AI-powered chatbots are leading digital transformation, offering significant benefits for the insurance industry [7].

More traditional users of insurance services still prefer and trust direct contact with the insurer and consider such an approach to be the standard of financial literacy, while probably lacking adequate digital literacy at the same time. However, new generations prefer indirect contact and consider everything they can do online to be a more accessible service, more adapted to the modern lifestyle. This means that insurers need to provide both methods of communication, the traditional direct contact with the insurer and the one enabled by conversational AI. Conversational AI tools will continue to develop in this parallel use and offer an ever-widening range of user support, thus becoming increasingly acceptable to a broader range of users. However, insurance services, especially in the voluntary insurance segment, require an individual approach, so the expertise of insurer employees is an indispensable factor in quality service. In addition, complex requests can only be resolved by highly qualified insurance experts, and due to the complexity and interdisciplinary nature of the subject matter, AI tools can hardly reach the level of comprehensive expertise that an experienced and educated insurance expert has. However, conversational AI makes the insurance service more accessible and resource-efficient. It raises the quality of service for users who prefer this type of communication, and there are more and more of them. AI application in insurance results in an enhanced consumer experience: smooth and efficient purchasing process; more accessible customer service; and chatbots available around the clock [3].

Claims Management. Claims management is one of the most demanding segments of the overall insurance industry. It requires a unique, interdisciplinary approach, experience, and expertise of the people who process claims. Processing claims involves processing a large amount of data and documents. AI tools can be used to automatically read, interpret, and process relevant documents and photographs, such as to extract the information needed from medical records or identity cards, to recognise vehicle types or licence plate numbers, or to evaluate whether the damage to a vehicle is a total loss [1]. Modern claims processing systems employ sophisticated machine learning algorithms that analyze historical claims data to identify patterns and anomalies [8]. AI can also classify claims and submissions by regulatory categories or insurer internal policies. This can save the insurance undertaking's time, money, and human resources. The well-known insure-tech lemonade became famous for its innovative use of generative AI in various insurance industry segments, especially in claims management. The virtual assistant AI Jim broke the record by solving one claim in 3 s. At the same time, Lemoned is aware of regulatory requirements and that AI Jim cannot solve more complex claims as a virtual alter ego of a human claims officer.

Human judgment, expertise, and experience are still indispensable for assessing the outcomes of AI decisions and ensuring regulatory compliance. But, according to the EIOPA Eurobarometer 2024, 52% of insurance consumers find the claim process easier and faster due to online automated processes. This percentage was even higher in 2023. (62% of consumers found the claims process easier due to digitalisation). Whilst it is positive that over half of EU consumers find that digital tools improve their experience, digitalisation may not always result in good consumer outcomes, especially for the less digitally literate [5]. Digital tools have simplified the claims process and sped up their processing, but consumers are not the most satisfied with the management and claims outcomes. This means that AI tools require improvement or that humans are irreplaceable at certain stages of the claims management process, especially regarding more complex claims. AI-driven decisions and claims management results should be understandable to policyholders, and expert oversight by insurer employees should be included.

Fraud Detection and Prevention. Insurance fraud is, unfortunately, common but difficult to detect, especially nowadays. As fraudulent schemes become increasingly sophisticated, traditional fraud detection methods, which rely heavily on rule-based systems and manual reviews, have struggled to keep pace [9, 10]. In the absence of human capabilities to quickly detect fraudulent actions, accident setup, intentional causing of insured events, organized fraudulent activities, etc., AI solutions come into play. AI-driven fraud detection solutions can analyse massive amounts of data from multiple sources, enabling insurers to spot and flag unusual patterns that a human might miss, thereby detecting possibly fraudulent claims [1].

AI is very efficient at finding correlations, particularly in large data sets that are too complex for humans to analyse [3]. This makes AI tools efficient in detecting suspicious patterns and errors, leading to the detection of attempted fraud or potentially fraudulent activities. AI algorithms can detect claims, data, and documentation anomalies and alert to possible fraud activity. Meanwhile, new technologies have caused the appearance of new types of financial scams that are outside of the traditional fraud detection approaches and methods, as well as increased perspectives of hacker attacks because of the vulnerabilities of network systems and web applications [11]. Therefore, developers of AI tools for the insurance industry must take into account all these new risks potentially involved in the insurance fraud scenario.

Operational Efficiency. Digital transformation in the insurance sector has delivered measurable improvements in operational efficiency and cost reduction [12]. AI sets a lot of opportunities for the insurers' efficiency. All benefits of AI application, mentioned above, lead to savings, added value, and operational, planning, and financial efficiency of the insurer. Using AI, insurers can speed up their operational processes, leading to cost savings and improved customer experience [13]. AI creates an innovative atmosphere and encourages insurers to develop new products and recognize the need for new types of insurance to meet the demands of the modern lifestyle and new risks. This may also cause new investments by insurers, which should be profitable in the long term, i.e., lead to savings and new profits.

AI tools can also be helpful in the insurer's internal governance models. The application of AI in insurance undertakings can speed up processes, facilitate procedures, optimize operations, save time, and simplify the daily performance of complex tasks. Insurers who understand the potential benefits of using AI in their business today will have a secure competitive advantage in the market in the future. This is a very responsible and, at the same time, risky request for the management of insurance undertakings. Indeed, with all the risks it entails, AI applications in the insurance industry can reduce costs, enhance consumer experience, detect and prevent fraud, and thus improve operational efficiency.

3.2 Legal Challenges

Technological breakthroughs throughout human history have brought both opportunities and harms [14]. The result is the same when looking at the impact of AI implementation in business. Paradoxically, while AI-driven applications may improve the quality of goods and services and increase (more informed) choice, such applications have great potential to do precisely the opposite [15]. So far, the most significant legal challenge has been the lack of legal regulation of AI and its implications in existing normative frameworks. This has resulted in an attempt to have a relatively rapid regulatory process to keep pace with technological development dynamics. The result is a broad framework of norms resulting in legal understatement. Quantity has prevailed over the quality of the legal norm.

The need to develop an adequate legal regulation of relations developing in the digital sphere, the definition of the boundaries and capabilities of AI involved in solving diverse tasks, is today a priority direction for the development of law, its theoretical foundations, and practical aspects in technologically developed countries of the world [16]. To address these challenges, legal frameworks must shift from broad, rigid regulatory approaches to more adaptable, principle-based regulations that evolve alongside technological advancements. Simultaneously, to develop an adequate legal framework for the AI application in business, including insurance industry, one should be aware of legal and related challenges such as ethical implications, suitability of an industry and its particular segment for the AI application, specific human resources, due diligence, customers' human rights, data protection, etc.

Regulatory Compliance. The insurance industry has a strict and comprehensive regulatory framework as part of the financial market. The legislative regulation of AI and its applications in business requires general regulation focused on regulating the specificities of AI and its implementation and impact on society. A tiered regulatory model, where AI applications are categorized based on risk assessment, could help ensure compliance while fostering innovation. Such a model would allow for flexible oversight, where low-risk AI applications in insurance, such as automated customer service, would require minimal intervention. In contrast, high-risk applications, like AI-Driven risk assessment affecting policyholder rights, would be subject to stricter scrutiny. Collaborative governance involving industry stakeholders, regulators, and technology experts is essential to creating practical, enforceable AI regulations that balance consumer protection, ethical considerations, and business efficiency.

It is necessary to ensure the practical application of sector legislation, considering proportionality and the specificities of the insurance sector [17]. However, this has become a complex task due to the increasingly widespread application of AI, the specifics of the insurance business, and the complexity of AI systems. A key challenge in AI regulation for the insurance industry is maintaining a dynamic approach accommodating innovation and consumer protection. Regulatory bodies should consider implementing a vertical framework that distinguishes between AI use cases based on their impact on policyholders and the market. The responsibility for regulatory compliance lies not only with the regulator itself but also with the insurance undertakings themselves. It should be borne in mind that not all segments of the insurance business are suitable for applying AI systems and tools. Human judgment, expertise, and experience are still indispensable for assessing the outcomes of AI decisions and ensuring regulatory compliance [3].

Human Resources and Due Diligence. Although the prevailing view is that AI saves resources, including humans, the application of AI may require additional investments in all business resources. Regardless of the unjustified fear that AI tools can replace humans, investing in human resources is essential to ensure the proper and ethical application of modern technological solutions in business. EIOPA survey, on the other hand, shows that the human role is irreplaceable in pre-contractual information and informed purchase choice. Further, the EIOPA Eurobarometer 2024 data shows that consumers value human interaction, with 70% of customers reporting they purchased insurance in person or over the phone [5].

In the insurance sector, the additional engagement of IT experts and the education of all employees are included in addition to investment in software. However, the most important things are management education and qualifications. They must consider due diligence and choose the best models for their internal governance of sectoral and AI regulations. The management is responsible for the legality of the business. Therefore, it is necessary to understand and have sufficient knowledge about all the risks involved in applying AI in business. To know the risks, one must know enough about the very cause or source of the risk – AI itself. According to company law in the most developed jurisdictions, company directors must also comply with (inter alia) the duty of care when deploying AI systems. Such duty implies the duty of due diligence and the duty to act on an informed basis [18]. Therefore, due diligence and the application of AI imply professional and well-informed management, additional investments, and long-term savings and profits.

Liability. An open question in AI's general application is the liability for errors and damages that AI systems may cause. This question can also be raised in the sectoral use of AI, such as insurance. Who is, therefore, responsible for the damage that an AI system causes to the user? is this responsibility borne by its developer or deployer, or, in this case, by the insurance undertaking as a kind of user of the AI system, or should we go to the extreme and place the burden of responsibility on the AI itself, implying its legal subjectivity? This is still a controversial and open question in the general application of AI. For the insurance industry, it is clear that the final user, the policyholder, can place the burden of responsibility for using the AI system on the insurance undertaking or its management. It is up to the insurance undertaking to further seek and determine responsibility for the AI itself. This can also cause an incentive for insurers to develop new products, i.e., liability insurance for AI use.

Data Protection and Privacy. The application of digital tools and AI is highly desirable in facilitating the processing of large amounts of data in insurance operations. Concurrently, this makes the insurance business very risky regarding privacy and protecting confidential data. An interesting case study is the recent data leak in the insurance market in the Republic of Croatia. In 2024, the public was informed about the unauthorized use of approximately 1.2 million personal data of individuals (names, dates of birth, addresses, etc.) and 2.4 million vehicle registrations. As stated in a public statement by the National Security Intelligence Agency (SOA), "it was an unauthorized creation and removal of copies of the database by persons who had access to the information system" [19], and there were no elements of a cyber-attack. so, it is a matter of human error and misuse of the information system. Indeed, in this particular case, it is not a matter of the shortcomings of digital tools, but of their misuse by people. However, data leaks are either the disclosure of customer data by third parties or data leakage through computer systems and various technical means [11]. The risk does not have to stem directly from the AI system but can be linked to its shortcomings. still, the EIOPA Eurobarometer showed that 58% of consumers trust that insurers will collect and use their personal data ethically when buying insurance online.

To prevent unauthorized use of personal data and protect the privacy of insurance service customers, an adequate risk assessment of information systems should be implemented alongside a higher level of control and supervision that includes control of the technological systems themselves and human-related factors. However, regardless of the prevention and implementation of all mechanisms above, a certain level of risk remains. Ultimately, we can only rely on integrity in business practices. Only insurers that base the use of AI in their business on a combination of preventive and protective mechanisms and ethical business practices will build a competitive image of trust and quality service regarding data protection and privacy. Of course, to provide transparency and trust in AI applications, insurance undertakings should inform their customers when, in delivering services, interaction with AI is implied.

Bias and Discrimination. As part of the privacy and data protection challenges, one must consider bias and discrimination concerns related to AI applications in insurance. The underlying data and methodologies used in AI systems, not the technology itself, cause these issues [3]. The possibility of data bias is widespread, and in insurance, it can lead to improper algorithmic processing and thus cause unfair assessment and discrimination. Data bias arises from historical factors and from how datasets are collected, annotated, and prepared for model training [20]. Discrimination and biased decision-making can occur in processes performed by both AI and humans [3]. Yet, we tolerate human imperfections more easily and expect perfection from machine solutions, especially advanced technological solutions like AI. To prevent these risks, continuous improvement and upgrading of AI systems should be undertaken, as well as indispensable human control, assessment, and oversight.

4 Regulation of AI Applications in the European Union

The European Union has been very active in its legislative actions regulating AI and its application. In October 2020, the European Parliament adopted several resolutions related to AI, including on ethics, liability, and copyright. In its Resolution on a framework of ethical aspects of AI, robotics, and related technologies, the European Parliament specifically recommended that the Commission propose legislative measures to harness the potential and benefits of AI and ensure the protection of ethical principles. The Resolution stated that EU legislators should refrain from over-regulation by only closing existing legal loopholes and increasing legal certainty for businesses and citizens, including mandatory measures to prevent practices that undermine fundamental rights [21]. This was followed in 2021 by adopting a proposal for a Regulation of the European Parliament and of the Council on establishing harmonized rules on AI (AI Act) and amending certain legislative acts of the EU. The AI Act was adopted in 2024 (Regulation (EU) 2024/1689), with the start of application from August 2, 2026. [22]. Some segments of the AI Act will be applicable earlier. For example, the ban on AI systems with unacceptable risk has been in effect since February this year. In the coming months, codes of practice and general-purpose AI rules will successively begin to be applicable.

Although at first it seems like the AI Act is a legislative act that should regulate AI as a whole, this is not the case. Namely, it is mainly about ethical principles translated into legal principles and regulations for the moral development, application, and use of AI, robotics, and related technologies. It also regulates some obligations and procedures for the specific certification of AI. Therefore, the aim and purpose of the AI Act is to establish standards for protecting consumers as users of AI. The AI Act sets out a clear set of risk-based rules for AI developers and deployers regarding specific uses of AI [23]. The AI Act defines four levels of AI system risks: minimal, limited, high, and unacceptable, causing specific levels of possible harm to safety, health, livelihoods, and/or fundamental rights.

The AI Act applies to all sectors of the economy, including insurance. In the context of the insurance industry, according to Article 2(1) of the AI Act, it can be interpreted that the Regulation applies in particular to those insurance undertakings that implement AI systems and are established or located within the EU, or in a third country where the result produced by the AI system is used in the EU; furthermore, to those who place on the market or put into use an AI system together with their product and under their name or trademark. Regarding consumers, the AI Act applies to all affected persons in the EU. The use of AI systems by insurance undertakings, classified as having minimal or limited risk under the AI Act, is subject to further regulation of the insurance sector.

In addition to the above, EIOPA's regulatory activities, as the EU insurance supervision authority, are significant in regulating AI applications for the insurance industry. On 12 February 2025, EIOPA launched a consultation on its Opinion on AI governance and risk management, which provides supervisors and insurance undertakings guidance on how to interpret and implement insurance sector provisions in light of the use of AI systems in insurance. The Opinion is in line with the underlying principles and requirements of the AI Act [24]. It is also consistent with Directive (EU) 2016/97 (IDD), Directive 2009/138/EC (Solvency II), and Regulation (EU) 2022/2554 (DORA).

The AI Act aims to implement horizontal unification and applicability to all segments of the economy. This can create specific challenges for the financial sector, including insurance, which is strictly and comprehensively regulated. It is now incumbent on all insurers to understand their place in the post-AI Act regulatory world, contribute responsibly and transparently to the debate on AI in insurance, and, most importantly, understand how AI will impact their business now and into the future as it grows in visibility and significance [25].

5 Digitalization and AI Application in the Insurance Market of Bosnia and Herzegovina

The legal regulation of the insurance market in Bosnia and Herzegovina (BH) is under the jurisdiction of two entities, the Federation of Bosnia and Herzegovina (FBH) and Republika Srpska (RS). Due to this fact, there is a certain level of legal inconsistency, non-harmonization, and two parallel insurance markets exist within one country. This makes the digitalization process very challenging. To identify the level of digital tools applied online in the insurance industry, we have analyzed the web platforms of active insurance undertakings in BH without going into the possible application of AI tools in internal business mechanisms. There are 10 registered insurance undertakings in FBH and 14 in RS. The research was related to the review of officially available tools in online insurance distribution channels and online claims on a sample of 24 undertakings' websites. The results related to online insurance offers are shown in the following table (Table 1 and Fig. 1):

Table 1. Overview of insurance undertakings that offer online insurance in BH

Online insurance	Insurance undertakings	
Type of insurance	FBH (10)	Rs (14)
travel insurance	8	6
assistance insurance	3	1
accident insurance	1	0
health insurance	4	0
home insurance	4	2
Other types of insurance	1	0

The results show that travel insurance is the most widespread online insurance. However, not all insurance undertakings offer online travel insurance, with only 80% in FBH and 43% in RS. According to the analysis, one undertaking in the FBH does not offer any online insurance, nor do six of them in the RS.

Online claims reporting is possible via the websites of seven insurance undertakings in the FBH, and only one is seated in the RS. Some of these undertakings offer only to download and submit a claim form online, rather than an actual platform for reporting and processing claims through an AI system. The fact that national regulators require communication by standard mail in claims proceedings makes these results expected. It is also important to note that only one insurance undertaking in the RS offers a web agent as a platform for AI communication, and only one in the FBH provides a fully developed user platform for comprehensive, systematic communication with consumers.

These elementary statistical analyses based on the authors' consumer review of 24 websites show that AI applications are not widespread in the insurance market in BH. The lack of application of digital tools is particularly noticeable in the RS (see Fig. 1). There are multiple reasons for this level of digital tools and AI application in the BH insurance market. For instance, the lack of harmonization of the overall insurance legislation, the low level of insurance culture and digital literacy, related resistance to digitalization, the lack of an adequate regulatory framework for the application of AI, the traditional approach to the insurance distribution channels, etc.

The results were expected given that the insurance market in BH is still based on the dominance of traditional methods of contracting insurance, where face-to-face negotiations prevail. On the path to EU membership, BH must harmonize its legislation with the EU legislation, which will undoubtedly bring new trends and adaptation to modern insurance market requirements. This certainly includes the application of AI with all its

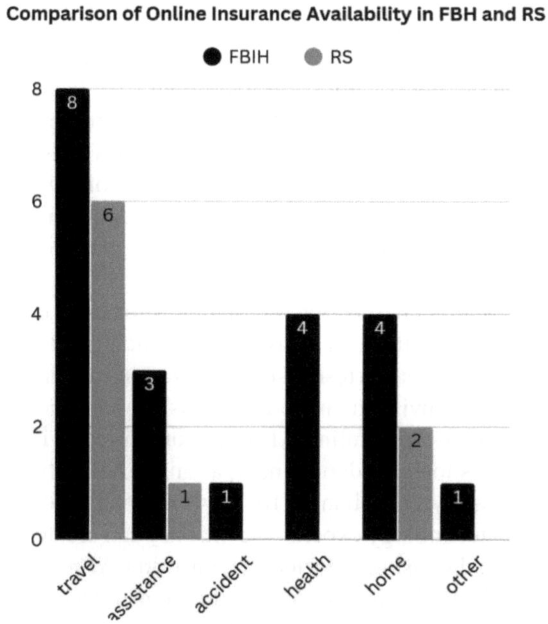

Fig. 1. Ratio of online insurance offers in Bosnia and Herzegovina: FBH and RS.

advantages and challenges. One such trend is, for example, the digital insurance policy, which was recently introduced in Croatia, an EU member state neighboring BH. A prerequisite for such innovations in the insurance market in BH is an appropriate legal framework, stability of the insurance market, and joint action of all stakeholders in this industry.

Research limitations. Since the leading distribution channel for online insurance services in BH is the websites of insurance undertakings, the research included a simple analysis of online tools available on the websites of all registered insurance companies. The sample size was 23 websites, as one registered insurance undertaking doesn't have a functional website. The analysis was conducted during February 2025, and verifying the accuracy of the data is challenging given the possibility of changes in the short term. It may not fully capture the long-term impact. The study was conducted with the general assumption of digital underdevelopment of the BH insurance market, so further study should include a comparative review with a more developed digital insurance market. These limitations require cautious interpretations and encourage further research.

6 Conclusion

To properly assess the results of the AI application in insurance, it is necessary to consider multiple factors. Achieving optimal balance between business benefits and transparent, ethical, legal regulation of AI in the insurance industry is a great challenge. This can only be achieved through clear, principle-based, but not too soft legislation. The real challenge is to find an appropriate balance between comprehensive legislation on AI and the stimulation of innovative development. This will undoubtedly be a matter of future growth and will change the law's nature and traditional role. In particular, care should be taken to ensure that the pursuit of quality legislation does not result in overregulation. This should mean that high-risk AI systems undergo rigorous validation, ethical review, and continuous monitoring while preventing overregulation of low-risk AI applications. Additionally, fostering collaboration between insurers, regulators, and AI developers will be crucial to refining regulations and ensuring they remain relevant in an evolving technological landscape.

A forward-thinking approach to AI regulation in insurance should focus on developing adaptable legal frameworks that can evolve with technological advancements. Regulatory sandboxes, where insurers can test AI-driven solutions under regulatory oversight, could provide a controlled environment to assess risks and benefits before full-scale implementation. Additionally, integrating AI ethics committees within insurance undertakings can help ensure responsible deployment, aligning AI applications with industry best practices and regulatory compliance. By fostering continuous dialogue between regulators, insurers, and technology experts, the industry can create a governance model prioritizing innovation and consumer protection, ensuring AI remains a beneficial tool rather than a disruptive force. Therefore, AI's future in insurance depends, among other things, on the digital education of all involved participants, including lawyers. This would involve stepping out of their comfort legal zone.

In the long-term process of balancing the business benefits and legal challenges of AI applications, it should be kept in mind that AI cannot replace the role of humans in any profession. Still, it should only help in performing that profession better. AI should retain its role as a business tool, not a performer of core business operations. Human resources are the best control mechanisms for the application of AI in business, so it should be the same in the insurance sector.

By all the above, this paper concludes with the quote of the famous OpenAI, ChatGPT: "*As AI continues to gain traction in insurance, there will likely be increasing legal scrutiny, and regulatory bodies may need to develop new frameworks specifically designed to address the unique challenge posed by AI technologies in the sector.*" In other words, the story never ends…

Disclosure of Interests. The authors have no competing interests to declare relevant to this article's content.

References

1. Insurance Europe AISBL: AI in the insurance sector (2021). https://www.insuranceeurope.eu
2. Bird & Bird: AI governance: Essential insights for organizations: Part I – Understanding meaning, challenges, trends, and best practices in AI governance. Lexology (2025). https://www.lexology.com/library/detail.aspx?g=7c454b4a-a3df-4ce6-9730-e368923e020d. Accessed 22 Feb 2025
3. Noordhoek, D.: Regulation of artificial intelligence in insurance: Balancing consumer protection and innovation. The Geneva Association (2023)

4. Barna, E., Barcău, E., Răvaru, R.: Predictive data analysis platform, for optimizing and automating the distribution of car insurance products, based on telematic data. In: Cavallucci, D., Brad, S., Livotov, P. (eds.) World Conference of AI-Powered Innovation and Inventive Design. TFC 2024. IFIP Advances in Information and Communication Technology, vol. 736. Springer, Cham (2025). https://doi.org/10.1007/978-3-031-75923-9_12
5. European Insurance and Occupational Pensions Authority (EIOPA): Consumers trend report 2024 (Report No. 0107262) (2025). https://www.eiopa.europa.eu/document/download/4f3b2964-455d-497e-b69f-b5c5939d7aee_en. Accessed 15 Apr 2025
6. EIOPA: Eurobarometer 2024: Consumer trends in insurance and pension services. https://www.eiopa.europa.eu/tools-and-data/eurobarometer-2024-consumer-trends-insurance-and-pension-services_en. Accessed 20 Jan 2025
7. Bandari, S.S.G.: Exploring Java for AI-powered chatbots in the insurance industry. Int. J. Sci. Res. Comput. Sci. Eng. Inform. Technol. (2025)
8. Sudabathula, B.: Revolutionizing insurance: the impact of AI on claims processing. Int. J. Sci. Res. Comput. Sci. Eng. Inform. Technol. (2025)
9. Joginipalli, S.K., Gummadi, V.: Advancing insurance fraud detection: leveraging machine learning and AI techniques. Int. J. Innov. Res. Sci. Eng. Technol. (2024)
10. Alekseenko, A.P.: Privacy, data protection, and public interest considerations for fintech. In: Chen, H.Y., Jenweeranon, P., Alam, N. (eds.) Global Perspectives in FinTech - Law, Finance and Technology, Palgrave Macmillan (2022)
11. Vamkeswaram, S.: AI-powered chatbots: revolutionizing Auro insurance policy selection and management. Int. J. Sci. Res. Comput. Sci. Eng. Inform. Technol. (2025)
12. Vamkeswaram, S.: AI-powered chatbots: revolutionizing auto insurance policy selection and management. Int. J. Sci. Res. Comput. Sci. Eng. Inform. Technol. (2025). Accessed 20 Feb 2025
13. Watson, R., Poorthuis, E.: AI Act: A new legal standard for artificial intelligence – Three key insights. Lexology (2025). https://www.lexology.com/library/detail.aspx?g=e18a57c3-ca46-4239-b6a5-fc822bb918ae
14. Bennis, S.: AI and the consumer. In: De Bruyne, J., Vanleenhove, C. (eds.) Artificial intelligence and the Law, Intersentia (2021)
15. Molchakov, N., Ryzhkova, E., Ryzhkova, E.: Problems of legal regulation of digitalization (the Case of AI). In: Baykov, A., Zinovieva, E. (eds.) Digital International Relations, Palgrave Macmillan (2023)
16. EIOPA in brief: Regulatory framework applicable to AI systems in the insurance sector (2024). https://www.eiopa.europa.eu/document/download/b53a3b92-08cc-4079-a4f7-606cf309a34a_en?filename=Factsheet-on-the-regulatory-framework-applicable-to-AI-systems-in-the-insurance-sector-july-2024.pdf. Accessed 17 Jan 2025
17. Pacielo, F.: Proposals for a new legal framework on AI: possible discrepancies between liability, compliance and duties of company directors. In: Bertolaso, M., Capone, L., Rodríguez-Lluesma, C. (eds.), Digital Humanism: A Human-Centric Approach to Digital Technologies, Palgrave Macmillan (2022)
18. Index.hr: SOA objasnila kako je došlo do ogromnog curenja podataka o vlasnicima auta, 15 December 2024. https://www.index.hr/vijesti/clanak/soa-objasnila-kako-je-doslo-do-ogromnog-curenja-podataka-o-vlasnicima-auta/2568528.aspx. Accessed 15 Dec 2024
19. AI ACTION SUMMIT: International AI Safety Report (2025). https://www.gov.uk/government/publications/international-ai-safety-report-2025/international-ai-safety-report-2025. Accessed 15 Apr 2025
20. European Parliament resolution of 20 October 2020 with recommendations to the Commission on a framework of ethical aspects of artificial intelligence, robotics and related technologies (2020/2012(INL))

21. Regulation (EU) 2024/1689 of the European Parliament and of the Council of 13 June 2024 laying down harmonised rules on artificial intelligence and amending Regulations (EC) No 300/2008, (EU) No 167/2013, (EU) No 168/2013, (EU) 2018/858, (EU) 2018/1139 and (EU) 2019/2144 and Directives 2014/90/EU, (EU) 2016/797 and (EU) 2020/1828 (Artificial Intelligence Act), OJ L 2024/1689
22. European Commission: AI Act. https://digital-strategy.ec.europa.eu/en/policies/regulatory-framework-ai. Accessed 20 Feb 2025
23. EIOPA: EIOPA is seeking feedback on its Opinion on Artificial Intelligence governance and risk management. https://www.eiopa.europa.eu/eiopa-seeking-feedback-its-opinion-artificial-intelligence-governance-and-risk-management-2025-02-12_en. Accessed 20 Feb 2025
24. Munich RE: New EU Act Regulates AI in Insurance. https://www.munichre.com/automation-solutions/en/resources/blog/EU-AI-Act.html. Accessed 24 Feb 2025

Application of a No-Code AI Model for Legal Research in International Insurance Claims

Ana Martinović[1] and Boris Martinović[2](✉)

[1] Postgraduate Specialist Study Programme Insurance Law, Faculty of Law, University of Mostar, Mostar, Bosnia and Herzegovina
ana.martinovic@euroherc.hr

[2] Postgraduate Doctoral Programme, University of Mostar, Mostar, Bosnia and Herzegovina
boris.martinovic@phd.sum.ba

Abstract. The research demonstrates an application of a no-code AI model in the field of international MTPL insurance claims. The model uses natural language processing (NLP) to analyze a custom-made case law database, create summaries, and provide translations into the Croatian language when needed. The AI model was developed using a Generative pre-trained transformer (GPT) and the effectiveness of the model was evaluated through two studies in which the participants were given a hypothetical cross-border insurance claim. The pilot study revealed, and the follow-up study confirmed, that the GPT significantly improves research efficiency and helps overcome language barriers in international MTPL claims handling.

Keywords: Artificial Intelligence · Custom GPT · No-Code AI Model · AI in Law · Legal Research

1 Introduction

Artificial intelligence (AI) is becoming a fundamental technology across industries as more and more businesses increasingly integrate it into their workflows and processes. AI offers advantages such as improved productivity, faster decision-making, the development of new business models, and process optimization [5], among others. With the acceleration of AI adoption comes the emergence of new tools and applications that reshape professional workflows, especially in data-intensive fields. Consumer-friendly AI tools, such as ChatGPT [2], demonstrate the potential of AI in text analysis and retrieval, enabling users to interact with vast legal databases through conversational queries. These developments are particularly relevant for international insurance claims, where cross-border disputes require the interpretation of multijurisdictional case law and regulatory frameworks.

D. Vasić and E. Brajković (Eds.): MoStart 2025, CCIS 2609, pp. 241–253, 2026.
https://doi.org/10.1007/978-3-032-02801-3_16

Previous research on the topic of using Artificial Intelligence in insurance focuses on topics such as fraud detection in auto insurance industry [1] and health insurance claims automation [13], among others. However, there are not enough data on the specific topic of legal research in international insurance claims, considering that it is a specific and relatively narrow topic. Beyond that, previous research does not include generally available tools and consumer-friendly tools, making implementation easier and less expensive compared to other, more specialized solutions.

This paper presents a no-code AI model for legal research in international motor third-party liability (MTPL) claims, which is designed to assist claims adjusters in retrieving relevant case law. The model also generates summaries and provides automated translations into Croatian if asked. Two studies were conducted in order to evaluate AI-assisted research versus traditional manual legal research, as well as to measure the efficiency, accuracy, and usability of the no-code AI model in question. The findings presented in the paper contribute to the ongoing discussion on AI-assisted decision making in insurance law and demonstrate both the benefits and limitations of AI-driven legal research.

2 Challenges in Legal Research for International MTPL Claims

Legal research plays a crucial role in international motor third-party liability (MTPL) claims where road traffic accidents involve vehicles and individuals from different countries. Determining liability and the applicable legal framework in such cases is complex. While many claims are settled out of court, a significant number escalate to litigation where judicial precedents serve as critical references for claims adjusters (and other legal professionals) in assessing liability, estimating compensation, and addressing jurisdictional issues.

Traditional legal research methods in this field are very time-consuming, as claims professionals must first locate the appropriate online database, navigate its search functions using relevant keywords, and browse numerous court judgments to identify potentially relevant cases. Once a case is selected, they must read through the full text, interpret the legal reasoning, and, in many instances, translate the decision to determine if the document is even applicable to the claim in question. These challenges introduce inefficiencies in claims handling and potential delays in claim resolutions.

Advancements in AI tools present an opportunity to address these inefficiencies. AI models capable of processing large legal databases, extracting relevant precedents, and generating structured summaries could significantly reduce the time required for legal research in international insurance claims. Building upon these advancements, we propose a custom GPT model specifically designed to streamline international MTPL legal research. The proposed custom GPT model automates case law retrieval, legal summarization, and translation, which allows claims adjusters to efficiently analyze case law. By integrating AI-driven automation, this approach has the potential to improve claims processing, reduce costs, and improve consistency in claim resolution. Through two studies, we assess the feasibility and impact of AI-driven legal research in optimizing the handling of international MTPL claims.

3 Development of the No-Code AI Model (Creating a Custom GPT)

3.1 System Overview

The main tool of choice used for this research is ChatGPT. Its system is based on GPT (Generative pre-trained transformer), a combination of transformers [14] and unsupervised pre-training [4]. GPT employs a two-step training approach: first, the transformer model is trained on a large amount of data without supervision using language modeling as a training signal, and then the model is fine-tuned using smaller supervised datasets to help solve specific tasks [9].

ChatGPT is a popular tool used by more than 400 million people [12], which will allow familiarity and ease of use. Another reason why ChatGPT is a tool of choice is the Custom GPTs feature. Custom GPTs are specialized and customizable types of ChatGPT that serve a specialized purpose, currently powered by GPT-4o. [10]. In addition, custom GPTs can interact with external systems, such as calling APIs. In this study, the Custom GPT is specifically utilized to analyze, extract, and store information from court decisions provided in PDF format that will pose as a searchable legal database.

3.2 System Architecture and Elements

The main elements of a custom GPT are the following: instructions, conversation starters, knowledge base, and selected capabilities. The detailed instructions provided to GPT and the legal database that was uploaded will be discussed separately.

Selected capabilities are additional actions that a GPT can perform in order to provide a more appropriate response. They include Web search, Canvas, Dall-E Image generation and code interpreter and Data analysis. For this GPT, all of them were enabled, as they can provide useful functionalities to response.

Conversation starters are elements of GPTs which are used to quickly start conversations and should involve the phrases or questions that most users could use. In addition, they are useful as a guide for users as to what specific capabilities this custom GPT includes. Since this GPT is related to the research and analysis of court decisions, the conversation starters involved are as follows.

1. Summarize the key points of a court decision.
2. Find cases related to liability in traffic accidents.
3. Retrieve court decisions discussing fraud cases.
4. Translate a case summary into Croatian.

GPT Instructions

Instructions are the elements that are essential for each GPT to fully function in a proper manner. They are guidelines for the GPT model on how to perform tasks, and they are written in natural language. However, the formulation of instructions is extremely important for the successful execution of the tasks. There are various important writing styles that need to be incorporate into the instructions, such as simplifying complex tasks into smaller, simpler chunks, using detailed steps in order to achieve more clarity, and avoiding negative expressions in order to reduce potential chances of confusion [3].

The instructions provided to the custom GPT were following:

This GPT is designed to analyze, store, and retrieve court decisions from uploaded PDF files, creating a structured and searchable legal database. The files uploaded by the user constitute the database, and this GPT will extract and analyze each court decision to be prepared for answering legal queries. It follows a multi-step process:
1. **Building the Legal Database:**

- Reads, extracts, and stores information from uploaded court decisions (PDFs).
- Structures and indexes the database by extracting key details such as:
- Case Title
- Court Name & Jurisdiction
- Date of Decision
- Factual Background (Circumstances of the case)
- Judgment & Legal Reasoning
- - Confirms when the database is successfully built and ready for use.

2. **Generating Case Summaries:**

- Provides concise and structured summaries of each stored case.
- Extracts key details from documents and generates a summary.
- Can translate summaries into Croatian upon request while maintaining legal accuracy.

3. **Implementing Search Functionality:** - Allows users to search the database using keywords, case numbers, legal topics, or specific laws cited. - Retrieves and summarizes the most relevant cases in a structured format:

- Case Title
- Court Name & Jurisdiction

- Date of Decision
- Factual Background
- Judgment & Reasoning
- Enables users to refine searches by jurisdiction, case type, or year.

4. **Handling New PDFs Uploaded by Users:**

- Reads new documents upon upload
- Provides case summaries and allows retrieval of case details upon user request.
- Provides an option to translate the summary into Croatian.
- All knowledge is derived from uploaded files; the GPT does not have external legal knowledge beyond what has been uploaded.

This GPT ensures efficient legal research by maintaining a structured legal database, offering concise case summaries, and enabling powerful search capabilities.

Legal Database

Knowledge base is an important part of the custom GPT since it houses the additional data that GPT can query based on user input. It accepts up to 20 files, where each file can be up to 512 MB in size. This was a potential limitation as 20 court judgments would not be sufficient to build the database. For this reason, it was important to collect and combine documents that share the same context in a single file to circumvent the file limit. At the moment, only text data are processed, which is sufficient in the vast majority of cases. Upon uploading the file, the GPT breaks the text into chunks, creates embeddings (a mathematical way to represent text) and stores them for later use [8].

There are two methods in which the custom GPT can query the knowledge base: Semantic search and document review. The semantic search returns relevant text chunks, in the case where a specific part of the source text is required. An example of this is a prompt with a direct question, where an answer is expected based on the data of the document. Document review is a more complex operation, which returns entire short documents, and/or relevant excerpts of larger documents are returned and included along with the prompt as additional context. It is used when a translation or summarization is needed, where a user expects more comprehensive data. In this custom GPT, both styles of interaction could be used, depending on the user needs [8].

The legal database for this custom GPT model consists of court judgments grouped into four key categories relevant to international motor third-party liability insurance claims: applicable law, fraud, liability, and material damage. Each category contains selected German court decisions, publicly available [6], that address frequent legal issues encountered in cross-border traffic accidents, such as determining which country's laws apply, assessing liability, identifying indicators of fraudulent claims, resolving disputes over compensable material damages, claimant obligations like damage mitigation, etc. Each judgment in the database includes the case title, court name and jurisdiction, decision date, factual background, text of the decision, and applied statutory provisions. By consolidating these judgments into structured text documents, the database circumvents limitations regarding the number and size of files allowed by the GPT platform.

4 Two Studies: AI-Assisted Vs. Manual Legal Research

To evaluate the effectiveness of the custom GPT model, we conducted two studies that measured efficiency, accuracy, and usability of AI-assisted legal research. The first, a pilot case study, involved two claims adjusters - one with and one without German proficiency - to assess how language barriers impact legal research and whether AI can bridge this gap. Based on these findings, a follow-up study was conducted with additional non-German-speaking adjusters to test whether the initial results could be replicated across a broader sample. The objective was to determine whether the custom GPT model improves legal research efficiency, particularly for adjusters handling cross-border claims where language barriers may pose challenges.

4.1 Hypothetical Claim Used in the Study

A hypothetical claim was designed to simulate a real-world cross-border insurance claim. The case involved a traffic accident in Croatia between a German-registered vehicle and a Croatian-insured vehicle, where the German driver sought full reimbursement for rental car expenses under the Visitors' Protection System. The Croatian insurer, citing domestic practice, disputed the claim and offered partial compensation. The claimant, arguing for full reimbursement under German legal standards, threatened litigation.

The research task required participants to locate relevant German court decisions supporting the Croatian insurer's position on two key legal points:

- Duty to Mitigate Losses - Whether the claimant must limit rental car expenses to minimize damages
- Recognition of Croatian Law - Whether German courts acknowledge the application of Croatian legal principles in cross-border insurance claims when the accident occurs in Croatia.

4.2 Pilot Study - Design, Methodology, and Results

Study Design and Participants

The pilot study was conducted with the assistance of two Croatian claims adjusters from an international claims department, selected to represent different levels of language proficiency:

- Adjuster A - A legal expert with no knowledge of German.
- Adjuster B - A claims specialist fluent in German.

The hypothetical case scenario was given to participants who were instructed to locate relevant German court decisions supporting the Croatian insurer's position.

Research Methods

Each adjuster conducted research using two different approaches:

- Manual research - Searching for case law through Google, legal databases, official court websites, and others.
- AI-assisted research - Using the custom GPT model designed for legal research, which was trained on German court decisions.

Both adjusters recorded the time it took to find the first relevant case and provided feedback on the usability of each research method. After completion of their research, the participants were asked to complete a short response survey to provide qualitative feedback on their experience.

The survey assessed key aspects of the research process, including:

- Success Rate: Were you able to find court decisions supporting the insurer's position?
- Time Efficiency: How long did it take to find relevant cases using traditional vs. AI-assisted research?
- Accuracy: How many relevant cases did you find using each method?
- Relevance: How applicable were the retrieved cases to the hypothetical scenario?
- Ease of Use: How difficult was it to conduct research manually vs. using AI?
- Preference: Which method would you choose for future cases?

This survey provided qualitative insights into the usability, effectiveness, and perceived benefits and limitations of both research approaches.

Results

The pilot study revealed significant differences in research efficiency between manual and AI-assisted legal research. Adjuster B (fluent in German) successfully found a relevant court decision via Google in 15–20 min, but only after switching from browsing the Internet in Croatian to browsing in German. Using GPT, they retrieved a relevant case in 2 min. Adjuster A (no German proficiency) failed to find any relevant case manually and stated that language limitations prevented any effective search queries. However, GPT provided a relevant case within 2–3 min.

Manual research was more time-consuming, particularly for the non-German-speaking adjuster who in the end gave up on further traditional research. Both adjusters reported higher ease of use and efficiency with AI-assisted research, and both adjusters found two relevant court decisions using our custom GPT model. When asked which method they would prefer for future cases, German speaking adjuster opted for combined research methods, and non-German speaking adjuster for AI-assisted research.

4.3 Follow-Up Study - Design, Methodology, and Results

Following the initial pilot study, another study was conducted to assess whether the results could be replicated across a broader group of non-German-speaking claims adjusters. The primary goal was to determine whether our custom GPT model consistently improved legal case retrieval efficiency and overcame language barriers in international claims handling.

Study Design and Participants

The follow-up study involved four non-German-speaking claims adjusters, selected to test whether the GPT model could bridge language barriers and improve research efficiency. Participants were given access to the custom GPT model and the same research task as in the pilot study. They were instructed to find relevant German case law supporting the Croatian insurer's position using both manual and AI-assisted research methods. After completion of the task, the participants were given the same survey.

Research Methods

The research methods in the follow-up study mirrored those used in the pilot study. Participants searched for case law using the same two approaches:

- Manual research
- AI-assisted research

Each participant was asked to record the time taken to find the first relevant case, to note the number of cases retrieved, and provide qualitative feedback on the usability of both research methods. Upon completing their tasks, participants filled out the same survey used in the pilot study.

Results

The follow-up study confirmed and reinforced the findings of the pilot study. The study demonstrated that AI-assisted legal research significantly improves research efficiency and helps overcome language barriers in international claims handling. Two participants attempted to use Google Translate [7] to assist in manual research, but the process was not fruitful and proved to be more difficult than anticipated. Two other participants also failed to retrieve any relevant cases manually, but reported that they did not try to use Google Translate at all. The four participants retrieved a relevant case in less than 5 min using AI-assisted research alone.

As demonstrated by the results shown in Table 1, 100% of the participants have found relevant court decisions only using AI-assisted research, rendering the traditional research method ineffective.

Table 1. Did you find relevant court decisions that would confirm insurers' stance?

Response	Response %
Yes, using traditional research	0
Yes, using AI-assisted research	100
Yes, using both	0
I didn't find any information	0

In reply to second question "How much time did it take to find relevant court decisions using the traditional method?", the participants were unable to provide any time as they could not find relevant court decisions. Table 2 shows the replies to the third question, which in contrast shows that the time needed to find relevant court decisions using the AI tool was under 5 min for all participants.

Table 3 shows that 50% of the participants managed to find one relevant court decision, while the other half managed to find two. This question was interesting since the results have shown that user's prompt is an important factor in generating results, as it can enhance or debilitate the query executed by AI tool. It is important to note that the AI tool always yielded at least one relevant court decision regardless of the prompt.

Table 2. How much time did it take to find relevant court decisions using the AI tool?

Response	Response %
I could not find any	0
Under 5 min	100
5 to 15 min	0
Over 15 min	0

Table 3. How many relevant court decisions were found using AI tool?

Response	Response %
None	0
One	50
Two	50
Three or more	0

Overall the survey responses provided the following qualitative insights:

- Manual research was for non-German-speaking adjusters perceived as difficult, inefficient, and impractical.
- AI-assisted research was preferred for its speed and ease of use.
- All indicated they would choose AI-assisted research over manual methods for future cases involving foreign legal systems.

5 Discussion and Limitations

The findings of this study highlight the potential of AI-assisted legal research in international insurance claims handling. The ability of the custom GPT model to retrieve relevant foreign case law within minutes improves efficiency, particularly for claims adjusters that are met with language barriers. The results suggest that AI tools can serve as a powerful resource for professionals who may lack proficiency in a foreign jurisdiction's legal system but still require access to relevant case law.

5.1 Key Insights and Implications

The findings from both the pilot and follow-up studies show the great potential of AI-assisted legal research in cross-border insurance claims handling. Several key insights emerged from the research.

AI-Assisted Legal Research Improves Efficiency

The most evident advantage of AI-assisted research was the reduction in time required to retrieve the relevant case law. Although manual research required extensive effort, the GPT model consistently retrieved relevant cases within minutes. This suggests that AI tools can expedite legal research processes and allow claims adjusters to focus on case analysis rather than search logistics.

AI Bridges Language Barriers in Cross-Border Claims Handling

Language barriers posed a significant obstacle for non-German-speaking adjusters. Even when aided by translation tools, participants struggled with legal terminology and identifying proper search queries. The AI model, trained on relevant legal texts, eliminated these challenges. This proves that AI can democratize legal knowledge by making foreign jurisprudence more accessible to professionals without multilingual expertise.

Accuracy and Relevance of Case Retrieval

Both studies demonstrated that AI-assisted research yielded accurate and relevant cases. These findings demonstrate the ability of the GPT tool to process specialized content such as court cases. When German-speaking adjuster conducted manual searches, the effectiveness of their results depended on their ability to formulate precise search terms. In contrast, the GPT model retrieved directly relevant court decisions with minimal input.

Increased Accessibility and Usability for Claims Adjusters

Survey responses indicated that adjusters found the AI model significantly easier to use compared to manual research methods. The participants described the GPT interface as intuitive and straightforward. This ease of use makes AI tools a practical solution for claims professionals who may not have formal legal training but require access to case law in international claims disputes.

Practical Implications for International Insurance Claims Handling

The study's findings have direct implications for the insurance industry, particularly in claims departments handling international cases. The ability to quickly and accurately retrieve foreign case law reduces the risk of misinterpretation and ensures more informed decision-making. This could lead to the following:

- Faster claim resolution and improved efficiency in cross-border disputes.
- More consistent legal arguments based on verified case law.
- Reduced reliance on external legal consultants for preliminary case research.

5.2 Limitations

The study has certain limitations that must be considered. Both the pilot and follow-up studies involved a small number of participants, which should be addressed in potential follow-up research to solidify the relevance of the research. While the consistency of the results suggests that AI-assisted research improves efficiency, a larger sample across multiple jurisdictions would provide a more robust evaluation of the tool's effectiveness. Furthermore, the performance of the custom GPT model is inherently tied to the quality and scope of its training data. While the model was trained on German court decisions, variations in legal reasoning across different courts and jurisdictions could affect the accuracy of the retrieved case law. Future studies should assess the model's ability to handle diverse legal contexts beyond the tested dataset. The research was conducted in a simulated environment where participants retrieved case law for a hypothetical scenario. Although this setup effectively measured AI efficiency, future studies should examine how AI-assisted research influences actual litigation outcomes.

Aside from limitations that stem from the study itself, there are other potential issues that can arise from the use of generative AI, such as hallucinations [11]. In order to deal with them in the most accurate way possible, the current solution is to verify the cited court decision manually. Although manual verification is not ideal, it remains a necessary step even in traditional manual legal research. Therefore, despite this additional step, the AI tool still accelerates the overall process of identifying relevant court decisions compared to standard manual methods. This efficiency gain, along with the ability to explore a broader range of documents in less time, underlines the practical value of the tool.

6 Conclusion and Future Work

The paper explores the implementation of a no-code AI model, a custom GPT, which was created with the aim of improving legal research in international MTPL claims. The paper presents two studies, the results of which demonstrate a significant improvement in research efficiency and usability when using AI-assisted search methods compared to traditional methods, such as browsing the internet or manual research. GPT effectively addressed language barriers and helped claim adjusters with no proficiency in foreign language to find relevant case law. The findings highlight the unexplored benefits of integrating AI in daily processes in the insurance industry. However, limitations regarding the scope of the dataset and the controlled research environment necessitate further studies that should expand the dataset, evaluate real-world case scenarios, and expand the number of study participants. Only then can the long-term efficacy and impact on actual litigation outcomes be verified. Also, it is particularly important to emphasize that the unique aspect of this AI model is a no-code solution. This means that it does not require involvement from software developers or programmers, and insurance professionals themselves can directly create, manage, and customize such tools. This signifies a fundamental advancement toward greater autonomy for non-technical professionals in using, more specifically in leveraging, AI to solve practical, real-life problems such as the one presented in this paper.

Based on the study's findings and limitations, several directions are proposed for future research and development. To further improve the reliability of the AI model, future iterations should incorporate more court decisions and relevant national laws. A larger data set would improve the adaptability of the model and ensure more comprehensive legal coverage. A key improvement would be linking the AI tool with official legal databases, which would allow the GPT to retrieve up-to-date case law directly from relevant sources. This would mean more credibility and accuracy of the retrieved information and would minimize the risk of outdated or incomplete data. A valuable next step would be testing the AI model in real-world claims disputes. Observing how AI-assisted research influences decision-making in active cases in negotiations or litigation. This would provide deeper insights into its practical application and long-term impact on legal efficiency, paving the way for a fully custom solution for legal research.

References

1. Aslam, F., Hunjra, A.I., Ftiti, Z., Louhichi, W., Shams, T.: Insurance fraud detection: evidence from artificial intelligence and machine learning. Res. Int. Bus. Financ. **62**, 101744 (2022)
2. Introducing ChatGPT — openai.com. https://openai.com/blog/chatgpt, Accessed 28 Feb 2025
3. https://help.openai.com/en/articles/9358033-key-guidelines-for-writing-instructions-for-custom-gpts , Accessed 09 Mar 2025
4. Dai, A.M., Le, Q.V.: Semi-supervised sequence learning (2015), arXiv:1511.01432
5. Dias, F.S., Lauretta, G.A.: The transformative impact of ai and deep learning in business: a literature review. arXiv preprint arXiv:2410.23443 (2024)
6. juris GmbH: Rechtsprechung im Internet — rechtsprechung-im-internet.de. https://www.rechtsprechung-im-internet.de/jportal/portal/t/ozp/page/bsjrsprod.psml, Accessed 13 Mar 2025
7. Google Translate — translate.google.com. https://translate.google.com/, Accessed 13 Mar 2025
8. https://help.openai.com/en/articles/8843948-knowledge-in-gpts , Accessed 09 Mar 2025
9. https://openai.com/index/language-unsupervised/ , Accessed 09 Mar 2025
10. https://openai.com/index/introducing-gpts/ , Accessed 04 Mar 2025
11. Maleki, N., Padmanabhan, B., Dutta, K.: Ai hallucinations: a misnomer worth clarifying. In: 2024 IEEE Conference on Artificial Intelligence (CAI), pp. 133–138. IEEE (2024)
12. https://www.reuters.com/technology/artificial-intelligence/openais-weekly-active-users-surpass-400-million-2025-02-20/ , Accessed 04 Mar 2025
13. Singh, J., Urolagin, S.: Use of artificial intelligence for health insurance claims automation. In: Advances in Machine Learning and Computational Intelligence: Proceedings of ICMLCI 2019, pp. 381–392. Springer (2020)
14. Vaswani, A., et al.: Attention is all you need (2023), arXiv:1706.03762

Usability Assessment of Video and GIS Integration from Wildfire Geolocalization Perspective

Antonia Bartulović[1](✉), Ljiljana Šerić[1], Antonia Ivanda[1], Damir Krstinić[1], and Selena Knežić Buhovac[2]

[1] Faculty of Electrical Engineering, Mechanical Engineering and Naval Architecture, University of Split, Split, Republic of Croatia
{Antonia.Bartulovic.00,Ljiljana.Seric,Antonia.Senta.00, Damir.Krstinic}@fesb.hr

[2] Faculty of Mechanical Engineering, Computing and Electrical Engineering, University of Mostar, Mostar, Bosnia and Herzegovina
selena.knezic@fsre.sum.ba

Abstract. In this paper, we investigated the factors affecting human accuracy in geolocalizing wildfires based on visual imagery. Through an online survey of 71 participants of diverse demographics, we evaluated three key hypotheses regarding wildfire location estimation. Participants were presented with images captured by the FireDetectAI system during the summer of 2022 and asked to mark estimated fire locations on a map using a custom Leaflet-based interface. Our analysis revealed that incorrectly marked fire alarms significantly reduced location accuracy (mean distance error of 7.86 km versus 9.89 km for other scenes). Camera misalignment also negatively impacted geolocalization precision, with misaligned scenes showing higher error values when outliers were excluded. The presence of landmarks improved estimation accuracy (mean distance error of 7.84 km versus 10.37 km for scenes without landmarks). Statistical analysis of the results reveals inherent challenges in relying solely on human visual assessment for wildfire location estimation, particularly in featureless terrain, and suggests that improved annotation accuracy, proper camera alignment, and landmark presence could enhance human geolocalization performance. These insights have important implications for the design of wildfire monitoring systems and emphasize the potential benefits of supplementing human assessment with automated detection and geolocalization technologies for more effective early warning and response.

Keywords: VGI · GIS · empirical study · geolocalization · video surveillance

1 Introduction

The rise of Volunteered Geographical Information (VGI) [1] has revolutionized our approach to gathering spatial data about the world. However, quality assur-

D. Vasić and E. Brajković (Eds.): MoStart 2025, CCIS 2609, pp. 254–267, 2026.
https://doi.org/10.1007/978-3-032-02801-3_17

ance remains a significant challenge for VGI datasets. Since contributors possess varying levels of expertise, technical proficiency, and familiarity with geographic areas, the accuracy and reliability of this information cannot be universally guaranteed. The contributor database comprises individuals from different backgrounds who have different levels of knowledge or familiarity with areas, which introduces potential inconsistencies in data quality. To effectively assess and validate VGI quality, researchers typically employ two principal methods: comparing it against authoritative reference datasets or conducting temporal evaluation across multiple iterations of the same VGI dataset to identify patterns of improvement or degradation.

Wildfires pose a significant environmental hazard, and their early detection is crucial for mitigating catastrophic damage to ecosystems. Traditionally, early response mechanisms have relied on human observation, either through incidental detection by citizens or systematic monitoring conducted by trained personnel. This human-centered approach highlights the need for more advanced and automated detection systems to complement traditional methods.

Many studies have explored the possibilities of fire detection using satellite sensors [2], ground-based cameras [3], or IoT-based smoke sensors [4]. Additionally, researchers have explored social media data analysis to extract critical information about emerging disasters, enhancing disaster management capabilities. The primary objective of fire detection systems is to provide accurate information to emergency services about the emergence, location, and extent of the fire. However, location data is frequently miscommunicated during fire reporting processes. When working with a wildfire video surveillance system, accurate fire location determination is aided by knowledge of camera positions. However, the ability of operators to correctly determine the fire location based on information shown has remained unexplored in scientific literature. The goal of this paper is to evaluate the usability of integrating wildfire video surveillance with Geographic Information Systems (GIS). To achieve this, we designed and conducted a survey where participants were tasked with marking fire locations on maps based on video surveillance imagery. The survey included 23 scenarios, each varying in terms of GIS integration accuracy and marking precision. For each participant's response, we calculated the error as the distance between their mark and the actual fire location. Our analysis focuses on three main hypotheses.

- **Hypothesis 1**: Marking the precise location of the fire on the video surveillance image contributes to the precise determination of fire location. This hypothesis can be checked by comparing the performance of fire geolocalization in scenarios with and without correct fire marking.
- **Hypothesis 2**: Displaying the correct cameras' field of view enables more accurate determination of fire location. This is checked by comparing the user's performance in scenarios with accurate field of view display to those without.
- **Hypothesis 3**: The presence of visible landmarks in the vicinity of a wildfire enhances the accuracy of geolocalization by providing reference points for triangulation. This is checked by comparing the performance of users in scenarios with visible landmarks to those without.

The hypotheses are checked by statistically comparing the survey results on scenarios representing opposite situations. Additionally, we compared the performance of various users based on their characteristics. The rest of the paper is structured as follows: In the next section, we provide a brief overview of related work. Section 2 describes the study area, design of the survey, and data analysis techniques utilized. Section 3 discusses the statistical comparison, providing support for the three posed hypotheses. In Sect. 4, we discuss the conclusions and limitations of the conducted survey. In the final section, an overview of findings is given with directions for future work.

1.1 Related Work

The ability of individuals to accurately determine the location depicted in an image has been the subject of various studies. Identifying an image's location is a crucial task in multiple domains, including civil protection and journalism. In the absence of appropriate metadata, people rely on visual clues within the image to infer its geographic location [5]. However, automatic geotagging remains a challenging problem. A computer vision-based approach to geolocalization, as proposed in [6], relies on landmarks, large datasets, and extensive processing to match images with known locations.

In recent years, geolocalized information quality has been primarily studied in the context of Volunteered Geographic Information (VGI). While VGI is a valuable source of information for environmental monitoring, social sciences, and disaster management, the lack of standardized quality assessment frameworks has hindered its widespread adoption.

Data quality is typically defined as the degree of alignment between individual data points and the aspects of reality they represent [7]. Quality assessment focuses on four key dimensions: accuracy, completeness, consistency, and timeliness. This assessment is often performed by comparing VGI data with authoritative sources, which are not always available. In various studies, collected data is enriched with metadata, and researchers use factors such as user demographics, socioeconomics, and other features for quality assessment [8].

The most common method for collecting VGI is through campaigns using map-based data input. However, this method relies on users' ability to accurately determine the location of the event they are reporting. A literature review in [9] highlights the importance of assessing data quality in relation to users' familiarity with maps, tools, and events.

With advancements in computer vision techniques, video surveillance systems are becoming valuable tools for automatic event assessment in both protected spaces and wilderness areas [10]. When deployed in wilderness environments, integrating such systems with Geographic Information Systems (GIS) [11] enhances their functionality and usability. However, accurately determining the location of objects within an image remains a complex challenge. Analytical methods for location assessment are prone to errors due to inconsistencies in camera intrinsic parameters. To address this, lookup tables are commonly used for camera calibration [12], but this approach lacks verification mechanisms and can introduce errors in geolocalization. Some proposed techniques for outdoor surveillance camera calibration rely on recognizable objects and are unsuitable for installations in remote wilderness areas [13].

The significance of precise geolocalization in assessing the usability of video surveillance with GIS integration is recognized in the literature [14], yet it has not been systematically studied. In this paper, we explore the quality of information provided by video surveillance systems by examining how accurately individuals assess the location of a fire in an image when the available information is of uncertain reliability.

2 Materials and Methods

Croatia faces a high risk of forest fires, especially during the summer seasons. The seven coastal counties are especially vulnerable, with its islands at even greater risk, due to densely-spaced conifer forests [3]. This study focuses on the Dalmatian region, which includes the Zadar (Zadarska), Šibenik-Knin (Šibensko-Kninska) and Split-Dalmatia (Splitsko-Dalmatinska) counties. The study area is shown in Fig. 1.

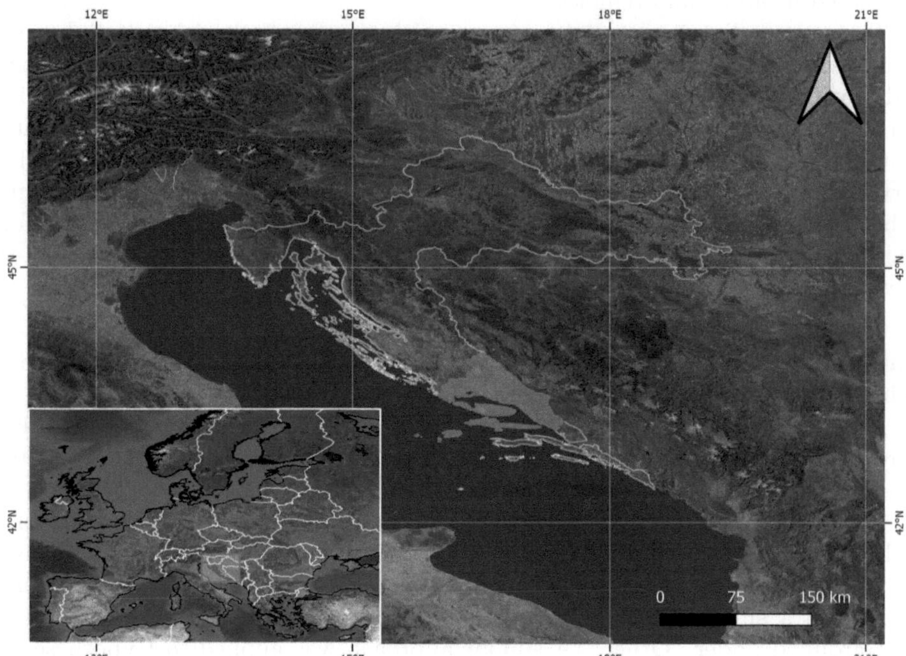

Fig. 1. Study area

Dalmatia, known for its natural beauty, is also the most susceptible region to wildfires. The combination of warm and arid summers, strong dry winds, and the characteristic Mediterranean terrain and vegetation of the region create ideal conditions for the ignition of fires and their rapid spread [15]. Due to this high fire risk, the Dalmatian region was specifically chosen for this study, where past wildfire events have severely impacted both the local environment and human settlements.

This region is also where most efforts to advance firefighting techniques are developed and tested. Thus, this area is equipped with wildfire video monitoring and surveillance cameras with advanced capabilities for smoke and fire detection, geolocalization, fire spread modeling, and other related functions.

2.1 Methodology

Survey Design. The survey was designed to evaluate participants' ability to estimate the location of wildfires based on images from the study area, captured using the FireDetectAI system during the summer of 2022. These images varied in complexity, featuring different visual elements such as landmarks and diverse terrain types. Participants were asked to mark their estimated fire locations on a graphical interface built with Leaflet, allowing for precise geolocalization assessments. The survey was hosted on a custom WordPress website, and participants completed it online and remotely.

To ensure a diverse range of responses, the survey was shared via a link with students from the Faculty of Electrical Engineering, Mechanical Engineering, and Naval Architecture in Split (FESB), as well as with friends and family. Participants were presented with a GDPR-compliant consent form outlining data protection measures and their rights before participating in the survey. The survey collected data on the accuracy of participants' location estimates in terms of both distance and proportion of error. The interface included a visual tool for marking fire locations, with an indication of the camera's position and field of view (FOV), as shown in Fig. 2.

Data Analysis. The survey data, extracted into a CSV file from the WordPress website, was analyzed using Python and Jupyter Notebooks.

Each scene was assigned one or more categories. Some of these categories were excluded from the hypotheses scenarios to prevent skewing the results. These categories are defined in Table 1.

Under Hypothesis 1, the categories "Opposite side" (o), "Zoomed in" (z), and "Slightly misaligned" (s) were removed from the scenario. The "Incorrectly marked" (im) and "Multiple fire sources" (mfs) categories were combined into a single "Incorrectly marked" category, while all other categories were grouped under "Other." A similar approach was applied to Hypotheses 2 and 3. In Hypothesis 2, the categories "Slightly misaligned," "Opposite side," and "Zoomed in" were grouped under "Misaligned," with all other categories placed under "Other." For Hypothesis 3, the "Opposite side," "Multiple fire sources," "Zoomed in," and "Slightly misaligned" categories were removed, with scenes labeled "Visible landmarks" (v) categorized as "Landmark," and all other scenes categorized as "No landmark."

Fig. 2. Survey interface

Table 1. Category Definitions

Category	Definition
o	Opposite side (camera view is looking in the opposite direction)
s	Slightly misaligned (misalignment in camera view, perspective, or orientation)
im	Incorrectly marked (fire alarm marked incorrectly)
v	Visible landmarks (roads, cities, or other reference points visible in the image)
n	No visible landmarks (absence of key reference points, such as roads or cities)
in	Invisible (fire source hidden behind terrain, such as a hill)
mfs	Multiple fire sources (more than one distinct fire in the area)
z	Zoomed in (image taken at a zoomed-in level of detail)

Each hypothesis included two types of error calculations: distance error and proportional error. Distance error (E_d) was calculated as the Euclidean distance between the actual fire location (x_a, y_a), obtained partly from pixel maps and real wildfire data provided by firefighters, and the estimated location (x_e, y_e):

$$E_d = \sqrt{(x_a - x_e)^2 + (y_a - y_e)^2} \tag{2.1}$$

Proportional (or weighted) error (E_p) was introduced to offer an additional perspective on the data, particularly for larger distances. It was defined as:

$$E_p = \frac{E_d}{d_{\max}} \tag{2.2}$$

where $d_{\max}$ represents the maximum possible distance within the given study area. Data for each hypothesis was visualized using Seaborn, and the results are presented in the next section.

3 Results

This section presents the results of the conducted survey, focusing on the precision of the fire geolocalization estimates of the participants under different conditions. Of the 71 participants, most (28) were 2029 years old, followed by 16 in the 3039 range and 10 in the 4049 range. The participants were almost evenly divided by gender, with 36 women and 32 men. Education levels varied, with 25 holding a Master's degree or university diploma, 23 having secondary school education, and 11 having a high school education.

Forty-one participants were employed, 25 were students, and 5 had other statuses. Most of the participants (58) had no previous experience with VGI, while 8 were unsure and 5 had experience. Thirteen participants were involved in Emergency Services, mainly firefighters, while the majority were civilians. The distribution of participant data is shown in Fig. 3.

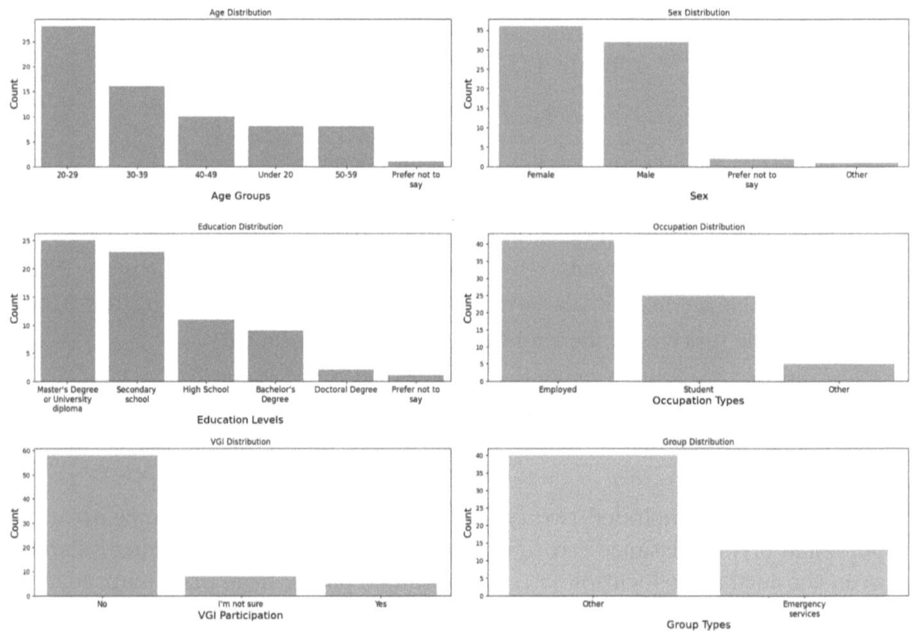

Fig. 3. Participant data distribution

We have structured the findings around three main hypotheses: (1) incorrect fire marking leads to lower accuracy, (2) misaligned camera previews result in lower accuracy, and (3) the absence of landmarks increases estimation error.

3.1 Hypothesis 1

The first hypothesis suggests that participants would be less accurate when fire locations are incorrectly marked in the scenes (referred to as "Wrong alarm" in the subsequent text). To test this, we define two scenarios: scenes with incorrect fire markings and all other scenes. Misaligned scenes are excluded from this hypothesis to avoid negatively impacting the results.

Table 2. Error metrics for Hypothesis 1.

Scenario	Items	Scenes	Users	Distance Error		Weighted Error	
				Mean	SD	Mean	SD
Wrong alarm	342	6	63	7.86	10.25	5.39	11.24
Other	915	16	67	9.89	19.76	4.78	16.05

Table 2 provides a detailed breakdown of error metrics for the two categories. The "Wrong alarm" scenario, which includes incorrectly marked fire locations, has a lower mean accuracy compared to the "Other" scenario. However, the "Wrong alarm" scenario has a higher weighted mean. This is partly due to the "Other" scenario containing three times as many items and scenes, resulting in a wider range of error in the unweighted case but a smaller difference when the values are weighted. For this reason, we have chosen to show a boxplot of weighted values for both scenarios to compare them.

Figure 4 compares the weighted error means for the "Wrong alarm" and "Other" scenarios, excluding outliers to prevent distortion of the graph's representation. As shown, the "Wrong alarm" scenario exhibits values in significantly higher ranges, suggesting that participants geolocalizing these scenes faced greater challenges in making precise estimations.

From this data, we can conclude that incorrectly marked fire locations lead to lower geolocalization accuracy, supporting the first hypothesis. This may be due to participants struggling to pinpoint the exact location for geolocalization, indicating that the accuracy of their guesses is influenced by the quality of the input data. As the alarm locations vary from scene to scene, participants' estimations become more variable. The trend holds even after excluding outliers, reinforcing its robustness. Ensuring accurate alarm marking is essential for improving geolocalization accuracy in wildfire detection systems and similar applications.

3.2 Hypothesis 2

The second hypothesis suggests that participants geolocalize alarms more accurately when provided with proper guidelines. These guidelines include a preview of the assumed field of view of the camera and the correct orientation of the camera. To test this hypothesis, we defined two scenarios: scenes with misaligned

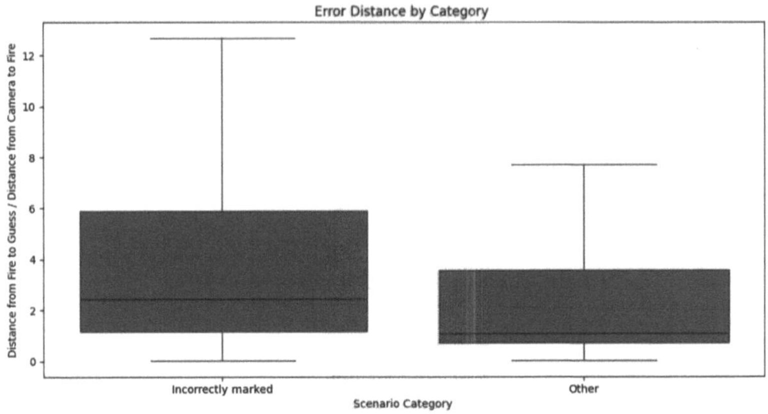

Fig. 4. Plot for wrong alarm scenes in comparison to other scenes

previews and all other scenes. No scenarios were excluded from the "Other" category, unlike in Hypothesis 1.

Table 3. Error metrics for Hypothesis 2.

Scenario	Items	Scenes	Users	Distance Error		Weighted Error	
				Mean	SD	Mean	SD
Misaligned	286	5	63	8.46	10.46	3.51	7.04
Other	1030	18	66	9.49	18.81	5.20	16.03

Table 3 follows a similar layout to Table 2. It shows that the "Other" scenario contains a significantly larger number of items as well as more than three times as many scenes as the "Misaligned" scenario. The mean values for both scenarios are relatively close, with "Other" having a slightly higher mean. The same trend holds for the weighted values, where "Misaligned" scenes have a lower mean and standard deviation.

However, despite these data points, Fig. 5 shows that, after excluding outliers, the "Misaligned" scenario exhibits relatively higher error values compared to the "Other" scenario. This is expected, given the large number of entries in the "Other" scenario. These findings suggest that participants had a harder time geolocalizing "Misaligned" scenes, whereas the "Other" scenario resulted in a wider range of guesses.

From these results, we can draw conclusions regarding Hypothesis 2. While participants made a smaller range of guesses for "Misaligned" scenes, it is important to note that this scenario only contained five scenes, whereas eighteen scenes were included in the "Other" scenario. This difference in sample size should be taken into account when interpreting the results.

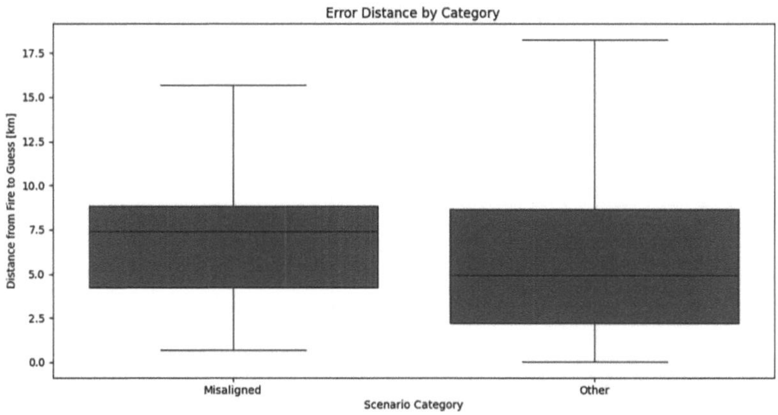

Fig. 5. Plot for misaligned scenes in comparison to other scenes

3.3 Hypothesis 3

The third hypothesis examines the impact of landmarks on participants' geolocalization accuracy. The assumption is that the presence of a landmark (e.g., a building, road, city, etc.) improves accuracy. To test this, we define two scenarios: scenes where a landmark is present and those without a landmark. Similar to Hypothesis 1, we excluded misaligned scenes to prevent them from skewing the results.

Table 4. Error metrics for Hypothesis 3.

Scenario	Items	Scenes	Users	Distance Error		Weighted Error	
				Mean	SD	Mean	SD
Landmark	511	9	63	7.84	12.78	5.62	13.72
No Landmark	746	13	66	10.37	20.35	4.48	15.64

Table 4 follows the same layout as Tables 2 and 3. There is slightly more 'No Landmark' scenes than 'Landmark' scenes, with a few additional participants contributing to the 'No Landmark' category. Examining the distance error means and standard deviations, we observe that, on average, scenes with landmarks result in lower errors compared to those without landmarks. However, the reversal of this trend in the weighted error suggests that landmarks tend to be located closer to the camera, causing errors to be exaggerated in proportion to distance.

Figure 6 supports these findings, showing that the "No Landmark" scenario exhibits a wider range of error values and a slightly higher average error. In contrast, scenes with landmarks are, on average, more precisely geolocalized, reinforcing the hypothesis that landmarks aid accuracy.

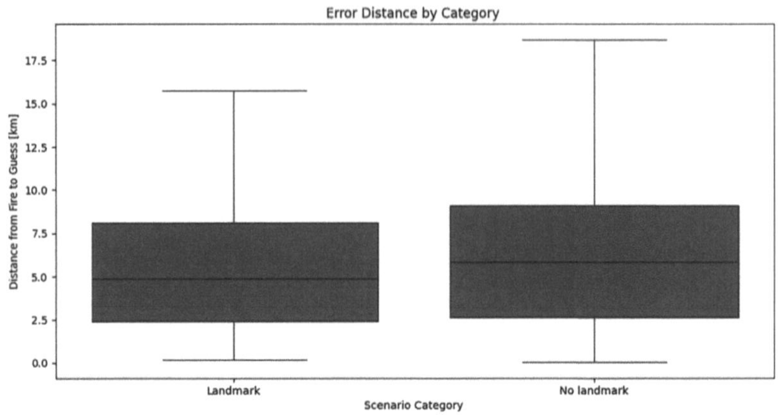

Fig. 6. Plot for scenes with landmarks and with no landmarks

4 Discussion

4.1 Incorrectly Marked Fire Locations and Geolocalization Accuracy

The results confirm that incorrectly marked fire alarms negatively impact geolocalization accuracy. Participants struggled more with estimating fire positions when the fire alarm was misplaced, leading to higher error values. This suggests that inaccurate annotations introduce confusion, causing participants to second-guess their estimates.

A potential explanation lies in the cognitive load associated with conflicting visual information. When a fire alarm is incorrectly placed, participants must not only estimate the fire's actual location but also assess the alarm's reliability. This additional cognitive step likely contributes to greater geolocalization errors.

These findings highlight the importance of accuracy in fire detection and reporting systems. Incorrectly placed alarms may not only mislead human operators but also degrade the performance of crowdsourced geolocalization efforts. Future applications could mitigate this issue by implementing automated validation methods, such as pixel-based fire location detection.

4.2 The Impact of Camera Alignment on Geolocalization Accuracy

The second hypothesis explored whether proper camera alignment and preview guidelines improve geolocalization accuracy. While the mean accuracy difference between properly aligned and misaligned scenes was not substantial, the variance in error suggests that misaligned previews made localization more difficult.

A key finding is that the "Other" category exhibited a wider range of errors compared to misaligned previews. This is likely because it included a greater diversity of scenes, leading to natural variation in geolocalization accuracy. However, after excluding outliers, it became clear that participants faced greater difficulty in the misaligned scenario. This aligns with expectations—when a camera's field of view is unclear or misleading, participants struggle to orient themselves, leading to more significant localization errors.

These findings suggest that accurate representation of the camera's orientation and improved preview tools could enhance the accuracy of volunteer-based geolocalization in fire detection systems. Ensuring that participants receive consistent, well-aligned previews may reduce uncertainty and improve response times.

4.3 Landmarks in Geolocalization Accuracy

The third hypothesis tested whether the presence of landmarks improves participants' geolocalization accuracy. The results strongly support this hypothesis, showing that participants performed better when landmarks were present.

An important observation is that the "No Landmark" scenario exhibited a wider range of errors, suggesting that participants used varied strategies to estimate locations in these scenes. Without clear reference points, participants may have relied on environmental cues such as terrain features or horizon positions, which vary in reliability. This variability likely contributed to the increased error spread.

While the mean distance error was lower for scenes in the "Landmark" category, the weighted error was slightly higher. This reversed trend could be explained by the fact that fires in landmark-containing scenes were generally closer to the camera. In such cases, even small geolocalization mistakes resulted in a larger proportional error. This suggests that while landmarks improve precision, their effect may depend on the scene's depth and scale.

5 Conclusions

In this paper, we analyzed how accurately individuals can geolocalize fire locations in images aided by GIS information and identified key factors influencing their precision. The data were gathered through a survey distributed to students, friends, and family, and analyzed based on three hypotheses: participants would be less accurate if fire locations were incorrectly marked, if the camera's field of view (FOV) was misaligned, and if there were no recognizable landmarks present. The findings confirmed these hypotheses, demonstrating that inaccurate fire alarms significantly reduce accuracy, misaligned camera previews introduce additional errors, and the absence of recognizable landmarks increases variability in distance estimation.

These results suggest that human geolocalization in wild, featureless areas is inherently imprecise, highlighting the challenges of relying solely on visual cues for fire detection. While trained personnel or geospatial tools might improve outcomes, the variability in responses indicates that human interpretation alone is insufficient for precise fire localization in such conditions. This underscores the potential benefits of automated video surveillance systems, which could provide more consistent and accurate fire detection, reducing reliance on subjective human estimation. Future research could explore the integration of AI-based geolocalization methods.

By addressing these challenges, we can improve fire monitoring strategies and enhance the effectiveness of early warning systems, ultimately contributing to more efficient wildfire response and management.

Acknowledgment. The authors would like to express their gratitude to the Split-Dalmatia County Firefighting Association for their contributions to this paper.

References

1. Goodchild, M.F.: Citizens as sensors: the world of volunteered geography. GeoJ. **69**, 211–221 (2007)
2. Wooster, M.J., et al.: Satellite remote sensing of active fires: history and current status, applications and future requirements. Remote Sens. Environ. **267**, 112694 (2021)
3. Stipaničev, D., Vuko, T., Krstinić, D., Štula, M., Bodrožić, L.: Forest fire protection by advanced video detection system-croatian experiences. In: Third TIEMS Workshop-Improvement of Disaster Management System, Trogir (2006)
4. Chan, C.C., Alvi, S.A., Zhou, X., Durrani, S., Wilson, N., Yebra, M.: A survey on iot ground sensing systems for early wildfire detection: technologies, challenges and opportunities. IEEE Access (2024)
5. Mehta, S., North, C., Luther, K.: An exploratory study of human performance in image geolocation tasks. In: HCOMP 2016 GroupSight Workshop on Human Computation for Image and Video Analysis, vol. 308, p. 1 (2016)
6. Hays, J., Efros, A.A.: Im2gps: estimating geographic information from a single image. In: 2008 IEEE Conference on Computer Vision and Pattern Recognition, pp. 1–8. IEEE (2008)
7. Fogliaroni, P., D'Antonio, F., Clementini, E.: Data trustworthiness and user reputation as indicators of vgi quality. Geo-Spatial Inf. Sci. **21**(3), 213–233 (2018)
8. Antoniou, V., Skopeliti, A.: Measures and indicators of vgi quality: an overview. ISPRS Ann. Photogrammetry Remote Sens. Spatial Inf. Sci. **2**, 345–351 (2015)
9. Tavra, M., Lisec, A., Galešić Divić, M., Cetl, V.: Unpacking the role of volunteered geographic information in disaster management: focus on data quality. Geomat. Nat. Hazards Risk **15**(1), 2300825 (2024)
10. Haering, N., Venetianer, P.L., Lipton, A.: The evolution of video surveillance: an overview. Mach. Vis. Appl. **19**(5), 279–290 (2008)
11. Milosavljević, A., Rančić, D., Dimitrijević, A., Predić, B., Mihajlović, V.: A method for estimating surveillance video georeferences. ISPRS Int. J. Geo Inf. **6**(7), 211 (2017)
12. Gartner, C., Mathew, J.K., Desai, J., Sturdevant, J., Cox, E.D., Bullock, D.: Methodology for georeferencing roadside pan-tilt-zoom cctv camera views to highway gps coordinates. IEEE Access (2024)
13. Shi, L., Lan, X., Lan, X., Zhang, T.: Quick calibration of massive urban outdoor surveillance cameras. ISPRS J. Photogramm. Remote. Sens. **214**, 231–243 (2024)

14. Suwaileh, R., Elsayed, T., Imran, M.: Role of geolocation prediction in disaster management. In: International Handbook of Disaster Research, pp. 1–33. Springer (2023)
15. Šerić, L., Ivanda, A., Bugarić, M., Braović, M.: Semantic conceptual framework for environmental monitoring and surveillance–a case study on forest fire video monitoring and surveillance. Electronics **11**(2), 275 (2022)

Advancing Medical Education and Planning Through Extended Reality: A Mini Review of XR Applications in Medicine

Irena Galić[1], Marija Habijan[1(✉)], Marin Benčević[1], Juraj Perić[1], Hrvoje Leventić[1], Krešimir Romić[1], Ivana Hartmann Tolić[1], Robert Šojo[1], Aleksandra Pižurica[3], Danilo Babin[4], Dario Muževič[2], Vjekoslav Kopačin[2], Maja Košuta Petrović[2], and Mirta Vujnovac[5]

[1] J. J. Strossmayer University of Osijek, Faculty of Electrical Engineering, Computer Science and Information Technology, Osijek, Croatia
marija.habijan@ferit.hr
[2] Clinical Medical Center, Osijek, Croatia
[3] Department of Telecommunications and Information Processing, TELIN-GAIM, Ghent University, Ghent, Belgium
[4] Department of Telecommunications and Information Processing, imec-TELIN-IPI, Ghent University, Ghent, Belgium
[5] III Gymnasium, Osijek, Croatia

Abstract. The integration of extended reality (XR) technologies, virtual, augmented, and mixed reality with artificial intelligence (AI) is transforming medical education, diagnostics, and surgical planning. This mini review explores how established AI methods such as convolutional neural networks (CNNs), recurrent networks (RNNs), generative adversarial networks (GANs), and reinforcement learning (RL) are being used to enhance XR systems for anatomical segmentation, realistic simulation, and autonomous interaction. It also examines emerging approaches, including diffusion models (DMs), vision transformers (ViTs), and multimodal learning (MML), which enable high-fidelity synthetic data generation, contextual scene understanding, and integration of heterogeneous inputs such as imaging, text, and sensor data. Through use cases in placenta accreta diagnosis and neurovascular intervention planning, we demonstrate how AI-enhanced XR systems can deliver immersive, intelligent, and personalized experiences for clinicians and trainees. We further outline technical challenges, including real-time performance, data variability, and interpretability, and discuss strategies to ensure safe, equitable, and effective adoption of AI-driven XR in healthcare.

Keywords: Artifical Intelligence · Augmented Reality · Extended Reality · Virtual Reality · Medical Education · Personalized Education

D. Vasić and E. Brajković (Eds.): MoStart 2025, CCIS 2609, pp. 268–282, 2026.
https://doi.org/10.1007/978-3-032-02801-3_18

1 Introduction

Extended reality (XR) is a term that includes virtual reality (VR), augmented reality (AR), and mixed reality (MR). These technologies merge digital information with the physical environment to varying degrees, providing immersive three-dimensional (3D) experiences [7,20]. In XR, VR typically refers to fully immersive simulations blocking out the real world, AR overlays digital content onto the real-world view, and MR blends interactive virtual objects into the real environment with spatial anchoring [1]. Recent advances in computing and display hardware have accelerated the adoption of XR in medicine [1,7]. Early applications demonstrated the benefits of XR's 3D visualization and intuitive interaction for medical tasks that are challenging with traditional 2D screens. For example, XR enables hands-free interaction with 3D anatomical models in sterile operating rooms, overcoming the limitations of desktops and tablets in these environments. Over the past decade, XR has evolved from experimental prototypes to practical tools in medical education and clinical practice [26,41].

This mini review explores state-of-the-art XR applications in two key areas: (1) medical education (such as anatomy learning, diagnostic training, and clinical simulations) and (2) surgical and clinical planning (including procedural rehearsal and image-guided interventions). We discuss how XR is being used to enhance learning and preoperative planning, examine the evidence of its benefits (and risks), and highlight current limitations. Section 2 reviews educational and clinical use cases, while Sect. 3 highlights how AI methods enhance XR systems. Section 4 present examples in placenta accreta diagnosis and neurovascular intervention, followed by AI pipeline integration in Section 5 and a discussion of challenges in Sect. 6. Section 7 concludes with future directions. The review aims to guide the development of accessible and scalable XR systems for medical education and practice.

2 XR in Medical Education and Clinical Planning

XR is widely used in teaching of anatomy, surgical skills, and clinical scenarios, often matching or surpassing traditional methods in effective learning engagement, and cost efficiency [7]. Tools like virtual anatomy platforms and AR overlays enhance spatial understanding and contextual learning, while increasing motivation and retention through multi-sensory interaction [43]. XR also improves access to high-quality simulation, offering portable, scalable alternatives to costly, centralized training labs. VR headsets allow for remote asynchronous practice, support standardized experiences, and reduce dependence on physical wear [40]. A range of XR tools support diverse educational needs: from VR surgical simulators (e.g. for endoscopy) to MR headsets such as HoloLens, which project interactive 3D anatomy for collaborative learning [15]. Virtual dissection tables bridge solo and group learning, further expanding XR's applicability. Evidence shows XR boosts procedural confidence and skill acquisition, with outcomes often comparable or superior to conventional teaching [19].

However, integration challenges remain, including the need for more research on mobile and multi-user platforms, curricular alignment, and soft skills training. As XR matures, it is poised to become a standard complement to medical education, particularly in anatomy and procedural instruction [25].

XR technologies are also becoming essential tools in surgical planning and image-guided procedures by enabling detailed, interactive visualization of patient-specific anatomy. VR allows surgeons to explore 3D reconstructions of CT/MRI scans, enhancing spatial understanding and supporting preoperative rehearsal [6]. AR and MR systems can project this data onto the patient during surgery, assisting with real-time navigation and improving precision. Studies across specialties, such as thoracic and urologic surgery, show that VR-based planning improves anatomical insight, surgical confidence, and outcomes, including reduced operative times and improved preservation of healthy tissue [10]. Intraoperatively, AR reduces the need to shift attention between monitors and patients by embedding navigation data directly into the surgeon's field of view [36]. Applications in neurosurgery and vascular surgery show promise, with benefits such as better alignment of surgical targets and more intuitive incision planning [34]. XR also supports interdisciplinary collaboration and patient education, enabling shared understanding through 3D models in *virtual consultations.* Despite its promise, XR faces challenges such as ensuring accurate hologram alignment, managing device ergonomics, and integrating systems into existing workflows. Nonetheless, early trials report positive outcomes and no adverse events, suggesting XR may soon become a standard aid in complex surgical planning and execution [9]. A structured comparison of VR, AR, and MR modalities in terms of their immersion level, educational and surgical applications, hardware, strengths, and limitations is presented in Table 1.

Table 1. Systematic comparison of XR methodologies in medicine

Feature	VR	AR	MR
Immersion level	Full immersion	Low to moderate	Moderate to high
Use in medical education	High-fidelity simulations, anatomy learning	Real-time overlays for anatomy and procedural steps	Interactive group learning with spatially anchored virtual content
Use in surgery	Preoperative planning, rehearsal	Intraoperative navigation and guidance	Real-time guidance with interactive overlays and tool tracking
Hardware examples	Oculus Rift, HTC Vive, Meta Quest	Smartphone-based AR, Microsoft HoloLens	Microsoft HoloLens 2, Magic Leap with spatial tracking
Strengths	Deep immersion, effective skill transfer, standardized training	Real-world integration, supports real-time feedback, cost-effective	High realism, spatial accuracy, user interaction with real-world context
Limitations	Lack of real-world context, motion sickness, hardware cost	Limited field of view, alignment challenges, requires stable tracking	High complexity, hardware cost, computational requirements

3 AI Methods for Medical XR

In this section we present eastablished and emerging AI methods. Established techniques, such as convolutional neural networks (CNNs), recurrent neural networks (RNNs), generative adversarial networks (GANs), and reinforcement learning (RL), have been foundational in tasks like image segmentation, temporal modeling, image synthesis, and interactive control. Meanwhile, newer paradigms like vision transformers (ViTs), diffusion models (DMs), and multi-modal fusion architectures are pushing boundaries by offering improved data representation, generative realism, and integrated understanding across diverse medical modalities. Together, these AI models enable XR systems to deliver more realistic, adaptive, and clinically relevant experiences for diagnosis, training, and intraoperative guidance.

3.1 Established AI Methods for Medical XR

Several well-established AI methods serve as the foundation for enhancing medical image interpretation, simulation, and interactivity in XR environments. Fig. 1 present a conceptual overview of established AI methods that drive innovation in medical XR.

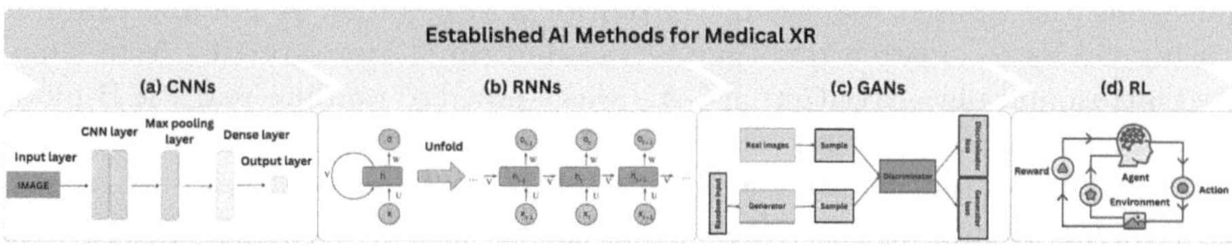

Fig. 1. Overview of established AI methods for medical XR applications: (a) CNNs for image analysis and segmentation, (b) RNNs for temporal modeling, (c) GANs for realistic image synthesis, and (d) RL for interactive control and simulation.

Convolutional Neural Networks (CNNs): CNNs form the backbone of many XR medical applications, especially for medical image segmentation and reconstruction. For example, U-Net architectures [32] are widely used to segment patient-specific anatomy (e.g. organs, vasculature) from volumetric scans, producing 3D models that can be visualized in AR/VR. In placenta accreta diagnosis, an nnU-Net (a self-configuring 3D U-Net variant) was applied to MRI data for automatic placenta segmentation, which improved diagnostic AUC beyond expert radiologists [37]. This segmentation allows the overlay of critical structures in the view of the clinician in XR, or the import of patient-specific models into simulators. CNN-based image analysis also supports XR by detecting and tracking instruments or anatomical landmarks in real time, enabling interactive feedback during simulation and image-guided interventions [30].

Recurrent Neural Networks (RNNs): While less common than CNNs in medical imaging, RNNs are employed in XR systems to model temporal dynamics and sequences. For instance, physics-informed deep networks combining CNN and LSTM layers have been used to emulate soft tissue behavior over time in surgical VR simulations [35]. By training on biomechanical simulation data, these models can predict tissue deformations and tool interactions with high fidelity, but at a fraction of the computational cost of finite element methods. This enables real-time haptic feedback and realistic tissue response in VR surgical trainers, which is crucial for interventions like neurovascular embolization that involve complex, time-dependent vessel and catheter interactions [14]. In general, RNNs can learn system dynamics, allowing XR environments to respond realistically to user actions (e.g. simulating physiologic changes or instrument motion over time).

Generative Adversarial Networks (GANs): GAN-based models are powerful for image generation and domain translation in XR medical systems [3]. They can synthesize realistic medical images or augment simulation visuals, addressing the limited realism of conventional simulators. A notable example is using GANs to create a real-time ultrasound simulation: starting from simulated ultrasound physics output, a GAN was trained to produce realistic B-mode ultrasound images that mimic speckle and tissue texture [23]. Moreover, GAN-based domain adaptation can translate between imaging modalities, such as generating ultrasound-like images from MRI scans, helping to improve multi-modal visualization in XR systems. These capabilities help create more immersive and varied XR simulations, from virtual patients with different anatomies to on-the-fly realistic imaging feedback during an AR-guided procedure [29,31].

Reinforcement Learning (RL): RL techniques are emerging as tools to automate and optimize interactions within XR simulations [11]. In medical training simulators, RL can be used to train virtual assistants or autonomous agents that demonstrate surgical maneuvers, adjust scenario difficulty, or control virtual patients [39]. For example, researchers have applied RL (using methods like Proximal Policy Optimization) to learn automated surgical subtasks in a virtual reality setting [4]. Such RL-driven automation within XR can provide trainees with an intelligent training partner or dynamically adjust simulations based on performance [27]. Beyond training, RL has been used for planning in image-guided therapy for instance, to optimize the path of a catheter or endoscope in a complex 3D vessel network. Overall, combining RL with high-fidelity XR environments enables skill acquisition through trial-and-error in simulation and can adaptively enhance realism and educational value in medical XR systems.

3.2 Emerging AI Techniques and Multi-Modal Systems

As medical XR continues to evolve, new AI paradigms are emerging that push the boundaries of what is possible in simulation, visualization, and interaction.

These cutting-edge approaches aim to enhance the fidelity, adaptability, and intelligence of XR systems by leveraging recent advances in generative modeling, vision architectures, and multi-modal integration. Fig. 2 present a conceptual overview of emerging AI methods that drive innovation in medical XR.

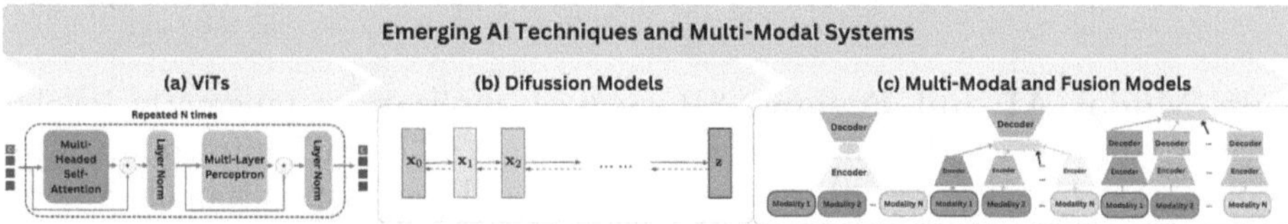

Fig. 2. Overview of emerging AI methods for medical XR applications: (a) Vision Transformers (ViTs) for capturing long-range dependencies in medical images, (b) Diffusion Models for high-fidelity generative tasks such as 3D volume synthesis, and (c Multi-Modal and Fusion Models capable of integrating diverse data types (e.g., text, imaging, and sensor data) to support intelligent XR systems.

Diffusion Models. Diffusion-based generative models represent a cutting-edge approach for creating high-quality synthetic medical data and enhancing realism in XR. Unlike GANs, diffusion models iteratively refine random noise into coherent images, often yielding higher fidelity and diversity. These models have shown state-of-the-art ability to generate realistic anatomy and even assist with tasks like sparse-view reconstruction and data augmentation [21,22,38]. In an XR context, diffusion models could generate diverse patient cases (e.g. various placenta shapes or vascular anatomies) for simulation training, or fill in missing visual details on-the-fly to improve graphical realism. They also enable multimodal image synthesis: for example, creating plausible MRI from ultrasound or vice versa, which could be used to enrich the visual feedback in AR fusion systems. While still an emerging research area, diffusion models hold promise for overcoming data scarcity and increasing the variability and authenticity of XR medical content [17].

Vision Transformers (ViTs). Transformer-based vision models have recently gained importance in medical imaging due to their ability to capture long-range dependencies and contextual information. ViT models and hybrid CNN-Transformer architectures (e.g. Swin UNETR) are now achieving or exceeding state-of-the-art performance on tasks like 3D segmentation and classification [16]. Transformers can be pre-trained on massive image datasets and fine-tuned with relatively small medical datasets, addressing data limitations. In XR systems, ViTs can enhance perception and understanding of the scene, for example, accurately segmenting organs or vessels in real-time to overlay onto a surgeon's AR display, or identifying clinical landmarks in a VR training scenario.

By integrating ViT models, XR platforms benefit from robust and efficient analysis of complex imaging data, ultimately providing more reliable visualizations (e.g. highlighting a suspected accreta region in an AR view) and interactions. As transformer models continue to evolve (becoming more computationally efficient and hybridized with CNNs), they are expected to play a growing role in XR for tasks requiring high precision and understanding of global context in images [33].

Multi-Modal AI and Fusion. XR medical applications inherently involve multiple data modalities combining medical images (CT, MRI, ultrasound), sensor data, text (medical records or instructions), and even haptic signals. Emerging AI methods aim to fuse these modalities into a coherent understanding or output [8]. In practice, a multi-modal XR system might take as input a 3D MRI, an ultrasound video stream, and perhaps physician voice commands, and produce an output such as an AR overlay aligned to the patient with diagnostic annotations. Initial strides in this direction include models that align different imaging modalities: e.g. a learning-based system to register and fuse MRI and ultrasound images for prenatal diagnostics [2]. These XR systems could not only display merged imagery but also understand and respond to complex combinations of inputs (visual, textual, auditory, haptic), leading to more intuitive and intelligent medical training and guidance platforms.

4 Clinical Applications of AI-Enhanced XR in Medicine

The following section presents concrete examples that illustrate how the integration of AI and XR transforms medical imaging and surgical planning, focusing on placenta accreta diagnosis (ultrasound/MRI fusion) and neurovascular simulation and embolization planning, through enhanced visualization, real-time guidance, and patient-specific modeling.

4.1 Placenta Accreta Diagnosis (Ultrasound/MRI fusion)

Placenta accreta spectrum (PAS) is a high-risk obstetric condition where the placenta invades the uterine wall, often requiring complex surgery. Accurate diagnosis and pre-surgical planning are critical [12]. Ultrasound (US) is the first-line imaging modality for suspected accreta, but it can be limited in deep invasion cases, whereas MRI provides complementary soft-tissue detail. Extended reality offers a novel way to combine these imaging modalities and assist clinicians [28]. In an XR diagnostic setup, a physician wearing an AR headset could perform a live ultrasound while seeing overlaid 3D information from a prior MRI on the patient [5]. This US/MRI fusion in AR provides a rich, spatially intuitive view for example, highlighting the placenta boundaries and areas of uterine invasion in 3D within the patient's body, rather than interpreting 2D images side-by-side. Early developments suggest that augmented reality overlays can indeed enhance the understanding of placental anatomy: in one report, real-time

AR visualization of a 3D placenta model during ultrasound improved diagnostic clarity for accreta [18].

To enable such XR fusion, AI methods are pivotal. A CNN (like U-Net) can automatically segment the placenta and abnormal invasion zones on the MRI, generating a 3D volume of the placenta accreta [42]. This model is then imported into the AR system and spatially registered to the patient's anatomy (using landmarks or sensor tracking). During the ultrasound exam, the AR headset displays the segmented placenta (from MRI) correctly aligned within the patient, while the operator simultaneously sees live ultrasound slices in their field of view. The result is a composite "X-ray vision" effect the physician looks through the abdomen and observes both the real-time ultrasound and the contextualized MRI-derived structures [13]. For placenta accreta, this could translate to better intraoperative planning (e.g. visualizing how deeply placenta penetrates and its relation to bladder or vessels), potentially reducing surprises during surgery. AI contributes further by analyzing the multimodal data. Beyond segmentation, machine learning classifiers can assess invasion depth or likelihood of placenta accreta from the images (using radiomic features or deep networks). The XR interface might also allow clinicians to interact with the data for instance, voice-querying the system for measurements like placental thickness or getting a projected blood loss risk based on AI analysis of the case. This tight integration of AI-driven analysis with immersive visualization exemplifies how XR can augment clinical decision-making.

4.2 Neurovascular Simulation and Embolization Planning

Neurovascular procedures, such as cerebral aneurysm coiling or AVM embolization, demand a high level of skill due to intricate cerebrovascular anatomy and the risks of navigation within blood vessels. XR technology is being applied to neurosurgery training and planning to enhance understanding of complex 3D anatomy and to allow rehearsal of interventions in a safe environment. A recent systematic review found that extended reality greatly aids endovascular neurosurgery education: VR simulations were used in the majority of studies (for procedural training on aneurysm coiling, thrombectomy, etc.), while AR/MR were used for visualizing patient-specific anatomy and intraoperative guidance [30].

AI is advancing neurovascular simulators by enabling patient-specific virtual environments. Using CT/MR angiography, CNNs can segment cerebral vessels and generate 3D models for VR, allowing trainees to practice on digital twins and test catheterization strategies. AI-driven simulations model real-time blood flow and contrast propagation, while generative models like diffusion networks can create diverse aneurysm scenarios to enhance preparedness [24].

In XR-based planning, surgeons can explore 3D holograms of patient vasculature, simulate device placement, and receive AI-driven guidance on risk zones or optimal fluoroscopy angles. When paired with haptics, AI models replicate tactile feedback, helping train fine motor skills needed for delicate tasks.

Reinforcement learning and RNNs improve realism by simulating catheter behavior and vessel response.

Intraoperatively, AR can overlay key anatomy onto the patient, offering "X-ray vision" during embolizations. Tracked catheter positions and real-time imaging can be integrated, though precise tool tracking remains a technical challenge. AI helps by improving registration accuracy and predicting instrument motion, supporting safer and more effective navigation.

5 Integration of AI Models into XR Pipelines

Incorporating AI into XR pipelines requires a delicate balance between data processing and interactive, real-time visualization. A general pipeline might look like: data acquisition → AI model inference → XR rendering, all potentially happening in real or near-real time as illustrated in Fig. 3.

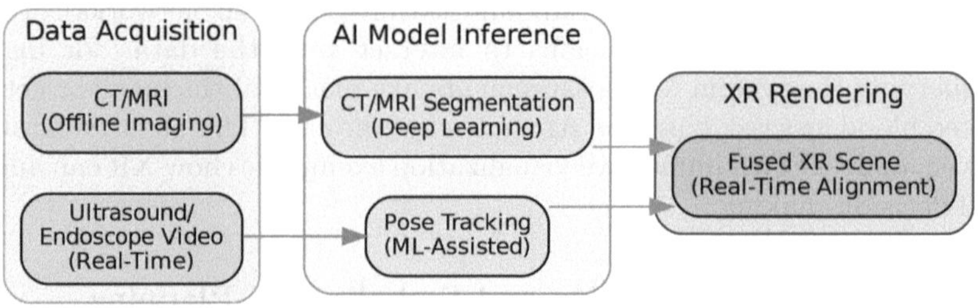

Fig. 3. AI-enhanced XR pipeline for medical visualization. The system integrates two data sources: offline imaging (CT/MRI) and real-time imaging (ultrasound or endoscopic video) which are processed by AI models for CT/MRI segmentation (via deep learning) and pose tracking (via ML-assisted methods). These outputs are combined in the XR rendering stage to generate a fused XR scene aligned in real time with the patient's anatomy, enabling accurate and immersive visualization for diagnostic or surgical guidance.

For example, consider an AR surgical guidance system: it acquires patient imaging (CT/MRI) offline and live data (ultrasound or endoscope video) in real time. Offline, a deep learning segmentation model processes the CT/MRI to produce 3D meshes of anatomy. In real time, a pose-tracking algorithm (often augmented by ML for robustness) continuously aligns the virtual content with the patient. A rendering engine then displays the fused scene to the user. Each of these stages can be improved or accelerated by AI.

Regarding real-time image analysis, XR systems often rely on understanding live sensor input (camera views, ultrasound streams). Latency is a major concern; many XR applications require < 50 ms pipeline delay to feel instantaneous. Here, efficient neural networks or even specialized hardware (GPUs, TPUs) are critical. Techniques like model quantization, distillation, and use of compact architectures (e.g. MobileNet, or neuron pruning in a U-Net) are employed to ensure AI models don't bottleneck the XR experience.

Moreover, regarding interactive graphics and image synthesis, it is important to emphesise that AI-generated content can be fed directly into the XR rendering stage. We saw how GANs can produce ultrasound images on the fly; similarly, diffusion models or neural radiance fields (NeRFs) might be used to render anatomy with realistic textures and lighting in VR. A challenge is to do this on demand as the user's viewpoint changes. One approach is to pre-compute a lot of variability (e.g. many angles of a surgical scene) and use lightweight interpolation during interaction. Another is to use neural rendering where part of the graphics pipeline is a neural network that fills in detail. This is cutting-edge in XR: research prototypes exist where a neural network helps render unseen viewpoints of organs by learning from CT data. Ensuring stability and avoiding flicker or artifacts is non-trivial; thus, often a hybrid pipeline is used (traditional graphics for baseline visualization + AI for refinement). The integration of AI-based denoising is already more common. For example, noisy ultrasound images projected in AR can be cleaned up by a deep denoising model in real time, making the overlay clearer. Ultimately, the XR pipeline becomes a mix of deterministic algorithms and AI modules, each feeding into the next.

Nevertheless, XR is not just visual. Many medical simulators involve haptic feedback (force, tactile simulation) to mimic procedures. Integrating AI here means using learned models to simulate physics faster or more realistically. Classical haptic engines might use physics equations that are simplified for speed. By training on high-fidelity simulations or real force measurements, a neural network can learn the mapping from user actions (e.g. how far a needle is inserted) to resulting feedback (resistance, tissue deformation). Once learned, this can be extremely fast to compute. For example, a deep model was trained to predict soft tissue deformation under various forces, achieving accurate results at interactive rates, whereas a full finite element simulation would be too slow for real-time use.

6 Current Challenges and Future Directions

Integrating AI with XR in medicine offers transformative potential but also presents several challenges. A primary concern is the limitation and bias in training data, which can hinder AI models' ability to generalize across diverse patient populations and devices. Variations in imaging equipment and clinical practices may further degrade performance. To mitigate these issues, researchers are exploring large-scale, multicenter datasets and domain adaptation techniques. Synthetic data generation, such as creating labeled 3D CT scans, shows promise but requires caution to prevent overfitting to artificial characteristics. The "black-box" nature of many AI algorithms raises concerns about interpretability and trust, especially when understanding decision-making processes is crucial in clinical settings. Efforts in Explainable AI (XAI) aim to provide insights into AI decisions by highlighting influential image regions and displaying confidence levels, thereby fostering clinician trust. Achieving real-time, high-resolution AI processing in XR environments remains challenging due to the computational demands of complex models, particularly with volumetric data.

Solutions include optimizing neural networks, leveraging edge or cloud computing, and developing specialized hardware to minimize latency and ensure seamless XR experiences. Additionally, AI-integrated medical XR systems must undergo rigorous validation to meet safety and efficacy standards set by regulatory bodies like the FDA. The opacity of some AI models complicates this process, necessitating transparency, robustness, and comprehensive testing across diverse scenarios for regulatory approval and clinical adoption. Ethical and training considerations are also paramount; balancing AI assistance with the preservation of fundamental clinical skills is critical. While AI and XR can democratize medical training, there's a risk of over-reliance, potentially diminishing essential competencies. Ensuring equitable access to these technologies and addressing data privacy concerns are essential. Techniques like federated learning, which allow AI models to learn from decentralized data without compromising patient privacy, are being explored to responsibly enhance XR systems. In summary, while AI and XR hold immense promise for transforming medical education and practice, addressing these challenges through ongoing research and ethical considerations is essential for their successful integration into healthcare.

7 Conclusion and Discussion

AI-driven extended reality is poised to revolutionize medical training and intervention, fusing the strengths of human intuition with the precision and breadth of machine intelligence. We now have XR simulators where convolutional networks provide patient-specific 3D anatomy, transformers and multimodal models fuse data into rich interactive experiences, and generative models populate virtual worlds with realistic scenarios that were once scarce or unimaginable. These advances enable a trainee to palpate a virtual organ with haptic feedback informed by real physics, or a surgeon to visualize hidden pathology floating before their eyes with AR confidence markers. The result is a more immersive learning environment and potentially safer, more effective patient care early studies already show improved procedural performance after AI-enhanced XR training. At the same time, our exploration of current limitations reminds us that this is a journey in progress. Ensuring that an AI model's superb accuracy in the lab translates to the chaotic variability of the real world is an ongoing endeavor. The future directions highlighted from creating larger and more diverse datasets, to developing explainable and trustworthy AI, to integrating these tools seamlessly into clinical workflows are being actively pursued by the research community. We can expect the next decade to bring XR systems that are more intelligent (with AI that can reason across modalities and scenarios), more adaptive (tailoring themselves to each user and patient), and more accepted in everyday clinical practice. Key to this will be maintaining a focus on the end-users: the medical professionals and patients. XR and AI should ultimately amplify the expertise of clinicians, providing support where humans have limitations (e.g. seeing the unseen, recalling vast case libraries), while preserving the empathy, judgment, and responsibility that only humans can provide.

In conclusion, the convergence of advanced AI methods with extended reality platforms is opening new frontiers in medical simulation, planning, and guidance. Current methods like CNNs, GANs, and RL have already shown how realistic virtual training and augmented guidance can be achieved, and emerging approaches like diffusion models, vision transformers, and multimodal learning are set to push these boundaries even further. The use cases of placenta accreta management and neurovascular interventions exemplify the tangible benefits from improved diagnostic confidence to hands-on rehearsal of high-stakes procedures that these technologies can deliver. By diligently addressing the challenges of generalization, interpretability, data curation, and validation, researchers and clinicians together can ensure that future XR systems are not only technologically impressive but also clinically impactful and safe. The ultimate vision is a healthcare ecosystem where learning and practice are enriched by immersive, intelligent tools: surgeons entering the operating theater having essentially "already performed" the surgery in VR with an AI tutor, and when the real procedure happens, having AI-augmented AR guidance to navigate complexity. Achieving this will mark a significant leap in how we train doctors and treat patients, fulfilling the promise of extended reality amplified by the power of machine learning.

Acknowledgements. This work was supported by the Croatian Science Foundation under the project number IP-2024-05-9492.

References

1. Andrews, C.E., Southworth, M.K., Silva, J.N.A., Silva, J.R.: Extended reality in medical practice. Current Treat. Opt. Cardiov. Med. **21**, 1–12 (2019). https://api.semanticscholar.org/CorpusID:89618916
2. B, J.K.D.K., G, D.C.L.U.N.: Real-time virtual sonography using MRI and ultrasound fusion imaging in the evaluation of CNS anomalies (2015). https://api.semanticscholar.org/CorpusID:26995384
3. Bengesi, S., El-Sayed, H., Sarker, M.K., Houkpati, Y., Irungu, J., Oladunni, T.: Advancements in generative AI: a comprehensive review of GANs, GPT, autoencoders, diffusion model, and transformers. IEEE Access **12**, 69812–69837 (2023). https://api.semanticscholar.org/CorpusID:265281267
4. Bourdillon, A.T., Garg, A., Wang, H., Woo, Y.J., Pavone, M., Boyd, J.H.: Integration of reinforcement learning in a virtual robotic surgical simulation. Surg. Innov. **30**, 94 – 102 (2022). https://api.semanticscholar.org/CorpusID:248503124
5. Castro, P.T., Júnior, E.A., Lopes, J., Ribeiro, G., Werner, H.: Placenta accreta: virtual reality from 3D images of magnetic resonance imaging. J. Clin. Ultrasound **50**, 119 – 120 (2021). https://api.semanticscholar.org/CorpusID:244402114

6. Chang, Y.Z., Wu, C.T.: Application of extended reality in pediatric neurosurgery: a comprehensive review. Biomed. J., 100822 (2024). https://api.semanticscholar.org/CorpusID:274605449
7. Curran, V.R., Xu, X., Aydin, M.Y., Meruvia-Pastor, O.: Use of extended reality in medical education: an integrative review. Med. Sci. Educ. **33**, 275 – 286 (2022). https://api.semanticscholar.org/CorpusID:254876440
8. Dai, Y., Gao, Y.: TransMed: transformers advance multi-modal medical image classification. Diagnostics **11** (2021). https://api.semanticscholar.org/CorpusID:232170589
9. D'Amico, R.S., Barrington, N.M., Langer, D.J.: Opinion: navigating the integration and impact of extended reality in neurosurgery. Surg. Neurol. Int. **15** (2024). https://api.semanticscholar.org/CorpusID:270684228
10. Elsakka, A., Park, B.J., Marinelli, B., Swinburne, N.C., Schefflein, J.: Virtual and augmented reality in interventional radiology: current applications, challenges, and future directions. Techn. Vasc. Intervent. Radiol. **26 3**, 100919 (2023). https://api.semanticscholar.org/CorpusID:264385482
11. Feng, B.: A deep reinforcement learning-based resource allocation mechanism for XR applications*. In: 2023 IEEE International Symposium on Broadband Multimedia Systems and Broadcasting (BMSB), pp. 1–6 (2023). https://api.semanticscholar.org/CorpusID:260933507
12. Fratelli, N., Fichera, A., Prefumo, F.: An update of diagnostic efficacy of ultrasound and magnetic resonance imaging in the diagnosis of clinically significant placenta accreta spectrum disorders. Current Opin. Obstet. Gynecol. **34**, 287–291 (2022). https://api.semanticscholar.org/CorpusID:251131704
13. Gadodia, G., Evans, M., Weunski, C., Ho, A., Cargill, A., Martin, C.: Evaluation of an augmented reality navigational guidance platform for percutaneous procedures in a cadaver model. J. Med. Imag. **11** (2024). https://api.semanticscholar.org/CorpusID:267715794
14. Gani, A., Pickering, O.J., Ellis, C., Sabri, O., Pucher, P.H.: Impact of haptic feedback on surgical training outcomes: a randomised controlled trial of haptic versus non-haptic immersive virtual reality training. Annals Med. Surg. **83** (2022). https://api.semanticscholar.org/CorpusID:252500398
15. García-Robles, P., et al.: Immersive virtual reality and augmented reality in anatomy education: a systematic review and meta-analysis. Anatom. Sci. Educ. **17**, 514 – 528 (2024). https://api.semanticscholar.org/CorpusID:267635560
16. Hatamizadeh, A., Nath, V., Tang, Y., Yang, D., Roth, H.R., Xu, D.: Swin UNETR: swin transformers for semantic segmentation of brain tumors in MRI images. ArXiv **abs/2201.01266** (2022). https://api.semanticscholar.org/CorpusID:245668780
17. Herur-Raman, A., Almeida, N.D., Greenleaf, W.J., Williams, D., Karshenas, A., Sherman, J.H.: Next-generation simulation–integrating extended reality technology into medical education. In: Frontiers in Virtual Reality (2021). https://api.semanticscholar.org/CorpusID:237425857
18. Huang, J., et al.: Deep-learning-based automatic segmentation of the placenta and uterine cavity on prenatal MR images. In: Medical Imaging (2023). https://api.semanticscholar.org/CorpusID:258016071
19. Jiang, H., Vimalesvaran, S., Wang, J.K., Lim, K.B., Mogali, S.R., Car, L.T.: Virtual reality in medical students' education: scoping review. JMIR Med. Educ. **8** (2021). https://api.semanticscholar.org/CorpusID:245610841
20. Kazemzadeh, K., Akhlaghdoust, M., Zali, A.: Advances in artificial intelligence, robotics, augmented and virtual reality in neurosurgery. Front . Surg. **10** (2023). https://api.semanticscholar.org/CorpusID:261194809

21. Kazerouni, A., Aghdam, E.K., Heidari, M., Azad, R., Fayyaz, M., Hacihaliloglu, I., Merhof, D.: Diffusion models in medical imaging: a comprehensive survey. Med. Image Anal. **88**, 102846 (2022). https://api.semanticscholar.org/CorpusID:253523207
22. Khader, F., et al.: Medical diffusion: denoising diffusion probabilistic models for 3D medical image generation (2022). https://api.semanticscholar.org/CorpusID:260444528
23. Lainé, N., Zahnd, G., Bernard, O., Orkisz, M., Liebgott, H.: Generation of realistic simulated b-mode image texture with a GAN. In: 2022 IEEE International Ultrasonics Symposium (IUS), pp. 1–4 (2022). https://api.semanticscholar.org/CorpusID:254155038
24. Lee, K.H., Muniyandi, P., Li, M., Saccenti, L., Christou, A.S., Xu, S., Wood, B.J.: Smartphone technology for applications in image-guided minimally invasive interventional procedures. Cardiovas .Interv. Radiol. **48**, 142 – 156 (2024). https://api.semanticscholar.org/CorpusID:274787363
25. Moro, C., Stromberga, Z., Stirling, A.: Virtualisation devices for student learning: comparison between desktop-based (oculus rift) and mobile-based (gear VR) virtual reality in medical and health science education. Austral. J. Educat. Technol. **33**, 1–10 (2017). https://api.semanticscholar.org/CorpusID:54012958
26. Nakaguchi, T.: The current state of the use of XR technology in medicine. Japan. J. Rehab. Med. (2024). https://api.semanticscholar.org/CorpusID:275365258
27. Nguyen, T.T., Nguyen, N.D., Bello, F., Nahavandi, S.: A new tensioning method using deep reinforcement learning for surgical pattern cutting. In: 2019 IEEE International Conference on Industrial Technology (ICIT), pp. 1339–1344 (2019). https://api.semanticscholar.org/CorpusID:57825757
28. Palaiologou, E., et al.: High resolution three dimensional imaging of placental villi using serial block face scanning electron microscopy. Placenta **45**, 84 (2016). https://api.semanticscholar.org/CorpusID:88963351
29. Parmar, T.: Generative adversarial networks for historical data generation in semiconductor manufacturing: applications and challenges. Int. J. Multidis. Res. (2024). https://api.semanticscholar.org/CorpusID:276413421
30. Patel, S.A., et al.: Advancing endovascular neurosurgery training with extended reality: opportunities and obstacles for the next decade. Front. Surg. **11** (2024). https://api.semanticscholar.org/CorpusID:272050580
31. Peng, B., Huang, X., Wang, S.Y., Jiang, J.: A real-time medical ultrasound simulator based on a generative adversarial network model. In: 2019 IEEE International Conference on Image Processing (ICIP), pp. 4629–4633 (2019). https://api.semanticscholar.org/CorpusID:202780747
32. Ronneberger, O., Fischer, P., Brox, T.: U-net: convolutional networks for biomedical image segmentation. ArXiv **abs/1505.04597** (2015) . https://api.semanticscholar.org/CorpusID:3719281
33. S, M., S, A., S, Y., T, A.S.K.: Transforming digital interaction: an in-depth exploration of extended reality(XR) technologies. In: 2024 5th International Conference on Data Intelligence and Cognitive Informatics (ICDICI), pp. 937–941 (2024). https://doi.org/10.1109/ICDICI62993.2024.10810916
34. Sueyoshi, T., Sugimoto, M.: [clinical application of metaverse and extended reality in neurosurgery: spatial image analysis, remote surgical assistance, and re-live training]. Brain and nerve = Shinkei kenkyu no shinpo **75 10**, 1129–1134 (2023). https://api.semanticscholar.org/CorpusID:264287126
35. Sundermeyer, M., Schlüter, R., Ney, H.: LSTM neural networks for language modeling. In: Interspeech (2012). https://api.semanticscholar.org/CorpusID:18939716

36. Tortora, M., et al.: Current applications and future perspectives of extended reality in radiology. La Radiologia medica (2025). https://api.semanticscholar.org/CorpusID:277409936
37. Wang, H., et al.: A deep learning pipeline using prior knowledge for automatic evaluation of placenta accreta spectrum disorders with MRI. J .Magn. Reson. Imaging **59** (2023). https://api.semanticscholar.org/CorpusID:258676898
38. Wang, H., Liu, Z., Sun, K., Wang, X., Shen, D., Cui, Z.: 3D MedDiffusion: A 3D medical diffusion model for controllable and high-quality medical image generation. ArXiv **abs/2412.13059** (2024). https://api.semanticscholar.org/CorpusID:274789446
39. Wang, Z., Wang, R., Wu, J., Zhang, W., Li, C.: Dynamic resource allocation for real-time cloud XR video transmission: a reinforcement learning approach. IEEE Trans. Cogn. Commun. Netw .**10**, 996–1010 (2024). https://api.semanticscholar.org/CorpusID:267124648
40. Wong, J.Y., Azam, A.B., Cao, Q., Huang, L., Xie, Y., Winkler, I., Cai, Y.: Evaluations of virtual and augmented reality technology-enhanced learning for higher education. Electronics (2024). https://api.semanticscholar.org/CorpusID:269265828
41. Ming Yang, J., et al.: Artificial intelligence in medical metaverse: applications, challenges, and future prospects. Current Med. Sci. (2024). https://api.semanticscholar.org/CorpusID:274711422
42. Zheng, C., et al.: Deep learning radiomic analysis of MRI combined with clinical characteristics diagnoses placenta accreta spectrum and its subtypes. J. Magn .Reson. Imag .: JMRI (2024). https://api.semanticscholar.org/CorpusID:267806822
43. Ziker, C., Truman, B., Dodds, H.: Cross reality (XR): challenges and opportunities across the spectrum. In: Innovative Learning Environments in STEM Higher Education, pp. 55 – 77 (2021). https://api.semanticscholar.org/CorpusID:232206002

Application of the Random Forest Algorithm for Team Role Classification Based on Belbin's Self-perception Inventory

Drina Ćavar Brajković[2], Emil Brajković[1](✉), and Tomislav Volarić[1]

[1] University of Mostar, Mostar 88000, BiH, Bosnia and Herzegovina
{emil.brajkovic,tomislav.volaric}@fpmoz.sum.ba
[2] IT Odjel Mostar, Mostar 88000, BiH, Bosnia and Herzegovina
drina.cavar.brajkovic@phd.sum.ba

Abstract. This study explores the application of the Random Forest algorithm for classifying dominant team roles based on Belbin's Team Roles Self-Perception Inventory. A synthetically generated dataset of 100,000 instances was used to train and evaluate the model, ensuring that the distribution of team roles reflects real workplace environments. The results demonstrated high classification accuracy, with an overall precision of 0.98725. The study found that roles with distinct behavioral characteristics, such as shaper and coordinator, were easier to classify, whereas roles with overlapping traits, such as monitor evaluator and plant, posed greater challenges.

The findings have significant implications for modern workforce management. By utilizing machine learning for team role classification, organizations can optimize team formation, enhance collaboration, and improve productivity. The model offers a data-driven approach to aligning employees with roles that match their strengths, reducing subjective decision-making in human resource processes.

Despite its effectiveness, the study acknowledges limitations, such as the reliance on synthetic data and the need for further validation using real-world datasets. Future research should explore deep learning models and integrate natural language processing techniques for improved role prediction. This study highlights the potential of AI-driven HR analytics to create balanced, high-performing teams in contemporary business environments.

Keywords: Team Role Classification · Random Forest Algorithm · The Belbin Team Roles

1 Introduction

In today's dynamic and competitive business environment, teamwork has emerged as a crucial factor for organizational success. Companies increasingly

D. Vasić and E. Brajković (Eds.): MoStart 2025, CCIS 2609, pp. 283–294, 2026.
https://doi.org/10.1007/978-3-032-02801-3_19

rely on teams to drive innovation, solve complex problems, and improve productivity. Effective teamwork fosters collaboration, enhances problem-solving capabilities, and ensures the efficient execution of tasks. However, simply assembling a group of skilled professionals is not enough. Understanding individual roles within a team is essential for maximizing efficiency and achieving organizational goals. By recognizing and leveraging the strengths of each team member, managers can create balanced teams that function cohesively, optimize workflow, and enhance overall performance.

1.1 The Significance of Teamwork in Modern Management

Teamwork plays a pivotal role in contemporary management strategies, enabling organizations to achieve their objectives more effectively. One of the key advantages of teamwork is the diversity of skills and perspectives that each team member brings. When individuals collaborate, they combine their expertise to generate innovative solutions that a single person might not achieve alone. This synergy fosters creativity and problem-solving, which are critical for companies operating in fast-changing industries.

1.2 The Impact of Understanding Team Roles on Efficiency

While teamwork is essential, its success largely depends on how well team roles are defined and understood. The Belbin Team Roles model, developed by Dr. Meredith Belbin, provides a framework for understanding the different contributions individuals make in a team setting [1]. According to Belbin, a well-balanced team should comprise individuals with complementary roles, such as the Shaper, who drives progress and challenges the status quo; the Coordinator, who ensures alignment and clarity in team efforts; and the Monitor Evaluator, who offers critical analysis and strategic thinking. In modern management, teamwork is more than just a collaborative effort—it is a strategic approach to achieving business success. Organizations that prioritize teamwork benefit from increased innovation, efficiency, and employee engagement. However, the true potential of teamwork can only be realized when team roles are clearly defined and understood. By leveraging frameworks such as the Belbin Team Roles model, managers can build well-balanced teams that capitalize on individual strengths, enhance collaboration, and drive superior performance. As businesses continue to navigate an increasingly complex and competitive landscape, investing in effective teamwork and team role understanding will remain a cornerstone of sustainable growth and success [2].

By understanding these roles, managers can assign tasks more effectively and avoid potential conflicts that arise from overlapping responsibilities or skill mismatches. For instance, if multiple team members exhibit dominant leadership traits, they may clash over decision-making authority, leading to inefficiencies. Conversely, if a team lacks individuals with planning and organizational skills, project execution may suffer from delays or mismanagement.

Furthermore, recognizing team roles helps in identifying skill gaps and areas for improvement. Managers can provide targeted training and development opportunities to enhance individual competencies, ensuring that the team remains adaptable and high-performing. It also enables better communication and collaboration as team members become aware of each other's working styles and strengths. This awareness fosters mutual respect and trust, reducing misunderstandings and improving overall team cohesion [3].

Moreover, teamwork enhances employee engagement and job satisfaction. When employees feel valued and included in decision-making processes, they become more motivated and committed to their work. Research has shown that organizations with strong teamwork cultures experience higher levels of productivity and lower employee turnover rates. Additionally, teams facilitate knowledge sharing and continuous learning, allowing employees to develop new skills and adapt to evolving business challenges.

Another significant benefit of teamwork is increased efficiency and performance. When tasks are distributed based on individual strengths and expertise, workflows become more streamlined, reducing redundancy and improving time management. Well-functioning teams also demonstrate greater resilience in the face of challenges, as they can collectively overcome obstacles and adapt to changing circumstances [4].

2 Enhancing Team Role Prediction with Random Forest Algorithm

In modern organizations, forming well-balanced and efficient teams is crucial for achieving high performance and productivity. One of the key challenges managers face is identifying the dominant roles of employees within a team to ensure an optimal mix of skills, strengths, and work styles. The Random Forest algorithm, a powerful machine learning technique, can significantly improve the accuracy of team role prediction, enabling managers to make more informed decisions when assembling teams[5].

The Random Forest algorithm is an ensemble learning method that operates by constructing multiple decision trees and aggregating their results to produce a more accurate and stable prediction. This approach is particularly beneficial for predicting dominant team roles, as it can handle complex patterns within large datasets, account for non-linear relationships, and reduce the risk of overfitting. By training a Random Forest model on historical data, such as self-assessment results, performance metrics, and work behavior indicators, organizations can more accurately classify employees into predefined team roles, such as those defined by the Belbin Team Roles framework.

One major advantage of using Random Forest for this purpose is its ability to process diverse data types and identify the most important features contributing to role classification.[6] For example, factors such as decision-making style, problem-solving approach, and communication preferences can be evaluated simultaneously to determine the most suitable role for each employee. This capability allows managers to make data-driven decisions rather than relying solely on subjective assessments or traditional personality tests.

Additionally, the predictive capabilities of the Random Forest algorithm can help managers identify skill gaps and potential mismatches within teams before conflicts arise [7]. By forecasting how individuals will perform in specific roles, organizations can proactively adjust team compositions, ensuring that all critical functions are adequately covered. This is particularly valuable in fast-paced industries where effective teamwork directly impacts project success and business outcomes.

Furthermore, the use of machine learning in team formation fosters a more objective and fair selection process. Instead of being influenced by unconscious biases, managers can rely on empirical data to determine the best candidates for specific roles. This enhances not only team efficiency but also employee satisfaction and engagement, as individuals are placed in positions that align with their strengths and work preferences.

Integrating the Random Forest algorithm into team role prediction can significantly enhance the accuracy and efficiency of team formation. By leveraging machine learning to analyze complex datasets and predict dominant team roles, organizations can build more cohesive, balanced, and high-performing teams. As businesses continue to embrace data-driven decision-making, the application of Random Forest in workforce analytics will play an increasingly important role in optimizing team dynamics and driving organizational success [8].

3 Research Methodology

3.1 The Belbin Team Roles

he dataset used in this research is based on the Belbin Team Roles Self-Perception Inventory, a widely recognized framework for identifying an individual's natural tendencies within a team. The Belbin model classifies individuals into nine distinct team roles: Shaper, Implementer, Completer Finisher, Coordinator, Teamworker, Resource Investigator, Monitor Evaluator, Specialist, and Plant. Each of these roles represents a unique contribution style, cognitive approach, and behavioral pattern within a team setting. The Belbin Team Roles: Self-Perception Inventory (BTRSPI) is a psychometric assessment tool developed by Dr. Meredith Belbin to identify an individual's preferred role within a team. The inventory helps in understanding how people contribute to teamwork based on their natural tendencies and behaviors. The Belbin Team Roles Model classifies individuals into nine distinct team roles, each of which represents a specific way of interacting and contributing within a team setting.

The Belbin Self-Perception Inventory consists of a series of statements that describe different types of behaviors within a team. The respondent is required to distribute 10 points per section among the statements that best reflect their behavior. The scoring method allows for flexibility, as an individual may distribute all points to one statement or spread them across multiple statements.

The inventory typically consists of seven sections, with each section containing eight statements. Each statement corresponds to one of the nine team roles, allowing for a comprehensive assessment of how an individual behaves in different team situations.

The statements in the BTRSPI are designed to assess how individuals naturally behave in a team rather than what they would ideally like to do. Some examples of these statements include:

- "I enjoy challenging others and pushing the team to achieve results,"
- "I thrive in high-pressure situations and help to keep the team focused,"
- "I am disciplined and ensure that plans are put into action,"
- "I prefer structured approaches and dislike inefficiency,"
- "I have high attention to detail and ensure that tasks are completed to perfection," and "I feel uneasy if there are errors or unresolved issues in a project."

Other statements include:

- "I like to take charge and ensure that everyone is contributing effectively,"
- "I believe in delegating tasks based on team members' strengths,"
- "I am good at maintaining team harmony and resolving conflicts,"
- "I enjoy working collaboratively and supporting my teammates,"
- "I am enthusiastic about exploring new opportunities and external resources," and
- "I enjoy networking and bringing in fresh ideas from outside the team."

Some statements focus on problem-solving and expertise, such as;

- "I take a logical and impartial approach to problem-solving," "I tend to weigh all options carefully before making a decision,"
- "I bring expert knowledge and skills that are crucial to the team,"
- "I prefer working on tasks where I can apply my deep technical expertise,"
- "I generate original ideas and solve problems in unconventional ways," and
- "I prefer to work independently to develop creative solutions."

Once the respondent completes the inventory, their scores across different team roles are calculated. The highest scores indicate the dominant team roles, while lower scores represent less preferred roles. A well-balanced team ideally consists of individuals with complementary roles to maximize efficiency and effectiveness.

The Belbin Team Roles: Self-Perception Inventory remains one of the most widely used tools in organizational psychology for enhancing teamwork and productivity.

3.2 Research Dataset

To conduct a large-scale machine learning analysis, a synthetic dataset comprising 100,000 records was generated. This dataset was designed to closely mimic real-world distributions of team roles in professional environments. The generation process ensured that the probability distributions of team roles reflected realistic occurrences in workplace settings. Studies on team dynamics suggest that roles such as Teamworker and Coordinator appear more frequently in organizations, while roles like Specialist and Plant are less common. The dataset was structured to align with these real-world tendencies. The dataset was created using the ChatGPT tool and AI Prompt Engineering. This prompt aims to generate a synthetic dataset for Belbin's Self-Perception Inventory (SPI), an assessment used to individual team roles within an organization. The dataset consists of 100,000 employees, each assigned a primary team role along with scores for all nine Belbin roles. This dataset is designed to support HR analytics, leadership development, and team composition studies. The dataset includes the following key attributes:

- Employee ID: A unique identifier for each employee.
- Primary Role: One of the nine Belbin team roles assigned as the dominant role.
- Belbin Team Role Scores: Each employee is assigned a score (1-10) for all nine Belbin team roles, simulating their strengths in different areas.

The dataset is generated using randomized distributions to ensure a realistic spread of scores. Each employee receives:A primary role selected randomly from the nine Belbin roles.Role scores generated using a normal distribution with a mean of 5 and a standard deviation of 2, ensuring variability while staying within the 1-10 scale. To introduce variability and prevent overfitting, random noise was added while maintaining structured role distributions. The dataset was compared to smaller, real-world HR analytics datasets to verify its statistical similarity in role distribution, ensuring a reliable foundation for training and testing machine learning models.

3.3 Random Forest

Random Forest is a supervised machine learning algorithm based on ensemble learning. It constructs multiple decision trees and aggregates their predictions to improve classification accuracy. This approach makes it highly effective for categorical classification tasks such as predicting an individual's dominant team role. The algorithm operates by training multiple decision trees on different subsets of the dataset created through random sampling with replacement. Each tree makes an independent prediction, and the final classification is determined by majority voting, making the model robust and less prone to overfitting. Unlike a single decision tree, which considers all features at every node, Random Forest selects a random subset of features for each split, ensuring diversity among decision trees and reducing variance [9].

One of the key strengths of Random Forest is its ability to rank feature importance, allowing researchers to identify which attributes, such as leadership skills, adaptability, or communication style, have the strongest influence on team role classification. The algorithm efficiently handles high-dimensional datasets, ensuring that even weakly correlated features contribute to classification decisions. Additionally, its scalability makes it well-suited for large datasets like the synthetic dataset used in this study, allowing it to process vast amounts of data while maintaining strong predictive performance.

3.4 Classification of the Dominant Role

In this research, the classification of an individual's dominant team role was based on the highest self-assessment score among the nine Belbin roles. Each participant in the dataset provided ratings for all nine roles, and the role with the highest score was considered their dominant role. This approach aligns with the principles of the Belbin Team Roles model, which suggests that while individuals may exhibit characteristics of multiple roles, they tend to have one predominant role that best represents their natural tendencies in a team setting.

To ensure that the classification process accurately captured the dominant role, additional data validation steps were applied. In cases where multiple roles had the same highest score, a tiebreaker mechanism was introduced, prioritizing roles based on their hierarchical importance in workplace dynamics. If a participant exhibited two or more roles with identical scores, the role that was most relevant to the specific industry or job function was selected. This ensured that the classification system mirrored real-world decision-making processes in team formation.

Once the dominant role for each individual was established, the dataset was split into training and testing subsets. The training data was used to build the classification model, while the testing data allowed for evaluating the model's accuracy. The dataset was balanced to prevent bias toward more frequent roles, as some team roles, such as Coordinator and Teamworker, naturally appeared more often than others. To address this, data augmentation techniques were applied to ensure that less frequent roles like Specialist and Plant were adequately represented, thereby improving model generalization.

During the training phase, the Random Forest model was optimized by adjusting key hyperparameters, including the number of trees, depth of trees, and the number of features considered at each split [10]. The model was initially tested with default hyperparameters, and subsequent tuning was performed to improve performance. Cross-validation techniques were used to ensure robustness, preventing the model from overfitting to the training data while maintaining generalizability to new data. Feature importance analysis played a crucial role in understanding which attributes contributed most to classifying an individual's dominant role. The Random Forest algorithm ranked features based on their influence in decision-making, revealing that attributes such as problem-solving ability, leadership preference, and communication effectiveness were among the most predictive factors. This insight provided further validation of the Belbin framework, as it confirmed that different team roles are strongly associated with specific behavioral characteristics (Fig. 1).

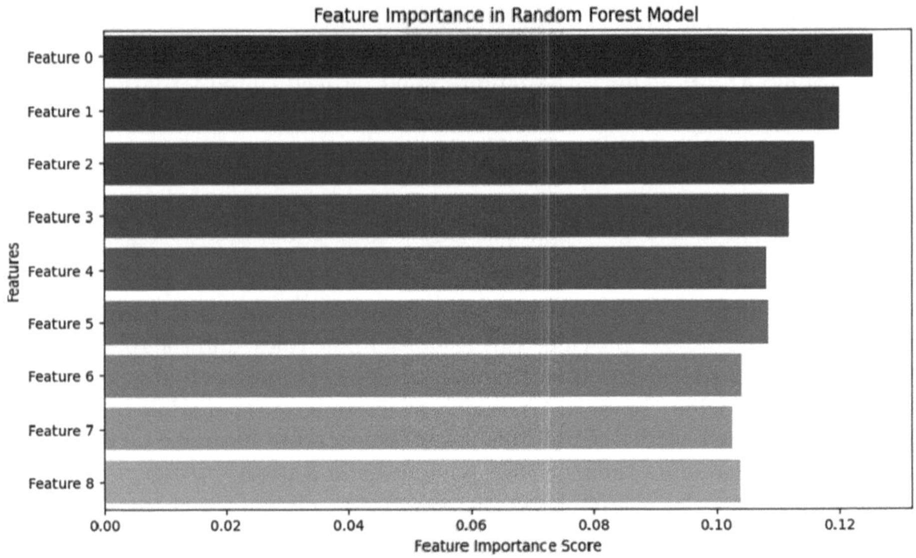

Fig. 1. Feature importance

4 Result

After training, the model was evaluated using multiple performance metrics, including accuracy, precision, recall, and the F1-score. The results demonstrated that the model achieved a high accuracy of 98.7%, indicating strong predictive power. The precision and recall scores across all nine roles showed consistent and balanced performance, meaning that the model successfully classified team roles without favoring any specific category (Table 1).

Table 1. Model Evaluation

Role	precision	recall	f1-score
Completer Finisher	0.99	0.99	0.99
Coordinator	0.99	0.99	0.99
Implementer	0.99	0.99	0.99
Monitor Evaluator	0.99	0.98	0.98
Resource Investigator	0.98	0.99	0.99
Shaper	0.99	1.0	0.99
Specialist	0.98	0.98	0.98
Teamworker	0.98	0.99	0.99
Plant	0.99	0.97	0.98

By employing a well-structured classification approach, this study demonstrated how machine learning can effectively predict an individual's dominant team role based on self-assessment and workplace behavior data. The application of Random Forest not only improved the accuracy of classification but also provided interpretability through feature importance analysis. These findings have practical implications for organizations seeking to optimize team composition, as they offer a data-driven approach to understanding employee strengths and ensuring that team members are placed in roles where they can contribute most effectively. A confusion matrix is a fundamental tool for evaluating the performance of classification models in machine learning. It provides a detailed breakdown of a model's predictions by comparing them to the actual class labels. The matrix consists of four main components: true positives (TP), where the model correctly predicts a positive class; true negatives (TN), where the model correctly predicts a negative class; false positives (FP), where the model incorrectly predicts a positive class when it should be negative; and false negatives (FN), where the model incorrectly predicts a negative class when it should be positive (Fig. 2).

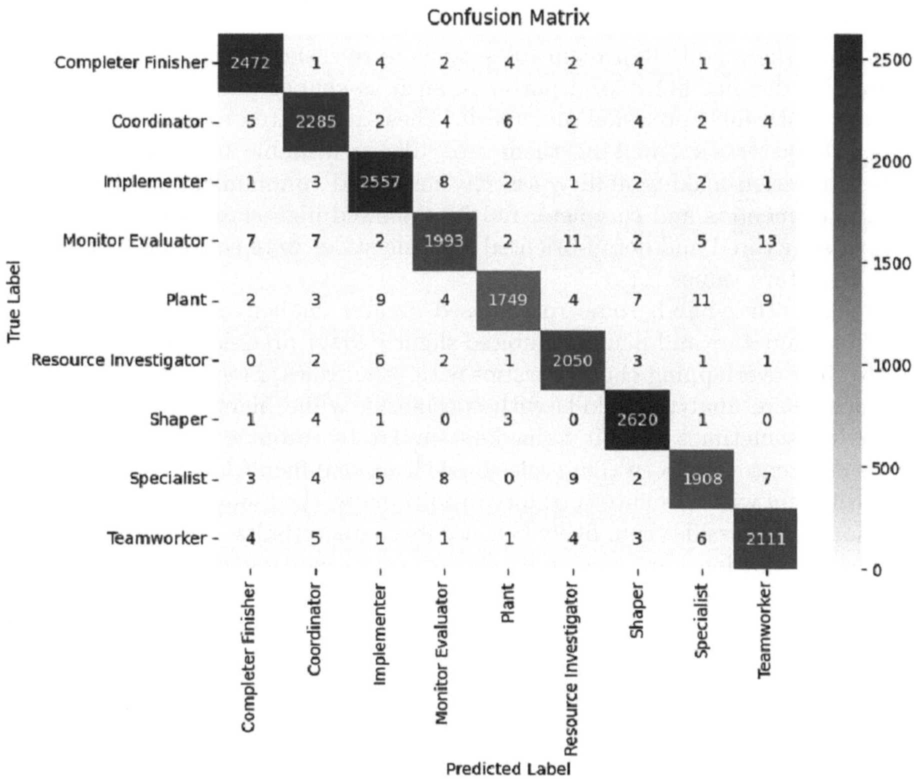

Fig. 2. Confusion matrix

The confusion matrix is particularly useful in assessing the balance between precision and recall. Precision measures the proportion of correct positive predictions out of all predicted positives, while recall indicates how well the model identifies actual positive instances. These metrics are essential in domains such as medical diagnosis and fraud detection, where false negatives or false positives can have significant consequences.

For multi-class classification, the confusion matrix extends to display predictions across multiple categories, helping identify misclassified instances. By analyzing the confusion matrix, data scientists can fine-tune models, adjust decision thresholds, or apply techniques such as class balancing to improve overall accuracy.

The high accuracy of the Random Forest model in classifying dominant team roles can be attributed to several key factors. First, the model's ability to handle high-dimensional data and capture complex relationships between features allowed it to effectively distinguish between different team roles. The large, synthetically generated dataset ensured that the model was exposed to a wide range of scenarios, improving its generalization capabilities. Additionally, the balanced distribution of team roles within the dataset prevented bias toward more frequent roles, contributing to consistent classification performance across all categories.

Among the nine Belbin team roles, some were easier to classify than others. Roles with distinct behavioral patterns, such as shaper and coordinator, were classified with high precision and recall. These roles often exhibit strong leadership characteristics, making them more distinguishable based on attributes such as decision-making ability, assertiveness, and communication style. Similarly, implementers and completer finishers showed high classification accuracy, as their structured and detail-oriented working styles were consistently reflected in their feature values [11].

On the other hand, some roles posed greater challenges for classification. Monitor evaluators and plants exhibited slightly lower precision and recall scores due to their overlapping characteristics with other roles. Monitor evaluators, for instance, share analytical skills with specialists, while plants, known for their creativity, sometimes exhibit behaviors similar to resource investigators. The subtle differences between these roles made it more difficult for the model to distinguish them with absolute certainty. Additionally, the teamworker role showed occasional misclassification, likely because its characteristics—such as adaptability and cooperation—are commonly shared across multiple roles.

Despite these challenges, the model's overall performance remained strong, demonstrating its ability to accurately capture role-specific traits. The feature importance analysis further validated that leadership tendencies, problem-solving skills, and collaboration levels were key factors in predicting dominant roles. These findings suggest that the Random Forest model is highly effective in assisting managers with team composition decisions, offering reliable insights into employees' natural strengths and work styles.

5 Conclusion

This research explored the application of the Random Forest algorithm for classifying dominant team roles based on Belbin's Team Roles Self-Perception Inventory. The results demonstrated that the model achieved a high level of accuracy, effectively distinguishing between different team roles with a precision rate of 0.98725. The use of a synthetically generated dataset with 100,000 instances allowed for a robust training process, ensuring that the model could generalize well across various workplace scenarios. The study found that certain roles, such as shaper, coordinator, and implementer, were more easily identifiable due to their distinct behavioral traits, while others, like monitor evaluator and plant, posed greater classification challenges due to overlapping characteristics with other roles.

The practical implications of these findings are significant for modern organizations that rely on teamwork to achieve strategic goals. By utilizing machine learning models such as Random Forest, companies can improve team formation processes by aligning employees with roles that best match their strengths. This approach reduces inefficiencies in team dynamics, enhances collaboration, and increases overall productivity. Furthermore, automated classification of team roles can assist human resource departments in making data-driven decisions about hiring, training, and employee development. Rather than relying solely on subjective assessments, organizations can leverage AI-driven insights to create balanced and high-performing teams.

Despite its effectiveness, the current model has limitations that should be addressed in future research. First, while the synthetic dataset was designed to reflect real-world distributions of team roles, it lacks the variability and complexity of actual workplace behaviors. Future studies should incorporate real-world data from diverse industries to validate the model's applicability across different organizational contexts. Second, while Random Forest proved to be a reliable classification algorithm, other machine learning techniques, such as deep learning models (e.g., neural networks), could be explored to further enhance accuracy, especially for roles with overlapping traits.

Another potential area for future research involves integrating natural language processing (NLP) techniques to analyze job descriptions, performance reviews, and other text-based data sources. By combining structured numerical data with unstructured text analysis, researchers can develop more comprehensive models for predicting team roles. Additionally, investigating the impact of team role classification on actual team performance would provide valuable insights into the real-world effectiveness of AI-driven team formation strategies.

Overall, this study highlights the potential of machine learning, specifically the Random Forest algorithm, as a tool for improving workforce management. By refining classification models and expanding the dataset to include real-world examples, future research can contribute to the development of even more precise and actionable insights for team optimization. The continued advancement of AI-driven HR analytics will enable organizations to foster more cohesive, efficient, and high-performing teams in an increasingly data-driven business environment.

References

1. Belbin, R.M.: Team Roles at Work. Butterworth-Heinemann, Oxford (2010)
2. Belbin, R.M.: Management Teams: Why They Succeed or Fail. Butterworth-Heinemann, Oxford (1981)
3. Fisher, S.G., Hunter, T.A., Macrosson, W.D.K.: The Structure of Belbin's Team Roles. J. Occup. Organ. Psychol. **71**(3), 283–288 (1998)
4. Aritzeta, A., Swailes, S., Senior, B.: Belbin's team role model: development, validity and applications for team building. J. Manage. Stud. **44**(1), 96–118 (2007)
5. Breiman, L.: Random forests. Mach. Learn. **45**(1), 5–32 (2001)
6. Ho, T. K.: *Random decision forests.* In: *Proceedings of the 3rd International Conference on Document Analysis and Recognition*, pp. 278–282 (1995)
7. Liaw, A., Wiener, M.: Classification and regression by random forest. R News **2**(3), 18–22 (2002)
8. Hastie, T., Tibshirani, R., Friedman, J.: The Elements of Statistical Learning: Data Mining, Inference, and Prediction. Springer, New York (2009)
9. Genuer, R., Poggi, J.M., Tuleau-Malot, C.: Variable selection using random forests. Pattern Recogn. Lett. **31**(14), 2225–2236 (2010)
10. Biau, G., Scornet, E.: A random forest guided tour. Test **25**(2), 197–227 (2016)
11. Belbin Associates. Belbin Team Roles. https://www.belbin.com/about/belbin-team-roles .Accessed 15 Mar 2025

Author Index

D. Vasić and E. Brajković (Eds.): MoStart 2025, CCIS 2609, pp. 295–296, 2026.
https://doi.org/10.1007/978-3-032-02801-3

MIX
Papier aus verantwortungsvollen Quellen
Paper from responsible sources
FSC® C105338
FSC
www.fsc.org

If you have any concerns about our products,
you can contact us on
ProductSafety@springernature.com

In case Publisher is established outside the EU,
the EU authorized representative is:
Springer Nature Customer Service Center GmbH
Europaplatz 3, 69115 Heidelberg, Germany

Printed by Libri Plureos GmbH
in Hamburg, Germany